# OBSCENE PROFITS

# OBSCENE PROFITS

## THE ENTREPRENEURS OF PORNOGRAPHY IN THE CYBER AGE

BY

FREDERICK S. LANE III

Routledge

New York
London

Published in 2001 by
Routledge
29 West 35th Street
New York, NY 10001

Published in Great Britain by
Routledge
11 New Fetter Lane
London EC4P 4EE

First Routledge hardback edition, 2000
First Routledge paperback edition, 2001
Copyright © 2000 by Frederick S. Lane III

Routledge is an imprint of the Taylor & Francis Group.

Printed in the United States of America on acid-free paper.

Book design by The Whole Works ®, New York

10 9 8 7 6 5 4 3 2 1

Library of Congress Cataloging-in-Publication Data

Lane, Frederick S., 1963–
     Obscene profits : the entrepreneurs of pornography in the cyber
age / by Frederick S. Lane, III.
        p.    cm.
     Includes bibliographical references and index.
     ISBN 0-415-92096-5 (alk. paper) 0-415-93103-7 (pbk)
     1. Pornography—Economic aspects. 2. Pornography—Technological
innovations. 3. Sex-oriented businesses. 4. Computer sex—Economic
aspects.    I. Title.
HQ471.L26    2000
338.4'37004538—dc21                                                    99-35383
                                                                          CIP

To my parents, Warren and Anne Lane,
for giving their children the confidence to choose
their own paths, and for their unflagging
support for the occasionally
unorthodox destinations.

# CONTENTS

# ACKNOWLEDGMENTS

It is with great pleasure and deep gratitude that I undertake the task of thanking the people who assisted me in the writing of this book. The past year and a half has helped me to understand that the writing of a book, although it appears at first glance to be a uniquely solitary endeavor, simply could not happen without the vision, encouragement, support, criticism, and patience of numerous others. I hope that these acknowledgments will help to illustrate my sincere appreciation to everyone who participated in this project.

First and foremost, the members of my immediate and extended family, who spent the past year and a half dealing with the long days, late nights, and frequent weekend absences that writing this book required. Writers can be a self-absorbed and demanding lot, so I offer thanks to the people closest to me who helped make it possible for me to do this work.

I would like to extend particular thanks to my agent, Martha Kaufman Amitay of Adler & Robin Books. From the moment of our first conversation, Martha has been a consistent source of calm encouragement and sound ideas. Although this project has undergone some fairly radical changes from the initial proposal, both in terms of content and deadline, Martha's support and enthusiasm have not wavered.

Equally special thanks are due my editor, Melissa Rosati, former publishing director of Routledge in New York City. Not only was Melissa willing to go to bat for a potentially controversial idea, but she was willing to do so with a first-time author. It took a terrific leap of faith, particularly when it was clear from my first submissions that I was well on my way to an unrequested new four-volume history of pornography. I suspect that when editors (and agents, for that matter) get together, they tell first-time author jokes: "How many first-time authors does it take to screw in a light bulb?" "Just one, but he needs an extension ladder." Throughout this long process, Melissa did a terrific job of offering encouragement in the midst of shifting schedules and multiple revisions. It has been a real pleasure.

Throughout this project, I have had the distinct privilege of working extensively with Linda Smith, a former writing instructor at the University of Massachusetts/Amherst and now the principal of Final Draft, a freelance editing service. Linda read every word of this manuscript at least twice, and her insightful criticisms on structure, style, and substance were invaluable. I can say with complete confidence that this is a far better book than it would have been without her help. Any remaining errors in form or content (including my law-school-induced fondness for semicolons, subordinate clauses, and of course, parentheticals) are mine and mine alone.

During the course of this project, I have had thoughtful input from a number of different people, some of whom have discussed various ideas with me and others who have read some or all sections of a draft. Among those whose comments and questions were influential in shaping this books were: Jessica Smith Lane, Dennis Heron, Keri Toksu, Chris McVeigh, Warren Lane, Anne Lane, Jon Lane, Rob Backus, Adam Snyder, Mark Hughes, Laurel Neme, David Smith, Lincoln Holmes, David Punia, Al Hudson, Judy Hudson, Kate Hudson, Geoff Hudson, Ralph Faulkingham, and Linda Faulkingham. It has been an enormous help to have a collection of interested and well-informed family members and friends with whom to discuss this occasionally discomfiting topic.

I would also like to thank the many adult Web site operators (many of whom appear in this book) for taking the time to answer numerous questions. Without exception, the people I interviewed were helpful, supportive, and very interesting.

Another enormously important part of this process was the environment in which I was fortunate to do much of my writing. I would like to extend my warmest thanks to the owners and staff of Muddy Waters, a coffee house on Main Street in Burlington, Vt. for creating such a terrific place for writing and communing with other writers, and for cheerfully refilling endless pots of tea.

The process of writing a book is not merely a creative process; it is also a mechanical one. A number of people deserve special recognition for helping to make the actual process of writing this book a little easier. Among them: Adam Snyder, whose timely offer of computer hardware assistance solved a difficult logistical problem and made writing this book so much more enjoyable (I will always be touched and honored by his act of generosity); Christine Rouleau, a freelance court reporter who transcribed a number of lively and "educational" interviews about the operation of online pornography sites; two used-book store owners, in particular, Dave Warden, co-owner of That Book Store in St. Johnsbury, Vt., which provided a number of useful reference books, and Debby Barnard, owner of Bygone Books in Burlington, for her interest and enthusiasm; Philip E. Varricchione for his patience and understanding of the writer's often erratic cash flow, and for his genuine interest and continuous encouragement; and the technicians at Computers Plus in Burlington and Ontrack Data Recovery in Minnesota, who at the very start of this project helped retrieve large amounts of essentially irreplaceable research. Although they wiped out a marvelous excuse ("The computer ate my homework"), they helped to keep this project from getting off on completely the wrong foot.

In addition, there are a number of software programs that helped make this project far easier than it would have been otherwise. Despite the occasional frustrations, a tip of the hat to the programmers of Microsoft's Win 95/98 (operating system); Corel Wordperfect 8.0 (word processing), Micro-Logic's Infoselect 5.0 (information management—a terrific program!), Netscape Communicator 4.5 (Web browser), Eudora 3.2 (e-mail), and Together Networks, my Internet service provider.

Finally, there are a number of different Web sites that I relied on frequently for news and research. Without these sites (and dozens of others like them) it would have been much more difficult, if not impossible, to write this book. Particular thanks are due to *The Boston Globe* (www.boston.com/globe), *The New York Times* (www.nytimes.com), CNN (www.cnn.com), *The Washington Post* (www.washingtonpost.com), *Wired* (www.wired.com), The Electronic Library (www.electroniclibrary.com), Amazon.com (www.amazon.com), Bibliofind (www.bibliofind.com), and the collector's narcotic, eBay (www.ebay.com).

# INTRODUCTION

## PORNOGRAPHY'S PROGRESS:
## FROM COTTAGE INDUSTRY TO ECONOMIC SECTOR

Strippers are not the first thing that leaps to mind when one thinks of the *Wall Street Journal*, but on at least two occasions in the last quarter-century, exotic dancers have featured prominently in the *Journal*'s generally dignified columns. In October 1974, the *Journal* reported on the exploits of Annabell Battistella, a former stripper who worked in Washington, D.C., under the stage name "Fanne Fox, the Argentine firecracker." Battistella came to the attention of the *Journal* (and the rest of the nation) when she took a well-publicized dive into the Tidal Basin in Washington, D.C., after a night out with Representative Wilbur Mills. Even then, the *Journal* might not have paid much public attention to the peccadillos of a congressman, but Mills happened to be the chair of the House Ways and Means Committee and was widely regarded for his knowledge of tax and tariff law, issues of particular interest to the *Journal* and its readers.

In May 1997, another former stripper was featured in the *Journal*. But this time, the *Journal*'s focus was not on her swimming ability or her relationship with the members of Congress. Instead, the *Journal*'s coverage of Danni Ashe focused on her business skills and her success in using a new medium—the Internet—to market sexually explicit images of herself and other models. Under a subheading proclaiming "Lessons for the mainstream," *Journal* reporter Thomas E. Weber described how Ashe's site, Danni's Hard Drive, was "bring[ing] in so much revenue that she has given up the stage and nude photo shoots."[1] Weber also implicitly praised Ashe's initiative, reporting that when she was dissatisfied with the appearance of her original Web site, she sat down and taught herself Hypertext Markup Language, the formatting language for the World Wide Web. The article concludes with an impressive recitation of the site's revenues: "Now the pay site boasts 17,000 members, putting Ms. Ashe on pace for more than $2 million in revenue [in 1997], she says." Weber's article also pointed out that sites specializing in sexually explicit materials were generally the only ones online that consistently made money.

The article about Ashe was hardly the first time that the *Journal* has covered the business workings and fiscal fortunes of a pornographer—Hugh Hefner, for instance, and his *Playboy*-based empire have frequently been covered by the *Journal*, particularly after Hefner successfully took the company public in 1971.[2] What is more significant is the tone of the *Journal*'s article. It's not merely that Ashe was credited for having the foresight and initiative to set up her adult Web site; it's that the *Journal*'s article, by juxtaposing the low costs of start-up and the potential returns, not so subtly suggests that Internet pornography is a lucrative entrepreneurial opportunity in general.

The goal of this book is to illustrate the various social and technological developments over the last 50 years that have made it possible for a former stripper and now pornography entrepreneur to wind up in an unabashedly positive front-page article in the *Wall Street Journal*. Even in the heady days of *Playboy*'s early success, there was no suggestion that others should try to emulate Hefner's own entrepreneurial beginnings. Part of that was simply realistic: By the early 1960s, when the media first began to cover the Playboy empire like any other business, *Playboy*'s share of the magazine market was so large that it would have been essentially impossible to start a competitor for *Playboy* on the same-sized shoestring that Hefner used. More important, even given *Playboy*'s success, the pornography business was still so socially unacceptable that few people would even have remotely considered becoming a pornographer.

The combination, however, of an enormously successful sexual entrepreneur (more on Hefner in a minute), a well-attended sexual revolution, and a steady flow of technological innovations to increase the privacy of pornography consumption have significantly reduced or eliminated much of the stigma attached to pornography. Pornography's progress over the last half-century, of course, has not been uniformly smooth: The industry has had to contend with the rise of religious and social conservative movements, 15 years of antagonistic administrations in Washington (including the infamous Meese Commission), and a supposedly disastrous U.S. Supreme Court opinion (1973's *Miller v. California*). Despite these impediments, however, the pornography industry has flourished, and by the middle of the 1990s, pornographers found themselves uniquely positioned to take advantage of the phenomenal production and distribution capabilities of the Internet.

Given the *Journal*'s focus on business and finance, its nonjudgmental coverage of online pornography should not be particularly surprising. Ashe and other online pornographers are the newest participants in an industry that over the last quarter-century has grown from approximately $2 billion in total annual revenues to at least $10 billion (although some estimate that the actual total today is somewhere between $15 billion and $20 billion). The sheer amount of money at stake makes the pornography industry newsworthy. Even at the conservative estimate of $10 billion per year in gross revenues, the pornography industry takes in about what Americans pay for sporting events and live music performances combined.

Of that industry total, adult Web sites contribute an estimated $1 billion to $2 billion per year, or between 5 and 10 percent of the total amount of money spent online in 1998. Although there is no suggestion that the online pornography industry will keep pace with online spending in general (doing so would put online sales of sexually explicit materials at somewhere between $50 billion and $100 billion in 2001, which seems unlikely), there is little reason to believe that the industry will not experience continued strong growth in the foreseeable future.

So if the *Journal* is touting the entrepreneurial possibilities of pornography, what does that say about the role of sex and pornography in American society in general? A fashionable pastime these days, particularly among such conservative pundits as Cal Thomas, Mona Charen, Pat Buchanan, and William Bennett is to perceive a vast moral decay engulfing American society in the last days of the second millennium. It is even more fashionable, if not *de rigueur*, to portray President Clinton (the first baby boomer president) as both symbol of and unrepentant contributor to the spreading rot. Baby boomers, so the argument goes, with their casual attitudes toward sex, perpetually rebellious attitudes, and compulsive need for self-gratification have brought the nation teetering on the edge of a moral abyss. One of the most frequently cited pieces of evidence in support of this view is the amount of pornography and sexual content available in print, on video, and online.

An important irony, of course, is that it wasn't the rebellious, unruly baby boomers who single-handedly transformed pornography from a largely underground enterprise into a multibillion-dollar industry; instead, it was their allegedly buttoned-down, strait-laced elders, who fought the Good War, voted for Ike and JFK, built Levittown, and purchased Hugh Hefner's *Playboy* by the millions. When Hefner published the first issue of *Playboy* in December 1953, the oldest baby boomers were just turning six years old.[3] As precocious as that generation of Americans has proved to be, it is doubtful that they purchased many of the more than 50,000 copies that Hefner sold of that first issue. By the time the first baby boomers were old enough to vote, in 1968,[4] Hefner was already a multimillionaire. Undoubtedly, many adolescent baby boomers sneaked a peek or two at Dad's copy of *Playboy*, but it certainly wasn't their generation that turned the magazine into a cultural icon and Hefner into one of the richest men in the country.[5]

To be fair, the baby boomers, whose enthusiastic embrace of the sexual revolution in the late 1960s and early 1970s so fundamentally changed American society, have helped to push the pornography industry far beyond anything Hefner might have imagined in 1953. If their fathers made pornography an industry, then the baby boomers have made it a full-blown sector of the economy. It is chiefly baby boomers, after all, who now rent more than $5 billion worth of adult videos each year, purchase $150 million worth of adult pay-per-view movies via cable and in hotel rooms, and whip out their credit cards to buy $1 billion to $2 billion worth of sexually explicit materials on the Internet.

The social impact of these new technologies has been profound. By eliminating inconvenient, potentially embarrassing, and occasionally unnerving trips to urban adult movie theaters, such innovations as cable television, the VCR, and later the CD-ROM have helped the pornography industry to dramatically expand its potential pool of customers (and not insignificantly, breathed new life and enormous value into the industry's stock of films, which could be transferred to videotape or CD-ROM and sold or rented repeatedly). The potential privacy of talking to a phone sex operator or watching an adult movie in one's own living or hotel room has made it a much more palatable activity for millions of people, most of whom would never have considered going to an adult movie theater either by themselves or with a spouse or friend.

## THE RETURN OF SEXUAL ENTREPRENEURSHIP

By far, the most famous (and to date, most successful) sexual entrepreneur has been Hugh Marston Hefner, who turned a $600 investment in 1953 into a multimedia empire worth hundreds of millions of dollars. The 27-year-old Hefner was a veteran of the magazine empire of George von Rosen, who published a variety of girlie and faux-nudist magazines including *Modern Man* and *Sunshine & Health*. Hefner did not intend to supplant existing methods of distribution or production; his intent, after all, was to produce and distribute a magazine. But Hefner was an innovator who had studied the competition and was convinced that he could offer a new product to a new market. The new product: a men's magazine featuring full-color photos of nude women (*Playboy* was one of the first men's magazines to publish photos in color) and emphasizing a sophisticated, urban lifestyle. Hefner's intended new market: the nation's swelling ranks of young male professionals, eager to believe *Playboy*'s seductive pitch of the good life (not least of which was the fantasy of an active sexual life).

The centerpiece of Hefner's new magazine was a color photo of a woman already well established as a national sex symbol. Using $500 of his $600 in cash, Hefner secured the reproduction rights to a garage calendar photo of Marilyn Monroe from the calendar's publisher (Monroe, not surprisingly, had no say about the use of her image). With the Monroe photo in hand, Hefner was able to raise an additional $10,000 from family and friends, which he used to produce and print roughly 70,000 copies of his magazine.

By any objective measure, Hefner's success was stunning: The first issue of *Playboy* in December 1953 sold more than 50,000 copies in a little more than four weeks. At 50 cents an issue, Hefner grossed more than $25,000 in his first month, which enabled him to pay back his investors and still print a second issue. Within two years, he was selling more than 600,000 copies per month. Just 13 years after founding *Playboy* in his living room, Hefner's personal worth crossed the $100 million mark (an amount that translates into more than $503 million in 1998 purchasing power). *Playboy* magazine was selling millions of copies each month, and Playboy Enterprises, Inc. (PEI) owned a growing chain of nightclubs that would help to turn *Playboy's* bunny logo into a three-dimensional cultural icon around the world. In 1966, Hefner purchased 919 North Michigan Avenue and made a nine-foot-high, illuminated "Playboy" sign part of the Chicago skyline for the next 23 years. And just five years later, in 1971, PEI would engage in that purest of capitalistic endeavors, a public stock offering.

Somewhat ironically, Hefner's overwhelming entrepreneurial success actually made it harder for other entrepreneurs to compete. Although a large number of different men's magazines were started in the 1950s, 1960s, and 1970s, none was able to achieve as a start-up anything close to what Hefner had achieved.[6] The same was generally true in the adult film industry: During the so-called "Golden Age of Pornography," from 1957 to 1973, the industry was dominated by a relatively small number of well-heeled (and allegedly well-connected) movie companies that could afford the typical $200,000 to $300,000 in production costs and, more important, had access to the rigidly controlled distribution channels.

The consolidation of the pornography industry was accelerated by the U.S. Supreme Court's decision in *Miller v. California* (1973). In *Miller*, the Court laid out the standard for determining whether sexually explicit material is obscene rather than merely pornographic:

> (a) whether the average person, applying contemporary community standards would find that the work, taken as a whole, appeals to the prurient interest; (b) whether the work depicts or describes, in a patently offensive way, sexual conduct specifically defined by the applicable state law; and (c) whether the work, taken as a whole, lacks serious literary, artistic, political, or scientific value.[7]

The significance of this three-pronged standard—which became known as the *Miller* test—is that it was a specific rejection of the Court's pronouncement 16 years earlier in *United States v. Roth* that before a work could be deemed "obscene," it had to be found to be "utterly without redeeming social importance."

The adoption of *Miller* and the subsequent well-publicized trial in Memphis, Tennessee of various people involved in the production and distribution of the hugely popular X-rated movie *Deep Throat* (including its stars Harry Reems and Linda Lovelace) did cause a temporary retrenchment by the nation's pornographers. The new legal test for obscenity was widely viewed as a limitation on what sexually explicit materials could safely be published, and most pornographers did change their product in an effort to lessen their legal exposure. The major magazines, for instance, made both their cover art and contents less explicit (at least temporarily), and adult movie distributors limited the geographic regions in which their movies played. Some West Coast adult film companies, for instance, did not distribute their movies outside of California for fear of prosecution under the federal antiobscenity laws.

As a general rule, the larger financial resources of established pornography businesses such as *Playboy* and *Penthouse* magazines gave them the ability to weather legal challenges in multiple jurisdictions, which in turn enabled them to maintain large distribution areas. At the same time, the decision in *Miller* narrowed the scope of what was legally acceptable, which meant that potential competitors had less opportunity to distinguish themselves from *Playboy* and *Penthouse* by offering more explicit or rawer images. As Larry Flynt demonstrated when he successfully founded *Hustler* in 1974, there was still some room left on the fringes of legality, but the numerous legal proceedings he has faced in his lifetime clearly demonstrate the risks of operating a pornography business at the fringes of obscenity. Most recently, Flynt and his brother Jimmy reached a plea agreement with Cincinnati prosecutors on a 15-count indictment. Under the terms of the agreement, the Flynts were allowed to substitute the *Hustler* corporation as the defendant and have the corporation plead guilty to two counts of pandering. In exchange, prosecutors agreed to drop all other charges against the brothers, including a count of selling obscenity to a minor, which under Ohio law carries a maximum sentence of 24 years in prison.[8]

The mere fact that Flynt was able to launch and operate a magazine as avowedly crude and misogynistic as *Hustler* is ample evidence, however, that it was impossible for the *Miller* court to turn the judicial clock back to 1957, when it handed down the *Roth* decision. In part because of the *Roth* decision itself, and in part because of broader social forces, the nation's attitudes toward sexually explicit materials underwent enormous changes in the 16 years between *Roth* and *Miller*. In 1957, for instance, Hugh Hefner's soft-focus and nonpubic *Playboy* was just four years old and still daring for its time; in 1974, Flynt's aggressively genital *Hustler* was edgy, often violent, and raw, but in most parts of the country, it was not obscene.

The goal of the *Miller* decision was to give local communities the ability to set their own standards as to what is obscene and what is not. In the years following the Court's decision, however, a variety of technological advances have severely undercut the ability of local communities to enforce their standards of obscenity. In particular, the telephone, cable television, the computer, and the Internet have made it possible for sexually explicit materials to enter a community without anyone but the specific consumer knowing they are there.

An even more significant consequence of these various technological innovations is that it is now very easy for virtually anyone to become a producer and distributor of sexually explicit materials. For less than $200, for instance, someone can purchase a camcorder, make a videotape of herself in the nude or having sex, send the video off to a distributor of amateur videos, and earn royalties on its sale. Although the initial investment is higher, the cost of distributing sexual images across the Internet is even lower, and the potential return is far greater. Despite what one might imagine as a glut of product, sexually explicit materials still sell at a premium over their nonsexual counterparts. As a result, as the costs of production and distribution have steadily fallen over the last 25 years, the financial attractiveness of the pornography business has steadily grown.

Not everyone with a camcorder or computer, of course, is starring in his own personal pornographic productions, just as not every owner of a still camera shoots nude photos of himself or herself. Still, if social and religious conservatives are correct in their estimate that there are now at least 60,000 adult Web sites online (more objective estimates are half that number), then there are a lot of people who have recently decided to become pornographers. It is a particularly startling illustration of the full extent of the change in American attitudes toward sexually explicit materials.

## DEFINING THE PRODUCT

Still left unanswered, of course, is the question of just what exactly these new sexual entrepreneurs are selling. Over the last 14 months, when I've told people that I'm writing a book about pornography on the Internet, even those who don't own computers have nodded knowingly. Clearly, most people carry around with them at least a working definition of pornography; there's no need, as they say, to draw them a picture.

That's a fairly vague standard, however, on which to build a business. After all, a sexual entrepreneur's entire business and personal freedom can turn on whether twelve jurors good and true believe that a particular image is obscene or merely pornographic. The distinction is hardly trivial: Under the United States Constitution, nonobscene materials, however pornographic, are protected by the First Amendment; obscene materials are not entitled to any First Amendment protection and their mere possession can result in fines and imprisonment. Distinguishing between the obscene and the merely pornographic is a problem that our society (and in particular, the legislatures and the courts) have been wrestling with for years.

Dictionary definitions are of only slight assistance. According to the *Oxford English Dictionary*, the first appearance of "pornography" in the English language occurred in 1857, when it appeared in an English medical dictionary with the accompanying definition, "a description of prostitutes or of prostitution, as a matter of public hygiene."[9] Seven years later, the word made its first appearance in the United States in Webster's dictionary, with the definition "licentious painting employed to decorate the walls of rooms sacred to bacchanalian orgies, examples of which exist in Pompeii."

The origins of the word "pornography" betray the moral assumptions that typically accompany its use. The word is a spin-off of "pornographer," which first appeared in 1850.[10] "Pornographer" is derived from the Greek, poruografh, "writing of harlots," and is defined in the *Oxford English Dictionary* as "one who writes of prostitutes or obscene matters; a portrayer of obscene subjects."[11] In turn, "obscene" is defined in part as "offensive to modesty or decency; expressing or suggesting unchaste or lustful ideas; impure, indecent, lewd."[12]

Over the last 140 years, the moral component of the definition of pornography has not changed dramatically, but the scope of the material included in the definition has expanded as technology has changed:

- 1927: "The description of prostitutes or prostitution; hence, obscene literature or art."[13]
- 1947: "1. The expression or suggestion of the obscene in speaking, writing, etc.; licentious art or literature. 2. Description of prostitutes and of prostitution as related to public hygiene."[14]
- 1961: "1. A description of prostitutes or prostitution; 2. a depiction (as in writing or painting) of licentiousness or lewdness: a portrayal of erotic behavior designed to cause sexual excitement."[15]
- 1966: "Obscene literature, art, or photography, esp. that having little or no artistic merit."[16]
- 1969: "Written, spoken, or other forms of communication intended to excite lascivious feelings."[17]
- 1977: "1. The depiction of erotic behavior (as in pictures or writing) intended to cause sexual excitement; 2. material (as books or a photograph) that depicts erotic behavior and is intended to cause sexual excitement."[18]
- 1992: "1. Pictures, writing, or other material that is sexually explicit and sometimes equates sex with power and violence. 2. The presentation or production of this material."[19]
- 1998: "Any material, pictures, films, printed matter, or devices dealing with sexual poses or acts considered indecent by the public."[20]

The most recent definition illustrates the challenge of defining the product that sexual entrepreneurs offer. What "public," after all, determines whether a particular sexual pose or act is "indecent"? That was precisely the issue the U.S. Supreme Court dealt with in *Miller*, when it announced the local community standard. The theory behind *Miller* is that since local communities are the ones that have to deal with the allegedly deleterious effects of the public display and sale of sexually explicit materials (lower property values, increased crime, effect on public morals, etc.), it should be the local communities—the points of sale for the pornography—that decide whether a particular movie, book, or magazine is in fact obscene.

Most of the new technologies, however, shift the point of sale for pornography from a storefront on Main Street to an individual's living room. For the purveyors of telephone sex, adult cable channels, and Internet pornography, there is no direct impact any longer on local communities, which calls into question the ability and the right of a local community to label a particular image or conversation as obscene. The U.S. Supreme Court has already glanced at this issue once, when it ruled in *Sable Communications v. FCC* that Congress's ban on obscenity applied to phone sex as well as other types of sexually explicit material. The Court rejected Sable's argument that it would effectively be subject to a national standard of obscenity imposed by the least tolerant community. "Sable," the Court said, "is free to tailor its messages, on a selective basis, if it so chooses, to the communities it chooses to serve."[21]

The question, of course, which is thrown into particularly sharp relief by the Internet, is whether communications technologies like the phone and the Internet serve whole communities or individual households. This question was only indirectly raised in *Sable*, but the time may well be approaching for it to be considered more directly. For instance, when a computer connects to the Internet through an Internet service provider, it is temporarily assigned a unique Internet identifier that has no relationship whatsoever to the computer's physical location. In the not too distant future, even phone numbers will lose their geographic organization. The explosion in demand for phone numbers has a number of telecommunications companies considering the implementation of permanent personal phone numbers, which people would take with them wherever they reside. Increasingly, the "local community" that should be deciding whether a particular image or sexual conversation is unacceptable is the individual who is actually purchasing it.

## A PERSONAL NOTE

It is ironic that 25 years ago, the nation's capital was also roiled by the news of a powerful Arkansas Democrat engaged in an extramarital affair. I have distinct recollection of my parents' refusal to allow me (age 11 at the time) to watch the evening news, despite my evident interest in knowing more about the "Argentine bombshell" and just what it was that she and the congressman had been doing. Normally, my parents encouraged my siblings and me to follow the news from Washington in great detail, so their disinclination to have me watch Walter Cronkite's report on Congressman Mills's misadventure was particular striking. To be fair, I don't know if my parents were trying to shield me from the news about Mills's extramarital activity or the broader realization that not all congressmen behave properly. On both fronts, it was a valiant but ultimately futile effort.

Today, as a parent myself, I face a similar predicament that is at the same time both more and less acute. My children are younger today than I was in 1974, which makes it easier to limit their exposure, but the information about the president's Oval Office dalliance with Monica Lewinsky is far more widely available, far more detailed, and far more explicit than anything broadcast 25 years ago. Every mainstream news program (let alone the more purposefully racy ones) has detailed the type of sexual relations engaged in by Clinton and Lewinsky, and has reported on which areas of her body were touched and for what purpose. I find it virtually impossible to imagine Walter Cronkite or John Chancellor offering similar descriptions in 1974. It is hard not to conclude that when it comes to descriptions of sex in the White House, more is somehow less.

Undoubtedly, there will be those who argue that precisely the same is true for this book, that it serves no good purpose to examine in detail and without particular condemnation an industry whose sole objective is to sell sexually explicit images and sexual fantasy to as many people as possible. If, as some argue, the prurient interest of the news media and the public in President Clinton is partly a result of the prevalence of pornography, why then give any thoughtful consideration to the businesses that produce and distribute it?

There are a number of different answers to the question, but two suffice. First, the pornography industry does not deserve all of the blame for the public's lascivious appetites. As this book illustrates, sex sold long before there was a United States. If anything, the existence of a pornography industry is a reflection of an immutable human characteristic, our reproductive drive. For reasons too complex and elusive for this book, fantasy is an integral part of that drive. The universality of sexual images underscores the importance of fantasy for all humans.

Of more immediate importance, the pornography industry is once again at the forefront of technological innovation and change. In their rush to limit the allegedly harmful effects of pornography, Congress and various state legislatures have overlooked the role that the pornography industry is playing in making the Internet a faster and more economically viable medium for all businesses. This is not intended to be an argument that illegal businesses should be left alone if they are economically successful; far from it. But any effort to rein in online smut should recognize the broader sociological and economic forces that are making the pornography industry an increasingly attractive entrepreneurial opportunity and should give due weight to the important role that these entrepreneurs are playing in shaping this new medium.

—Frederick S. Lane III

Burlington, Vermont

13 May 1999

# NOTES

1. Weber omitted to point out, however, that Ashe has not given up nude photo shoots altogether. Ashe's Web site contains numerous nude photos of her.

2. The success of the stock offering was spurred in part by the fact that the stock certificate for Playboy featured a reclining nude; at the time of the offering, nearly 20,000 people bought a single share as a collector's item. New certificates (without the nude) were issued in 1990, but many shareholders refused to give up their original certificates.

3. According to the *American Heritage Dictionary of the English Language* (3d ed.), the post–World War II baby boom ranged from 1947 to 1961. Other sources stretch the baby boom in each direction, from as early as 1946 to as late as 1963.

4. The voting age was not lowered to 18 until the adoption of the 26th Amendment to the U.S. Constitution on July 1, 1971.

5. Baby boomers cannot even be given credit for inventing illicit presidential dalliances: Seventy-five years before Monica Lewinsky first walked into the White House, there were widespread (and accurate) reports that President Warren Harding was often illicitly closeted with presidential secretary Nan Britton. Unlike his Starr-crossed successor, of course, Harding did not have to face the possibility of impeachment for his extramarital activity, in part because it would not have occurred to anyone then that he should and in part because he died two years into his term.

6. *Playboy's* two chief competitors, *Penthouse* and *Hustler*, were able to make significant inroads into Hefner's market share for two different but equally important reasons: Bob Guccione, the owner of *Penthouse*, did not launch an American edition of the magazine until after several successful years of publishing the magazine in Great Britain; and Larry Flynt successfully carved out a segment of the market that felt underserved by the tonier adult publications like *Playboy* and *Penthouse*. Moreover, as Flynt has demonstrated with his recent campaign to expose what he perceives as sexual hypocrisy on Capital Hill, he has a genius for self-promotion.

7. 413 U.S. 15, 24–25 (1973).

8. Terry Kinney, "Flynt reaches plea agreement, videos to be removed," *Boston Globe*, May 12, 1999.

9. *Oxford English Dictionary*, s.v. "pornography."

10. *Oxford English Dictionary*, s.v. "pornographer."

11. *Oxford English Dictionary*, s.v. "pornographer."

12. *Oxford English Dictionary*, s.v. "obscene," def. 2.

13. *The New Century Dictionary*, s.v. "pornography."

14. *Funk & Wagnalls New Practical Standard Dictionary*, 1947 ed., s.v. "pornography."

15. *Webster's Third New International Dictionary*, s.v. "pornography."

16. *The Random House Dictionary of the English Language*, unabridged ed., s.v. "pornography."

17. *The American Heritage Dictionary of the English Language*, s.v. "pornography."

18. *Webster's New Collegiate Dictionary*, s.v. "pornography."

19. *The American Heritage Dictionary*, 3d ed., s.v. "pornography."

20. *The 1998 Grolier Multimedia Encyclopedia*, s.v. "pornography."

21. 492 U.S. 115, 125 (1989).

# 1

# A BRIEF HISTORY OF PORNOGRAPHY AND TECHNOLOGY

The thing that hath been, it is that which shall be;
and that which is done is that which shall be done;
and there is no new thing under the sun.
Ecclesiastes 1:9

On August 7, 1908, archaeologist Josef Szombathy discovered a small limestone figurine lying deep in the mud of the Danube River outside the town of Willendorf, Austria.[1] Carbon dating of the sedimentary layer in which the figurine, nicknamed the "Venus of Willendorf," was found put the object's age at somewhere between 24,000 and 22,000 B.C.E., making it one of the earliest depictions of the human form ever discovered.

Even with the passage of more than 240 centuries, there can be no doubt that the figurine Szombathy discovered is a depiction of a human female. Although seven long braids encircle the figurine's head and obscure the face, the body's chief distinguishing characteristics—an upright torso, large pendulous breasts, and prominent mons pubis with a distinctly rendered vulva—are unmistakably human and unequivocally female. The rest of the figurine is no less remarkable: thin, almost nonexistent arms draped across the breasts; round and well-padded buttocks; an ample stomach; rolls of fat along her sides; and corpulent thighs, pressed together but not obscuring her genitals.

On the basis of age and craftsmanship alone, the Venus was a remarkable discovery. It is one of the earliest examples of humanity's ability to create images in three dimensions, and it was executed with compelling skill and attention to detail. Its diminutive size and final resting place, in soil far from the oolitic limestone from which it was carved, suggests that it was intended as a piece of portable art. Perhaps most compellingly of all, the figurine was clearly designed to highlight and accentuate female sexual characteristics.

Over the last 150 years, approximately 200 similar figurines have been found in locations ranging from France and Spain in the west to the Urals in the east. Vast amounts of research grant dollars have been spent and small forests have been leveled in the debate by archaeologists and anthropologists over the significance of these figurines.[2] Scholars debate their possible significance as religious or cult icons, fertility totems, rites of passage, realistic or stylized portraits, and tribal identifiers. Some even suggest that they are little more than prehistoric Barbie dolls. Given the skill and artistic detail with which the Venus of Willendorf was executed, it is tempting to surmise that a skilled pre-historic sculptor might have profitably traded figurines for food, fire, shelter, and other necessities. The lack of a written historical record, however, makes it unlikely that definitive answers to these questions will ever be found.

As is often the case, the labeling and description of these figurines reveals far more about contemporary attitudes toward sexual imagery than those of their creators.

The nickname "Venus," for instance, was first used to describe a prehistoric figurine by a French archaeologist, the Marquis de Vibraye, who discovered a similar statuette at Abri de Laugerie-Basse in 1864. By the turn of the century, the term had become standard archaeological shorthand for each new female Paleolithic figurine.[3] Christopher L. C. E. Witcombe, a professor of archaeology at Sweet Briar College, explains that:

> To identify the Willendorf figurine as "Venus," then, was a rich male joke that neatly linked the primitive and the female with the uncivilized and at the same time, through implicit contrast with the Classical Venus, served as a reassuring example to patriarchal culture of the extent to which the female and female sexuality had been overcome and women effectively subjugated by the male-dominated civilizing process.[4]

When the figurines weren't being mocked for their depiction of the female form, they were being effectively censored for the explicitness of their renderings. Despite the obvious historical and artistic importance of the Venus of Willendorf, for instance, the nudity and unequivocal sexuality of the figurine kept it out of beginning art textbooks for nearly 60 years. While the ostensible reason for the figurine's omission was the belief that it was not typical of its period,[5] the primary (albeit unspoken) objection was to the carving's explicitness and thinly veiled eroticism.

As the sexual revolution swept the nation in the late 1960s, easing attitudes toward the depiction of sexual imagery, the Venus of Willendorf not only gained her rightful place in entry-level art texts but also became something of a cultural phenomenon. The figurine was adopted by many as a symbol of the Mother or Earth Goddess, a concatenation of multiple prehistoric female deities carrying heavy overtones of fertility fetish and erotic charm.

Thanks in large part to Jean Auel's popular Earth's Children series, best known for its first book, *The Clan of the Cave Bear*, the Venus as Goddess is now probably the most widely accepted explanation for the figurines.[6] In the second book of the series, for instance, Auel's hero Jondolar carries a Venus figurine with him on a ritual journey with his brother:

> As he spoke, Jondalar unconsciously reached into the pouch attached to his belt and felt for the small stone figurine of an obese female. He felt the familiar huge breasts, her large protruding stomach, and her more than ample buttocks and thighs. The arms and legs were insignificant, it was the Mother aspects that were important, and the limbs on the stone figure were only suggested. The head was a knob with a suggestion of hair that carried across the face, with no features.
>
> No one could look on the awesome face of Doni, the Great Earth Mother, Ancient Ancestress, First Mother, Creator and Sustainor of all life, She who blessed all women with Her power to create and bring forth life. And none of the small images of Her that carried Her spirit, the donii, ever dared to suggest Her face.
>
> Jondalar absentmindedly caressed the pendulous stone breasts of the donii in his pouch, wishing for luck as he thought about their Journey.[7]

Today, the Venus of Willendorf's role is more commercial than spiritual. With her image having passed into the public domain centuries ago, more than 200 hundred sites on the World Wide Web alone display the image of the Venus of Willendorf or offer Venus-adorned products for sale. The Venus can now be found, for instance, on jewelry of every description (brass, pewter, gold), on T-shirts, posters, postcards, and paper dolls, and even molded into glycerine soap. Even prehistoric sex, it appears, sells.

## THE GREEKS AND THE ROMANS

The commercial use of sexual images in Western civilization reached its height in Greek and Roman culture. By the time they consolidated their political and military control over the Aegean peninsula circa 800 B.C.E., the Greeks had already established widespread trade in goods and services.

Thanks to extensive archaeological excavations over the last century, numerous ancient Greek household and decorative items have been uncovered. Even a cursory examination of these ordinary objects makes clear that sex was a commonplace theme. Sexual imagery adorns wine coolers, dinnerware, and even children's drinking bowls and plates.[8] The Greeks also carved sexual images and fertility symbols into stone statuettes and figurines, beat them into bronze bowls and mirror covers, and molded them into clay lamps. Sexual activity or symbols were not the only subject depicted on vases and other household objects, of course—Greek artists also depicted scenes from everyday life, famous battles, and myths and legends—but sex was clearly a common and unremarkable theme.[9]

With the destruction of Corinth in 146 B.C.E., the territories of Ancient Greece came under the control of Rome, which quickly established itself as the preeminent military and economic power in the Mediterranean. Aided by a superb system of roads stretching thousands of miles, an efficient postal system, the Roman legions, a common currency, and low tariffs, Roman businesses traded goods from one end of the empire to the other and with many of the neighboring civilizations. As with the Greeks before them, the Romans showed little reluctance to produce artistic works containing often frank descriptions of sexual activity. The poems of Roman writers such as Catullus, Martial, and Juvenal, for instance, have inspired schoolboy snickers for generations, and have stretched the editorial abilities of classical scholars. Among Catullus's least scabrous lines, for example, are the following:

> I entreat you, my sweet Ipsitilla,
> my darling, my charmer,
> bid me come and spend the afternoon with you.
> And if you do bid me, grant me this kindness too,
> that no one may bar the panel of your threshold,
> nor you yourself have a fancy to go away,
> but stay at home and have ready for me
> nine consecutive copulations.
> And bid me come at once if you are going to at all:
> for I'm on my bed after lunch, thrusting through tunic and cloak.[10]

In addition, many of the objects produced by Roman artists and businesses were sexual in nature or adorned with explicit sexual images. The fertility cult of Priapus was important to the Romans, and artisans worked the cult's chief symbol (an erect or semierect penis) into wax votive candles, jewelry, wall carvings, hanging lamps, ornaments, mosaics, and even belt buckles.[11] And as the excavations at Pompeii clearly reveal, Roman sexual imagery was not limited to household items but also adorned household walls in the form of paintings, murals, and frescoes. A strenuous argument was made that such images appeared only on the walls of Roman brothels, a view poignantly captured by poet James Dickey in his poem "In the Lupanar at Pompeii":

> As tourist, but mostly as lecher,
> I seek out the dwelling of women
> Who all expect me, still, because
> They expect anybody who comes.
> I am ready to pay, and I do,
> And then go in among them

Where on the dark walls of their home
They hold their eternal postures,
Doing badly drawn, exacting,
Too-willing, wild-eyed things
With dry-eyed art.[12]

When that argument was conclusively rejected, the fallback position was that sexually explicit materials appeared only in rooms that were used exclusively by adults (and preferably just by men and prostitutes). However, further research has made it clear that erotic images took their place with less explicit works of art throughout the home. The discoverers and custodians of Pompeii could do little about the unfortunate artistic choices of the long-dead Romans, but they did their best to shield modern sensibilities. As late as 1964, the rooms adorned with sexually explicit frescoes and paintings were still roped off to most visitors, although men could usually gain entrance by plying the site custodian with a small gratuity.[13]

Given the profound impact that Greek and Roman culture and thought have had on virtually every other aspect of Western civilization, it is noteworthy that the commercial use of sexual imagery in the U.S. has still not matched those ancient cultures in its scope or frankness. A number of powerful factors—the birth of a charismatic leader, the sexual excesses of a long string of dissipated Roman emperors, the collapse of the Empire's political and military dominance, and the phenomenal growth of an ascetic religion—combined to virtually eliminate sex as an aesthetic and commercial theme for more than a millennium.[14] So powerful was the cultural shift that it has only been in the last 30 years that the use of sex in commerce has approached its pre-Christian levels.

## NO NUDES IS GOOD NUDES

In Palestine, around 34 to 38 C.E., a Jewish teacher named Jesus of Nazareth attracted thousands of followers with his message of the advent of the Kingdom of God and his promise of God's pardon and the eternal reward of heaven for repentant sinners. His popularity was a cause of concern for the Romans, who governed the region following their conquest of the Jews in 63 B.C.E., but even more so for the religious leaders of the Jews. Jesus's teachings, with their emphasis on repentance over ritual, were perceived as a challenge to the Torah. The dispute over religious doctrine was ultimately a significant factor in Jesus's subsequent betrayal, arrest, and crucifixion.

As is often the case with charismatic leaders, however, Jesus's death energized his followers. From its center in Jerusalem, the Christian movement spread rapidly throughout the eastern Mediterranean. By the middle of the first century C.E., the new religion had become popular enough to attract the unfavorable attention of Emperor Nero.[15] Although the number of Christians was still fairly small, the religion's rate of growth and worship of "Christ the Lord" instead of the emperor as god were seen as inherent threats to Roman social stability. Force-feeding Christians to the lions in the Colosseum, however, proved to be only a short-term solution: "The blood of the martyrs," the Carthage-born Christian writer Tertullian (160?–240? C.E.) later said, "became the seed of the church."[16]

It proved to be prolific seed. Christianity's rapid growth and swelling political power (it was adopted as the official religion of the Roman Empire in 324 C.E. by the Emperor Constantine) coincided with the empire's own steadily declining stability. Racked by internal dissensions and threatened repeatedly by outside aggressors, the Roman Empire was split in two in the fourth century, and what was left of the Western Roman Empire fell to the Germanic tribes in 476 C.E. As the Roman Empire lay in tatters from the Atlantic Ocean to the Dardanelles, the commercial and political infrastructure that had supported it rapidly disappeared. Gone, for instance, were the highly skilled engineers who built an elaborate system of roads from one end of the empire to the other; gone were the Roman Legions, who kept the roads largely free of brigands and thieves; and long gone or much diminished were the markets around the Mediterranean interested in or capable of supporting the sculptors, painters, and potters who helped decorate and equip empire villas.

The disintegration of Rome's central authority and Europe's rapid economic retrenchment left the Christian Church as the only institution capable of exerting authority or influence across a wide geographical region. Over the next thousand years, Christianity's preeminent position in Western European culture helped to fundamentally change the attitudes of Western civilization toward sex and sexuality. Nudity, for instance, which was celebrated in both Greek and Roman culture and art, became a powerful taboo.[17] Depictions of sexual behavior of any description, let alone of such "deviant" practices as masturbation, orgies, or homosexuality were completely unacceptable.

Prohibition against nudity and the depiction of sexual activity were part and parcel of Christianity's more restrictive attitudes toward sex in general. Largely gone, for instance, were the fertility cults of Greece and Rome that celebrated and encouraged a wide variety of sexual activity. In the views of the early Christians, sex was a necessary evil to be tolerated grudgingly only for its role in procreation. The church's general attitude can best be summed up Saint Paul's cheerful admonishment to the Romans: "To be carnally minded is death."[18]

If moral strictures were somehow insufficient to control the content of artistic works, the church was also in a position to exert powerful economic influence over artists. As a multinational institution collecting tithes and donations throughout Europe, it had relatively large resources for commissioning works of art, which of course gave it direct control over content. The majority of artworks created in the Early Middle Ages were ordered by the church, and a significant portion of the works not directly commissioned by the Church were intended as gifts from the faithful. As a result, the Church was able to exert strong direct and indirect economic influence over the paintings and sculptures of the period. Not surprisingly, the art of the Early Middle Ages reflects Christian attitudes toward sex and sexual themes to an extent unmatched since.

In one creative field, the Christian Church's control was particularly effective. Literacy was one the greatest casualties of the Early Middle Ages, and what little reading and writing took place was largely limited to the monasteries that dotted the European landscape.[19] Moreover, the only books produced during that time were made by monks hunched over in a monastery *scriptorium*, laboriously copying from ancient texts and scrolls. As with art in general, literary reproductions were almost entirely limited to titles that met with the Church's approval (or at least that of the local bishop or abbot).

The Church's literary and artistic monopolies were eventually broken through a combination of education and technology. During the first millennium following Christ's birth, education (like almost every other facet of Western civilization) was under the control and direction of the Church. In the 11th and 12th centuries, however, the first secular universities were founded. Even though the new schools were often outgrowths of Church institutions, the Church's control over the content of the curriculum slowly began to slip. More importantly, the steady increase in the number of universities created a tremendous demand for texts which the monasteries simply could not meet. The economic opportunity presented by the demand for books was met to a large extent by lay copying centers, which further loosened Church control over the content of written materials.

Technology dramatically accelerated this trend. In 1450, Johannes Gutenberg became the first European to print using hand-set metal type. Although the casting and setting of type was a slow and laborious process, Gutenberg's invention made the production of multiple copies of a given page far faster than copying each page out by hand. With the demand for texts steadily growing, Gutenberg's press helped to lower the cost (at least in labor) of reproducing text and illustrations. Although it would be centuries more before a printed page could equal the beauty of a hand-crafted illuminated manuscript, the speed with which the press could produce serviceable texts made monasteries (and by extension, the Church itself) an increasingly irrelevant part of the medieval publishing process.

The Church's views on the morality of a given publication were hardly irrelevant, of course (it was no accident that Gutenberg's first work was a Bible), but in the heady intellectual atmosphere at the dawn of the Renaissance, people were increasingly willing to risk clerical disapproval. Among the very first printed books, for instance, were Giovanni Boccaccio's *Decameron* (written in 1371 C.E.) and Geoffrey Chaucer's *Canterbury Tales* (written from 1386 to 1400 C.E.). Both books are highly salacious in parts, and both have a strong anticlerical tone.

By the middle of the 16th century, in fact, the amount of obscene literature was sufficiently alarming to the Church that Pope Paul IV established the

*Index Librorum Prohibitorum*, the church's list of forbidden books. Although initially drafted to prevent Catholics from reading heretical protestant works, the *Index* was expanded in 1563 to include "[books] which professedly deal with narrate or teach things lascivious and obscene." The *Index*, however, did little to stop the spread of salacious materials, and may actually have had the opposite effect: Pope Pius IX (1792–1878), asked to help promote the sales of a friend's book, jokingly promised to list it in the *Index*.[20]

# SEX AND TECHNOLOGY IN AMERICA

In England, the course of the Protestant Revolution was altered by the sexual appetites of the reigning monarch. King Henry VIII, who lusted after his wife's lady-in-waiting Anne Boleyn, used the Catholic Church's refusal to grant him a divorce from Catherine as an excuse to set himself up as the head of an Anglican Church. In the decades following the separation from Rome, however, some English Protestants came to believe that not enough had been done to purge Roman Catholic doctrine and practices from the Church of England. Although the reformers were splintered into numerous groups by the end of the 1500s, the most numerous and most vocal of the critics came to be known as Puritans. When the Puritans wound up on the losing side of the ensuing doctrinal debate with the Anglican Church, the resulting persecution chased them first to the Netherlands and ultimately across a storm-tossed Atlantic to Plymouth, Massachusetts.

## AMERICA'S PURITAN FOUNDATION

Three hundred and seventy–odd years later, the adjective "puritanical" has become one of the most overused words in the debate over the Internet. The term is favored by free-speech advocates as a way of describing both legislation such as the 1996 Communications Decency Act and its supporters. It is something of a bum rap for the Puritans, who did not in fact condemn all sexual enjoyment or equate sex per se with humanity's fall from grace.[21] Like most English Protestants, they felt that the Catholic Church's bar against marriage by clergy was unrealistic, and they also believed that the Church had not done enough to discourage "deviant" sexual behavior (i.e., anything other than the time, place, and manner described by St. Augustine). While constantly preaching moderation (lest couples begin enjoying sex purely for its own sake), Puritan leaders in the New World recognized the role that sex played in maintaining a strong marital bond and promoting procreation.

The source of the Puritans' dour reputation was their strong prohibition against *extra*marital forms of sexual activity, and their prohibition against any artistic work or social activity that might describe or encourage such behavior. For instance, though the Puritans were generally not opposed to dancing, they were suspicious of its potential to lead people astray. "Dancing was not disapproved of by all Puritans," said Jon Lane, the former director of public programs at Plimouth Plantation. "Many considered it to be good exercise. The problem was that country dancing was often filled with kissing, clipping, eye contact, et cetera. It was the 'Dating Game' of the 17th century. It was that behavior that the Puritans objected to."

For a period of time, colonial religious leaders were able to enforce their ban on sexually suggestive or explicit behavior much like the Christian Church had been able to do in the early Middle Ages.[22] At the beginning of the 17th century, the European population in the New World was small, the colonies were relatively isolated, and the supply of books and other artistic works was low. In addition, for more than a century, the Puritan church was a powerful partner of New England governments and courts (and in fact, they were often one and the same). Over time, the Bay Colony's religious leaders used their influence and authority to encode Puritan moral precepts into the secular legal code (a process that the Moral Majority and Christian Coalition have been striving to emulate for the last 15 years). As early as 1711, for example, the Massachusetts Bay Colony prohibited the "Composing, Writing, Printing or Publishing, of any Filthy Obscene or Prophane Song, Pamphlet, Libel or Mock-Sermon, in Imitation or in Mimicking of Preaching, or any other part of Divine Worship."[23]

The effort to codify religious precepts was driven in part by the realization that the church's authority in society was steadily diminishing. Unlike Europe in the early Middle Ages, the population of the colonies was growing at a tremendous rate. As a result, it was increasingly difficult for any one social or religious group to completely restrict access to texts or to prevent the dissemination of potentially scandalous materials. From 1620 to 1700, for instance, the European population in the colonies grew from a few dozen to approximately 262,000, and by 1781, to 3.5 million. Just as the growth of trade with Eastern and Arabic cultures in the 12th and 13th centuries exposed Europeans to intellectual concepts and sexual materials that had been suppressed or forgotten, population growth and trade between the colonies and Europe offered colonists access to materials which could not be produced in the New World.

## THE IRREPRESSIBLE DR. FRANKLIN

Few individuals better embodied the shift in social and sexual mores of the colonies than Benjamin Franklin. Born in 1706 in Puritan-dominated Boston, Franklin went on to become, among his other staggering accomplishments, one of the nation's great wits and most infamous roués. Despite Franklin's lusty embrace of life in general (during his life, he acknowledged fathering numerous children out of wedlock) and European culture in particular, his more salacious literary efforts remained unpublished in North America for decades after his death. The difference in what could be published in America and what was generally available in Europe sharply illustrates the impact of Puritan beliefs on North American culture.

During the first century of European settlement on North America, the printing press was almost exclusively under the control of religious leaders, which severely limited the materials that could be published. However, by the early 1700s, the cost of printing presses and, more important, the metal type used in the presses had fallen to a level that made it possible for some private individuals to own and operate their own presses. The increased privatization of printing presses helped to expand the range of printed materials, but laws like the one passed in 1711 by the Massachusetts Bay Colony made printing a potentially risky business.

Franklin had firsthand experience with such risks. In 1719, at the age of 13, Franklin was apprenticed to his brother James to work on the printing press that James had recently imported from England.[24] Two years later, he and his brother began publishing the *New England Courant*, a politically liberal tract that frequently earned the wrath of Massachusetts officials. For a short period in 1722, in fact, Franklin published the *Courant* on his own while his brother served a jail term for an issue that colonial authorities found particularly offensive. Following a dispute with his brother, Franklin moved to Philadelphia in 1723. After a brief visit in London to further his education as a printer, he returned to Philadelphia in 1726, and six years later, began publishing the well-known *Poor Richard's Almanack*.

Although the Quakers (the primary religious group in Pennsylvania) took a more liberal approach to sex than did the Puritans (which may have been one reason why Franklin's relocation from Boston to Philadelphia was permanent), there were still generally accepted limits to what might properly be printed. In April 1745, for instance, Franklin wrote a short essay titled "Advice to a Young Man on Choosing a Mistress," in which he extolled the charms of older women (including his famous final line: "and lastly—they are so grateful"). Franklin's essay, however, was not publicly printed in the United States until early in the 20th century.[25] At about the same time, Franklin wrote another essay, "The Speech of Polly Baker," in which a young woman defends herself for having produced a fifth illegitimate child.[26] "The Speech of Polly Baker" was published in the *Gentleman's Magazine* in London in 1747, but it was not printed in the United States. Also unprinted but very much in the same vein was Franklin's 1761 essay, "A Letter to the Royal Academy at Brussels," in which Franklin speculates about the benefits of different perfumes for flatulence.

In contrast, to America's literary repressiveness, there were plenty of overtly sexual printed materials circulating in Europe in the mid-1700s.[27] The stories of Boccaccio and Chaucer remained popular, as did the work of Italian poet and writer Pietro Aretino, whose *Il Modi* (*The Postures*) had been published in 1527. *Il Modi* consisted of a series of lewd sonnets written to accompany sixteen engravings by Giulio Romano, each depicting a different sexual position.[28]

Thanks to the efforts of printers throughout Europe, Aretino's *Postures* enjoyed widespread and enduring popularity.[29]

At about the same time, a new literary form was slowly emerging in Western Europe: the novel. Although the designation of "first novel" is hotly disputed (candidates include *Don Quixote* [1605 and 1615] and Pilgrim's Progress [1678–84]), no such mystery surrounds the identity of the first "adult" novel. Between February 1748 and March 1749, a destitute Englishman named John Cleland was confined to debtor's prison. He passed the time writing an erotic novel titled *Fanny Hill, or the Memoirs of a Woman of Pleasure*, which chronicled a young woman's successful rise from destitution to a middle-class life through a career in prostitution.

In the finest tradition of pornographers since, a major part of Cleland's motivation for writing *Fanny Hill* was financial, and he accomplished his objective—he was paid twenty guineas for the rights to the novel, enough to get him out of debtor's prison. But in a scenario that would become all too familiar in years to come, the real money lay in the production and distribution of Cleland's novel; the purchaser of the rights, publisher Ralph Griffiths, is reported to have earned more than £10,000 from the sale of *Fanny Hill*.[30] In 1749, a warrant was sworn out for the arrest of Cleland and Griffiths, but they were released on payment of £100.[31] Cleland went on to write three more erotic novels, but none had the success or staying power of *Fanny Hill*, which in 1998 marked its 250th year in print.[32]

Whether Franklin read Cleland's novel or any of the other sexually explicit materials circulating in Europe is difficult (if not impossible) to determine. But given the length of time he spent in Europe and his generally libidinous approach to life, he doubtless was familiar with the genre. It would be some years, however, before people with similar tastes could indulge in such books in the New World.

## THE FIRST STIRRINGS OF A PORNOGRAPHY INDUSTRY

Despite the generally cavalier attitude of U.S. publishers to foreign copyrights in the 1700s and 1800s, no one in the United States was earning money from the publication of *Fanny Hill*. The book's frank description of sexual activity and its unrepentant portrayal of the prostitute as heroine were completely unacceptable to civic leaders, particularly in New England.

Word of *Fanny Hill* (or perhaps the book itself), however, had clearly reached America. As early as 1786, a well-known American publisher was trying to get his hands on a copy. A London bookseller wrote to Isaiah Thomas of Worcester, Massachusetts, rejecting his request for a copy: "If you must have *The Memoirs of a Woman of Pleasure*, I must beg you will apply to some of the Captains coming here, as it is an article I do not send my customers if I can possibly avoid it."[33] Thomas apparently succeeded in finding a captain willing to import the book, because he reportedly printed his own copies of *Fanny Hill* in 1810.[34] However, whether out of an excess of caution or modesty, Thomas did not put his name on his publication, reproducing instead a fake imprint used by the original publisher Griffith for *his* own protection in the mid-1700s: "G. Fenton 1747."[35] Thomas's caution was clearly justified: in 1820, two itinerant booksellers were prosecuted in Massachusetts for selling copies of *Fanny Hill*, a transgression which earned one a fine and the other six months in jail.[36] A year later, a Massachusetts publisher named Peter Holmes was prosecuted and jailed for printing what he described as the "first American edition" of *Fanny Hill*.[37]

As every adolescent who has read *National Geographic* knows, one way to get around strictures on the publication of sexually explicit material is to cloak it in scientific study or social outrage (i.e., the "redeeming social importance" argument). Thanks to such stratagems, by the early 1800s, the domestic production of sexually explicit literature was much larger than might have been imagined. Spurred by a growing desire for smaller families and an interest in improving overall health (including sexual health), America's increasing literate population purchased hundreds of thousands of copies of so-called "advice literature." Among the popular titles were Dr. Charles Knowlton's *Fruits of Philosophy; or the Private Companion of Young Married People* (1832); William Alcott's *Young Man's Guide* (1833); Dr. Frederick Hollick's *The Marriage Guide* (1850); Russell Trall's *Sexual Physiology* (1866); and Alice Stockham's *Tokology: A Book for Every Woman* (1883). Also popular were such nonfiction titles as Dr. William Sanger's *History of Prostitution* (1858), which was the first such study conducted and printed in the United States.[38]

The age-old practice of accusing one's enemies of sexual aberrations or atrocities made a highly profitable American debut in 1836, with the publication of Maria Monk's *Awful Disclosures of the Hotel Dieu Nunnery*. Ostensibly an autobiography, Monk's *Awful Disclosures* claimed to reveal the terrible truth of life behind the walls of a Montreal Catholic convent. Monk used her exposé as an opportunity to describe a wide variety of sexual activity, up to and including rape of the nuns by priests, and the murders of nuns and children. By today's standards, the descriptions of sexual references were extremely elliptical, but for the 1830s, they were apparently quite titillating. Monk's book found a ready market among the nation's Protestant majority, who were quickly becoming concerned and resentful about the large numbers of Catholic immigrants arriving in the United States in the 1830s and 1840s.[39]

The first edition of Monk's book was published by Howe and Bates, a dummy corporation set up and run by two employees of Harper and Brothers (the forerunner of today's HarperCollins). Harper reportedly was concerned about the reaction of its Catholic customers to the book but did not want to miss out on what it believed would be a highly profitable title.[40]

Harper's assessment of the book's economic potential was accurate. Within seven months, *Awful Disclosures* sold 26,000 copies and became a rallying cry for anti-Catholic sentiments. By the start of the Civil War 25 years later,

Monk's book had sold more than 300,000 copies. A second book, *Further Disclosures of Maria Monk*, also sold well.[41]

The combination of a growing population and the success of books like *Awful Disclosures* helped to make it easier, at least temporarily, to publish books that lacked even a superficial socially redeeming purpose. In 1846, an Irish surgeon named William Haynes took advantage of the freer atmosphere when he immigrated to New York City and published another American edition of *Fanny Hill*. Like Hefner almost exactly a century later, Haynes's timing was superb. Not only was Haynes not prosecuted for publishing *Fanny Hill*, the venture was so successful that Haynes was able to set up a publishing house that specialized in lascivious works. Over the next three decades, Haynes published more than 300 titles (many of which he is purported to have written himself),[42] and his annual sales by 1871 were reported to be in excess of $100,000.[43] Among the titles that Haynes published were *Amours of a Modest Man: By a Bachelor; Venus in Boston: A Romance of City Life; Fanny Greely: or, Confessions of a Free-Love Sister written by herself; The Delights of Love: or, The Lady Libertine;* and *The Bridal Chamber, and its Mysteries: or, Life at Our Fashionable Hotels*.[44]

American production of sexually explicit literature (which was only just beginning to be known as "pornography") was off and running.

## COMSTOCKERY

The sudden rise of pornography publishing in America caught many civic leaders by surprise. Many states, including New York, did not have laws on the books specifically forbidding the publication and sale of obscene materials, relying instead on common law prohibitions. Concerned about the impact of such materials on society in general and young men in particular, religious and civic leaders scrambled to fill the gap. In New York, for instance, the Young Men's Christian Association launched an antiobscenity campaign after the end of the Civil War and, in 1868, successfully lobbied for the passage of a state statute barring the sale of obscene materials. The YMCA's pride in its legislative accomplishment, however, was quickly tempered by the state's lackluster enforcement of the new law. What the organization needed, YMCA leaders realized, was someone who would spur law enforcement officials to prosecute the producers and sellers of obscene materials. To the surprise and delight of these leaders, just such a person showed up on the doorstep of the YMCA in early 1872.

On March 7, 1844, two years before Walter Haynes arrived in New York City, Anthony Comstock was born in New Canaan, Connecticut, to parents of Puritan descent. Comstock established a name for himself as an unofficial arbiter of morals while still in his teens. In 1862, at the age of 18, Comstock broke into a saloon and general store in Winnipauk, Connecticut, and spilled the establishment's liquor onto the floor. Had the Civil War not intervened, Comstock might have preempted Carrie Nation (only two years his junior) as the leader of the nation's temperance movement. Instead, Comstock served briefly in the Union Army and then returned to Connecticut, where he became a clerk and bookkeeper in a New Haven dry goods store. In 1867, Comstock moved to New York, and in January 1871 he married 37-year-old Margaret Hamilton and settled in Brooklyn.[45]

Shortly after arriving in New York, Comstock became active in the area that would consume much of the remainder of his life and with which his name would be perpetually linked. Through various sources, Comstock learned of the tremendous volume of "obscene" materials being distributed in the city of New York and indeed, around the nation. Apparently outraged by the scope of the perceived problem and its effect on the young men who consumed such materials, Comstock undertook a personal crusade to rid New York and the rest of the country of indecent materials.[46] Shortly after the passage in 1868 of New York's antiobscenity law, Comstock succeeded in having a bookseller—the first of many—arrested for the sale of obscene materials. Although he aggressively pursued his campaign, he grew frustrated by the sheer number of booksellers peddling obscene materials and by the fact that at the same time he was gathering evidence at the front of a store, the police were providing a warning at the back.[47] Comstock concluded that the best way to deal with the problem was to go after the publishers of obscenity.[48]

At the time, William Haynes was perhaps the leading American publishers of indecent materials. According to Comstock biographers Haywood Broun and Margaret Leech, in the summer of 1872, Haynes received a note that read: "Get out of the way. Comstock is after you. Damn fool won't look at money." Haynes was found dead the following morning, reportedly by his own hand.[49] It is somewhat difficult to imagine why Haynes would have been so fearful of Comstock at that early stage in Comstock's antipornography career, since the nature of Haynes's business could hardly have been a secret. Comstock's zeal in attempting to stamp out indecency, however, was apparently ferocious, and Haynes may have feared the very real consequences of a criminal conviction under the New York antiobscenity statute. The possibility of having driven Haynes to suicide did not faze Comstock in the least; in fact, toward the end of his career, he would boast that his antismut campaign was responsible for the suicide of 16 producers or sellers of what he considered to be immoral materials.

The Brooklyn activist was happy to wage war against indecency by himself, but he recognized that he could be more effective with financial backing. Aware of the YMCA's campaign against vice, Comstock wrote to the organization for support. His hastily scrawled letter came to the attention of one of the YMCA's leaders, Morris K. Jesup, who sent Comstock a check for $500. Comstock used the money to purchase the plates from which Haynes's books were printed, which he later destroyed. In late 1872, Comstock met with Jesup and the other leaders of the YMCA, a collection of prominent New Yorkers that included such men as William E. Dodge, Jr., J. Pierpont Morgan,[50] and Robert R. McBurney. It was a perfect match: Comstock acquired extensive financial backing and a certain legitimacy for his efforts, and the YMCA obtained the services of an apparently tireless zealot.

Under the aegis of New York's antiobscenity statute, the YMCA had founded the New York Society for the Suppression of Vice. Comstock was installed as the secretary of the society, which gave him authority under New York State statute to search homes and businesses, to seize articles which in Comstock's sole view were in violation of the law, and to arrest the offenders. It was an unprecedented amount of police power for a private citizen to exercise, and Comstock did so with relish.

In addition to his confrontational raids on New York's porn purveyors, Comstock also spent a portion of 1872 in Washington, D.C., where he lobbied Congress on behalf of the YMCA for the passage of a stricter national law against obscenity.[51] He found a receptive audience. Congress, concerned about the consumption of pornography in the ranks during the Civil War, had passed a law in 1865 forbidding the use of the mails to ship obscene books and pictures. (As in New York, however, effective enforcement was lacking.) On March 3, 1873, President Ulysses S. Grant signed "An Act for the Suppression of Trade in, and Circulation of, obscene Literature and Articles of immoral Use," which broadened and strengthened the provisions of the 1865 law. In a backroom deal consummated prior to the adoption of the act, additional money (approximately $3,000) was appropriated for a "special agent" to enforce the act, but only with the express understanding that if the act were adopted, Comstock would receive the appointment.[52] For the next 42 years, Comstock's unique position as a "special agent" of the U.S. Post Office and secretary of the Society for the Suppression of Vice made him one of the most powerful moral censors in the nation's history.

Comstock's enthusiasm for his work was simply astonishing. By January 1874, less than a single year after his initial appointment, Comstock reported that he had confiscated and destroyed "134,000 pounds of 'books of improper character,' along with 194,000 pictures and sundries like 60,300 'rubber articles' and 5,500 'indecent' playing cards."[53] In 1913, just two years before his death, Comstock boasted that he had destroyed more than 160 tons of obscene literature and had convicted enough individuals to fill nearly 61 passenger cars with 60 seats each.[54] In his headlong rush to stamp out obscenity (a goal that was increasingly Sisyphean by the end of the 19th century), Comstock ruined or badly damaged countless lives and ran roughshod over a wide array of constitutional freedoms.

## THE COUNTRY OUTGROWS COMSTOCK

By the turn of the century, what had been public indifference or even tacit approval of Comstock's censorship efforts was rapidly turning into derision and dismay. Public perception of Comstock was not helped by an indirect brush with the acerbic George Bernard Shaw, who coined the word which is now Comstock's chief legacy. In September 1905, a New York Public Library employee decided that public access to Shaw's works (and particularly, to *Man and Superman* [1903]) should be restricted. The London correspondent for the *New York Times* wrote to Shaw asking for his response to the library's action. Shaw's reply, which the *Times* subsequently published, sealed Comstock's place in history:

> Nobody outside America is likely to be the least surprised. Comstockery is the world's standing joke at the expense of the United States. Europe likes to hear of such things. It confirms the deep-seated conviction of the Old World that America is a provincial place, a second-rate country-town civilization after all.[55]

In a nation imbued with a sense of Manifest Destiny and flush from the socially liberating effects of the Gay Nineties, Comstock's moral outrage at smut and indecency looked increasingly old-fashioned.

The real problem for Comstock was not so much the actual production of pornography but instead the increasing ease with which sexually explicit materials could be shipped to retailers and consumers. The strength of the 1873 Comstock Law lay chiefly in the fact that at the time of its passage, the U.S. Post Office was still one of the most efficient means of shipping goods from one location to another. Only four years earlier, however, in 1869, two hard-driving railroad companies had tied together the two ends of the country at Promontory Point, Utah, and within 20 years, more than 166,703 miles of railroad track would be laid in the U.S.[56] The distribution of sexually explicit goods would soon become even faster and more difficult to control: The Wright brothers made their first flight on December 17, 1903, and in 1908, Henry Ford introduced the Model T, sales of which would top 15 million by 1927.

Each new development had the pleasant effect for pornographers of lowering the overall cost of distribution and of offering less risky alternatives to the use of the U.S. mails. Most railroads and steamboat companies, for instance, offered shipping services that were beyond the reach of Comstock's attention, as were the services of privately owned shipping companies like Wells Fargo (founded in 1852) and United Parcel Service of America (1907). With the advent of the private automobile, it became even easier to ship materials without risking the wrath of the postal inspectors.

The new forms of transportation and shipping did not mean that the pornography business was by any means risk-free. Many states did, after all, have (and still have) antiobscenity statutes which could be used to seize materials physically located in the state, regardless of how the materials were transported there, and the very convenience and low cost of sending items through the U.S. mails meant that Comstock and his successors had plenty of work to keep them busy. In the end, however, the ability of a pornography producer to throw a box of photos, stereoscopes, dirty comic books, or even a grainy stag film into the back of a car and drive from town to town so decentralized the distribution of pornography that in the end, Comstock's job became impossible.

## COMSTOCK V. SANGER:
## THE FIGHT OVER BIRTH CONTROL

The real danger of Comstock (and his intellectual descendants) lay in the self-described scope of his mission. Comstock did not limit his censorship efforts to what is traditionally considered to be pornography; both he and his supporters (particularly the Young Men's Christian Association) were also concerned about the use of contraception and contraceptive devices, which they blamed for a decrease in the number of births.[57] And in fact, when Congress passed the Comstock Law in 1873, it included contraceptive materials (both products and information) in the list of items which could not be sent through the mails. During his tenure, Comstock and the U.S. Post Office confiscated hundreds and thousands of medical journals, pamphlets, brochures, advertising circulars, and contraceptive devices.[58]

Comstock's campaign against contraceptive information, like his campaign against pornography, was never completely successful; even in 1890, at the height of Comstock's influence, the widely read *Police Gazette* carried advertisements for both condoms and diaphragms.[59] Comstock did succeed during his lifetime in making it much more difficult to obtain safe and reliable information about contraception. At the very end of his career, however, Comstock ran up against a social activist every bit as determined as he was: a 34-year-old New York nurse named Margaret Sanger.

Sanger began writing about female sexuality in November 1912 for a socialist newspaper, the *New York Call*. The newspaper was seized under the Comstock Law, and Sanger made the first of two hastily arranged trips to Europe. After researching contraception abroad, she returned to the United States and began publishing a magazine titled *The Woman Rebel*, which dealt exclusively with issues of sexual behavior and reproduction. Following her publication of a pamphlet titled *Family Limitation* (which included explicit information on the use of various contraceptive methods), she was indicted on nine counts of violating the Comstock Law, each count carrying a sentence of up to five years in prison. Once again, Sanger left for Europe. Her departure did not slow the spread of contraception information; by the beginning of 1915, Sanger's allies in the Socialist Party had distributed more than 100,000 copies of *Family Limitation*.[60]

Frustrated in his efforts to capture Sanger, Comstock set his sights on her husband, William. In early 1915, Comstock sent one of his agents to William Sanger to request a copy of *Family Limitation*. When he obligingly provided one, Comstock arrested him and charged him with violating the federal obscenity law. Comstock offered to drop the charges if William would tell him where Margaret was, but William refused. He was tried in September, found guilty, and sentenced to 30 days in jail. Upon hearing of her husband's incarceration, Margaret Sanger returned to New York, where she was arrested and her case set for trial. Her arrest and her husband's jail sentence, however, galvanized Sanger's political and social compatriots, and the ensuing outcry forced the federal prosecutor to drop the charges against her. Sanger did not have the satisfaction of seeing Comstock's reaction to her victory. During William's obscenity trial, he took ill with pneumonia, and he died on September 21, 1915, prior to her return from Europe.[61]

In addition to raising the intensity of the debate over sexual practices and reproductive rights, Sanger was instrumental in challenging various provisions of the Comstock Law in court. In 1917, Sanger founded the National Birth Control League, which in 1942 became the Planned Parenthood Federation of America. In 1929, she helped establish the National Committee on Federal Legislation for Birth Control, an organization that used a combination of legislative lobbying, educational campaigns, and court cases to advocate for more liberal birth control laws. The National Committee made limited progress in Congress and the state legislatures, but was successful in gaining the support of state and regional social organizations across the country (ranging from the ACLU to the General Council of Congregational and Christian Churches). The courts also proved to be a valuable ally: in 1930, the National Committee helped persuade a federal appeals court to rule that companies could ship and advertise birth control devices for legal use without fear of prosecution under the Comstock Law.[62]

The impact of the court's decision was heightened by the nation's economic troubles: concern over the consequences of large families during the Depression drove up demand for contraceptives, and by the mid-1930s, American condom manufacturers were producing 317 million condoms per year.[63] In 1936, the National Committee was again victorious when Judge Learned Hand declared in *United States v. One Package* that the anticontraceptive portions of the Comstock Law were unconstitutional.[64]

The *One Package* decision meant that the U.S. postal inspectors could no longer seize information about contraception or contraceptive devices from the mails, and no one could be prosecuted in federal court for sending them.[65] However, it was still a crime under numerous state laws to use a contraceptive device or possess or distribute information about contraception. Those laws remained in effect until 1965, when the U.S. Supreme Court ruled in *Griswold v. Connecticut* that state laws forbidding contraceptives to married couples violated their federal constitutional right to privacy.[66]

Judge Hand's decision may have limited the scope of the Comstock Law, but as of 1999 (the 126th anniversary of its passage), the bulk of Comstock's Law remains in effect. U.S. citizens are still barred from mailing "every obscene, lewd, lascivious, indecent, filthy or vile article, matter, thing, device, or substance," as well as "every article or thing designed, adapted, or intended for producing abortion, or for any indecent or immoral use."[67]

## HOW 'YA GONNA KEEP 'EM
## DOWN ON THE FARM?

Fewer than 40 years passed between the death of Anthony Comstock (September 1915) and the publication of the first *Playboy* (December 1953). It is unlikely, however, that Comstock would easily have recognized the nation that he fought so hard to cleanse. The four decades between his death and the publication of *Playboy* were among the most tumultuous in the nation's history: two World Wars, the Great Depression, the Roaring Twenties, a riotous but failed experiment with Prohibition, the invention and use of the atomic bomb, the Berlin airlift, and the start of the Cold War. The pace of technological change, spurred by military necessity, accelerated appreciably.

What with all of the social and technological change taking place, it was a great time to be a pornographer. Between 1915 and 1953, the population of the United States grew from roughly 100 million people to more than 152 million, a 50 percent increase in the potential market. The motion picture, an exciting new technology with enormous economic potential for the skin trade, was just beginning to come into its own when Comstock died. In the decade following, Hollywood would flirt with sexual themes and an occasional flash of nudity before the Hays Office drove sex underground into the stag market. The improvements in the transportation system that had so confounded Comstock continued: thousands of more miles of railroad track, an extensive network of roads, and a growing number of commercial flights.

The most beneficial change for pornographers lay in the shift in social attitudes, including those toward sex and sexual materials. Even before the start of World War I, large numbers of young men and women had moved from the countryside to the cities in search of work. Their rising numbers helped spur the growth of numerous public amusements—"dance halls, amusement parks, pleasure steamers, and nickel movie houses"[68]—where young men and women could meet and interact in ways that would have been unthinkable only a few years before.

World War I, however, raised the age-old concern that Europe posed a particular risk to the morals of even the steadiest youth, which is why in 1919 the nation was ruefully singing "How 'Ya Gonna Keep 'Em Down on the Farm? (After They've Seen Paree)":

> How 'ya gonna keep 'em down on the farm,
> After they've seen Pa-ree?
> How 'ya gonna keep 'em
> Away from Broadway,
> Jazzin' aroun', and paintin' the town?
> How 'ya gonna keep 'em away from harm?
> That's a mystery.
> They'll never want to see a rake or plow

And who the deuce can parleyvous a cow?
How 'ya gonna keep 'em down on the farm,
After they've seen Pa-ree?[69]

The concern was justified. Not only did the population shift from the country to city continue, but after the war ended in November 1918, the United States underwent a general relaxation of morals that came to be known as the "Roaring Twenties."

The general tumult of the Roaring Twenties was spurred in large part by public reaction to the 18th Amendment, which prohibited the sale or consumption of virtually all alcohol. While Prohibition did cut down on the amount of alcohol consumed in the United States, the societal cost was high: Bootleggers and crime bosses like Al Capone and "Bugs" Moran became cultural heroes and hundreds of thousands of citizens became lawbreakers by frequenting illegal saloons known as "speakeasies" and buying bootlegged liquor.[70] The changes were evident throughout American society: Skirt lengths rose (along with the stock market), dances grew more risqué, Hollywood churned out a seemingly endless supply of titillating films, and readers devoured newly legalized and provocative books like *Mademoiselle de Maupin* (1835) and *The Well of Loneliness* (1928).[71]

The decision in 1933 to allow the importation and printing of James Joyce's epic *Ulysses* proved to be particularly significant. When Judge John M. Woolsey of the U.S. District Court for the Southern District of New York ruled that James Joyce's *Ulysses* could be published in the United States,[72] he abandoned the legal test previously used by the courts—whether any single word or phrase in the book was obscene—and took the novel approach of looking at the book as a whole. Although books would continue to be barred from the United States off and on for 30 years (it was not until 1966, for instance, that the Supreme Court held that *Fanny Hill* was not obscene),[73] Judge Woolsey's decision laid the legal and intellectual foundation for a long series of decisions that has essentially freed literature from the threat of censorship on the grounds of obscenity.

The magazine industry was particularly aggressive in its use of sexual imagery and themes. In 1931, the American Sunbathing Association began publishing *The Nudist* (later renamed *Sunshine & Health*), and a number of so-called "art photography" publications followed. And in 1933, *Esquire* magazine was founded by 29-year-old Arnold Gingrich, who hit upon the then provocative combination of top-notch writing,[74] risqué cartoons, and drawings of scantily clad women. Despite a rather high cover price of 50 cents (particularly for a nation in the throes of a depression), *Esquire* went on to sell more than 10 million copies in its first three years.

Even mainstream periodicals got into the act, although in a much smaller way. In 1933, the Czechoslovakian movie *Ecstasy*, starring Austrian Hedy Kiesler, earned the dubious distinction of becoming the first film to be blocked by U.S. Customs. A somewhat sanitized version successfully entered the country in 1936 and did very well at the theaters in which it appeared. *Ecstasy's* distribution was limited, however, because it lacked a seal of approval from the Motion Picture Producers and Distributors of America (MPPDA), and requests for one were denied.[75] Ironically, thanks to the existence of the country's free press, millions of people across the country were saved the trouble of seeing the movie when the photo magazines *Life* and *Look* covered the controversy and published photos of Kiesler's controversial nude swimming scene. A major uproar resulted from the fact that Kiesler's nipples are visible in the photos.[76]

The gradual rise of sexual content in the national news and entertainment media had two primary effects: First, it became harder for individuals to become sexual entrepreneurs, as larger businesses were able to take advantage of their economies of scale in producing and distributing sexually oriented materials. Why would someone pay $6.60 or even $8.80, for instance, for a collection of nude photos or "French postcards" if one could purchase a magazine full of nude sunbathing photos for 25 cents each month? The second primary effect of these changes answers that question: The photos, postcards, or film would have to show something that a sunbathing magazine or nickel feature would not—pubic hair, for instance, more explicit poses, or even intercourse.[77] As illicit sexual materials grew more explicit, of course, their production and sale grew riskier, since state obscenity laws were still in effect and still enforced; the trade-off was that the increased risk translated directly into higher prices and higher profits.

As we'll see in the next chapter, a number of different media remained open to sexual entrepreneurs. In addition to the ever-popular sexually explicit photos and postcards, entrepreneurs from this era specialized in stag films (which often depicted full frontal nudity and intercourse) and the infamous Tijuana Bibles, which cartoonist Art Spiegelman describes as follows:

> The Tijuana Bibles probably weren't produced in Tijuana (or Havana, Paris or London, as some of the covers imply), and they obviously weren't Bibles. They were clandestinely produced and distributed small booklets that chronicled the explicit sexual adventures of America's beloved comic-strip characters, celebrities, and folk-heroes. The standard format consisted of eight poorly-printed 4"-wide by 3"-high black (or blue) and white pages and covers of a heavier colored stock.[78]

Nor were these thrills particularly cheap. "A new Bluesie," Spiegelman wrote, "would reportedly set you back between a hefty two bits (enough for a shave and a haircut or five loaves of bread) to as much as five bucks—whatever the local traffic might bear."[79] Surreptitious admission to a so-called "blue" movie came at similarly inflated rates.

The producers and distributors of stag films and other forms of sexually explicit materials were actually helped by the decade's chief crackdown on smut.

Since the mid-1920s, religious and civic leaders had complained about the increasing sexual content in Hollywood films. The film industry gained some breathing room in 1922 by hiring Will B. Hays, the postmaster general under President Harding,[80] and appointing him head of the newly formed MPPDA.[81] Hays instituted a production code that detailed what could and could not be shown in a given film; but filmmakers could skirt the code by showing illicit conduct (suggestive dancing, occasional nudity, implied sex, etc.) so long as a proper moral message was conveyed by the end of the last reel.[82] Not surprisingly, this winking attitude towards morality was unsatisfactory to many critics of the industry.

Their solution, which would set an example for future pornography protesters, was to attack the economic rewards of cinema. In 1934, a coalition of Catholic, Protestant, and Jewish religious leaders founded an organization called the Legion of Decency, which drafted a new and more stringent production code. Later that year, the coalition helped to organize a boycott of all films in Philadelphia to protest Hollywood's lack of adherence to the new code. After movie revenues in the city dropped by 40 percent in a single week, the MPPDA created the Production Code Administration on July 1, 1934, to issue seals of approval to films that adhered to the terms of the Legion of Decency's production code.[83] No member of the MPPDA could release, distribute, or exhibit a film without a seal from the code administration. Since most stag film producers didn't give a hoot about the production code, the effective shackling of Hollywood by the religious coalition helped eliminate a large and well-financed competitor for the next 25 years.

# THE BIRTH AND GROWTH OF AN INDUSTRY

## THE "PLAYBOY" GENERATION: SHOW ME THE BUNNY!

The onset of World War II did more than simply help to jolt the nation's economy out of the Great Depression; it accelerated the steady liberalization of the nation's sexual mores and helped to complete pornography's expansion into a full-blown industry.

Never slow to leap on a cultural trend, various magazines began to produce more openly risqué materials for "the boys at the front." In August, 1941 for instance, *Life* printed one of the most famous pinup photos in history, the shot of film star Rita Hayworth kneeling on a bed, dressed only in a satin slip.[84] Two years later, *Life* published a pinup of blonde actress Chili Williams in a polka-dot swimsuit that upon casual inspection appeared to be tucked into the lips of her vulva. *Life* reported that the photo generated 100,000 letters, and the ensuing publicity helped Williams land some small parts in Hollywood.[85]

Take hundreds of thousands of young men, mostly between 18 and 25, transport them thousands of miles away from family, friends, and female companionship for months and years at a time, and it should be no surprise that sex would become a major topic of interest. Hollywood did its bit for the boys, sending some of its most voluptuous and ribald performers to entertain the troops under the auspices of the United Services Organization (USO).[86] The bulk of the demand, however, was satisfied by the nascent pornography industry, which understandably saw the armed services as an enormous and essentially captive market. The industry scrambled to provide soldiers with a combination of illicit photos, films, and especially magazines. The period's chief innovation was the "girlie" magazine, which despite occasional pretension toward social commentary or exposé journalism, was primarily a vehicle for photos and drawings of attractive women in lingerie or less. Although some were aimed specifically at servicemen, the majority were available on the nation's newsstands as well. Titles like *Laff* (founded 1939), *Beauty Parade* (1941), *See* (1941), *Eyeful* (1943), *Titter* (1943), *Sir* (1944), *Glamorous Models* (1945), *Hit* (1945), *Whisper* (1946), *Flirt* (1947), and *Showgirls* (1947) all helped to introduce the country to the idea of readily available risqué and even nude photos.[87] In turn, soldiers and sailors made their own use of sexual imagery, painting nudes on the nose cones of planes and on various pieces of explosive ordnance (hence the term "bombshell"), and carving pinups into the soft volcanic rock on the island of Iwo Jima.

By the time the war ended, the pornography genie was easing her way out of the bottle. Attracted by the traditionally attractive mix of opportunity and potentially high profit, entrepreneurs started literally hundreds of different girlie magazines. The last four decades have taken their toll on the girlie magazine industry; only one begun prior to 1960 (*Playboy*) is still in print. For a short time, it looked as though the honor might go to a publication started by George von Rosen, a New York publisher who prior to the war built a business specializing in unofficial (and probably spurious) nudist magazines such as *Modern Sunbathing & Hygiene* and pseudo-art periodicals such as *Art Photography*.[88] In 1951, however, von Rosen launched *Modern Man*, which would become by far his most successful publication. *Modern Man* was notable for two reasons: one, von Rosen was probably the first to publish a magazine that combined articles on the outdoors with photographic spreads of seminude models and starlets, and totally nude "art studies"; and two, a few months after starting *Modern Man*, von Rosen hired a 26-year-old named Hugh Hefner as the magazine's promotion manager.[89]

Hefner's stay at *Modern Man* lasted less than a year. In 1952, he quit the $80-a-week job to take a position with a children's magazine. Although lower paying, the new job gave him more time to work on his own magazine. An avid reader of men's magazines, Hefner was convinced that he had the formula for a magazine of that genre that would be unlike anything on the market. He envisioned a magazine that focused on the great indoors, that acclaimed the sophisticated urban male, and that equated male sexual prowess and female availability with economic success.[90] And so, in the summer of 1953, Hefner sat down on his living room floor and began laying out a magazine.

The first *Playboy* (the name Hefner settled on after his first choice, *Stag Party*, sparked a threatening letter from *Stag*, an existing men's magazine) was a mixture of articles written by Hefner himself and public domain stories from authors such Arthur Conan Doyle, Ambrose Bierce, and Giovanni Boccaccio, whose 14th-century *Decameron* was still on the blacklist of the National Organization of Decent Literature. The magazine's chief draw, however, was not its prose, but the now-famous centerfold, a color pinup of a nude Marilyn Monroe, the rights to which Hefner had purchased for $500.[91] Hefner demonstrated his business skills early on, by parlaying the Monroe centerfold into initial investments from friends and family of more than $10,000.[92]

The Monroe photo helped in other ways as well. Based on Hefner's description of it, magazine distributers around the country placed large orders for the unpublished magazine; by the early fall of 1953, Hefner had advance orders for more than 70,000 copies, which would instantaneously make *Playboy* one of the best-selling men's magazines in the nation. Since all of the orders were contingent upon unsold copies being returned, however, Hefner's risk was still substantial. Moreover, he was so concerned about the possibility of a criminal prosecution for distributing obscene material that the first issue of *Playboy* is both undated and unsigned—Hefner's name doesn't appear anywhere on it.[93]

Hefner's caution proved unnecessary. Within two weeks of hitting the newsstand, *Playboy* had sold 50,000 copies and the magazine's debut went unremarked by law enforcement. Emboldened by his success, Hefner dated the second issue of *Playboy*—January 1954—and listed his name on the masthead as publisher.[94] On the one-year anniversary of the publication of the first *Playboy*, Hefner printed 175,000 copies, and on the second year anniversary, 400,000. At 50 cents a copy, an empire was born.

Hefner's success spawned a variety of imitators: *Ace, Bachelor, Casanova, Cavalcade, Dude, Frolic, Gent, Monsieur, Nugget, Rogue, Swank,* and *Tiger,* to name just a few. While none managed to capture the elusive mix of sophistication and sexuality that was associated with *Playboy*, they collectively contributed to the growing freedom of Americans to view sexually oriented materials. There were, however, still some limits; depictions of sexual intercourse, for instance, were still restricted to back-alley photos or postcards, and to the ever-present stag films. If anything, the increasing ease with which soft-core publications such as *Playboy* could be purchased helped to push more hard-core images farther to the margins of commerce.

## FROM ROTH TO LOVELACE: THE "GOLDEN AGE" OF PORN

The 16-year period between 1957 and 1973 has frequently been referred to as the "Golden Age of Porn." From the point of view of technology, it was not a particularly innovative time for pornographers; the media used to create and distribute pornography were essentially the same at the beginning of the Golden Age as they were at the end. But this was the time when pornography matured as an industry. As the players in the business grew in size and resources, they diversified into other forms of adult entertainment. The industry grew increasingly sophisticated about legal issues and formed useful alliances with free speech activists to challenge governmental censorship. And most importantly, from an economic point of view, the industry worked aggressively to take advantage of the tremendous social turmoil and tumult of the era, as changing sexual mores made it possible to produce and widely distribute materials that were more explicit than anything that had been seen in the previous 1,500 years. The freedom the industry enjoyed led to excesses that would in time cause significant religious and political backlash. But the industry's economic success during the '60s and early '70s would give it the resources and the experience to fight later efforts to shackle it.

Much of the industry's strength during this period is directly attributable to the U.S. Supreme Court's 1957 decision in *Roth v. United States*.[95] Samuel Roth was a pornographer who got his start in the 1930s, developing a highly successful business publishing erotic and pornographic literature. In 1951, when Senator Estes Kefauver convened a congressional committee to investigate organized crime (including its role in the pornography industry), Roth testified that his business had developed a mailing list of more than 40,000 names.[96]

Three years later, Roth was indicted in New York on 26 counts of sending obscene materials through the mail (including pictures, magazines, and books). He was convicted, fined $5,000, and sentenced to five years in federal prison. Roth's conviction was upheld by the U.S. Court of Appeals for the Second Circuit, although one justice, Jerome Frank, expressed his dismay about the invasions of privacy that resulted from attempts to legislate morality. In conjunction with a man named David Alberts, who had also been convicted in California of mailing obscene matter, Roth took his case to the Supreme Court.[97]

By a 6-3 vote, the convictions of Roth and Alberts were upheld. At first glance, Justice William Brennan's opinion appeared to be a victory for the forces of censorship; not only had two men been sent to jail for distributing fairly mild sexual materials, but the Court had expressly declared that obscenity was not entitled to First Amendment protection.

From the defense lawyer's perspective, however, Brennan's definitions had two or three truck-sized holes. In the course of attempting to define "obscenity," Brennan said that the test was "whether to the average person, applying contemporary local standards, the dominant theme of the material taken as a whole appeals to prurient interests."[98] In addition, Justice Brennan declared that in order for something to be obscene, it must be "utterly without redeeming social importance."[99]

Justice Brennan's decision proved to be a powerful tool for the pornography industry. By emphasizing the latitude offered by words and phrases like "dominant theme," "taken as a whole," and "utterly," defenders of sexually oriented materials were able to use the *Roth* decision to free a wide range of materials that previously had been banned, including such magazines as *Sunshine & Health* (which beginning in the early 1950s had stopped airbrushing out the pubic hair of the people in its photographs), books like *Lady Chatterley's Lover, Tropic of Cancer,* and *Fanny Hill,* and the comic monologues of comedian Lenny Bruce. *Roth* also provided a legal basis for freeing up works of cinema, including Louis Malle's *Les Amants* and the film version of *Lady Chatterley's Lover.* Filmmakers also used *Roth* as an excuse to produce and distribute (much as the magazine industry had before them) pseudodocumentaries about the nudist lifestyle: in 1957, only a few months after *Roth* was decided, the first major nudist colony film, *Garden of Eden,* was released. It ran in 36 states before being banned in New York, a decision that was subsequently overturned by the New York Court of Appeals. Following the court's decision, a large number of other nudist films, including *My Bare Lady* and *The Nude and the Prude,* made their way into second- and third-run theaters.[100]

The grudging but unequivocal approval that these works received in the Supreme Court meant less harassment of pornographers by law enforcement, since officers were reluctant to undertake prosecutions that would simply be overturned on appeal (or thrown out in the first place). As a result, the amount of sexual materials available to all consumers (and not simply those willing to brave an urban red light district) rose dramatically.

The clearest sign of the nation's post-*Roth* mores was the 1959 return of nudity to mainstream cinema, when filmmaker and former Playboy photographer Russ Meyer shot and released *The Immoral Mr. Teas.* Like *Playboy* before it, *The Immoral Mr. Teas* not so much established a genre (the so-called "nudie cutie") as made it acceptable for public consumption. The film was a huge financial success. Meyer made the film for $24,000 and made a profit of $1 million on its first release. In the process, Meyer introduced American audiences to the idea that nudity could appear in films that were relatively well-made and even humorous. Meyer's economic success proved so enticing that within three years, more than 150 imitations had been produced.[101]

The Golden Age may have started in the dry language and marble hall of the Supreme Court when Justice Brennan read his *Roth* opinion, but it shifted into high gear on February 29, 1960, when Hugh Hefner opened the first Playboy Club, at 116 E. Walton in Chicago, Illinois. The Playboy Clubs (Hefner eventually opened 35 more clubs, along with five resorts) played to Hefner's strengths: young, attractive women stuffed into revealing costumes, upscale and gleaming surroundings, and well-stroked male egos. Again, Hefner's timing was superb; as the nation's economy headed into the exhilarating "go-go" years of the late '60s, successful businessmen were looking for ways to tangibly reward themselves for their success. Thanks to more than a decade of savvy marketing by Hefner, sex (or at least the illusion of it) was considered to be one of the reasonable rewards of business success, and holding a key to a Playboy Club was a tangible symbol of having "made it." Moreover, the clubs flourished (particularly later in the decade) because they served as a safe way for many members to participate in the sexual revolution that was swirling around them. Walking into a Playboy Club and flirting with buxom bunnies was just sufficiently naughty and rebellious to serve as a middle-class, middle-age substitute for dropping out and joining a free-love commune in Haight-Ashbury. The clubs were a huge success; in the last quarter of 1961, for instance, more than 132,000 people visited the Chicago night club, making it the busiest in the world at the time.[102]

The clubs were emblematic of *Playboy's* continued domination of the pornography industry. It started the Golden Age with nearly 1 million subscribers and finished it with close to 6 million (after peaking in November 1972 at more than 7 million). The profits from this business enabled Hefner to purchase a 48-room mansion on Chicago's Gold Coast, to purchase and sybaritically redecorate a $6 million private jet, and lease nearly half of a 37-story skyscraper in the heart of downtown Chicago. In the process, Hefner's personal worth crossed the $100 million mark, making him by far the most economically successful pornographer in history.

Much of that revenue was derived from the myriad offshoots of the hugely successful *Playboy*. Hefner was the first pornographer to establish widespread brand identity (the *Playboy* Rabbit Head has become one of the most widely recognized corporate symbols in the world), and he used that economic success to produce and market a broad array of products. Beginning with cufflinks in 1954, the Rabbit Head has adorned hundreds of different items, from bar glasses to playing cards to T-shirts to car air fresheners.

By the mid-1960s, it was clear that Hefner had essentially locked up the market for the mainstream "Girl Next Door" men's magazine; a wide variety of competitors appeared, published for two or three years (or less), and then succumbed to *Playboy's* overwhelming domination of the market. In order to compete in the marketplace (and there was clearly a perception that the demand was there), publishers had to find a way to differentiate themselves from *Playboy*. The solution for *Playboy's* most successful competitors, including *Penthouse*, was to offer sexual images that were more explicit and more hard-core than those offered by *Playboy*.

The ability of competitors to publish more explicit images was greatly aided by two additional decisions of the U.S. Supreme Court. In 1966, the Court ruled for the first time that the *Memoirs of Fanny Hill* was not obscene and could be legally sold in the United States. In the process, the Court created a new three-part test for obscenity: 1) a work had to appeal to a reader's "prurient interest" in sex; 2) it had to be "patently offensive" to the average adult; and 3) it had to be (as Justice Brennan had said in *Roth*) "utterly without redeeming social value."[103]

Would-be censors worried that the test would prove even more lenient than the one announced in *Roth*, and their fears were realized in 1967, when the Court decided *Redrup v. New York*.[104] Robert Redrup, a newsstand operator, had been convicted for selling two allegedly obscene books, *Lust Pool* and *Shame Agent*. The books were published by San Diego pulp paperback mogul William Hamling, who funded Redrup's defense. Without opinion, the justices reversed Redrup's conviction, thereby effectively holding that Hamling's books were not obscene. Moral leaders were horrified; if *Lust Pool* and *Shame Agent* were not obscene, then it was difficult to imagine any book that was.[105] Relying on Redrup, the Supreme Court swiftly overturned another 30 obscenity convictions without opinion (causing the word "redrupping" to temporarily enter the legal vocabulary).

With *Roth*, *Memoirs*, and *Redrup* paving the way, pornographers realized that they could compete with *Playboy* by producing and distributing much more explicit materials. In 1965, for instance, Berth Milton published *Private*, which by its ninth issue would become the first periodical to legally publish images of sexual penetration.[106] Bob Guccione founded *Penthouse* in London that same year, and brought it to America in 1969. The photos in *Penthouse* were markedly different from those in *Playboy*; although they did not go as far as those in magazines such as *Private*, they were more realistic and more overtly sexual, and the magazine gained subscribers rapidly. *Penthouse*'s growth accelerated in August 1971, when it became the first of the major men's magazines to publish a centerfold photograph that actually showed the model's pubic hair.

Fueled in part by the controversy surrounding the photo, *Penthouse*'s subscriptions soared to 1.5 million and sparked a circulation battle with *Playboy* that became known in the industry as the "Pubic Wars."[107] *Playboy* first tried to change its photos to mimic *Penthouse*'s explicitness. Then, in 1972, it launched *Oui*, a magazine designed specifically to compete against *Penthouse*. It soon became clear, however, that *Oui* was doing a better job of attracting *Playboy*'s own readers. Hefner, who had never been comfortable with the direction in which *Playboy*'s photos were going, decided to stop trying to match *Penthouse* and return to the softer-edged photos that had helped establish *Playboy* in the first place.[108] It was an excellent business decision; *Playboy* lost the battle—for a short time, *Penthouse*'s subscriptions actually exceeded those of *Playboy*—but it has clearly won the war.[109]

The field became both more crowded and more hard-core in the spring of 1974, when a Cincinnati strip-club owner named Larry Flynt invested $100,000 to start a new men's magazine called *Hustler*. Flynt purposely positioned his magazine as the opposite of *Playboy*'s self-styled sophistication, and his class-based attacks on *Playboy* quickly found an audience. Within a year of its founding, the magazine's explicit photographs of women and raunchy brand of humor had attracted 2 million subscribers.[110]

Periodicals were not the only type of pornography that was getting more hardcore; the push toward more explicit materials was being felt in all aspects of the industry. By the 1960s, the venerable stag films were known as "loops," and gradually shifted from the early black-and-white to color. By the end of the decade, the producers of loops would split into two camps: the ones producing short 8- to 12-minute films for use in the peep show booths (installed by the thousands around the country in the 1970s), and the ones producing full-length sexually oriented features.

Prior to *The Immoral Mr. Teas*, the number of established theaters in the United States that would show a "sexploitation" film numbered about 60.[111] But the Meyer film had illustrated just how profitable nudity could be, and a number of legitimate theaters converted to all-adult fare in the early-'60s.[112] By 1970, the number of adult theaters in the country had risen to more than 750, thanks in large part to the well-known chain of Pussycat Theaters. In addition, despite outcries from antipornography activists, the country's appetite for adult film fare did not seem to be diminishing. The Grove Press distributed the unabashedly sensual *I Am Curious (Yellow)* in 1968, and in 1969 Russ Meyer released the successful softcore film *Vixen*.

Hollywood could not be oblivious to the revenues that such films were generating. Largely as a result of the growth of television, attendance at movies had been falling steadily for years, and the industry was desperate to find some way to entice people back to the theaters.[113] One way was to offer audiences something they couldn't see on their television sets. Despite concerns about being associated with the producers of sexually oriented films, Hollywood produced a number of X-rated movies that did extremely well. For instance, in 1969, *Midnight Cowboy* (starring Jon Voight and Dustin Hoffman) became the first X-rated film to win the Best Picture Oscar. The following year, *A Clockwork Orange* (starring Malcolm McDowell) earned the New York Film Critics Award for Best Picture, and Marlon Brando earned kudos for his role in the 1973 *Last Tango in Paris*. The industry also latched onto Meyer's successful formula (and helped legitimize both the director and his work) when Twentieth Century Fox distributed his *Beyond the Valley of the Dolls* in 1970.

None of these films, as bold as they were for their day, helped prepare Hollywood or the pornography industry for the reaction to the 1973 film *Deep Throat*. The film, which chronicles the discovery by Linda Lovelace's character that she can't reach orgasm through vaginal intercourse because her clitoris is actually located in her throat, is by far the most financially successful X-rated move in history. Shot by stag-film producer Gerard Damiano in Miami for about $25,000, the film has since grossed an estimated $100 million in combined theater and video revenues.

To an extent unprecedented for a sexually explicit film, *Deep Throat* succeeded in attracting a mainstream audience, including a large number of women. The film's popularity was attributable to a number of factors: the release of the movie at a time when large numbers of both men and women were both ready and curious to see a feature-length adult film; the uncertainty of how the film squared with the U.S. Supreme Court's recent decision in *Miller v. California*[114] and the willingness of the film producers to promote *Deep Throat*'s leading performers, Lovelace and Harry Reems, as full-fledged movie stars.

The marketing of Lovelace in particular was an unqualified (albeit temporary) success; in relatively short order, she appeared on the cover of *Esquire*, *Time*, and *Newsweek*, did a photo spread for *Playboy* (which generally resisted featuring porn stars), and appeared on *The Tonight Show*.[115] Although Lovelace's star quickly dimmed, the industry's promotion of her and Reems helped establish a star system for the adult film industry that persists today. The film's own iconic status was confirmed the following year when Bob Woodward chose the title as the pseudonym for his as-yet-unidentified administration source on the Watergate coverup by President Nixon and his staff.

## HOW TECHNOLOGY SAVED THE PORNOGRAPHY INDUSTRY

In the years since the success of *Deep Throat* and *The Devil in Miss Jones* (also 1973), however, no other film with an X or NC-17 (the MPAA's trademarked replacement for "X") has done a significant fraction of the sales that those two movies did. Part of the reason, as we'll see in the next chapter, was technological. With the advent of cable and videotape (both of which brought adult films directly into the home), the adult film segment of the pornography industry lost much of its motivation to fight for access to screens around the country. The more important factor, however, was that in 1973 the Supreme Court handed down a decision that made those fights more frequent, more costly, and more difficult to win.

In California, obscenity charges were brought against Marvin Miller, a publisher of pornographic materials who had gotten his start in the industry by distributing sexual materials that had entered the public domain. After a brief (but successful) run-in with Barney Rosset and Grove Press over the Victorian classic *My Secret Life*, Miller expanded his business, and began selling pornography by mail.[116] Among the people who received Miller's explicit brochures (all unsolicited) were a number of postal inspectors and agents for antipornography groups. Miller was convicted under a California law of distributing obscenity, and he appealed his decision all the way up to the U.S. Supreme Court.

The Court that heard Miller's appeal was very different from the ones that had heard *Roth* and *Redrup*. Chief Justice Earl Warren had retired in 1969, and then-President Richard Nixon appointed Warren Burger, a much more conservative jurist, to replace him. Chief Justice Burger was soon joined by three other conservative Nixon appointees: Harry Blackmun (1970), Lewis Powell (1972), and William Rehnquist (1972). These new members of the Court gave Burger the votes that he would need to roll back some of what he considered to be the excesses of the Warren Court. Chief among them was the earlier Court's approach to obscenity, which Burger felt was simply too lenient and made it too difficult to obtain convictions.

*Miller v. California*[117] presented Chief Justice Burger with just the opportunity he needed. It had all the requisite elements: a relatively unsympathetic and gleefully unrepentant defendant, explicit sexual images, and the unsolicited receipt of explicit sexual materials in homes around the country. In the process of upholding the lower court's convictions, Burger set out a new standard for judging whether a particular item is obscene:

> (a) whether the average person, applying contemporary community standards, would find that the work, taken as a whole, appeals to the prurient interest; (b) whether the work depicts or describes, in a patently offensive way, sexual conduct specifically defined by the applicable state law; and (c) whether the work, taken as a whole, lacks serious literary, artistic, political, or scientific value.[118]

The two most significant changes lay in the adoption of the community standard as one of the prongs for judging obscenity (thereby largely removing the role of the federal courts as the national arbiters of decency), and the reworking of Justice Brennan's "utterly without" doctrine in *Roth*.

By adopting the "local community standards" language, the Court effectively reintroduced the concept of the local censorship board, not only for films but for all sexually explicit materials. More importantly, the Court effectively created a system whereby any particular community with, as legal scholar Edward de Grazia put it, "a low tolerance for candid sexual expression"[119] could affect the sexual content of artistic works for the entire country. If a federal jury, for instance, applied local community standards to a film and declared it obscene, and the jury's decision was ultimately affirmed by the Supreme Court, that community's judgment would be binding on the entire nation.[120] And in fact, no prosecutions were necessary for the attitudes of less tolerant jurisdictions to have an effect. With the emphasis increasingly on national distribution of periodicals, books, photos, and films, it was simply too risky and too expensive for major pornography producers to try to tailor their product to every possible jurisdiction. As a result, most major pornography producers tried to package their products (or change the contents) to minimize the chances that even the most antagonistic jurisdictions would object. Art directors at *Playboy*, *Penthouse*, *Screw*, and other sexually oriented publications, once informally competing to create the most salacious covers, now directed their efforts to toning down the covers enough to keep their publications out of court.[121] In some cases, the *Miller* decision even resulted in the cancellation of a project: Negotiations for a movie version of Hubert Selby's book *Last Exit to Brooklyn* promptly stopped, since no studio wanted to run the risk of producing a film about working-class Brooklyn that featured prostitution, homosexuality, and transvestism.[122] Another popular response to *Miller* was to exclude hostile jurisdictions from the distribution of a particular project. For instance, *Last Tango in Paris* was canceled in Utah following the *Miller* decision after local law enforcement agencies warned that theater owners would be prosecuted for showing it.

In the short run, *Miller* was an economic boon to pornographers, as hundreds and thousands of customers lined up to purchase sexually explicit materials that they believed would soon be permanently banned. But the longer-term economic (and legal) impact of *Miller* can best be illustrated by what happened with the movie *Deep Throat*. Although it did very well at the box office in late 1972 and early 1973, the Court's decision greatly reduced the number of theaters willing to show the film, which in turn limited its box office receipts. Moreover, in order to avoid the legal restrictions placed on *Deep Throat*, Lovelace's 1974 sequel, *Deep Throat II*, carried an R rating and depicted little nudity or sex. Lacking the daringness and novelty of the original (and lacking most if not all of the attributes of good film in general), *Deep Throat II* disappeared after a brief release, and Lovelace's stardom (at least temporarily) went with it. Two years later, the specter of a local community as national arbiter of sexual mores raised its head when Larry Parrish, an assistant U.S. attorney in Memphis, Tennessee, successfully prosecuted a number of people associated with the film for violating federal obscenity laws.[123]

The *Miller* decision and the subsequent *Deep Throat* prosecution made it clear that the federal antiobscenity laws had new teeth, developments which encouraged some pornographers to limit distribution to their own states. For instance, the classic adult film *Behind the Green Door* (produced and directed by Jim and Artie Mitchell and starring Marilyn Chambers) was originally shown only in California to eliminate the possibility of federal prosecution for shipping obscene materials across state lines.

The risks associated with distributing sexually explicit materials across state lines helped to accelerate the involvement of organized crime in the pornography industry. In a throwback to the early days of stag films, organized crime set up a system of "checkers" and "sweepers" to distribute the movie by hand. A checker would carry the movie across state lines to an adult theater, where mob reps would be stationed to count customers and collect receipts. Sweepers would travel a circuit from rep to rep, collecting the mob's share of the proceeds and forwarding it to headquarters.[124]

The need for such an elaborate system of distribution, however, quickly disappeared. Despite the fears of social and sexual libertarians, and despite the very real impact of *Miller* on the explicitness of artistic works, the Court's decision was only a brief pothole in the steady growth of the industry's revenues. A major reason for *Miller's* limited impact was that it came too late: *Playboy* had been on newsstands for 20 years, most libraries owned copies of books that had been banned for decades or for centuries, and in a 14-year stretch, a significant portion of the country had paid to see films ranging from *The Immoral Mr. Teas* to *Deep Throat*. The Court may have handed off the determination of obscenity to the local community, but the standards of most local communities had fundamentally changed. As a result, law enforcement officials (except in the most restrictive communities) were inclined to allow consenting adults to purchase or watch whatever they chose.[125] *Playboy*, for instance, was never forced from a community by the *Miller* decision; the most effective protest against the magazine would be an economic boycott organized during the Meese Commission's study of the industry in 1986.

A major reason that magazines were relatively immune from the threat of *Miller* prosecutions was that their sale and consumption had little visible impact on local communities. It is a relatively simple matter, for instance, for *Playboy* or *Penthouse* to be sold under the counter or with an opaque cover (as many states today require), and consumption of the magazine generally takes place in the privacy of the purchaser's home. In 1973, however, the only way to make money with a sexually explicit film was to show it in a theater or other public place, which made sexually explicit films disproportionately vulnerable to community censors. On top of everything else, despite the efforts of the Pussycat Theater chain to clean up the image of adult theaters, most local planners considered adult theaters to be a blight on the community.

What adult film makers needed was a means of distribution that offered the same relative anonymity enjoyed by adult magazines. They got their wish in 1975, when Sony released its videocassette recorder. It quickly became an enormously popular technology; although still less than 1 percent of all Americans owned a videocassette recorder in 1979, that number grew to nearly 60 percent in 1988, and 87 percent a decade later.

The pornography industry was quick to recognize the economic potential of video: 60 years of stag films, loops, peep shows, and the early 1970s surge of big-screen productions had left pornographers with a vast library of sexually explicit moving images. Transferring the images from film to videotape was relatively simple and inexpensive, and the resulting cassettes could be sold for as much as $300 each in the late 1970s.[126] In addition, the potential market for sexually explicit cassettes was much larger than the market for adult films. Unlike adult films, which had to be viewed in theaters that generally were in unsavory urban areas, adult videos could be viewed in the privacy of one's home. Another benefit was the discreet size of cassettes, which meant that they could be rented or sold with the same discretion enjoyed by sexually explicit magazines; an adult film sold or rented from the back of a book store or magazine shop was far less likely to excite official disapproval than a XXX marquee on Main Street.

Most importantly, the new technology greatly reduced the costs associated with the adult film industry as a whole. As the technology matured, an adult feature could be shot on videotape for as little as one-tenth the cost of shooting the same feature on film. When combined with a much larger potential market, video technology dramatically increased the profitability of producing and distributing adult movies. As the 1997 film *Boogie Nights* illustrated, there were some directors who thought the shift to video, as lucrative as it was, came at the cost of artistic integrity. However, as adult video rentals climbed into the stratosphere (from November 1997 to November 1998, Americans rented approximately $4.2 billion worth of adult videos),[127] artistic concerns largely vanished.

Also fueling the growth of the pornography industry (although to a much lesser extent) was the development of cable television, another medium that allowed adult materials to viewed in the privacy of the home. Adoption of cable technology has been somewhat slower than that of VCRs; in the late 1980s, when 60 percent of Americans owned VCRs, only about 20 percent subscribed to cable television. Today, the number of cable subscribers approaches 67 percent, but adult content on cable accounted for only approximately $100 million in revenues in 1997.[128]

Unlike adult video, which is readily available to everyone in the country, adult cable channels are available only on certain cable systems. The top three content providers—the Playboy Channel, the Spice Channel, and Adam & Eve—are all now owned by Playboy, which acquired the latter two channels when it bought Spice Entertainment for $95 million in early 1998. Although the high revenues generated by such channels are attractive to cable system operators, consumer complaints and technical difficulties in limiting exposure to children have restricted the spread of adult cable channels; as of August 1998, only about 36 million households in the U.S. (roughly 1 in 3) had access to adult cable channels.[129] The adult channels have found a lucrative alternative source of revenue by selling their content to hotel chains as pay-per-view movies. This often-overlooked distribution channel for pornography is highly profitable for both the pornography industry and hotel chains like Sheraton, Hilton, Hyatt, and Holiday Inn. Pay-per-view movies generated more than $175 million in 1997 alone, with the hotel chains keeping up to 20 percent of each sale.[130]

Although it has not proved to be much of an impediment, viewing an adult video still generally requires a trip out into the community, which carries a small risk of personal embarrassment. Adult videos are generally stored in a separate section of a video store, which one can be seen entering or leaving, and rental often requires carrying a distinctive card or other marker up to the front of the store. And even if the head of your child's PTA isn't there to perkily ask, "So, what are you watching tonight?" there's always the disturbing possibility that an overzealous prosecutor will someday try to subpoena the store's records.

Technology is in the process of removing even these minor impediments to the consumption of pornography. With the development of the World Wide Web in 1994 and the creation of the first graphical browser in 1995, the distribution of pornography on the Internet became extremely easy. Although the amount of bandwidth[131] available has chiefly limited online pornography to text and still images, video images are already being shown, and a variety of technological improvements are in the works which will greatly enhance the ability of pornographers to distribute video over the Web.

Without question, pornography has been the World Wide Web's major economic success. According to *U.S. News and World Report*, online pornography generated $1 billion in revenues in 1998, or somewhere between 5 and 10 percent of all online sales. The potential for growth is still enormous: The number of households with computers is still comparatively low (roughly 50 percent in 1998) and out of those, only about a third have Internet access. On average, one out of every six Web surfers visits adult entertainment sites, and 20 percent of all visitors are women. (The vast bulk of online pornography is aimed at men, but a steadily growing percentage of sexually explicit sites are being designed specifically for women.) As the number of Internet users continues to climb at a steady pace, the online pornography industry has the potential to dwarf other sectors of the industry.

## NOTES

1. Christopher L. C. E. Witcombe, "Women in Prehistory: The 'Venus' of Willendorf" (1998), online at http://www.arthistory.sbc.edu/imageswomen/willendorfdiscovery.html. The Natural History Museum in Vienna, where the Venus of Willendorf now resides, maintains a Web site (http://www.nhm-wien.ac.at/NHM/index5.htm), which contains images of the Venus. The first couple of Web pages are in German, but the pages on Paleolithic art are in English.

2. Among the various issues being debated are whether these figurines were intended to be depictions of actual women or idealized images of womanhood; whether the figurines were images of women who are pregnant or fat; whether the figurines were fertility idols; and whether the figurines were created by men or women.

3. Michael Bisson and Ronald White, "Female Imagery from the Paleolithic: The Case of Grimaldi" (n.p., ca. 1997), online at http://www.insticeagestudies.com/readings/techsoci/techmain.html.

4. Witcombe site. The "Classical Venus" refers to the Venus of Praxiteles's statue the *Venus de Milo* (c. 150–100 B.C.E.) and to Sandro Botticelli's painting *The Birth of Venus* (c. 1480).

5. Witcombe site.

6. People continue to find their own unique meaning in the Venus's curves. In the early 1990s, for instance, the Venus was adopted as a mascot for the fat acceptance movement by Marilyn Wann, the publisher of *Fat! So?*, a periodical designed to encourage hefty people to take pride in their size. The zine's Web site is at http://www.fatso.com. A "zine" (rhymes with "teen"), incidentally, is a publication that does not fit into the mainstream of magazine publishing; the word is a truncation of the more well-known "fanzine," which the *American Heritage Dictionary* defines as "[a]n amateur-produced fan magazine distributed by mail to a subculture readership and devoted to the coverage of interests such as science fiction, rock music, or skateboarding." Zines published on the World Wide Web are often referred to as "e-zines" and cover a wide range of topics.

7. Jean Auel, *Valley of the Horses* (New York: Bantam Books, 1992), pp. 36–37.

8. H. Montgomery Hyde, *A History of Pornography* (New York: Farrar Straus Giroux, 1964), p. 41.

9. Part of the popularity of sex as an artistic and commercial subject lay no doubt in simple enjoyment of the underlying activity, but a more fundamental reason lay in Greek attitudes toward fertility. Having by now had several thousand years of experience with domesticated animals, males were finally beginning to understand (and, predictably, inflate) their role in procreation. One consequence of this understanding was the appearance of fertility cults in which model phalluses played an important symbolic role. There are even reports of a Greek fertility festival in which all of the food was phallus-shaped. Catherine Johns, *Sex or Symbol: Erotic Images of Greece and Rome* (Austin: University of Texas Press, 1982), p. 42.

10. "The Poems of Gaius Valerius Catullus," No. 32, translated by Francis Warre Cornish, in *Catullus, Tibullus, Pervigilium Veneris*, 2d ed., revised by G.P. Goold, (Cambridge, Mass: Loeb Classical Library, Harvard University Press, 1988), p. 39.

11. See Johns, *Sex or Symbol: Erotic Images of Greece and Rome.*

12. James Dickey, "In the Lupanar at Pompeii," reprinted in James Dickey, *The Whole Motion: Collected Poems, 1945–1992* (Hanover, N.H.: Wesleyan University Press, 1992), p 97.

13. Hyde, p. 10.

14. In an appropriate twist, the sexual activities of the Roman nobility have offered fertile material for contemporary publishers and filmmakers. Caligula, for instance, had his story made into a 1980 XXX-rated movie written and produced by *Penthouse* owner Bob Guccione, and Messalina has been the breathless subject of no fewer than a dozen paperback biographies. Even the British Broadcasting Corporation reveled in the sexual peccadillos of the royal family when it made Robert Graves's *I, Claudius* into a miniseries in 1976.

15. Nero falsely blamed the Christians for the fire that burned two-thirds of Rome in 64 C.E., and used the allegations as an excuse for embarking on a campaign of religious persecution.

16. Quintus Septimius Tertullianus, *Apologeticus*, p. 50.

17. One of the first signs of Adam and Eve's fall from grace in the Garden of Eden, after all, is the realization that they are naked: "And the eyes of them both were opened, and they saw that they were naked; and they sewed fig leaves together, and made themselves aprons." Genesis 3:7.

18. Romans 8:6. St. Paul's view was ratified in the fifth century by Saint Augustine, who wrote at length about the inherent "shame" associated with sexual intercourse. Similarly, in the 13th century, the Christian saint and theologian Thomas Aquinas wrote that God approved of sex only when it met the following conditions: first, when it was for the proper purpose (i.e., for procreation); second, when it was with the right person (i.e., one's spouse); and third, when it was done the right way (i.e., face-to-face coitus). Any sexual activity, which did not comport with each of these conditions was "unnatural" and "sinful."

19. Reay Tannahill, *Sex in History* (New York: Stein and Day, 1980), pp. 137–38.

20. Hyde, 204. The Pope's comments echo present-day reports that the voluntary rating system adopted by the television networks is used most frequently by children to find the types of shows that they want to watch. See Jeannine Aversa, "TV ratings may entice kids to watch wrong shows, study finds," *Detroit News*, March 27, 1997.

21. John D'Emilio and Estelle Freedman, *Intimate Matters: A History of Sexuality in America* (New York: Harper & Row, 1988), p. 4. It is worth noting, of course, that the Puritans were not the first permanent English settlers in America; that honor belongs to the settlers of Jamestown, who arrived in 1607. The settlers in Jamestown and colonists who joined them in that region were generally members of the Church of England rather than Puritans.

22. Sexual transgressions were dealt with particularly harshly; when 16-year-old Thomas Granger was convicted in the Massachusetts Bay Colony of buggery with "a mare, a cow, two goats, five sheep, two calves and a turkey," the sheep were paraded in front of Granger so that he could identify his accomplices. The court then ordered that both Granger and the sheep be hanged. D'Emilio and Freedman, p. 17.

23. *Acts and Laws of Massachusetts Bay Colony* (1826).

24. James Franklin's press was one of the first private presses in the colonies.

25. By contrast, comtemporary mainstream magazines are awash in articles about the ins and outs of adultery. In the December 1998 issue of *Men's Health*, for instance, is an article called "The Promise Breakers," in which six men discuss the techniques they use for cheating on their spouses.

26. Some suggest that "The Speech" was quasi-autobiographical, given the number of Franklin's own by-blows. See David Loth, *The Erotic in Literature* (New York: Julian Messner, Ltd., 1961), p. 114.

27. As Franklin well knew: Franklin represented colonial and U.S. interests in Europe for 26 of his 84 years: in England from 1757 to 1762 and from 1764 to 1775, and in France from 1775 to 1785.

28. By way of example, Aretino's 16th sonnet reads something like this:

> She:
> My legs are wrapped around your neck,
>   Your cazzo's in my cul, it pushes and thrashes,
>   I was in bed, but now I'm on this chest.
>   What extreme pleasure you're giving me!
> But lift me onto the bed again: down here
>   my head hung low, you'll do me in.

The pain's worse than birth-pangs or shitting,
Cruel love, what have you reduced me to?
**He:**
What are you going to do?
**She:**
Whatever you like.
**He:**
Give me your tongue a little, darling.
Reward who served you silently and well.
**She:**
The potta will want its share of pleasure,
Otherwise potta and cul will stay at war.
Push harder, your cazzo's slipping out.
If I had to wait
One minute longer for release,
I swear I would have died, sweetheart.

The Chapel Perilous Web site contains reproductions of the translations of a number of Aretino's Sonnets. Online at http://www.sepulchritude.com/chapelperilous/aretino.html.

29. The Church's reaction to "Aretino's Postures" illustrates the role that education and social class play in attitudes toward sexual materials. At about the same time that Titian's *Venus of Urbino*, a full frontal nude done in the classical style, was hanging behind a drape in the pontiff's house for display to a select few, the Church was actively trying to suppress the public distribution and sale of "Aretino's Postures" and other similar salacious works. It is a distinction that has repeatedly arisen in the discussion of sexual materials. As a result of the Church's efforts, not a single original copy of "Aretino's Postures" is known to exist.

30. Hyde, p. 97.

31. See "John Cleland," The World of Penguin (n.d.), online at http://www.penguin.co.uk/Penguin/Authors/108.html.

32. Hyde, p. 190.

34. Bernhardt J. Hurwood, *The Golden Age of Erotica* (Los Angeles: Sherbourne Press, 1965), p. 131.

35. Hurwood, p. 131.

36. Hyde, p. 99. Whether they were copies of *Fanny Hill* published by Thomas or copies imported from England is unknown. Hurwood (pp. 131–32) believes it was the former.

37. Walter Kendrick, *The Secret Museum* (New York: Viking Press, 1987), p. 128 and n.3.

38. Hollick's book alone went through 300 editions in just 25 years. See D'Emilio and Freedman, pp. 55–73. "Tokology," incidentally, is the science of childbirth. On Sanger's work, see pp. 133, 136. See also *The American Catalogue*, under the direction of F. Leypoldt and compiled by Lynds E. Jones (New York: A. C. Armstrong & Son, 1881), p. 351 (listing title and price ($5) of Sanger's book). Coincidentally, Margaret Sanger, a tireless advocate for birth control information in the early 20th century, was married to an architect named William Sanger.

39. Peter Gardella, *Innocent Ecstasy: How Christianity Gave America an Ethic of Sexual Pleasure* (New York : Oxford University Press, 1985), p. 25–26.

40. Ruth Hughes, "The Awful Disclosures of Maria Monk" (n.d.), online at http://dept.english.upenn.edu/~traister/hughes.html.

41. *Ibid.*

42. Heywood Broun and Margaret Leech, *Anthony Comstock: Roundsman of the Lord* (New York: Albert & Charles Boni, 1927), p. 84.

43. Kendrick, p. 100; Hyde, p. 107. By contrast, the salary of the president of the United States in 1871 was $25,000; it was doubled in 1873.

44. Hyde, p. 107.

45. Kendrick, p. 131.

46. Broun and Leech, p. 84.

47. Broun and Leech, p. 83.

48. More than a century later, feminists Andrea Dworkin and Catherine MacKinnon would use

the same reasoning as a basis for promoting their antiobscenity ordinance in communities like Indianapolis and Minneapolis.

49. Broun and Leech, p. 84.
50. Ironically, Hyde lists Morgan as one of the two foremost American collectors of pornography (the other was Henry E. Huntington). Hyde, p. 181. If true, it is unclear whether Morgan did so for personal enjoyment or (like Andrea Dworkin today) as a means of documenting the scope of the problem.
51. Kendrick, pp. 133–34.
52. Kendrick, p. 135.
53. Kendrick, p. 130, citing Broun and Leech, p. 153.
54. Kendrick, p. 136.
55. Kendrick, pp. 147–48, quoting Letter to Robert W. Welch, ca. September 22–23, 1905, in Dan H. Laurence, ed., *Bernard Shaw: Collected Letters 1898–1910* (London: Max Reinhardt, 1972), pp. 559–61. It is remarkable that 90 years later, virtually identical sentiments are being expressed in newspapers around the world, as nations watch the way in which the United States has reacted to President Clinton's affair with a White House staffer.
56. Charles Johanningsmeir, *Fiction and the American Literary Marketplace* (Cambridge, UK: Cambridge University Press), 1997, p. 20.
57. D'Emilio and Freedman, p. 60.
58. D'Emilio and Freedman, p. 174.
59. D'Emilio and Freedman, p. 61.
60. A copy of Sanger's publication (6th ed.) is online at http://www.lib.msu.edu.spc/digital/radicalism/hq766.s321917.htm.
61. D'Emilio and Freedman, pp. 222–23.
62. See *Youngs Rubber Corporation v. C.I. Lee & Co. Inc.*, 45 F. 2d 103 (C.C.A. 1930).
63. Tannahill, p. 411.
64. *United States v. One Package*, 86 F. 2d 737 (C.C.A. 1936). It took Congress 45 years, however, to remove the references to contraception from the Comstock Law. See Pub. L. 91–662 (1971) (deleting references to contraception).
65. D'Emilio and Freedman, pp. 245–46.
66. See *Griswold v. Connecticut*, 381 U.S. 479 (1965). The ruling was extended to unmarried individuals in a case arising out of Massachusetts: *Eisenstadt v. Baird*, 405 U.S. 438 (1972).
67. 18 U.S.C. §1461.
68. D'Emilio and Freedman, p. 195.
69. Tune by Walter Donaldson, lyrics by Sam M. Lewis and Joe Young.
70. So popular were the speakeasies and other sources of illicit alcohol that by 1926, the amount of liquor being illegally consumed in the United States was estimated to be worth $3.6 billion per year.
71. Interestingly, all of the great literary censorship cases of the 1920s and early 1930s involved books written in Europe, a continuation in part of the long-standing conflict between Europe's greater freedom for sexually explicit (or at least provocative) materials and the fears of American religious and civic leaders towards the same. To a lesser degree, American books were also growing more daring—some of the highlights of the decade included *Winesburg, Ohio* (Sherwood Anderson, 1919), *The Great Gatsby* (F. Scott Fitzgerald, 1925), *Main Street* (Sinclair Lewis, 1920), and *The Sun Also Rises* (Ernest Hemingway, 1926)—but none addressed sexual issues as directly as their European peers.
72. *United States v. One Book Entitled "Ulysses,"* Opinion A. 110–59, slip op. (S.D.N.Y. December 6, 1933) (Woolsey, J.).
73. *Memoirs v. Massachusetts*, 383 U.S. 413 (1966) (reversing decision by the Massachusetts Supreme Judicial Court that the book was obscene).
74. The first issue featured a short story by Ernest Hemingway; other early contributors included William Faulkner, F. Scott Fitzgerald, Aldous Huxley, H.L. Mencken, Dorothy Parker, and John Steinbeck.
75. Frank Miller, *Censored Hollywood* (Atlanta: Turner Publishing, Inc., 1994), p. 82.
76. The infamous photo can be seen online at http://www.HedyLamarr.AT/070.html. The

ensuing commotion was so fierce, in fact, that when Kiesler came to Hollywood to pursue her film career, she changed her name to "Hedy Lamarr" in part to distance herself from *Ecstasy*. In addition to her more obvious attributes, Lamarr is also known as one of the inventors of "frequency hopping," an integral part of today's cell phone technology. She and composer George Antheil received a patent for the idea in 1942, but it was nearly a quarter-century before technology developed to the point where practical use could be made of their idea. In recent years, Lamarr and Antheil (posthumously) have received a number of awards for their contribution.

77. As we'll see, this is the same progression that took place from *Playboy* to *Penthouse* to *Hustler* some 40 years later.

78. Art Spiegelman, introduction to Bob Adelman, *Tijuana Bibles: Art and Wit in America's Forbidden Funnies, 1930s–1950s* (New York: Simon & Schuster, 1997).

79. Spiegelman in Adelman, *Tijuana Bibles*.

80. The irony, of course, is that President Harding made his own indelible contribution to the nation's sexual history by allegedly carrying on an affair with Nan Britton in a White House cloakroom.

81. In more recent times, both the television and Internet industries have undertaken similar efforts at self-policing to help stave off congressional action.

82. For example, the libidinous heroine might flee her lover and renounce a life of sin; supposedly single lovers might be revealed to have been married all along; or a dashing cad might come to a bad end.

83. Miller, p. 82.

84. Gay Talese, *Thy Neighbor's Wife* (New York: Dell Publishing Co., 1981), p. 59.

85. Williams was one of a long string of actors who have willingly made provocative photo appearances for the opportunity to be discovered. As is frequently the case, however, the anticipated film career never really materialized: Williams appeared in four films in 1945, but only three more in the next seven years. Her last role was a bit part in the 1952 sci-fi flick, *Captive Women*, about three tribes that fight for control of a postapocalyptic New York.

86. Given the risqué nature of much of the material used by USO performers (to say nothing of its delivery), it is ironic that one of the founding groups of the USO was the YMCA. For a terrific example of what the USO was all about, see Bette Midler's first song in the 1991 movie *For the Boys*.

87. See Alan Betrock, *The Illustrated Price Guide to Cult Magazines, 1945-1969* (New York: Shake Books, 1994).

88. Talese, p. 60. There was considerable doubt about von Rosen's affiliation with nudism, since many of the photographs in *Modern Sunbathing* were taken indoors and used models more likely to be strippers than nudists.

89. Talese, pp. 58–62.

90. Talese, pp. 89–90.

91. Talese, p. 96.

92. Talese, p. 97.

93. Talese, pp. 97–99.

94. Talese, p. 101.

95. 354 U.S. 476 (1957).

96. Hyde, p. 185.

97. Talese, pp. 126–27.

98. 354 U.S. 476, 489 (1957).

99. 354 U.S. 476, 484 (1957).

100. Luke Ford, *A History of X: 100 Years of Sex in Film* (1999), "Chapter One." The first three chapters of *History of X* are available online at http://www.lukeford.com/main.html. Click on the "Luke Ford" button, and then select "Chapter One," "Chapter Two," or "Chapter Three" from the drag-down menu. All references herein are to the online version of the text. In June, 1999, *History of X* was published in hardcopy by Prometheus Books of Amherst, N.Y.

101. Miller, pp. 196–97.

102. Playboy Club FAQ, Playboy Web site.

103. Talese, pp. 442–43.

104. 386 U.S. 767 (1967).

105. Talese, p. 457.

106. Ford, *History of X*, "Chapter One."

107. Edward de Grazia, *Girls Lean Back Everywhere*, (New York: Random House, 1992), pp. 577–79.

108. de Grazia, p. 579.

109. In 1995, *Playboy* was the 15th-best-selling magazine, with a little more than 3.2 million U.S. subscriptions. *Penthouse* was 69th, with approximately 1.1 million subscriptions.

110. Talese, p. 563.

111. Ford, *History of X*, "Chapter One."

112. Miller, p. 197.

113. Robert Sklar, *Movie-Made America: A Cultural History of American Movies* (New York: Vintage Books, 1975), pp. 300-302.

114. Sklar, p. 299.

115. Justin Plouffe, "Porn Yesterday," *The Nassau Spigot*, Vol. 19, Issue 7 (n.d.), online at http://spigot.princeton.edu/ns/19-7/cover-porn.html. Similar promotional efforts were also made on behalf of Georgina Spelvin, the star of 1973's other major mainstream adult hit, *The Devil in Miss Jones*. Although *Miss Jones* actually out-earned *Deep Throat* at the box office (finishing an astonishing sixth out of all the films released in the U.S. that year, while *Deep Throat* was 11th), Spelvin never gained the celebrity status that Lovelace did. Sklar, p. 299.

116. Talese, p. 467.

117. 413 U.S. 15 (1973).

118. 413 U.S. 15, 24–25 (1973).

119. de Grazia, p. 570.

120. de Grazia, p. 570. The same risk prevails today with respect to online materials. If one community determines that a certain kind of sexual material is obscene, that community can effectively prevent every other community from seeing it.

121. Talese, p. 473.

122. Talese, p. 472. Standards, however, continue to change. *Last Exit* made it onto the big screen in 1989, starring Stephen Lang, Jennifer Jason Leigh, and Jerry Orbach.

123. Ford, *History of X*, "Chapter Five."

124. *Ibid.*

125. de Grazia, p. 571.

126. John Tierney, "Porn: The Low-Slung Engine of Progress," *New York Times*, Jan. 9, 1994, at B1.

127. Richard Winton, "Porn Goes Mainstream." *Los Angeles Times*, August 18, 1998, Metro p. 1.

128. *Ibid.*

129. *Ibid.*

130. Eric Schlosser, "The Business of Pornography," *U.S. News and World Report*, February 10, 1997.

131. "Bandwidth" refers to the capacity of a communications system to transmit data. For instance, a fiber-optic cable, which can transmit millions of bits per second, has a higher bandwidth than a copper phone line, which is generally limited to approximately 56,000 bits per second.

# 2

# VOYEUR
# VIEWING
# PLEASURE

Much of our American progress has been the product of the
individual who had an idea; pursued it; fashioned it; tenaciously
clung to it against all odds; and then produced it, sold it, and
profited from it.
Hubert H. Humphrey in address to
U.S. Junior Chamber of Commerce, Detroit, June 1966

## WORTH A THOUSAND DIRTY WORDS

### THE INVENTION OF PHOTOGRAPHY

Over the last 160 years, a number of technological developments have tremendously enhanced our ability to create and transmit images of the world in which we live. The changes wrought by these inventions have been profound; our very perception of the world in which we live has been irrevocably altered by photography, film, video, cable television, and increasingly, the Internet. The role the pornography industry played in popularizing the VCR is often cited, but the impulse to take and even to sell sexually explicit images is evident from the earliest days of photography.

On the corner of an eerily empty Parisian street, a man stood with his foot on a shoe-shine box. Seen from a window overlooking the street, he was unaware that he had just become the first person ever to have his photograph taken (an honor accorded him because he was the only person in view who stood still long enough for his image to register on the primitive film). It was the summer of 1839, and the image was taken by Louis Daguerre, who had only a few months before disclosed to the French Academy of Sciences his method for capturing clear and detailed images.[1]

The French government, in a stunning display of generosity, gave Daguerre's invention to the world in August 1839 by simultaneously publishing in eight languages the instructions for making photographic images. In a pattern that would be emulated a century and a half later with the World Wide Web, people rushed out to buy the equipment and supplies needed to create their own images.

The images, which became known as "daguerreotypes," created a tremendous sensation around the world. For the first time, people could actually see places half a world a way. Without leaving the privacy of their home, people could visit the pyramids of Egypt, gaze at the Acropolis, or see the statues in the British Museum. Over the following half-century, literally millions of daguerreotypes would be taken of subjects all around the world.

Daguerre's invention had a profound impact on the 19th century psyche; it literally changed the way people saw their world. Images of the world—paintings, etchings, engravings, and so on—were available prior to the invention of photography, of course, but only to those with the skills to create them or the resources to purchase them. While the printing press did a great deal to lower the cost of purchasing printed images (including sexual explicit images like those created for *Il Modi*), consumers were limited to the images created by others.

When the news of Daguerre's invention first reached the United States, Samuel F. B. Morse, the inventor of the electromagnetic telegraph, traveled to France to learn Daguerre's method of capturing images. He and his partner, John W. Draper, were among the first in this country to take photographs. In 1840, Alexander Wolcott and James Johnson filed for a U.S. patent for an improved version of Daguerre's camera and opened the first photography studio in New York City.

As in Europe, daguerreotypes offered American entrepreneurs a lucrative opportunity. The start-up and operating costs, although not cheap, were not prohibitive; the skill required to take reasonably good pictures did not take particularly long to develop; and the novelty of the item commanded a premium price (as much as $2 per daguerreotype at the beginning of the 1840s).[2] As a result, large numbers of professionals, shopkeepers, and tradesmen opened daguerreotype studios on the side.[3] Supply and demand had its natural effect, however, and by the end of the 1840s, so many people were taking daguerreotypes that the average price had dropped to two for a quarter.[4] In 1853, the *New York Tribune* estimated that Americans were taking more than 3 million daguerreotypes each year.[5] Two years later, a survey indicated that New York could boast of more than 90 daguerreotype galleries, and most other large cities had at least one gallery. In the mid- to late 1800s, three new formats—stereoscopes,[6] the palm-sized "cartes-de-visite,"[7] and postcards—helped to further popularize photography and make it less expensive. To varying degrees, all of these new formats were used for the distribution of erotic images.

## THE COMMERCIALIZATION OF SEXUAL IMAGES

In Europe, where the nude body had been the subject of renewed artistic inter-est for more than 400 years, some of the earliest photographic images were of naked people. By some estimates, the first nude daguerreotype was take less than two years after the French government announced Daguerre's invention.

Reports from the era (along with the sheer volume of surviving nude photographs) make it clear that nude photography was not merely an amateur hobby but a commercial activity as well. At first, as with sexually explicit litera-ture in the United States, a gloss of scientific or educational value was necessary to minimize the hostile attention of civic leaders. N.P. Lerebours, for instance, a Parisian optical instrument maker who opened the first public photography stu-dio in 1841, specialized in so-called "Academies" or "academy studies"—nude photographs that were ostensibly designed to assist art students in studying the human form.[8] Henry Hyde reported in his *History of Pornography* (1964) that "the discovery and development of photography led to the 'manufacture and dis-tribution of erotic and indecent photographs on an enormous scale, thereby lay-ing the foundations of the business in "feelthy pictures" and postcards which has continued to flourish unabated to this day.' "[9] Among the examples he cites of this industry is an Englishman by the name of Henry Hayler. When Hayler's photography studio was raided in 1874, police confiscated more than 130,000 "obscene" photographs and 5,000 "obscene" slides.

In addition to their use by artists, risqué photos were also produced specifically for sale to tourists who were not able to find similar materials in their own country. The practice of producing and selling "artistic studies" to tourists (one that Lerebours apparently pioneered) was so successful that less than three years after the invention of the daguerreotype, the United States Congress passed the Customs Act of 1842, which specifically forbade the importation of "obscene or immoral . . . pictures."

If Congress thought that banning the importation of immoral or obscene pictures would rid the nation's streets of smut, it was sorely mistaken. In New York City in the late 1840s, for instance, daguerreotypes of women in var-ious stages of undress could be purchased not only in stationery stores but also from the numerous pushcart vendors working the city's streets.[10] The problem lay in the fact that Congress couldn't ban the most subversive import: the knowl-edge of how to make daguerreotypes in the first place. Although there is some dispute about the volume of U.S. domestic production of nude images in the mid- to late 19th century, it is clear that at least some of the photos available were of local origin. On August 9, 1846, for instance, the *Police Gazette* reported that a man had been arrested in Boston "for taking and exposing daguerreotypes of naked women." The *Police Gazette* noted that "[t]his practice is not confined to Boston, but is practised [*sic*] in New York to a great extent by several good daguerreotypists."

As with risqué literature, the popularity of sexual images in the United

States was spurred by the social disruption of the Civil War. With a significant portion of the nation's men deprived of female companionship while at the front (notwithstanding the efforts of "Hooker's Division," the prostitutes who worked Washington's red-light district), the demand for pornography was high. Although the lurid stories from Dr. William Haynes and his competitors supplied much of the demand, soldiers could also for the first time in history see the charms they had left behind (if not their beloved's in particular, then at least those of her gender).

Not everyone was thrilled with this addition to camp life. During the war, Captain M.G. Tousley, an officer in the Union Army, was so outraged by the volume of explicit materials circulating through the ranks that he wrote to his commander in chief and complained that the Army was not doing enough to "checkmate and suppress" the "obscene prints and photographs" that were "quite commonly kept and exhibited by soldiers and even officers."[11] To assist President Lincoln in understanding the scope of the problem, Captain Tousley thoughtfully included a sample of the brochures circulating in the Army, which offered "New Pictures for Bachelors." According to the circular, a customer could purchase a single image for 12 cents or a dozen for $1.20.[12] The pictures consisted of images of young women frolicking partially unclothed and nude in various natural settings.[13] There is, unfortunately, no report of what action (if any) President Lincoln took on Captain Tousley's complaint.[14]

One person who did find a sympathetic ear on Capital Hill was Postmaster General Montgomery Blair, who complained to Congress that " 'great numbers of obscene books and pictures' were being 'sent to the Army.'"[15] Congress responded by passing a law in 1865 banning the mailing of obscene goods, a law that would be later expanded at the urging of Anthony Comstock into a more comprehensive ban on the mailing of "Every letter, packet, or package, or other mail matter containing any filthy, vile, or indecent thing, device or substance."

## SEXUAL IMAGES ON (AND UNDER) THE NEWSSTAND

One of the reasons that Comstock had such a difficult time stamping out pornography was that throughout the 19th and beginning of the 20th centuries, the production and distribution of sexual images was almost entirely the province of the daring individual or small-business owner.

The lack of mass production for risqué photographs was hardly a major impediment for sexual entrepreneurs. With the development of celluloid film by George Eastman in 1889, the process of making prints from negatives became much faster and much less expensive. The developed prints could then be sold in any of a number of potential retail outlets. For instance, an arrangement might be worked out with the owner of the corner newsstand or cigar shop to sell photos under the counter, or with the madam of the local bordello to sell photos as a sideline (the madam in turn may have provided photographic subjects as a form of advertising or for a cut of the profits). Other popular sources for titillating pictures were pool halls, which became popular in the late 19th century, and all-male saloons and gentlemen's clubs.[16] Another common (albeit riskier) outlet was the classified-advertisement section of certain newspapers: An advertisement might be placed, for instance, in a publication such as the *Police Gazette*, the 19th century equivalent of today's *National Enquirer* or *Star*. Ad copy typically read something along these lines:

> 20 Female Photos, latest out. Full length pictures. 10 cents. F. B. Teel. Hurleyville, N.Y.
> 30 full form pictures (very rare) actresses in tights. Cab. size. 15c. J. R. Hay. Box 1905. San Francisco, Cal.
> 20 pictures sweet self. 10c. Lock Box 10. August, Me.[17]

A century or more later, it's impossible to know how successful such ads might have been (or for that matter, just how explicit the photos in fact were). But clearly, sex and the entrepreneurial spirit were already working hand in hand.

The tide began to turn against photographic entrepreneurs on March 4, 1880, when the *New York Daily Graphic* used the halftone process to publish the first photograph on newsprint. Seventeen years later, the *New York Tribune* became the first newspaper to print halftone illustrations on a power press, making the wide-scale and inexpensive distribution of photographs possible for the first time. The impact was not immediately felt by the producers of sexual explicit images; given the social and legal climate at the beginning of the 20th century, it would have been extremely difficult for a pornographer to sell enough product to justify the cost of using a press on the scale employed by the *Tribune*. As the social climate began to change in the years following World War I, however, the risks associated with publishing risqué materials diminished. As a result, the potential economic rewards of offering titillating materials to a regional or national audience became increasingly attractive.

One of the first publications to successfully exploit the greater cultural freedom on a national scale was *Sunshine & Health* ("The Official Organ of the American Sunbathing Association"), which began publication in 1931. Although obviously not intended as a direct competitor to the sellers of sexually explicit photos, *Sunshine & Health* made more nude photographs available in one place and at a lower cost (25 cents) than any other source of the day. The publisher made a nod to postal regulations by (mostly) erasing pubic areas, but otherwise, no effort was made to hide the nudity of the people in the photographs.[18]

More overtly sexual national publications soon followed the path blazed by *Sunshine & Health*, among them *Esquire* in 1933, *Modern Man* in 1951, and of course, *Playboy* in 1953. While these publications never completed eliminated the market for amateur or semiprofessional photo sets of sexual activity, particularly depictions of hardcore activity, the enormous reproduction and distribution advantages enjoyed by the national men's magazines made it very difficult for individual publishers of photographs to compete. One compensating factor was that the growth of men's magazines increased the opportunities and potential revenues for both photographers and models. However, competition was (and is) fierce, and the supply of photographers and models has consistently exceeded demand.

In the last four years, ironically, the market for sexually explicit photographs has come full circle. The Internet has greatly diminished one of the chief advantages of the national men's magazines—the economies of scale that enable them to produce and distribute sexually explicit photographs each month for less than it would cost the average person to process the roll of film used to take the photographs in the first place. Now, with an initial investment of less than $2,000 and a free afternoon, an individual can make dozens or even hundreds of sexually explicit photographs available to a worldwide audience. As we'll see, however, the national men's magazines have not lost all of their advantages: a well-established brand name is a powerful tool in a chaotic environment like the Internet.

## MOVING DEPICTIONS OF SEX: STAGS, PEEPS, AND TAPES

### STAG FILMS

In December 1895, a group of Parisians had the honor of watching the first public screening of a movie. The concept of watching moving images on a screen was so novel that when a head-on shot of a rushing train appeared, it frightened some members of the audience. The film was created by two French photographers and manufacturers of photographic equipment, Louie and Auguste Lumière, as a means of demonstrating their new invention, the *cinématographe* (from which we get our word "cinema"). The film was part of an effort by the Lumières to compete with the well-known American inventor Thomas Edison, whose kinetograph had been introduced the previous year. The Lumières's invention succeeded in large part because their device for taking moving pictures was lighter and more portable, used less film, was quieter, and could be set up to project the finished product to a large audience. By contrast, the kinetoscope (Edison's device for viewing films made with the kinetograph) could be viewed only by a single individual at a time.[19] Thanks to the *cinématographe*, France would dominate the world market for cinema for nearly a decade.[20]

The type of movies envisioned by the Lumières and others like them quickly proved to be enormously popular entertainment. Within 15 years, filmmakers from around the world (particularly France, Germany, Italy, Denmark, and the U.S.) were competing vigorously for audiences. As with photographers a half-century before, the idea occurred fairly quickly to filmmakers in a number of different countries (but particularly France) that filming and displaying nudity was a potentially lucrative activity. As early as 1896, for instance, the French film *Le Bain* showed actress Louise Willy as she disrobed. At about the same time, German producer Oskar Messter made a number of films that depicted women bathing, exercising, and disrobing. Many of Messter's films appeared in the United States;[21] although the content of these movies was often condemned,[22] that did not prevent them from being shown publicly.[23]

Over the next 50 years, the stag film became a cultural institution in the U.S. The form and content of the stag film remained essentially unchanged: a single, relatively short reel (usually 10–15 minutes in length), amateur participants, and heterosexual intercourse (albeit in a variety of positions and locations). The production of stag films was, as Di Lauro and Rabkin put it in their book *Dirty Movies*, "a cottage industry."[24] Most of the stag films were shown first in the region in which they were produced, and then only slowly in other regions or countries. The industry received an important boost in 1923, when Kodak introduced a 16mm camera, projector, and film. The ready availability of the new movie technology to the public resulted in one of the first surges in the production of stag movies.[25]

Whereas brothels provided regular audiences for stag films in Europe, the primary market for stags in the United States was the so-called "smoker" or "stag party." The audience at these gatherings was almost always all-male, and generally belonged to one of two types of groups: community organizations such as the Legionnaires, Elks, and Rotarians, and college fraternities.[26] According to Di Lauro and Rabkin, $50 to $100 was enough in the 1920s and 1930s to cover the cost of renting a projector and two to three hours of stag films.[27] There may have been entrepreneurs who rented stag films and charged members of the public admission to see them, but the number was certainly small, given the very real risk of arrest and prosecution. The much more common practice was for the stags to be rented by an organization for the pleasure of its members.[28]

A variety of technological innovations helped diminish the market for publicly shown stag films. In the late 1950s, 16mm cameras and film gave way to the smaller and lighter 8mm, a camera specifically marketed to families for the purpose of taking and viewing home movies. Pornographers got their first glimpse of the future: By the beginning of the 1960s, the sale of stag films to individuals for home viewing exceeded rental earnings.[29] As the decade progressed, the 8mm market benefited from the general easing of social restrictions on sexually explicit materials, and a thriving mail order business advertised in classified ads under the code words "private films," "mail orders," or "eights."[30]

With slightly less cumbersome technology and a slightly more liberal social climate, 8mm films might have sparked the surge in home pornography consumption that would later turn adult videotapes into a multibillion-dollar industry. 8mm technology, however, never became much more than a hobbyist's activity, in large part due to the cost of negatives, developing and printing films, and the equipment required to shoot and then play back the finished product. While the lack of a critical mass of 8mm owners limited the pornography industry's ability to sell directly to consumers (there were, for instance, very few retail outlets that offered 8mm films for sale or rental), the late 1960s and early 1970s were nonetheless boom years for sexually explicit 8mm films. The demand was driven by a simple but savvy realization: if the pornography industry could not bring its product to the consumer's living room, then it would bring the consumer to the product. Even better, it would offer the consumer the temporary rental of the functional equivalent of his living room: the peep show booth.

## LOOPS AND PEEPS: THE INDUSTRY TAKES OVER

As the founder of *Playboy* and host of innumerable well-publicized parties at the Playboy Mansion, Hugh Hefner was (and still is) one the most identifiable representatives of the pornography industry. The tremendous success of his magazine helped lay the groundwork for the industry's remarkable growth in a number of different sectors. For understandable reasons, however, not all of the major figures in the pornography industry have been as fond of the media spotlight as Hefner. One of the most reticent—but most influential—figures was Cleveland-born Ruben Sturman, who began distributing sex magazines in the late 1950s (including, incidentally, *Playboy*) and over the next 30 years built one of the largest pornography empires in the nation's history. In 1991, *Time* estimated that Sturman's empire grossed roughly $1 million per day "from the sale of lewd magazines, videos and marital aids."[31] According to porn industry chronicler Luke Ford, Sturman's personal fortune was estimated to be as high as $200 million to $300 million.[32]

A significant portion of Sturman's wealth was earned a quarter at a time, using technology that Thomas Edison and William Dickson developed in 1891 when they perfected the kinetoscope.[33] The first demonstration was held on April 14, 1894, when Edison and Dickson gave people the chance to watch a 13 second film clip of Annie Oakley and Buffalo Bill.[34] Although a number of kinetoscope parlors opened in various cities around the world (since the average price of viewing the contents was a nickel, the parlors became known as "nickelodeons"), the kinetoscope quickly gave way to the more lucrative projection system. The true economic potential of the peep show booth was not fully realized until 1971, when Sturman teamed with Swede Lasse Braun to produce the ubiquitous "peep booths," a simple combination of a coin-operated projector, a small screen, and a lockable door.[35] By the early 1970s, Sturman was distributing booths to adult book stores and sex shops in virtually every state in the country. In a typical arrangement, Sturman would offer to provide a shop owner with one or more booths for free, in exchange for half the receipts the booth generated; customers were generally charged 25 cents for 30 seconds to two minutes of viewing. The booths proved phenomenally popular: By some estimates, peeps grossed $2 billion during the 1970s alone, roughly four times the amount earned during the same decade by such full-length adult movies as *Deep Throat* and

*Behind the Green Door*. As both the primary manufacturer and distributor of the booths and a significant supplier of the sex shorts (known as "loops"),[36] Sturman made money hand over fist.

By the 1980s, the Justice Department believed that Sturman was the largest distributor of hardcore pornography in the entire country. Exactly how much Sturman earned over the years in the pornography industry will probably never be fully known, but in 1989 the federal government successfully tried and convicted Sturman for failing to pay $29 million in taxes. Shortly after being sentenced to prison, Sturman staged a daring helicopter escape. Recaptured eight weeks later, Sturman died in a Lexington, Kentucky, prison on October 25, 1997.

By building and distributing thousands of what were essentially miniature movie theaters, Sturman can be credited with doing for adult films what Hefner did for adult magazines: he created an industry. The demand for sexually explicit films to stock the booths created enormous opportunities for filmmakers interested in making such films, which in turn created a demand for actors. In 1954, Ted Paramore (son of Hollywood screenwriter Edward E. Paramore, Jr.) was one of the first to begin shooting loops. The content was affected by prevailing social mores: The first loops were of women in bikinis, then pasties, and then entirely nude. Even then, though, the film had to be airbrushed to eliminate the actor's pubic hair.[37] As the sexual climate changed in the 1960s, the explicitness of loops increased dramatically, forming an artistic bridge to full-length hardcore features such as *Deep Throat* and *Behind the Green Door*.

The shift from stags to loops changed the economics of sexually explicit films as well. Unlike stag films, which were primarily a regional product, a successful loop might easily be seen simultaneously on thousands of peep show screens from one end of the country to the other and, in the process, earn hundreds of thousands of dollars. The possibility of national distribution heightened the competition among filmmakers, particularly because the distribution of films to the peep show booths was controlled by a relatively small number of people (primarily Sturman, who was importing large numbers of loops from Sweden). If Sturman bought a filmmaker's loop, there was a good chance that it would make a sizable amount of money; if he didn't, then the amount of money that could be earned dropped precipitously.

Thanks to the increasingly ubiquitous 8mm home movie technology, Sturman's success did not completely wipe out the ability of individual sexual entrepreneurs to make sexually explicit films and profitably sell copies of them to other interested individuals through classified ads, clubs, and other outlets. In some ways, in fact, the ability of the home movie entrepreneur to compete with a national loop distributor such as Sturman was better than an amateur photographer's ability to compete with Hefner. Purchasing a copy of *Playboy*, with its professionally done photographs and consistently attractive models, was far easier than ordering a set of naughty photographs by mail, even if those photographs would show something *Playboy* wouldn't. By contrast, someone who wanted to see a dirty movie had the option of buying an 8mm film by mail or traveling to a seedy section of town and walking into a dark peep show booth. The power of national distribution can't be overstated; there is no evidence that amateurs were selling anything close to an average of $200 million worth of sexy home movies in the 1970s, whereas for every year in that decade, an average of 800 million quarters were dropped into peep show slots. Nonetheless, the unsavory environment in which peep booths were generally found helped keep the market for mail order films alive.

## THE AMATEUR VIDEO MARKET

The introduction of videotape technology fundamentally changed the production and distribution of sexually explicit films for both professionals and amateurs. The changes hit the professional adult film industry first, as videotape technology began to replace film in the mid-1970s (a transition dramatized in the 1997 film *Boogie Nights*, in which Burt Reynolds plays a adult filmmaker who resists the shift to videotape). The shift from film to video was driven by two main considerations: (1) the fact that videotape technology opened a virgin market of home movie viewers; and (2) the fact that it cost far less to produce an adult video than it did an adult film.

The first forays into consumer videotape occurred in the mid-1960s, when Sony, Panasonic, General Electric, 3M, and Phillips all introduced home taping systems. The systems, which consisted of some combination of a camera, recorder, and monitor, retailed for more than $1,000 and did not sell particularly well.[38] The technology continued to improve, however, and in 1975, Sony introduced the first Betamax videocassette recorder. Although the Betamax originally retailed for $1,300, it was far easier to use than the systems introduced a decade before. Sony had the market to itself for two years, until JVC (Japan Victor Company) introduced its videocassette recorder, which used VHS-format cassettes. The VHS system, which offered longer recording times (up to six hours) was incompatible with Sony's Beta system. When RCA and Panasonic chose to adopt the VHS standard, the stage was set for one of the century's major industrial standard battles.[39] In a relatively short time, the VHS format triumphed over Beta (although, as Macintosh users wistfully point out, Beta is still the preferred choice of format for high-end video productions, including most television studios).[40]

As the price of VCRs dropped steadily in the late 1970s, the number of units in American homes steadily rose. One of the first to recognize the potential of the new technology was David Friedman, a longtime veteran of exploitation and nudist camp films who founded an adult videocassette company called TVX in 1977. Within six months, he told *Film Comment*, he had a dozen competitors.[41] Friedman's assessment of where the industry was going was highly accurate; by 1985, the X-rated-home-video market (including both sales and rentals) was approaching the $1 billion mark, a figure that rose to an estimated $3.1 billion in 1995.

The enormous demand for adult videocassettes (driven largely by convenience and privacy) and the existence of an untapped market alone would have been enough to encourage adult film producers to shift to video. But an equally compelling factor was the enormous cost savings that video introduced to the industry. The savings resulted in large part from the fact that a video camera records images by storing an electronic signal directly onto a magnetic tape, much as a tape recorder stores sound or a computer stores information on a floppy disk. With the appropriate equipment, videotaped images can be played back and edited immediately, which sharply reduces the time and cost required for postproduction. By contrast, when a movie is shot on film, the images are first captured on a negative, which must be developed and processed before it can be edited. As the credits of most Hollywood films illustrate, the postproduction work for film requires a large number of people, all of whom add to the cost of film as a recording medium. As a result, the cost of shooting a video can be as little as one-tenth the cost of shooting a comparable film. By 1985, videotape was being used in more adult productions than film, and today virtually every adult production is shot on videotape.

The enormous drop in production costs, together with the tremendous profit margins traditionally associated with sexually explicit material, drew an increasingly large number of people into the adult film industry. Prior to the introduction of video cameras, only a relatively small number of people could obtain the $100,000 to $300,000 required to shoot the average feature-length adult film.[42] Finding $30,000 or $40,000 to shoot straight to video, however, was another matter altogether, and by the mid-1980s, the cost had plunged even further, to as little as $15,000. The surge in the number of adult filmmakers can be gauged in part by the growth in the number of sexually explicit movies: in 1976, approximately 100 new porn features were released; in 1996, the adult movie industry released more than 8,000 new titles. Thanks in large part to the sheer number of titles released each week, the United States is, according to *U.S. News and World Report*, the world leader in the production and distribution of adult videos.[43]

Even though a $15,000 shooting budget represented a significant drop in the cost of making an adult movie, it was enough to keep all but the most avid amateur out of the adult film industry. Unlike photography, which was inexpensive enough to be practiced by nearly anyone with the inclination to do so, the cost of purchasing and renting professional video equipment in the 1970s and early 1980s was still beyond the reach of most people. In the mid-1980s, however, the budget required for making an adult movie was reduced to little more than the cost of a blank videotape, a bottle of wine, and some baby oil. In 1983, Sony introduced the camcorder, a video camera aimed specifically at the home market. Within two years, consumers purchased nearly 500,000 camcorders, a figure that increased to 3 million in 1990.[44]

The first use of a camcorder to record sexually explicit material undoubtedly occurred at least as quickly, if not more so, than with the camera a century and a half earlier. After all, an enormous advantage of capturing images on magnetic tape is that it does not require development; as soon as an image is recorded by a video camera or camcorder, it can be replayed. As a result, video is a very rapid, very inexpensive, and very private technology. Almost overnight, it became possible for millions of people to produce and view sexually explicit videos.

The growth in the number of potential pornography producers was more than matched by the growth in the number of potential outlets for sexually explicit video. In the early 1970s, at the tail end of the so-called Golden Age of Pornography, a feature-length adult film could be seen on 1,200 to 1,300 screens, roughly 1,000 of which were under the control of the Pussycat Theater chain. By contrast, there were tens of thousands of screens on which a given loop might be seen. However, the distribution channels for loops were even more tightly controlled than those for adult films. In part because of the cost, but also in part because of the limited number of outlets, only about 100 or so feature-length adult films were produced and distributed each year. A chief result of the small number of adult titles produced each year was that amateur production and distribution of sexually explicit film was essentially limited to the underground 16mm and 8mm markets.

The introduction of the VCR, however, opened up completely new distribution possibilities for adult movies. Instead of playing on a few hundred full-size screens or even tens of thousands of peep show screens, an adult movie can now play on any of about 81 million screens around the country (based on surveys showing that a little more than eight out of ten households own a VCR). With that large a potential market, it is essentially impossible for any company or even group of companies to completely dominate the distribution of adult videos. While there are certainly a few large companies that produce and distribute the majority of titles (i.e., Vivid Video, Metro, Cal Vista Film), there is ample room in the $3.1 billion market for the distribution and sale of videos by smaller companies and even amateurs.

As with the old 8mm movies, the chief means by which amateur video is distributed is by mail,[45] with advertisements distributed by mail, in alternative newspapers, or over the Internet. The major distinction lies in the fact that over the past 30 years, the social climate has made the sale of such movies increasingly acceptable, which in turn has made the advertising of adult videos less risky. One of the first companies to specialize in amateur video (and one of the most successful) is Video Alternatives. Robert Scott founded the company in 1987 as a means of publishing amateur videos, and his initial stock consisted chiefly of travel and instructional videos. He quickly began receiving requests for adult videos, however, and offered a few titles on a trial basis. The response was extremely positive, and Scott decided to focus exclusively on amateur adult materials.

Until recently, Video Alternatives published an annual catalog, *The Ultimate Amateur*, which served as a useful barometer of the scope of amateur adult video activity. At its peak, the catalog listed more than 1,000 different titles. The producers of the amateur videos were paid in one of two ways: either through a purchase of the rights of the video by Video Alternatives or a royalty plan under which Video Alternatives would market the video and pay the producer(s) a percentage of the proceeds. The purchase price varied depending on such factors as the video's length and the amount of editing required, while royalties were paid monthly based on the video's sales. In a 1997 handbook for amateur producers, Video Alternatives said that some videos had been earning royalties for more than seven years, with total payments reaching into the thousands of dollars. The company was careful to make it clear that few if any producers of amateur videos can expect to get rich; even the most popular amateur video is unlikely to generate more than $2,000 to $3,000 in royalty payments, and any revenues that are received are usually spread over several months or years. Despite the relatively low returns, however, it was clear that Video Alternatives had its choice of a fairly large number of amateur sex films.

Although Scott and his wife Kim have not offered a public explanation for their decision to discontinue *The Ultimate Amateur*, it is not too difficult to surmise. The very success of distributors of amateur videos like Video Alternatives has not gone unnoticed by the distributors of professional adult videos. Over the last several years, companies like Vivid Video and Metro have produced large numbers of adult videos that purport to depict amateurs engaged in a variety of sexual activities. Even if one is justifiably skeptical about the amateur status of the people involved, the ready availability of such videos undoubtedly reduced the potential market for Video Alternative's mail-order business. After all, why would someone mail off $20 or $25 to purchase an amateur video from Video Alternatives when something substantially similar is available at the local video store for $4.50 for a three-night rental? At the same time, the Internet is also making it far easier for amateur moviemakers to market their products directly. An advertisement for an amateur video on a Web page reaches a far larger audience than *The Ultimate Amateur* catalog ever reached, new products can be added to the Web page in just a few minutes, and there is no need for the producers to pay 15 to 20 percent to a distributor like Video Alternatives.

In the years prior to the development of the Internet, a catalog like *The Ultimate Amateur* could succeed because it was a highly efficient marketing tool for producers of amateur adult video. It concentrated the risk of prosecution, reduced marketing costs for individual producers, and most importantly, offered a convenient way for interested consumers to locate a somewhat hard-to-find product. *The Ultimate Amateur*, however, will not be the only catalog to fall victim to the Internet's low cost and globe-spanning scope.

# SEX GOES ELECTRONIC

Unlike photography and film, computers were slow to play a role in the pornography industry. When the U.S. Army developed the Electronic Numeral Integrator and Computer (ENIAC) in 1946 (generally considered to be the world's first electronic computer), its purpose was to assist in the calculation of such mundane matters as missile trajectories. Even after Remington Rand purchased the ENIAC from the government and began marketing it to businesses under the name Univac, short for Universal Automatic Calculator, the cost and sheer complexity of the device made it impractical for anything other than high-level number crunching.

Although computers gradually grew less expensive and more prevalent over the next several decades, they remained the domain of government agencies, colleges and universities, and large corporations. Most of these organizations (with the exception of Playboy Enterprises, Inc.) were not in the business of producing or distributing pornography, and the role of computers in the pornography industry remained small to nonexistent.

A number of factors slowed the use of computers by pornographers. For much of their early development, computers were large and enormously costly investments, and businesses could ill afford to have them used for frivolous purposes. Equally important was the fact that very few people had access to a computer outside of work and even fewer had the skills and access required to program a computer to do something illicit. It's not that sex didn't occasionally enter the picture at work (an early piece of computer-related fiction, for instance, described how a programmer used his company's mainframe computer to keep track of birthdays and gifts for his wife and two mistresses), but the practical opportunities to combine a computer and sex were relatively limited. Most important, early computers were essentially incapable of working with and producing the sights and sounds that are integral to much of pornography. It is only relatively recently that the graphical capabilities of computers have developed to the point where pornography can be viewed and even created using computers.

With the development of first video games and then the personal computer in the late 1970s and early 1980s, individuals gradually gained the ability and the freedom to use and program computers for their own purposes in the privacy of their homes. As with other technologies, the decentralization of governmental and corporate control over computers made it possible for the adult entertainment industry to use the new technology, first for entertainment, and then for the storage and distribution of sexually explicit materials.

## VIDEO GAMES

The first significant migration of computing power from the office to the home was fueled by video games. In 1972, Nolan Bushnell founded a small northern California software company named Atari and released an arcade game called Pong.[46]

Shortly after he installed his first console version of Pong in a bar, Bushnell received a call from the bartender telling him to come get the game, since it had stopped working. When Bushnell examined the game, he discovered that the coin box was so full that it wouldn't accept any more quarters; Bushnell cleared out the box and Atari was off and running.[47]

For many Americans, Atari provided their first personal contact with computing when it released the home version of Pong in 1975. At the time, Atari did not have the resources to market and distribute Pong on its own, so it went searching for a retailer to assist them with the sale of the game. The company's big break came when Sears Roebuck decided to feature Pong in its 1975 Christmas catalog and placed an order for 150,000 units. By January 1976, Pong was by far and away the top-selling video game in the country.[48]

Bushnell sold Atari to Warner, Inc. that same year for $28 million, and in 1977, Atari released its hugely popular VCS 2600.[49] The Atari VCS 2600 remained in production for more than 14 years, sold hundreds of thousands of units, and millions of game cartridges.[50] At its height in 1980, Atari reported profits in excess of $2 billion per year. After being split into a home and arcade division and then sold by Warner in 1984, the Atari home division was purchased by Time-Warner and rechristened as Time-Warner Interactive. Following additional sales and a reverse merger in 1996, the once-mighty Atari became a division of the San Diego–based JTS Corp. In turn, JTS Corp. sold all of the Atari intellectual property rights to Hasbro in February 1998 for just $5 million.

The vast majority of the games released for the VCS 2600 were relatively innocuous, but the Atari's open standard provided the adult entertainment industry with its first opportunity to generate computer-based revenues. In 1982 and 1983, a Los Angeles company named American Multiple Industries (AMI) produced a number of sexually explicit game cartridges for the 2600. The games, which sold for $49.95 each,[51] were marketed under the name "Mystique/ Swedish erotica" and included such titles as Bachelor Party, Beat 'Em and Eat 'Em, Gigolo, Jungle Fever, and Custer's Revenge. By the end of 1982, Mystique's first three releases (one of which was Custer's Revenge) had sold nearly 750,000 copies.

The objective of the games is not difficult to deduce from their titles: in Bachelor Party, for instance, an erect bridegroom-to-be tries to "touch" as many women as possible, while in Custer's Revenge, the object is to steer the lust-filled general through a hail of arrows and a forest of cactus plants to reach a Native American woman who is bound to a stake. If the general reaches his objective, the player can "pump" the joystick to rack up bonus "rape" points.

AMI's products caused the first computer-sex controversy. In 1982, the group Women Against Pornography (WAP) and a number of Native Americans protested outside a New York electronics show where AMI was displaying new products. The owner of AMI, Stuart Keston, was apparently puzzled by the protest. "There's no violence or venereal disease," he said. "We have entertainment in mind."[52] He also pointed out that the Mystique cartridges are sold in sealed boxes and labeled "Not for sale to minors."[53] In 1983, AMI sold its line of "Mystique" cartridges to a competitor, Playaround, which attempted to mollify consumers by offering double-ended cartridges (with a separate game on each end), and to silence some critics by bringing out sexually explicit games for women (i.e., Burning Desire, Bachelorette Party).[54] Playaround's success can be gauged by the fact that today, collectors of VCS 2600 game cartridges rate all of the Mystique/Playaround cartridges as "extremely rare."[55]

## FROM WORDS TO PICTURES: HOW LEISURE SUIT LARRY HELPED TO DEFINE A GENRE

Much of Atari's success stemmed from the fact that the 2600 and its successors were specifically designed to use the graphical capabilities of television screens, which made it possible to create visually attractive games. By contrast, early personal computers simply lacked the ability to display complicated graphical images.

The lack of graphics proved only a minor impediment for programmers. Building on Adventure,[56] a text-based computer game first written for a mainframe computer in the mid-1970s, companies like Infocom (founded in 1979) produced dozens of text-based games with themes ranging from underwater treasure hunts to deep-space exploration. Infocom's most famous game, Zork, was first released for the Apple II in 1981; the company's sales peaked in 1985 with gross revenues of $11.5 million.[57]

Given the demographics of early computer users—young, usually single, and overwhelming male—it is not particularly surprising that sexually oriented parodies of text adventure games appeared. The object of these parody games was not to slay the dragon or find some rare hidden treasure; instead, players attempt to engage in a variety of improbable sexual acts with the characters in the game while avoiding muscle-bound bouncers and invariably fatal social diseases.[58] The most well-known and long-lasting example of this genre is Softporn, an X-rated version of Adventure originally written for the Apple II in 1984 by Chuck Benton.

By 1986, however, the death knell for Softporn and other purely text-based games had already been sounded (albeit fuzzily). Five years earlier, IBM had introduced its Color/Graphics Adapter (CGA), which allowed programmers to use a whopping four colors at a time (out of a total palette of 16). In 1984, IBM introduced its Enhanced Graphics Adapter (EGA), which extended the PC's graphics capability up to 16 colors at a time out of a pallette of 64. Today's widely adopted video standard was introduced in 1987, when IBM released the Video Graphics Array (VGA). Using VGA technology, a screen can display up to 256 colors out of a pallette of 262,114 different colors.[59] In addition to offering greater color choices, each improvement in graphics capability also offered higher screen resolutions, which translated into better-looking and more realistic games for the personal computer.

As the largest of the commercial text-based game publishers, Infocom did its best to keep up with the times. In 1986, for instance, it released Leather Goddess of Phobos, a pulpy space opera that could be played at various levels of naughtiness, from "G" up to a saucy "R." But Infocom's foray into the risqué was too little and much too late. The company's strategic decision to stick with text-based games (despite customer requests to the contrary[60]) proved fatal; between 1987 and 1989, the company lost approximately $200,000 per quarter, and by June 1989, had effectively ceased to exist.[61]

As it turned out, one of the first widely successful graphical PC games was a variant of Softporn. The rights to Benton's game were purchased by Ken Williams, the president of Sierra Online, who then released a commercial version of the game known as Softporn Adventure. A short time later, Sierra Online hired Al Lowe to add graphics to the program, which was then renamed Leisure Suit Larry. Although the female characters are predictably buxom, the most explicit part of the game is actually the language; there is very little nudity and the sex (assuming a player helps Larry do well) is hidden under blankets or behind signs that say "Censored." The addition of the graphics helped to make Leisure Suit Larry and its five sequels a phenomenon in the gaming world;[62] in 1991 alone, the game and its sequels grossed between $20 million and $25 million.

The success of Leisure Suit Larry is a direct result of Sierra Online's ability to create a game that is titillating but not sexually explicit. By keeping the game "R-rated," Sierra Online preserved its ability to distribute Leisure Suit Larry through mainstream distribution channels like software catalogs and retail stores, an advantage not enjoyed by more blatantly sexual computer games. For example, in 1987, Jon Wesener and Jim Hunter released Astrotit, a shoot-'em-up video game featuring a penis that fires sperm at a variety of politically incorrect targets. For obvious reasons, Astrotit never made it onto the shelves of Staples or Egghead Software.

The fact that a program like Astrotit was and is still available, however, helps to illustrate the powerful ways in which computers are changing retailing. An important outgrowth of the nation's computer bulletin board system was the development of a new distribution channel known as "shareware." The basic theory behind shareware is that a computer programmer places a fully or partially functioning version of her program on a bulletin board (or today, a Web site on the Internet). Interested consumers are encouraged to download a copy of the program and try it out. If the user likes the program and is interested in continuing to use it, he or she is expected to voluntarily send in a payment (generally less than $30, although some are more expensive) to obtain a licensed copy of the program. The shareware model proved successful and continues to work in large part because people are basically honest, but also because of the unique nature of the product: once a computer program is written, the marginal cost of distributing hundreds or even thousands of copies of the program from one computer bulletin board system to another is negligible.[63] Even if only a small fraction of a shareware program's users actually register the program, the revenues are generally sufficient to make the creation and distribution of the program a financial success.

Some companies have done very well distributing their programs as shareware. Jim Knopf, for instance, who essentially invented the shareware concept in 1982 with the distribution of his database program, PC-File, founded a company called Buttonware that by the early 1990s was grossing $4.5 million per year. Although it eventually sold some programs through mainstream channels, Buttonware's primary means of distribution remained shareware. In fact, distribution costs are so much lower using the shareware model that even today, a number of companies still use that as their primary means of distribution, and even larger companies use it as a secondary distribution channel for demos and add-ons.

While it was and is possible for the producers of X-rated computer games to make money by distributing them as shareware, the continuing success of Leisure Suit Larry nonetheless illustrates that the real money still lies in more traditional distribution channels. The challenge for programmers is to figure out where to draw the line between a game that is sufficiently titillating to add to its sales, and yet not so explicit that major retail outlets such as Wal-Mart[64] or Staples will refuse to carry it. As with so many other areas of entertainment, the line of what is permissible continues to shift (albeit generally in the direction of more explicit material). Although it may be a long time, if ever, before a computer game such as Astrotit would show up on the shelves of Wal-Mart, many of the most popular games today feature characters (particularly females) and plots that are increasingly sexual in nature. The line between what is permissible and what is not is often only a few pixels wide.

## THE SHAPE OF THINGS TO COME:
## LARA CROFT, RIANA ROUGE, AND ULTRAVIXEN

In the 1985 movie *Weird Science*, Michael Anthony Hall and Ilan Mitchell-Smith lived every computer geek's dream when they used their computer equipment to create a real live woman. Predictably, the end product of the computer's calculations (fueled in part, appropriately enough, by Hall's stash of *Playboy* magazines) was a statuesque redhead played by Kelly LeBrock.[65] In one memorable scene, when Hall and Mitchell-Smith are inputting the specifications of their ideal woman, they use the computer's software to expand the figure's breasts to outlandish proportions. Even by 1985 standards, the movie's $16.3 million box office was disappointing, but it did help to illustrate some of the more creative uses to which computer graphics could be put.

In a perhaps disturbing long-term trend for the software industry, the vast majority of today's teens aren't programming their computers to create a real or even virtual woman. They don't have to; instead, they are collectively spending millions of dollars each year to purchase and play software that already contains a female lead character of Valkyrian proportions. Lara Croft, the heroine of the hit game Tomb Raider, is a gun-toting, backpack-wearing action figure who favors a hormone-inflaming wardrobe of short shorts, sleeveless T-shirts and tank tops pulled tight across the chest, tiny bikinis and short pants, and a knowing smirk beneath her small oval sunglasses.

Tomb Raider, which was first released in 1996, was created by the British software firm Core Design Ltd. and is distributed by Eidos Interactive, a subdivision of the publicly traded London company Eidos (NASDAQ: EIDSY). In a little more than two years, Tomb Raider and its sequel, Tomb Raider II, have grossed $200 million in sales, and Tomb Raider III was released in 1998. The success of the games has propelled Lara Croft to a surreal international superstardom. She has been featured on at least 80 magazine and newspaper covers, and more than 100 Web sites are now devoted to her and the Tomb Raider games. A Lara Croft comic book has been issued, a five-inch action figure is available from Toy Biz, and Eidos supplements its video game earnings by selling Croft-inspired T-shirts and bomber jackets ($400) on its Tomb Raider Web site. In addition, Eidos teamed with Prima Games in the summer of 1998 to publish *Lara's Book: Lara Croft and the Tomb Raider Phenomenon*. The coffee-table-sized book is combination pin-up and strategy guide, and features original prose by Douglas Copeland, pop culture savant and author of *Generation X*. Other mediums await to be conquered: Paramount Pictures acquired the worldwide rights to a movie version of Tomb Raider in the spring of 1998 and announced plans to produce a live-action film based on the Lara Croft character.[66] In addition, Eidos is currently considering offers for an animated series featuring Croft.

Less authorized projects have also been in the works. Fifty and 60 years ago, comic strip characters and even movie stars made unauthorized appearances in the era's Tijuana Bibles, the small cartoon booklets that featured nudity and explicit sexual activity.[67] The changes in the social climate and technology (i.e., computers) have eliminated the need to sell sexual parodies out of the trunk of a car or in the backroom of a local bar but the motivation to create sexual parodies remains. In today's high-tech equivalent, fans of Lara Croft have set up numerous Web sites containing nude images of Lara Croft, and some enterprising programmers have even written patch programs[68] that allow users to play Tomb Raider with the Croft character naked throughout the game. Among its many other advantages, a sexual parody Web site offers one advantage that most Tijuana Bibles did not have: the potential for advertising revenues. While most Web sites containing nude images of Lara Croft appear to be the work of amateurs, who are happy to simply share their achievements and their obsession with other Croft-heads, a few have turned their parody into a business by selling advertising space.

The appeal of a nude Lara Croft (possible pitch: "She's all silicon!") for the game's players is apparently enormous; the most well-known parody site,

NudeRaider.com, claimed to have received more than 5 million visitors. A victim of its own notoriety, NudeRaider.com was shut down on March 19, 1999 after the site's owners were threatened with legal action by Core Design, the creators of the Tomb Raider series.

The success of Tomb Raider and the role ascribed the Croft character in fueling sales of the game has had one extremely predictable effect: imitation by other gaming companies, with each pushing the limits of sexual content slightly further. Lara Croft is already competing (or soon will be) with a variety of other cantilever-bosomed heroines, including Rinn from Psygnosis's Drakan, Lotos Abstraction from Playmate Interactive's Meat Puppet, and Allison Huxter from Ripcord's Space Bunnies Must Die. As computer graphics continue to improve and the market for adventure games grows more competitive, programmers are going to be increasingly tempted to push even further the limits of explicitness in the characters that they create or the scenarios that they include in their game. In Fallout 2, for instance, a game described by publisher Interplay Productions as "a post-nuclear role playing game," one of the advertised strategies is "Fall in love, get married, and then pimp your spouse for a little extra chump-change. Hey, it's a dark and dangerous world."[69]

Although the sexual content of mainstream games continues to grow, there is still a fine line between sexy and sexual, and games that cross the line pay the price in more restrictive software ratings and fewer distribution channels. A good example is the game Riana Rouge, published by Black Dragon Productions. The game is a live-action adventure game, in which players use a device called an "emotivator" to change the heroine's actions. Depending on the player's choices, different "R" and "NC-17" video clips are played to advance the action of the game. The character Riana Rouge is played by Gillian Bonner, the game's developer and owner of Black Dragon Productions (as well as *Playboy's* Playmate of the Month for April 1996).

In 1997, Bonner struck a deal with Eidos to distribute Riana Rouge in the fall of that year. By the end of the 1997, however, the deal had fallen through, largely because Black Dragon was unwilling or unable to change the game enough to avoid an "adult" rating, which would keep the game out of major retailers such as Wal-Mart.

The consequences of not having a major distributor are evident: despite a high-profile launch at a Chicago Playboy mansion party in December 1997, Black Dragon sold less than 50,000 copies of Riana Rouge in the following year. By comparison, Tomb Raider (which despite its fondness for skin-tight clothing did not have to contend with an "adult" rating) sold 2.3 million copies in its first year alone.

The Internet, however, has helped Riana Rouge to develop a loyal fan following. The game and its sequel are promoted on Black Dragon's Web site (www.blackdragon.com), where fans can access erotic true stories, digital art and photographs, chat with Bonner, and read a diary of her experiences as a

Playmate. Although current sales figures for the game are not available, Bonner reported in June 1998 that the Black Dragon Web site received about 80,000 visitors per month.

At the far end of the gaming spectrum is UltraVixen, by Pixis, Inc., which describes the game's general plot as follows:

> A beautiful college student is snatched out of time by the evil sex fiend OverLord and thrust into a future of erotic slavery. She escapes and vows vengeance, assuming a new identity. ULTRAVIXEN—a super-hot sci-fi sex star whose powerful SuperClimaxes can warp both time and space.
>
> The dark OverLord has been using a vast network of time portals to torture and enslave young girls in his maniacal, mechanical sex machines. Now, UltraVixen must use her tremendous sexual powers to seal the time portals and bring the dark OverLord to his knees. There's just one catch. She needs YOU to master the incredible array of erotic tools and weapons that will unleash her SuperClimax and destroy the evil sex machines forever. The fate of the universe is in your hands.[70]

Pixis, not surprisingly, is marketing the game itself on the game's Web site, where users can use a credit card to purchase a seven-day license for different sections of the game ($6.95 each) or order the complete game on CD-ROM ($49). Although UltraVixen has not received the extensive media coverage that Lara Croft has enjoyed, she did have the unique honor of becoming the first digital centerfold when she appeared in the January 1998 issue of *Rage*.[71]

Ironically, despite the vast graphical gulf between them, the authors of Astrotit and UltraVixen are using essentially the same method for advertising and distributing their programs. The difference lies in the fact that when Wesener and Hunter released Astrotit, the distribution channel was a loose network of individual bulletin board systems; although strangers helped to distribute the program, the only way Wesener and Hunter could be certain the program wound up on a particular system was to put it there themselves. Even if someone did download the game, the authors were relying on the user to then send in the licensing fee.

Pixis, by contrast, does not have to rely on the kindness of strangers to distribute its software. The structure of the World Wide Web makes it possible for potential consumers to obtain UltraVixen directly from the Pixis Web site, rather than from widely scattered bulletin board systems. This has a number of advantages for both consumers and software producers. Obtaining the software directly from the manufacturer ensures that potential customers will receive the latest version of the program and lessens the risk of viral infection, one of the more annoying risks of frequent BBS downloads. At the same time, distributing software from a Web site enables a company to easily keep track of how many people have actually downloaded the software, use registration forms to determine the identity of potential customers, and generate revenue through the direct sale of the program and on-site advertising.

## CHEAP AND EASY: THE ELECTRONIC DISTRIBUTION OF SEXUAL IMAGES

### A PUBLISHING HOUSE IN EVERY LIVING ROOM

"If you ever cruise the Net and see everything that's available, it's glutted [with sleaze]," Larry Flynt complained to Seth Lubove in a December 1996 interview for *Forbes*. "It's a nightmare out there. This has to be affecting the revenues of people like myself."

Putting aside the obvious irony, Flynt's assessment of the impact of the Internet on print pornography publications is exactly right. As the Internet has become an increasingly accessible medium over the last 15 years (a process that has accelerated dramatically since the development of the World Wide Web in 1994), it has grown into a source of staggering numbers of sexually explicit images.

The threat to the circulation of print magazines, however, began long before the average consumer had an opportunity to connect to the World Wide Web. On February 16, 1978, the first computer bulletin board system (BBS) was opened in Chicago by Randy Seuss and Ward Christiansen. Seuss set up the hardware and Christiansen wrote the software to operate the board, including a program called Xmodem, which became the first widely available method for transferring files between personal computers.[72] The new creation became known as the Computerized Bulletin Board Service (CBBS) and broke new ground by allowing callers to play games (using the computer's eight-inch floppies) and exchange messages with each other electronically. More important, the creation of Xmodem (the first of a number of different file transfer protocols for the personal computer) allowed users to send files from their own computers to CBBS, where other users could download them. For the first time, a computer user could quickly and efficiently share a new program, utility, game, or image with anyone else who used the bulletin board. In 1981, Hayes Microcomputer Products released its first consumer modem, the MicroModem 100, and participation in bulletin boards began a slow and steady increase that accelerated dramatically in the early 1990s.[73] By the end of 1992, an estimated 45,000 BBSs were in operation around the United States,[74] servicing the calls of approximately 12 million computer users. The BBS subscribers paid out approximately $100 million in fees to the BBSs, and installed nearly 5 million new phone lines, which in turn generated more than $850 million in revenues for local phone companies.[75]

Pornography played an important role in the growth of the BBS industry. At first, most BBSs were set up and operated by hobbyists, and access was generally free. As demand rose and the cost of providing access increased (new equipment, more lines, etc.), system operators ("sysops") began charging access fees. One of the first to do so was Bob Mahoney, who built his Exec-PC BBS into a $2 million–per-year business by 1993, with more than 30,000 subscribers from around the world.

Sysops, including Mahoney, quickly realized that computer users would be more likely to pay the access fee to a BBS if the system contained images and information that the user was interested in downloading. In 1993, for instance, Exec-PC had between 10,000 and 12,000 customers, each paying an average of $75 per year for access to the bulletin board's files. According to the company's current president, Greg Ryan, some of the most popular images were those that featured nudity or sexual activity.

"One of the main draws [of the Exec-PC BBS]," Ryan said, "was its large collection of adult materials. We really didn't advertise the adult materials. The word just got around pretty quickly. One of our main claims to fame was that we had—to my knowledge—the largest collection of adult material anywhere."

In addition to Exec-PC, one of the earliest and most successful purveyors of online pornography were Jim Maxey, whose Event Horizons BBS grossed more than $3.2 million in 1993. Maxey employed ten people to assist him in scanning photographs, formatting them, and putting them online for his users to download.

The practice of downloading sexual images from a BBS illustrates the compelling power that the combination of pornography and technology can have. In the early 1990s, many BBSs charged by the minute or the hour for access to the system. Image files are often quite large, the modems of the time were slow, and the calls were often long-distance; taken together, those factors meant that the cost of downloading even a handful of sexually explicit images could easily exceed the cost of a single issue of *Playboy* or *Penthouse*. Moreover, the quality of the images printed in most magazines is far superior to the quality of the images displayed on most computer screens even today, and the gap was far greater with the computers that were generally in use in the late 1980s and early 1990s. Users needed some faith and no little imagination to figure out what was being displayed on their screen.

Despite these drawbacks, however, people were willing to pay to have access to a seemingly endless supply of erotic images in the privacy of their home. In the process, the BBS industry, long-distance phone carriers, local phone companies, modem manufacturers, and a host of other computer-related businesses all benefited directly from the distribution of sexual images.

Another significant consequence of the growth of BBSs was a profound increase in the amount of pornography generally available. Prior to the introduction of scanners, a sexually explicit photograph printed in a book or magazine stayed there, and if someone wanted to look at it, they had to find a copy of the actual publication. That's not a particularly tough challenge; *Playboy* alone has printed more than one and half *billion* copies of its magazine over the last 45 years. But with the development of scanners (the early sales of which were almost certainly fueled by the desire to scan sexually explicit images), a *Playboy* photo could be converted into electronic bits and multiple copies could be transmitted anywhere in the world. More important, a far larger number of pictures than *Playboy* or all of its competitors would ever publish in a single year could easily be transmitted from one end of the country to the other in just a few days (using 1992 modem speeds) or a few hours (using 1998 technology). In less than a decade, anyone with a computer, a phone line, and a credit card could access unparalleled numbers of sexual images and could share their own sexual photos with the rest of the country.

One of the more subtle, albeit profound, effects of the BBS system was to shift thousands of computer users from consumers of pornography to publishers and distributors. In order to quickly build larger libraries of adult materials (the prevailing assumption was that size did matter), BBS operators would trade users the right to download more images or longer access time to the BBS in exchange for images uploaded to the system by users.

"Much of [Exec-PC's adult library] was just uploaded by our customers," Ryan said. "We gave 4-to-1 byte compensation and, I think, 1-to-1 time compensation. . . . If you were interested in downloading lots, it behooved you to look around for files that we didn't have and upload them to us."

As Ryan acknowledged, this practice was risky, since users might upload illegal materials such as child pornography or copyrighted materials such as *Playboy* photos. "We'd check to make sure that there was no illegal pornography," he said. "For example, kiddie porn, animals."

Protecting a BBS against potential copyright claims took on a particular urgency after *Playboy* obtained a $500,000 infringement settlement in 1993 from one of Exec-PC's main competitors, the Event Horizons BBS. "Bob and I developed a kind of rule of thumb for figuring out if we should kill photos or not," Ryan explained. "And essentially what it boiled down to was if the photos showed women that were so absolutely gorgeous and that the photography was so beautiful, and you know, there were no blemishes on their skin and the lighting was perfect, we just took it off."

Despite the risks of prosecution and litigation, soliciting images from customers proved to be a highly efficient way to quickly build a large library of sexually explicit photos. The net effect of the practice was that hundreds and even thousands of people scanned photos from a variety of sources—books, magazines, postcards, and even personal photos—and uploaded them to BBSs around the country. In the process, each person helped to create a vast electronic pool of sexually explicit images.

While the BBS as a venue played an important role in the transformation and distribution of sexual images, its structure was still an impediment to truly efficient distribution. By and large, most BBSs were not connected to one another and provided access numbers only in the region in which they were located. As a result, computer users frequently had to dial long-distance to access popular systems. Since long-distance charges were particularly difficult to hide from parents or a spouse, they often constrained use of bulletin boards. Unbeknownst to most computer users in the early 1990s, however, a system was already in place that would allow access to and the distribution of materials for little more than the cost of a local phone call.

## FREE PORNOGRAPHY:
## A MAGAZINE PUBLISHER'S NIGHTMARE

On October 4, 1957, the Soviet Union launched into space a smooth, 184-pound metal ball. Called Sputnik (Russian for "traveling companion"), the beach-ball-sized device was the Earth's first artificial satellite, and its launch came as a profound shock to Western nations. The United States, which had gauged Soviet space capability to the same fine degree it more recently estimated Indian nuclear prowess, was particularly shaken, and a chastened space program initiated a number of crash programs to close the gap.

Among the projects established was the Advanced Research Project Agency, which was designed to assist the Department of Defense (with which it was affiliated) in developing science and technology that might be of use to the military. One of the areas in which DoD was particularly interested was a new network technology called "packet-switching," which was being developed in a number of locations around the world in the mid-1960s. The basic concept of the technology—breaking messages and computer files into smaller units called "packets"—offers a number of advantages over traditional networking methods.[76] The DoD authorized funding for practical research on a packet-switching network in 1968, and the first network node was installed at UCLA on September 2, 1969. A second node was set up at the Stanford Research Institute, and on October 1, 1969, the first connection was made between the two machines at the then-blazing speed of 50 kilobits per second.[77]

Over the next couple of months, two additional nodes were installed at the University of Utah and the University of California at Santa Barbara, and the ARPANET was born. In addition to serving as a working laboratory for packet-switching research, the primary purpose of ARPANET was to enable researchers at the various institutions to rapidly share data and resources, since access to the network allowed researchers to use computers on campuses other than their own.[78]

ARPANET remained exclusively a military research network until 1983, when it was split into two separate networks: Milnet, for military installations, and ARPANET for nonmilitary DoD contractors and academics. Even after 1983, it was still extremely difficult for people not connected with the military to connect to ARPANET, largely because of the amount of classified material traveling through the network. This created problems on campus, as some faculty members had access to this terrific communication and research tool and others didn't. To help find a solution, the National Science Foundation set up a networking office in 1984 and by 1986 had constructed its own network (NSFNET). By and large, any educational or nonprofit organization with the resources to do so could connect to NSFNET. Over the next three to four years, most of the organizations on the ARPANET switched over to NSFNET, and in 1990, ARPANET was shut down.[79]

Out of the NSFNET has grown (and continues to grow) what today is generally known as the Internet. What makes the Internet such a remarkable communication tool is that over the last five years, access to the Internet has moved from the organizational level (government, education, and business) to the home. As with most technology, broader access to the resources of the Internet by the general public has resulted in uses that in all likelihood were not anticipated by the network's creators.

The first surge in the widespread availability of pornography on the Internet can be traced to 1979, when various programmers at the University of North Carolina at Chapel Hill, including Steve Bellovin, Steve Daniel, Jim Ellis, and Tom Truscott, developed a series of programs designed to ease the flow of information between UNC and Duke. These programs came to be known as the Usenet (from Unix User Network), and together formed the core of one of the earliest systems for automatically distributing information including images.[80]

Before the Usenet could be used to exchange images, however, two technical hurdles had to be overcome. First, the Usenet is essentially a publicly accessible e-mail system, and the software was originally written to handle text only. Before an image could be sent across the Usenet, it had to be converted into something that looked like text to Usenet's software. In addition, when Usenet was being developed in the early 1980s, the combination of high memory costs, slow transmission speeds, and limited computer storage made it impractical for the system to handle large messages. As a result, most messages were limited to no more than 64 kilobytes in size.[81] Many images, however, require more than 64 kilobytes of storage space when they are converted to electronic form. The practical result was that a special software program had to be used to break up an image into files less than 64 kilobytes in size so that the image could be transmitted across the Usenet. Computer users interested in viewing the image then had to find each piece, use another software program to put them back together in the correct order, and then use a separate program to actually view the image.[82]

The compelling attraction of pornography is illustrated by the fact that a number of different software programs were written specifically for the purpose of shipping images across the Usenet, and by the fact that large numbers of people were willing to deal with the time and frustration required to extract a single dirty picture from the electronic haze of a newsgroup's messages. In fact, the distribution of images across the Usenet became so popular that by August 1996, five sexually oriented newsgroups were among the ten most popular newsgroups on the Internet; one, alt.sex, was estimated to have approximately half a million readers per day.[83]

Despite the fact that the software machinations required to obtain sexual images from the Usenet made it highly unlikely that someone would accidentally stumble across pornography while online, the sheer volume of material available (and the fact that kids were particularly good at using software) began to alarm parents, legislators, and activists of all descriptions. Those fears were dramatically heightened on July 3, 1995, when *Time* magazine ran a cover story titled "On a Screen Near You: Cyberporn." The bold headline was accompanied by a drawing of a pop-eyed child, perhaps seven or eight, macabrely illuminated by the glow of a computer screen (on which, presumably, naked bodies are writhing). Relying on a study published in the *Georgetown Law Review* by Marty Rimm, senior *Time* writer Philip Elmer-Dewitt reported, "On those Usenet newsgroups where digitized images are stored, 83.5 percent of the pictures were pornographic."[84]

Just three weeks later, Elmer-Dewitt wrote a follow-up to his cover story in which he conceded that "serious questions have been raised regarding the study's methodology, the ethics by which its data were gathered and even its true authorship."[85] Elmer-Dewitt went on to admit that an analysis of Rimm's study by Vanderbilt University professors Donna Hoffman and Thomas Novak revealed that a more accurate assessment of the number of pornographic images transmitted across the Usenet was one-half of 1 percent of the total number of messages.[86]

From a public policy point of view, however, the damage was already done. The original but erroneous figure of 83.5 percent was published just weeks after the U.S. Senate voted to approve a bill put forward by Senator James Exon (D-Neb.) that came to be known as the Communications Decency Act. The *Time*/Rimm statistic is widely credited with helping to spur final passage of the bill in the House of Representatives.

## THE WORLD WIDE WEB AND INTERNET COMMERCIALIZATION

As a means of distributing information, the Usenet is a powerful tool. It is vast, relatively uncomplicated, easily expandable and, on the surface, at least, free. It can be used to post messages to a worldwide audience in a matter of seconds, and recent improvements in Usenet software have eliminated the early restrictions on size and content, so sending images across the Usenet is now almost as simple as sending a plain text message.

As a means of conducting business, however, the Usenet has some important limitations. The most obvious limitation is the transitory nature of Usenet messages: They are automatically removed by the host computer after a period of time, generally five to seven days. Also problematic is the fact that the computer system that posts a message to the Usenet retains the ability to cancel the message until the message is automatically removed from the Usenet system.[87] Since most terms-of-use agreements prohibit Usenet messages that contain indecency or obscenity, trying to run a pornography business solely through Usenet messages would be a difficult task.

In general terms, setting up and running a business (whether online or not) requires a predictable location (so customers can find the business), some means of displaying merchandise, an adequate number of potential customers, and some method for collecting payment. Within a five-year period, all of those elements fell into place for the Internet, and pornographers of all descriptions wasted little time in exploiting the new technology.

The groundwork for extensive commercial activity on the Internet was laid in 1989 when Timothy Berners-Lee, then a researcher at Conseil Européen pour la Recherche Nucléaire (CERN), circulated a memo describing a new system for information storage and retrieval across the network at CERN. The purpose of Berners-Lee's proposal was to make it easier for the people at the research facility to store, locate and retrieve project data.[88] A more formal proposal was drafted the following year, and Berners-Lee chose the name World Wide Web for his new system of organizing and accessing information.[89]

The concept was straightforward but incredibly powerful: The specific location of a particular document or image, regardless of the actual location of the computer on which it was stored, could be embedded in another document displayed on a computer anywhere else in the world. In order to implement his revolutionary concept, Berners-Lee created Hypertext Markup Language (HTML).

HTML is a set of protocols for displaying information on the computer screen, and for linking one document to another. For instance, the availability of additional resources is indicated by some type of visual clue in the text of a document, such as an underlined word or a word displayed in a different color. The underlined or highlighted word constitutes an electronic link between the information being viewed and related information. When the user clicks on the link, a command is sent from the user's computer to the computer where the information is stored requesting a copy of the information, which is then displayed on the user's computer. The strength of HTML lies in its flexibility: the links can be embedded in words, sentences, small buttons or icons, entire images or even in portions of an image (for instance, a map of the United States might contain a different link to the home page of each state).

Unlike the Usenet, a business can use HTML to create a permanent Web site, which serves as the functional equivalent of a store on Main Street. As a general rule, a well-designed Web site is a relatively stable corner of cyberspace. Although a variety of things can go wrong (and often do), businesses can use Web sites to establish relationships with customers and can be reasonably confident that customers will be able to find them again later.

A successful online business also needs the means to display merchandise and a suitable pool of potential customers. Both of those requirements were met with the development of software to "browse" sites that use HTML. A browser interprets the HTML commands used by a Web site and uses the commands to display the information on the user's computer.

In addition to creating the software protocols that would enable the sharing of information, Berners-Lee also helped write the first Web browser. The original browser implemented at CERN was designed to retrieve text only, but the concept was quickly extended to allow retrieval of graphical images, programs, and other nontext resources. After some initial testing, CERN released its WWW software on its central machines on May 17, 1991.[90] By January 1993, there were about 50 Web servers (computers set up to distribute hypertext information), and a half-dozen different browsers available or under development.

The Web's real boost came the following month, however, when Marc Andreesson and a team of programmers at the National Center for Supercomputing Applications at the University of Illinois released the first version of Mosaic.[91] What made Mosaic different from earlier browsers was that it was the first graphical Web browser and allowed the display of more than one type of information on the screen at the same time. This capacity gave creators of Web pages the ability to combine text, graphics, color, and even sound on the same page.

In the fall of 1993, Macintosh and Windows versions of Mosaic were developed, and the supercomputing center made the programs available for free. Within 18 months, more than 2 million people began using Mosaic, and the explosive growth of the World Wide Web was under way.

Sensing the economic possibilities, the software manufacturer Spry released its own version of Mosaic in January 1994 as part of its "Internet in a Box," a suite of programs which featured a version of the Web browser Mosaic and a half-dozen or so other programs for accessing different types of online resources, including e-mail, gopher, and newsgroups. The "Internet in a Box" suite made accessing online resources much easier, and as the media coverage at the time repeatedly pointed out, for a little more than $100 in software, a computer user could access any of the materials located on the Internet.

Andreesson also saw the economic potential of supplying the software for accessing the Internet and left the University of Illinois in December 1993 to start his own company. With the help of Silicon Valley veteran Jim Clark, Andreesson founded Mosaic Communications (later renamed "Netscape") and in November 1994 released the first version of Netscape Navigator, a Web browser with many more features and capabilities than Mosaic. On August 9, 1995, just two years after releasing a Windows version of Mosaic, Netscape Communications went public, selling $2 billion worth of stock.

The widespread success of Mosaic and the Netscape helped to spur the realization that there was in fact a potentially lucrative pool of customers using the World Wide Web. As the number of Internet users climbed rapidly above 2 million, individuals and businesses began setting up Web sites to offer information and services for sale, and the media and the public began devoting a lot of attention to the new medium.

As the number and variety of online resources increased in the mid-1990s, a large number of commercial enterprises arose to provide Internet access to members of the public, and many of the nation's BBSs created electronic gateways to give their subscribers Internet access. The growth of Web-related Internet traffic in 1993–94 was nothing short of phenomenal: Estimates peg it at a rate of 341,634 percent.[92] Although the pace has inevitably slowed, the Internet has become one of the most quickly adopted technologies in the nation's history. For example, it took 38 years before 50 million Americans listened to radio, and 14 years before that many were watching television. The Internet crossed the same threshold in just four years.

Most industries, from automobiles to sunglasses to banking, have been quick to appreciate the advertising potential of the Internet (particularly in light of the highly attractive demographic profile of Internet users). In 1998, for instance, advertisers spent an estimated $1.92 billion in online advertising, up 112 percent over the previous year's $906.5 million. The amount spent on Internet advertising now exceeds the amount spent on outdoor advertising.[93]

The pornography industry, with its ubiquitous banner ads and click-through programs, accounts for a significant portion of that figure. The pornography industry's impact, however, is not limited to the number of advertising dollars it helps spread around the Internet (advertising dollars, incidentally, that help highly popular mainstream sites such as Yahoo! and AltaVista to pay their own bills), nor to the vast amount of free pornography that is available on sites that generate all of their income through advertising.

The true significance of the online pornography industry lies instead in its success in demonstrating the economic potential of the Internet both as a catalog supplement and replacement (i.e., displaying items for sale online that are then purchased by telephone or mail and shipped to the customer by land or air) and as a storefront, where goods and services can be purchased directly online. In doing so, the industry has convincingly demonstrated (to an estimated tune of $2 billion in 1998 alone) that consumers are willing to shop online and are willing to use credit cards to make purchases. In the process, the pornography industry has served as a model for a variety of online sales mechanisms, including monthly site fees, the provision of extensive free material as a lure to site visitors, and the concept of upselling (i.e., selling related services to people once they have joined a site). In myriad ways, large and small, the pornography industry has blazed a commercial path that other industries are hastening to follow.

## WHERE SIZE ISN'T EVERYTHING

The pornography industry also offers a good demonstration of the leveling impact of the Internet. In the so-called real world, the economic resources and revenues of a business have a tremendous impact on its ability to service its existing customers and attract new ones. Larger economic resources translate direct-ly into larger storefronts, larger distribution networks, more employees, better price discounts, a larger advertising budget, bigger catalog mailings, and so on. Even online, of course, the amount of financial resources available to a business still affects the business's size and the quality of the site it can make available to its customers. The structure of the Internet, however, makes it easier for busi-nesses with smaller resources to compete with more affluent organizations.

The chief reason for this lies in the unique nature of the Internet and the software that runs it. For instance, on the Yahoo! page listing the distributors and retailers of amateur adult videos, about 36 companies are listed. In reality, these companies are located all over the country, and all have different levels of financial resources. But for the purposes of a directory like Yahoo!, they all look basically the same, which means that smaller companies are competing on an equal footing with larger ones. In addition, thanks to the speed of today's com-puters and communications network, there is no appreciable difference in the time required to access a Web site in New York and one in California (or Budapest, for that matter). And unlike in the real world, the Internet does not have neighborhoods into which a user is unwilling to go; at least in the abstract, there is no distinction between one piece of virtual "real estate" and another.

Smaller businesses also are able to compete more effectively with larger businesses because the Internet significantly reduces two major sources of expense: advertising and distribution. In essence, a Web site is an almost infi-nitely expandable display ad that a business can set up for only a few dollars a month. Without links to the site, of course, a Web site is little more than a col-lection of words and pictures floating in the vast reaches of cyberspace. Fortunately, there are numerous ways to establish links to a Web site (which will be discussed in more detail in Chapters 5–9). With relatively little effort, a small business owner can establish a high-profile online presence.

To be fair, the Internet does not completely eliminate the effects of dis-parate resources. The amount of money a business has available to it does play a significant role in determining the speed and reliability with which customers can access its Web site, issues of particular concern to pornographers. A smaller business may share access to its Web site with numerous other businesses on a local Internet service provider, while large businesses like Playboy Enterprises, Inc. and Hustler, Inc. can set up their own Web servers to handle incoming traf-fic. Since even normal activity on the Internet can be slow (a well-known nick-name for the Web is the "World Wide Wait"), online customers are very sensi-tive to how long it takes to access a particular Web site.

In addition, a business's financial resources will determine the extent to which it can purchase and implement new technologies. Although the cost of creating a Web site for text and images is quite low, the expenses can rise quite quickly if the business wishes to offer animated Web pages, professional design, interactive video or chat online ordering, and so on. Even greater expenditures are required if an online business is successful, because then additional computer hardware and software is required to handle the influx of new customers. Having the latest bells and whistles is not essential to making money online, particularly in the pornography industry, but the high level of competition makes it vital that a site provide useful and informative content that changes regularly or that the site offer customers online resources that are not available elsewhere. If George Orwell had lived to see to see the development of the Internet and World Wide Web (he died in 1950), he might well have applied his famous maxim from *Animal Farm* to the Internet: While all Internet addresses are equal, some are more equal than others.

Increasingly, Web sites are serving as the functional equivalent of a real-world retail outlet, where people can make purchases of goods and services. As it turns out, the pornography industry is uniquely suited to take advantage of the new technology, because its products are easily convertible to electronic form. In the real world, larger businesses often have a competitive advantage in the distribution of goods, because the volume of business that they offer shipping companies translates into lower costs. In cyberspace, by contrast, the cost of transmitting each bit of information is theoretically the same for Playboy and the smallest distributor of sexual images. While this may change in the not-too-distant future (some suggestions have been made, for instance, to charge for Internet access based on volume of traffic generated by a particular business), the low entry costs and low overhead have made the Internet an attractive option for a large number of people, a surprising number of whom have decided to specialize in one or more aspects of the pornography industry. The next chapter outlines some of the sociological changes that have made that decision easier for people to make.

# NOTES

1. Peter Pollack, *The Picture History of Photography* (New York: Harry N. Abrams, Inc., 1977), pp. 20, 21. The original of Daguerre's photograph was destroyed during World War II; a copy exists at the George Eastman House in Rochester, N.Y. The earliest known surviving photograph of a human being is believed to be a self-portrait taken by the American Robert Cornelius in November or December 1839, when he jumped in front of a daguerreotype camera set up in his front yard. William Welling, *Photography in America* (New York: Thomas Y. Crowell Co., 1978), p. 14.
2. Martin W. Sandler, *The Story of American Photography* (Boston: Little, Brown and Company, 1979), p. 18. By comparison, a train or steamer trip between Boston and New York cost about $7.
3. Sandler, p. 14.
4. Sandler, p. 18.
5. Cited in Al Di Lauro and Gerald Rabkin, *Dirty Movies* (New York: Chelsea House, 1976), p. 41.
6. Stereoscopic photographs consist of two photographs placed side-by-side on a single card. The photographs are taken by a camera with two lenses, each focused at a slightly different angle. When the stereoscopic photographs are viewed through a special device known as a stereoscope, the image in the photographs appears to be three-dimensional.
7. The "carte de visite" was invented in 1853 by the Frenchman Adolph-Eugène Disdéri; the palm-size cards were intended primarily for use as calling cards (as their name implies), but

their small size made them convenient for more surreptitious viewing.

8. Helmut Gernsheim and Alison Gernsheim, *The History of Photography* (New York: McGraw-Hill, 1969), p. 117.

9. Hyde, pp. 110–111.

10. N.R. Kleinfield, "Campaign to Curtail Smut Trade Never Ends," *New York Times*, March 1, 1998, p. 28.

11. John D'Emilio and Estelle Freedman, *Intimate Matters: A History of Sexuality in America* (New York: Harper & Row, 1988), pp. 131–132, quoting Capt. M.G. Tousley to Abraham Lincoln, 23 March 1864, copy of typescript in Vertical File, Institute for the Study of Sex, Gender, and Reproduction, Indiana University, Bloomington.

12. At that price, pornography was relatively expensive, given that in 1863, the annual income of an American family averaged about $500. By contrast, a single issue of *Playboy* (which contains roughly two dozen sexually explicit photos) cost approximately $5 in 1996 (less by subscription); for the same year, the median annual income of the American family was $38,782.

13. D'Emilio and Freedman, p. 132.

14. The battle over the availability of sexual materials to soldiers continues today. In 1996, Rep. Roscoe Bartlett (R-Md.) introduced the Military Honor and Decency Act, which bans the sale of sexually explicit magazines, films, and tapes on military bases. A U.S. District Court in New York concluded that the law was unconstitutionally vague, but that decision was reversed on a 2-1 vote by the Second Circuit Court of Appeals. On June 26, 1998, the U.S. Supreme Court upheld the Second Circuit's decision.

15. Montgomery, p. 191.

16. D'Emilio and Freedman, p. 132

17. See the reproduction of a portion of a page from the *Police Gazette* in D'Emilio and Freedman, fig. 25. Unfortunately, the excerpt is undated.

18. One intriguing feature in *Sunshine & Health* (as well as other magazines of the period) is the classified advertisements for the confidential development of photographs and movies. It is not unlikely that some sexual entrepreneurs would have used such services for more commercial purposes.

19. In a development that anticipated the peep show parlors of the 1960s and later (at least in form if not in substance), a number of kinetoscope parlors opened around the country. The parlors were stocked with multiple machines in which patrons could view short movies.

20. Di Lauro and Rabkin, p. 45.

21. Arthur Knight, *The Liveliest Art* (New York: The New American Library, 1957), p. 28.

22. As was Edison's *The Kiss*, a kinetoscope film he made of a scene from a play in which two people are shown kissing.

23. Di Lauro and Rabkin, p. 43.

24. Di Lauro and Rabkin, p. 52.

25. Di Lauro and Rabkin, p. 53.

26. Di Lauro and Rabkin, p. 54. On occasion, theaters would attempt to cash in on the phenomenon by showing stag movies for local college students. One Amherst alumnus, for instance, recalls attending a "blue movie" night at the Amherst Cinema in the early 1960s.

27. Di Lauro and Rabkin, p. 55.

28. Another benefit of renting stag films to community service organizations was the likely presence in the audience of various law enforcement officials and town fathers, which dramatically reduced the possibility of interruption or harassment by the police.

29. Di Lauro and Rabkin, p. 55.

30. Di Lauro and Rabkin, p. 111.

31. "Porn King Gets Off," *Time*, November 4, 1991, p. 37.

32. Luke Ford, "Reuben Sturman," (n.d.), online at http://www.4porn.net/c48.html.

33. The kinetoscope's design differed only slightly from today's version. Viewers peered through a small lens on the side of a box while images on film passed between the lens and a light at the back of the box. Public Broadcasting System, "The American Experience Technology Timeline," (n.d.), online at http://www.pbs.org/wgbh/pages/amex/technology/techtimeline/.

34. The History Channel, "This Day in History" (n.d.), online at http://www.historychannel.com/thisday/today/980414.html.

35. Ford, "Reuben Sturman." Di Lauro and Rabkin, however, report that at least one peep show arcade (using curtains and carefully placed projectors) was operating in Chicago in the early 1950s. *Dirty Movies*, p. 117. The idea of having people come to a stag film or loop instead of the stags traveling to the people undoubtedly occurred to others in the intervening years, although having a fixed location for viewing adult films would have made the operation more susceptible to raids by the police.

36. "Loops" got their name from the fact that given enough quarters, each 10- to 15-minute movie will run in a continuous loop on the projector.

37. Luke Ford, *History of X*, "Chapter One."

38. The Consumer Electronics Manufacturers Association, "The History and Technology of the VCR" (n.d.), online at http://www.cemacity.org/mall/product/video/files/hstryvcr.htm.

39. Consumer Electronics Manufacturers Association.

40. Economists are still debating the precise reasons for the market's choice of the VHS format. The leading theory appears to be that companies such as JVC and Panasonic were better positioned than Sony to meet consumer demand. For a more detailed examination of this debate, see Michael A. Cusumano, Yiorgos Mylonadis, and Richard S. Rosenbloom, "Strategic Maneuvering and Mass-Market Dynamics: The Triumph of VHS over Beta," *Business History Review*, Spring 1992, pp. 51–94.

41. David Chute, "Tumescent Market for One-Armed Videophiles," *Film Comment*, Sept./Oct. 1981, p. 66.

42. One of the things that made *Deep Throat* such an industry sensation, however, was the fact that it cost only $25,000 to make. But the movie's big screen success suggested to adult filmmakers that audiences wanted adult films to more closely emulate mainstream features.

43. Eric Schlosser, "The Business of Pornography," *U.S. News and World Report*, February 10, 1997, online at http://www.usnews.com/usnews/issue/10porn.htm.

44. Peter Nulty, "The New Look of Photography," *Fortune*, July 1, 1991, p. 36.

45. Sensing a trend, most if not all of the major adult video producers also make or distribute "amateur" videos.

46. Ironically, Bushnell's initial investment in his new business was the same amount that Hefner paid for the rights to Monroe's nude calendar photograph—$500 (although some sources claim that Bushnell founded his multimillion-dollar business on an even smaller shoestring—$250).

47. Sylvain de Chantel, "The 'Real' Pong FAQ," November 10, 1997, online at http://www.classicgaming.com/museum/realpongfaq.shtml.

48. de Chantel, "The 'Real' Pong FAQ."

49. de Chantel, "The 'Real' Pong FAQ." "VCS" stands for "video cartridge system."

50. Atari's focus on gaming may have caused it to miss one of the great opportunities of the computer industry. Steve Jobs was hired by Atari to work on new video games (including the highly popular "Breakout"). Jobs and his friend, Steve Wozniak, used surplus Atari components to put together the Apple I in 1976. Kevin Maney, "From Pong to pow: Video game evolution," *USA Today*, April 23, 1998, pp. 4B. When Atari showed little interest in the project, Jobs and Wozniak set up shop in Jobs's garage and in 1977, released the enormously popular Apple II.

51. As with other types of pornography, the adult titles by Mystique sold for $10 to $15 more than the most expensive mainstream video games. Ann Hornaday, "X-rated Computer Games," *Ms.*, January 1983, p. 21.

52. "Mystique" (n.d.), online at http://www.atarihq.com/2678/3party/mystique.html.

53. "Mystique."

54. "Mystique."

55. See, e.g., "VGR's Giant 2600/7800 List" (n.d.), online at http://www.clark.net/pub/vgr/lists/ht/atari/Mystique.htm.

56. Adventure, which is available for free from a variety of software sites on the Internet, features a maze of rooms or caves that players can wander through by typing commands like "north," "south," "up," "down," etc. (In fact, one of the first challenges in playing a game like

Adventure is figuring out the words and sentence syntax the program is capable of recognizing.)
Some of the rooms are stocked with various items that the player can pick up and carry, and the
game is designed so that a particular object may or may not be useful in solving puzzles or getting out of traps along the way.
57. "Infocom Timeline" (n.d.), online at http://www.csd.uwo.ca/Infocom/Articles/ timeline.html.
58. Many of these parodies (and their more straitlaced counterparts) are still available as free-
ware on various Internet sites and bulletin boards.
59. See Peter Dyson, *The PC User's Essential Accessible Pocket Dictionary* (2d ed.), (San Francisco:
Sybex, 1994).
60. See Infocom, "Leather Goddesses of Phobos: Hitchhikers Guide with Sex," *The Status Line*,
vol. v, No. 3, Summer 1986, p. 1, online at
http://www.csd.uwo.ca/Infocom/Articles/NZT/lgop.html.
61. "Infocom Timeline."
62. There are, for instance, more than a half-dozen Web sites devoted to Leisure Suit Larry, and
most offer some explanation for why Sierra Online skipped Leisure Suit Larry IV. The longlast-
ing appeal of the game is difficult to explain, but may lay in the cheerful cheesiness of the
graphics (particularly in the first three episodes) and the outrageousness of the lines that Larry
uses in his effort to score with various female characters.
63. Back when bulletin boards ruled the earth, another significant factor was the fact that much
if not most of the distribution of shareware programs was done by complete strangers who
would upload programs to bulletin board systems in exchange for additional credits. In addition, system operators ("sysops") of the various BBSs would routinely swap hot shareware programs to keep their boards up to date.
64. Thanks to its enormous buying power, Wal-Mart exerts strong influence on the content of
music CDs, videos, and even cover art.
65. LeBrock's character was named "Lisa," after the computer used in the movie, an Apple Lisa.
The Internet Movie Database, online at http://us.imdb.org. The Lisa was a very short-lived predecessor to the Apple Macintosh.
66. A heated debate is already taking place among Croft-heads about which buxom British
actress or model should play Croft. For a while, the inside track appeared to be held by Rhona
Mitra, a 23-year-old British model hired by Eidos Interactive in 1997 to pose as Lara Croft at
various gaming shows and press events. As the popularity of the character grew, however, Eidos
distanced itself from Mitra and is reported to be favoring British actress and Estee Lauder
model Elizabeth Hurley. More recently, rumors have surfaced that the role will be offered to
Welsh beauty Catherine Zeta-Jones. The decision is eagerly awaited by adolescents of all ages.
67. The true 1990s equivalent of the Tijuana Bibles are the works of fiction circulated on the
Usenet. For instance, there are hundreds if not thousands of sexually explicit stories on the Web
involving one or more characters from *Star Trek: The Next Generation, Xena: Warrior Princess,
The Simpsons,* and other cultural icons.
68. A "patch" program is a utility program written for a specific piece of software that changes
the way that the software performs.
69. Interplay Productions advertisement, *Computer Gaming World,* July 1998, pp. 212–13.
70. "The story," UltraVixen Web site at http://www2.ultravixen.com/index2.html.
71. *Rage,* a publication of Larry Flynt's media company, Larry Flynt Publishing, Inc., was
intended as a competitor for *Playboy.* The issue in which UltraVixen appeared, however, was the
magazine's last.
72. Henry Edward Hardy, "The History of the Net," master's thesis, School of Communications,
Grand Valley State University, September 28, 1993. Online at
http://vrx.net/usenet/thesis/hardy.html. In fact, many of the commands that Christiansen
developed for his bulletin board software are still in general use today. See Rey Barry, "The origin of Computer Bulletin Boards," last updated January 13, 1998, online at
http://www.freewarehof.org/ward.html.
73. Modems offer a particularly good example of how technology has changed. In 1983, a state-
of-the-art modem—for instance, the Hayes Smart Modem 1200—could transmit and receive
data at 1,200 bits per second and cost $700 (although it could be found as "cheaply" as $525).

Fifteen years later, the top-speed modems transmit data at 57,600 bits per second and cost less than $100.

74. By the end of 1993, just prior to the introduction of the World Wide Web, analysts estimated that the BBS industry peaked at 60,000 systems. Over the last five years, the number of BBS systems has been cut at least in half.

75. Jack Rickard, "Homegrown BB$," *Boardwatch* (n.d.), available online at http://www.wired.com/wired/1.4/departments/electrosphere/bbs.html.

76. First, each packet can follow the fastest route available at the instant it is sent, regardless of the route earlier packets have taken, which has the effect of speeding up network transmissions. Second, the use of packets allows multiple users to share a single network connection, since the packets from one user can be mixed with those of another and sorted out on the way to their various destinations. Third, messages sent in packets reduce the consequences of transmission error; if a particular packet is missing or corrupted, the receiving computer can send a request for the retransmission of that one packet, rather than the entire message. And fourth, each packet can accumulate data on its travel about how it got to its destination and how fast. Such information is very useful in helping network administrators evaluate weaknesses or defects in the network.

77. Anderberg, "History of the Internet and Web."

78. There is widespread belief that a second reason for the development of the Internet was that the Defense Department wanted a communications network that would be able to continue functioning even if a portion of the network were destroyed by nuclear attack. There is a fair amount of circumstantial evidence supporting that theory (beginning, of course, with the Defense Department's involvement in the first place [calling Mr Stone . . . ]) and the objective fact that no single node on the Internet is so important that its destruction will shut down the network (something which is even more true today than it was thirty years ago). However, the postapocalyptic theory has been categorically rejected by Frank Heart, one of the people who worked on the creation and installation of the Internet's predecessor, the ARPANET. See, e.g., Hiawatha Bray, "BBN: Present at the (Net) Creation," *Boston Globe,* May 7, 1997.

79. See Jack Rickard, "Ring That Bell . . . ," *Boardwatch,* June 1995, online at http://www.boardwatch.com/mag/95/jun/bwm.htm.

80. "History of the Internet" (n.d.), online at http://www.ccit.arizona.edu/internet/inthist.html.

81. Gareth Sansom, "Illegal and Offensive Content on the Information Highway," Spectrum, Information Technologies and Telecommunications Sector, June 19, 1995, online at http://xinfo.ic.gc.ca/ic-data/info-highway/general/offensive/offens_e.html.

82. A particularly popular program for this process was UUencode, which converts binary files into text and then split each file into as many parts as necessary to keep each part under the magic limit of 64 K. On the receiving end, users decode the messages using a program like UUencode's reciprocal, UUdecode, and then use another program (such as Paint Shop Pro) to actually view the picture.

83. The other four sex newsgroups are alt.sex.stories, alt.binaries.pictures.erotica, alt.binaries.pictures.erotica.female, and rec.arts.erotica, all of which carried large numbers of sexually explicit immages. See Mistress Blanca and Peter (Green Way), "Pointer to Sex Info on the Net," November 15, 1996, online at http://www.viaverde.com/sex/ptsiotn.txt. As various researchers have pointed out, determining the precise number of readers of a particular newsgroup is essentially impossible.

84. Jonathan Wallace and Mark Mangan, *Sex, Lies, and Cyberspace* (New York: Henry Holt, 1996), p. 126.

85. Philip Elmer-Dewitt, "Fire storm on the computer nets: A new study of cyberporn, reported in a *Time* cover story, sparks controversy," *Time,* July 24, 1995, p. 57.

86. Elmer-Dewitt, "Fire storm." For a thorough and well-written discussion of the original *Time* article and the controversy that swiftly arose, see *Sex, Laws, and Cyberspace,* Ch. 6.

87. An example of this occurred in March 1998, when America Online (AOL) canceled a number of hostile and threatening Usenet messages following the bombing death of a 17-year-old in Fairhaven, Vermont. In AOL's view the messages constituted a violation of the sender's "terms of use" agreement with AOL, and AOL was within its rights to cancel the messages. Insofar as the

messages were potentially relevant to a capital murder case, of course, AOL's decision to delete the messages from the Usenet system raises some disturbing questions. The effort was not entirely successful; the messages could still be located in the online Usenet archive DejaNews at http://www.dejanews.com, and about a week later, the original sender reposted his messages from a different account.

88. Timothy Berners-Lee, "Information Management: A Proposal," March 1989 and May 1990, online at http://www.w3.org/History/1989/proposal.html.

89. "A Little History of the World Wide Web," 1995, online at http://www.w3.org/History.html. Among the names Berners-Lee considered but rejected were Information Mesh, Mine of Information, and Information Mine.

90. "A Little History."

91. The first version of Mosaic was written for X-Windows, an MIT windowing program generally found on Unix systems.

92. Anderberg, "History of the Internet and Web."

93. Cyrus Afzali, "IAB: Internet Ad Revenues Reach $1.92 Billion for '98," *Internet News*, May 3, 1999, online at www.internetnews.com, search Advertising Report Archives.

# 3

# THE THIN
# BLUE LINE

O tempora! O mores!
Marcus Tullius Cicero (106–43 B.C.E.),
*In Catilinam, I.i*

## PORNOGRAPHY AND CELEBRITY

During the 60-year period stretching from 1865 to 1925, the United States entered the age of mass media. With relentless intensity, each technological development increased the ease with which information could be spread from one location to another: the web press (1865), radio and film (both 1895), and television (1925).

In their search for ways to sell newspapers and advertising, publishers, broadcasters, and filmmakers quickly discovered that the American public had an unquenchable interest in the lifestyles of the rich and famous. As Calvin Coolidge once observed, "the business of America is business," and tales of economic success (and excess) have always been particularly compelling to the nation's residents.[1] More important, the development of the nation's mass media coincided with the growth of massive transportation (J. Pierpont Morgan, Cornelius Vanderbilt), manufacturing (Andrew Carnegie, J. Paul Getty), and media (William Randolph Hearst) empires. Readers eagerly snapped up stories about the rich: the parties, the fashions, the mansions, and the business deals. The fact that many (if not all) of these fortunes were made through the use of dubious if not outright illegal means did little to diminish public interest in the nation's newly minted multimillionaires. In an era remarkably free of government regulation and labor laws, business was business, and the roguish nature of the so-called robber barons just added to their appeal.

In the defiant days of Prohibition, it was only a small step to accord celebrity status to individuals whose conduct was purposefully criminal. Thanks largely to the enormous profits associated with the bootlegging trade (as well as drugs, prostitution, and various other rackets), the incomes and lifestyles of such well-known criminals as Al Capone and "Bugs" Moran were so outrageously extravagant that reporters wrote about them despite (or perhaps partly because of) the taint associated with the money. In 1927 alone, for instance, Capone had a personal income of $105 million, smashing Henry Ford's earlier single-year record of $70 million. Even in a decade so rife with conspicuous consumption that it became known as "The Roaring Twenties," fortunes on the scale enjoyed by Capone and his ilk made for fascinating reading.

In the early years of this century, the men and women who ran or participated in the pornography industry received little if any press attention. The occasional editorial might be written about the unfortunate availability of dirty postcards, stag films, and the like, but no reporter would have been dispatched to chronicle the pornographer's lifestyle or business operation. In part, the inattention stemmed from a lack of star power among the nation's pornographers; the diffuse nature of the business meant that no single pornographer was earning anything like what Capone earned from selling illegal booze. More importantly, however, the sex trade lacked the air of civil disobedience that helped make speakeasies and other sources of bootleg liquor so successful; making money in the sex trade was still considered to be both socially and morally unacceptable.

But the power of celebrity was slowly breaking down the taboos against sex in the news media, largely as a result of public fascination with Hollywood. In the 1920s, for instance, the nation was riveted by stories of the San Francisco manslaughter trial of actor Fatty Arbuckle. The popular actor was charged in the death of fellow actor Virginia Rappe, who died from peritonitis resulting from a ruptured bladder that she suffered at a Labor Day weekend party hosted by Arbuckle. Reports on the case ran constantly in the newspapers of publishing magnate William Randolph Hearst, who used the salacious case to boost circulation.[2] Other newspapers followed suit, running stories about Hollywood behavior that might not otherwise have appeared in print: quickie divorces, rapid remarriages, drug use, and wild parties. The ostensible purpose of such articles was to condemn the behavior described, but the real purpose was to use taboo themes (particularly sex) to sell newspapers.

It required only the tiniest of leaps for the news media to go from covering the sexual misadventures of celebrities to covering individuals as celebrities because of their sex appeal. The practice started in the earliest days of Hollywood: Early actors like Theda Bara, Clara Bow, Joan Crawford, and Barbara Stanwyck owed a fair measure of their popularity to their sex appeal.

When Harlean Carpenter (better known by her stage name, Jean Harlow) arrived in Hollywood, however, she took the concept of sex appeal to a whole new level. After an indifferent beginning to her career, Harlow signed with MGM and was teamed several times with Clark Gable, most notably in the 1932 film *Red Dust*. An actor whose striking platinum hair and low-cut gowns led to the coining of the phrase "blond bombshell," Harlow quickly became a popular box office draw.

Concerned about the popularity of MGM's attractive addition to its stable of actors, Paramount Pictures in 1932 signed a bawdy Broadway actor named Mae West. Although not as classically beautifully as Harlow, West's unabashed sexuality and racy double-entendres proved enormously popular with the general public. Although by today's standards, West's one-liners were more clever than dirty, the moralists of the period saw in West's dialogue (most of which she wrote herself) the seeds of social decay. Concern over the effects of West's films and other racy Hollywood productions helped spur the creation of the Production Code Administration, an industry organization founded in 1934 to issue seals of approval for films to ensure that they conformed to the tenets of Hollywood's Production Code.[3]

The creation of a supervisory organization and stricter enforcement of the Production Code did reduce (temporarily) the level of sexually titillating dialogue and sexual situations in films, a development that seriously damaged West's career. However, neither effort did anything to diminish the fascination of Hollywood or the public with sex symbols. The trail blazed by Harlow and West was quickly followed by a bevy of sex symbols, including Rita Hayworth, Lana Turner, Betty Grable, Jane Russell, and of course, Marilyn Monroe. Along the way, Hollywood and the rest of the country grew increasingly comfortable with the idea, long familiar to pornographers, that sexuality was as much a commodity as grain or frozen orange juice.

## THE PORNOGRAPHY MOGULS: THE HEFNERS, GUCCIONE, AND FLYNT

Hollywood moguls, of course, were not the only ones to recognize the economic potential of Monroe's sexuality. The master stroke of Hefner's decision to start a new men's magazine was his decision to purchase the rights to Monroe's nude calendar photo. With just a small investment, Hefner guaranteed himself a wide audience eager to see more of Monroe (who had had her first leading role in the successful *Gentlemen Prefer Blondes* just a few months earlier). Ironically, the very success of the Monroe issue of *Playboy* helped to underscore the commercial potential of sexuality in general and Monroe's in particular, a development that undoubtedly influenced the course of her career.

As Hefner built on the success of his first issue, the mainstream media of the time needed only the gauziest of excuses to cover *Playboy*'s growing empire in breathless detail. The Algeresque origins of the magazine were intriguing, of course, but far more compelling was the enormous financial success that Hefner enjoyed. Any business capable of selling millions of copies of a magazine per year, running multiple members-only clubs and casinos around the country, inhabiting an office tower in the heart of Chicago, and flying its own customized jumbo jet was perceived as legitimate news, regardless of (or perhaps precisely because of) the business's primary product. And in truth, perhaps the only surprising thing is that it took as long as it did; the first serious look at Hefner's venture did not appear until the May 1957 issue of *Fortune*.

By 1961, Hefner was being accorded celebrity status by the mainstream media, the first purveyor of sexual materials to be treated in that fashion. While moralists and would-be censors around the country decried *Playboy*'s growing popularity, Hefner's very success resulted in dozens of articles detailing his business accomplishments in the same matter-of-fact terms usually reserved for such sober subjects as automobile dealerships and electric utilities. In one article in 1961, for instance, *Time* headlined an article about Hefner with his boast that he was "The Boss of Taste City," and detailed his growing entertainment empire. "Hefner's members-only Playboy key club has become the largest employer of entertainment talent in Chicago," *Time* reported, "and is the prototype of more girl-filled clubs to follow in virtually every major city in the country."[4]

In a 1967 cover story, an unnamed *Time* reporter visited Hefner's Playboy Mansion in Chicago and described it as "the monument to a major American business success story."[5] The five-page article that followed described in detail Hefner's sybaritic lifestyle, the successes and failures of Playboy Enterprises, Inc., the *Playboy* philosophy, and Hefner's work ethic. The article also analyzed in detail the magazine's place in the nation's sexual landscape. Nothing in the article suggests that Hefner's gains were ill-gotten; indeed, the article makes a point of noting that "[o]ne of the more surprising facts is that *Playboy*'s readers include quite a number of ministers," to whom Hefner apparently offered subscriptions at 25 percent discounts.[6] In fact, if there is any criticism of either Hefner or the magazine, it is for having what one commentator called a "midwestern Methodist's vision of sin," the implication being that Hefner wasn't particularly daring.[7]

Two years later, Hefner was being described as an "American legend," living a life replete with the jet, two mansions (the original in Chicago and a new one in Los Angeles), and a bevy of bunnies at his beck and call. He was the host of a television show (the short-lived *Playboy After Dark*, which Hefner himself described as "better than the 'Johnny Carson show'"), and was actively scouting for a movie studio in which to invest. As *Time* pointed out, he could afford it: *Playboy* at the time was selling more than 5.5 million issues per month.[8]

Hefner built his empire by bringing nudity and sex to Main Street. In 1971 however, he made history by being the first pornographer to establish a financial presence on Wall Street. Playboy Enterprises, Inc., the holding company for *Playboy* magazine and Hefner's other ventures, announced that in November of that year it would offer 1.1 million shares to the public. With an average sale price of $25, Hefner's remaining stock in Playboy Enterprises gave him a personal fortune (albeit only on glossy paper) of about $168 million, making the 45-year-old publisher one of the five or six richest self-made men in the country.[9]

Media fascination with the Playboy empire did not stop with Hugh Hefner; it also extended to his daughter, Christie. In December 1973, writer (and now film critic) Roger Ebert[10] profiled Christie Hefner, then a senior at Brandeis University, for *Esquire* magazine. Eight years after graduating Phi Beta Kappa, Christie Hefner again made news when her father made her president of Playboy Enterprises at the age of 29.[11] The article announcing her promotion to president is so matter-of-fact that it is possible to read the entire article, which outlines the various business challenges she faced, without having the slightest idea that a major part of the company's revenues stemmed from the sale of pictures of naked women.

To a much lesser degree, the favorable news media coverage that enveloped Hefner and his daughter has also extended to his two chief rivals, Bob Guccione and Larry Flynt, although neither was immediately depicted with the mixture of admiration, disbelief, and outright envy with which Hefner was portrayed. Both provincialism (Guccione is British) and class snobbery (Flynt was widely perceived as crude and unsophisticated, particularly in comparison to the slim, silk-pajama-clad Hefner) helped to color portrayals of Hefner's rivals. The tone of articles and reports about the publishers was also influenced by the fact that both Guccione's *Penthouse* and Flynt's *Hustler* used much more explicit photos than *Playboy* and by the fact that *Hustler* in particular was far raunchier, cruder, and violent.

Over the years, however, both Guccione and Flynt have gained favorable attention (at least within media circles) for their unwavering and often expensive work in support of the First Amendment. Their defense of free speech was obviously fueled in large part by economic self-interest (a strong First Amendment being crucial to the success of the pornography industry), but also by their genuine belief that adults should have the right to read and view whatever they choose. Since that belief is also one of the fundamental prerequisites for a free press, many in the news media came to see Guccione and Flynt as regrettably crude but undeniably valuable allies.

Just how valuable became clear in 1987 and 1988, when Flynt spent more than $2 million in legal fees alone to appeal a jury verdict holding that he and *Hustler* had inflicted emotional distress on the Reverend Jerry Falwell by printing a mock advertisement claiming that Falwell's first sexual experience was with his mother in an outhouse.[12] At stake was not merely a large sum of money (the jury awarded Falwell $150,000 in damages), but more importantly, the ability of magazines such as *Hustler* (and, by extension, of comedians such as Jay Leno and David Letterman) to parody and satirize public figures without worrying about whether the jokes will hurt their feelings.[13] In 1988, a unanimous U.S. Supreme Court agreed with Flynt that as a "public figure," Falwell could recover only if he could show that *Hustler* published false facts about Falwell "with actual malice." The Court also rejected Falwell's argument that the fake ad was so "outrageous" as to be outside the scope of protection of political speech. Writing for the Court, Chief Justice Rehnquist pointed out that:

"Outrageousness" in the area of political and social discourse has an inherent subjectiveness about it which would allow a jury to impose liability on the basis of the jurors' tastes or views, or perhaps on the basis of their dislike of a particular expression. An "outrageousness" standard thus runs afoul of our longstanding refusal to allow damages to be awarded because the speech in question may have an adverse emotional impact on the audience.[14]

Flynt's victory over Falwell helped to cement his position as a stalwart defender of the First Amendment. Eight years later, in the film *The People vs. Larry Flynt* (1996), director Milos Forman took the story of Flynt's life (and particularly his battle with Falwell) and turned it into a major Hollywood release starring Woody Harrelson as Flynt and Courtney Love as his fourth wife, Althea Leasure.[15] The film was widely hailed by free speech advocates, but as numerous critics pointed out, the film glossed over most of the least savory aspects of Flynt's life, including *Hustler*'s relentless misogyny. As the nomination period for the Academy Awards approached at the beginning of 1997, a number of highly critical articles and editorials appeared (including an infamous anonymous ad in *Variety*), and a movie that was often cited at its release as an Oscar contender received only two nominations in minor categories. *The People vs. Larry Flynt* was a box office disappointment as well, earning only slightly more than $20 million against production costs of more than $35 million.

Nonetheless, the fact that a major director and a major studio would release a movie which unabashedly celebrated the free speech contributions of one of the nation's biggest and most often reviled pornographers is a remarkable commentary on the increased legitimacy of the pornography industry. Before the returns for *Larry Flynt* were in, at least three other big-budget looks at the pornography industry were planned: *The Mitchell Brothers,* a bio-pic about Jim and Artie Mitchell (who produced *Behind the Green Door,* starring Marilyn Chambers); *Good Vibrations,* about the pornography industry in general; and an unnamed film about Linda Lovelace.[16] Whether those projects will go forward following the disappointing returns from *Larry Flynt* is unclear. What is relatively certain, however, is that this will continue to be an area of fascination for Hollywood and the rest of the mainstream media.

## NAKED AMBITION

The perception of the pornography industry has been shaped not only by news coverage of the industry's moguls, but also by increasing participation in the industry by mainstream celebrities. As the media began to make celebrities out of pornographers, and as the industry took on a certain cachet stemming from impressive profits and its place in the vanguard of the sexual revolution, the lines between traditional entertainment and the pornography industry began to blur.

In the 1950s and 1960s, for instance, the economic success that Hefner realized with his magazine made it possible for him to offer substantial fees to starlets and starlet-wannabes to pose nude. In addition to the economic benefits (*Playboy* has consistently paid some of the highest, if not the highest, model fees), Hefner was able to pitch an appearance in his magazine as a career move, a means of attracting the attention of Hollywood. Thanks largely to *Playboy*'s phenomenal success and the economic resources that he had available, Hefner largely succeeded in his efforts to legitimize *Playboy*'s pictorials (a process accelerated by the fact that the pictorials were interspersed with some outstanding fiction and interviews of various influential figures).

As early as 1965, attitudes toward pornography had changed to such an extent that even established film actresses were making appearances in men's magazines. By posing nude or seminude in *Playboy* and its competitors, such actors as Jane Fonda, Shirley MacLaine, Kim Novak, Elke Sommer, Liz Taylor, and Ursula Andress all contributed to the perception that participating in the pornography industry was not merely for the fallen but also for the rising.[17] As a result, over the last 35 years, a startling number of actors and public figures have posed nude including Brigitte Bardot, Kim Basinger, Joan Collins, Cindy Crawford, Patty Davis (the only daughter of a president to pose), Bo Derek, Linda Evans, Farah Fawcett, Melanie Griffith, Margaux and Muriel Hemingway, Barbara Hershey, Natassja Kinski, Ann-Margret, Jenny McCarthy, Bernadette Peters, Victoria Principal, Vanessa Redgrave, Jane and Stephanie Seymour, Sharon Stone, Raquel Welch, and Vanna White.[18] Even if a model's *Playboy* appearance fails to generate much publicity at the time, it is a potent résumé item: The fact that an ex-*Playboy* model is involved in a particular project all but insures coverage today by powerful entertainment outlets such as *People, USA Today,* and *Entertainment Weekly* (all of which, for instance, devoted extensive and breathless coverage to Jenny McCarthy's short-lived sitcom).

Over the years, in fact, so many popular actresses and celebrities have appeared in *Playboy* and even *Penthouse* that the stigma once associated with posing nude in a national men's magazine has largely faded. The last celebrity to visibly suffer from posing nude was Vanessa Williams, whose 1984 appearance in *Penthouse* caused her to be stripped of her Miss America crown. The damage, however, was hardly permanent. Aided in part by the publicity resulting from the controversy, Williams has since been nominated for multiple Grammy awards for her albums; sung the Oscar-winning song from Disney's *Pocahontas,* "Colors in the Wind"; starred in a number of films; and appeared in the widely acclaimed Broadway hit *Kiss of the Spider Woman.*[19]

Fifteen years later, the more typical attitude is the one expressed by Olympic skater Nancy Kerrigan's lawyer, Victor Polk, Jr., in announcing that Kerrigan would sue a Web site for posting a faked nude photo of her: "It really is a foul picture. This isn't *Playboy*. This isn't *Penthouse*. This is gutter."[20] While there has been no suggestion whatsoever that Kerrigan would consider posing for *Playboy* (to be fair, not everyone considers it a seemly thing to do), one of Kerrigan's longtime skating rivals did. In its December 1998 issue, *Playboy* published ten pages of nude photos of the German skater Katherina Witt, a two-time Olympic gold medalist.

"I'm sure that some of my skating audience, when they hear I've taken off my clothes for *Playboy*, will be shocked," Witt stated in a piece accompanying her photos. "They may be uncomfortable with it, or they might ask, 'Why?' I don't know what to say, except that I was ready to do this. But I also think that once people see the photos, they'll feel differently. The pictures are beautiful and pure and natural. They're nude, but they still have a feeling of innocence. They're set in nature, in Hawaii, so it's appropriate that I'm naked, and I felt very relaxed."[21]

In a throwback to the sentiments of the '60s, some women have even asserted that they posed nude in *Playboy* as a form of feminine empowerment or political statement: Both Nancy Sinatra and Farah Fawcett, for instance, have recently done pictorials in part to demonstrate the continuing attractiveness of women over 50, and in January 1998, Pietra Thornton, the estranged wife of actor Billy Bob Thornton, said that her pictorial was intended to raise awareness about domestic abuse.[22]

As remarkable as the involvement of mainstream celebrities in the pornography industry has been, it has really only been the magazine sector of the industry that has benefited from any amount of celebrity crossover (and even then, really only *Playboy* and, to a much lesser degree, *Penthouse*). Despite periodic rumors to the contrary, for instance, there is no firm evidence that any well-known Hollywood actress has ever appeared in a porno flick or stag movie.[23] The rumors have swirled most strongly around Marilyn Monroe, who some believe appeared in a 16mm stag movie in 1948, a short time before her first Hollywood film, *Love Happy*, was released.[24] However, there is no conclusive proof, and the pictorial evidence from the 50-year-old film is ambiguous at best.[25]

The reverse, for the most part, has also been true: Until recently, no successful porn actor had been able to establish a significant career in mainstream films or television. Buoyed by the mainstream success of *Deep Throat* (1973), the adult film industry harbored high hopes that its stars would gain widespread popularity and that a genre of adult mainstream films would be established. At first blush, the treatment that Linda Lovelace, the star of *Deep Throat*, received from the mainstream media seemed to confirm the industry's hopes. However, the mainstream success of *Deep Throat* proved to be an aberration, and in the intervening quarter-century, only a few porn stars have made appearances in nonporn productions. Marilyn Chambers,[26] for instance, starred as a psychotic blood-sucking killer in the 1977 film *Rabid*, and appeared as an extra in *Angel of H.E.A.T.* (1982) and *Who Shot Patakango?* (1990). Also in 1990, Ginger Lynn Allen (a veteran of 69 adult films) appeared in *Young Guns II* as a saloon girl, and a year later as a prostitute in director Ken Russell's NC-17-rated film *Whore*. She has also starred in a couple of horror/slasher films (*Bound and Gagged: A Love Story* [1992] and *The Sorority House Murders* [1993]), and has had a recurring role as Chief Technician Rachel Coriolis in the live action *Wing Commander* video game series (appearing alongside such well-known names as Mark Hamill, Malcolm McDowell, and John Rhys-Davies). Most recently, the well-known porn star Nina Hartley appeared in *Boogie Nights* (1997) as William Macy's aggressively unfaithful wife.

Male porn actors, as a general rule, have had an even tougher time making the transition to mainstream productions, but Ron Jeremy (aka "The Hedgehog") has appeared in a variety of Hollywood film and TV productions, including most recently the Rodney Dangerfield vehicle, *Meet Wally Sparks* (1997), and Turner Network Television's *George Wallace* (1997). He also served as a consultant on the film *Boogie Nights*.

Remarkably, the most successful graduate from the ranks of porn flick actors is Traci Lords, who at one time was widely considered to be one of the most bankable stars in the sex film industry. That was before the revelation that virtually all of her hardcore films had been shot before she was 18, and some reportedly before she turned 16. A panicked video industry stripped the entire stock of Lords' films from the shelves almost overnight. Lords has parlayed her notoriety into appearances in a number of B- and C-grade movies (*Not of This Earth* [1988], *Shock 'Em Dead* [1991], and *Raw Nerve* [1991]) and several TV series (*Wiseguy, MacGyver,* and *Roseanne*), then into much more substantial roles. In 1993, she was one of the stars (along with Jimmy Smits) in the made-for-TV movie *The Tommyknockers*, which led the following year to a 16-episode appearance as "Rikki" on *Melrose Place*. Most recently, she has starred on the NBC television series *Profiler*, and she appeared with Wesley Snipes and Kris Kristofferson in *Blade*, a 1998 live-action remake of the comic book of the same name.

Although the anticipated crossover between adult and mainstream fare never materialized, *Deep Throat* did mark the beginning of the adult film industry's own star system. In the heady days following the 1972 release of *Deep Throat*, Linda Lovelace appeared in a *Playboy* pictorial and on the cover of *Esquire*, began writing an advice column on sexual matters, appeared in the first paperback printed with a centerfold, shot a softcore sequel to *Deep Throat*[27] and got the Rolls-and-red-carpet treatment in Los Angeles for the premier of *Last Tango in Paris* (which she thought was "disgusting").[28] Similarly, the box office success of *The Devil in Miss Jones* (which actually outgrossed *Deep Throat* in 1973) and *Behind the Green Door* helped Georgina Spelvin and Marilyn Chambers to became well-known names in the early 1970s. Nor was all the attention focused on female performers; Lovelace's costar Harry Reems became a reliable box office attraction, as did the man the industry simply referred to as "The King," John Holmes.[29]

The growth of a porn star system was greatly aided by the contemporaneous growth of VCR and videotape technology. As the number of competing adult titles steadily rose, producers relied on the notoriety of established porn stars to help boost sales and rentals. Over time, the star system for porn actors has come to resemble the one for mainstream stars, including publicity agents, trade journals, celebrity appearances, and so forth.

## SALUTING THE SEXUAL ENTREPRENEURS:
## MANSFIELD, ASHE, AND WARSHAVSKY

News coverage of online pornography began somewhat more quickly than coverage of *Playboy* 40 years earlier. Within two years or so of the start of the World Wide Web, articles began to appear detailing the growth of online pornography and profiling the people who were making it happen. The articles carried two basic messages: A lot of money was being made by online pornographers, and some of the most successful pornographers were just average folks. Although the positive coverage has been balanced (or more than balanced) by a steady procession of articles describing the concerns of parents, social and religious activists, and politicians, the reports of easy money have drawn and continue to draw large numbers of people into the industry.

Even before the introduction of the World Wide Web, media outlets were writing breathless stories about the amount of sex available on the Internet. A few articles, among them *Time*'s infamous "On a Screen Near You: Cyberporn," focused on the legal and social concerns raised by the growth of online pornography. The majority focused instead on the novelty of cybersex and the variety of resources available. In 1983, more than a decade before the Web started, Lindsy Van Gelder described her experiences with "Compusex,"[30] and other articles later explored the sexual possibilities of AOL chat rooms and Internet Relay Chat.[31] The Usenet has received particular attention, thanks both to the volume of messages posted each day[32] and the explicitness of the material that could be found in some of the sexually oriented groups.

News coverage of Internet pornography did not really take off, however, until 1996, when journalists realized that online pornography as a whole (and some sites in particular) were making huge amounts of money with the new technology. In August of that year, for instance, John Simons of *U.S. News and World Report* described in detail the sharp contrast between online pornography, which experts projected would generate more than $50 million in sales, and most other types of online businesses, which were finding it very difficult to generate any sales at all.[33] Four months later, a front-page story in the *Boston Globe* estimated earnings for online pornography in 1996 at $100 million.[34] The *Wall Street Journal* also got into the act, writing in the spring of 1997 that:

> Cyberporn is fast becoming the envy of the Internet. While many other Web outposts are flailing, adult sites are taking in millions of dollars a month. Find a Web site that is in the black and, chances are, its business and content are distinctly blue. That has legions of entrepreneurs rushing to cash in, from former phone-sex marketers gone digital to new-media mavens to a onetime stripper whose thriving Web site brings in so much revenue that she has given up the stage and nude photo shoots.[35]

At almost exactly the same time, the *New York Times* ran an article about the profitability of the online sex trade and quoted one industry analyst as saying, "It's a good business to be in right now."[36]

Even during the heyday of the adult movie industry in the early 1980s, when adult videos could be made for $15,000 or even less, and then rented and sold around the country for tens or even hundreds of thousands of dollars, neither the *Times* nor the *Journal* was running articles stating that the adult video market was a "good business" to be in. Though it is unlikely that many online pornographers would say that they started their businesses because the *Times* or the *Journal* said it was a good idea, articles such as these have gone a long way toward creating an atmosphere in which the online pornography industry is judged more by traditional business measures and less by moral or religious standards.

The favorable coverage of the industry as a whole has been reinforced by the flattering profiles published of many of the men and women who have set up successful Internet pornography sites. The underlying message of these articles is that average folks are using the new technology to make impressive amounts of money, and that it a relatively simple matter for others to do so as well.

The media's favorite examples in this regard has been Beth Mansfield, a Tacoma, Washington homemaker and mother of two who founded the adult Web site Persian Kitty in 1995. Persian Kitty is a directory to adult Web sites on the Internet, which Mansfield supports by selling advertising. In 1997, Mansfield estimated that her site would earn almost $1 million in gross revenues, approximately 70 percent of which is profit. As one of the most successful online entrepreneurs of any description, Mansfield has been interviewed and profiled in dozens of articles online and off. Although an occasional interviewer will ask Mansfield's position regarding online sex and children, the vast majority of the interviews focus squarely on the business end of her operation, including the equipment she uses, the mechanics of advertising, and her plans for the future.

When asked why she runs a site identifying sexual materials on the Internet, Mansfield is refreshingly candid. She told Matt Richtel of the *New York Times* in April 1997 that she created her Persian Kitty site "to see how many people I could bring to my corner of the Web."[37] She chose to focus on adult materials, she said, because she was told that those were the most heavily visited sites.

Another popular journalistic theme is the "stripper with the brain of gold." A useful alternative to interviewing a homemaker-turned-pornographer is to interview a stripper-turned–Web site operator. The most frequently interviewed person in that category has been Danni Ashe,[38] who turned a part-time fan club into one of the Web's most successful adult sites. Profiles of Ashe have recounted with glee the fact that she taught herself HTML while vacationing in the Bahamas and then started a Web site called Danni's Hard Drive that today grosses more than $4 million per year. Ashe's business acumen has garnered her the bulk of attention, but a number of other male and female strippers and porn stars have also appeared in the mainstream press thanks to the success of their Web sites. Very few of those same strippers and actors had ever been interviewed for their success in their primary profession.

The last general category of positive news coverage is the online porn tycoon story. The chief examples in this genre are the profiles of Seth Warshavsky, a former phone-sex business owner who has taken an early lead in the development of adult video conferencing sites. Warshavsky, who founded and runs Internet Entertainment Group, has been described as both "the virtual Hugh Hefner"[39] and as "the Bob Guccione as the 1990s."[40] At one time, being compared in print to two infamous pornographers might have been grounds for a libel suit; however, there is little question from the tone of the articles that the writers meant the comparisons as compliments. The characterizations of Warshavsky reflect how much journalistic attitudes toward the pornography industry have changed, but even more so, how the attitudes of the general populace have changed.

# MEDIA GLAMORIZATION OF PROSTITUTION AND SEX

Journalists, of course, have not been solely responsible for society's more liberal attitudes toward pornography. While the matter-of-fact tone with which journalists have discussed the pornography industry may have helped to lessen the stigma traditionally associated with the industry, the entertainment industry has played a more significant role in changing public attitudes toward sex in general and the sex trade in particular.

## LETTING OUR HAIR DOWN

The arts offer a particularly powerful yardstick for gauging the changes that have occurred in our nation's attitudes toward sexuality. When Hefner started *Playboy* in 1953, two of the most popular songs were "That's Amore," by Harry Warren, and "(How Much Is That) Doggie in the Window," by Bob Merrill. On television, Ozzie and Harriet, Donna Reed, Dobie Gillis, and the Cleavers helped to define cultural norms. Undoubtedly, some pulses were being raised by the surf-washed smooches of Deborah Kerr and Burt Lancaster in *From Here to Eternity* (1953), but by and large, the sexual content of the arts was fairly low.

The surface tranquility, however, masked swirling undercurrents of sexuality that helped set the stage for the tumultuous years ahead. Social interaction for teens, for instance, moved from the tentative "dating" of the 1930s and 1940s to "going steady," and over the following decades, the limits of sexual exploration moved inexorably from kissing and petting to heavy petting and intercourse. The nation's economic prosperity and surplus production capacity helped make the automobile an essential part of both family life (making it possible, for instance, to move to the suburbs) and courtship (making other types of moves possible).

It didn't take long for the entertainment industry to appreciate the economic possibilities of sex and sexuality, if only at a subliminal level. In 1955, Bill Haley ("Rock Around the Clock") and Chuck Berry ("Maybellene") helped to jump-start the rock 'n' roll era (with all of its attendant eroticism), and in 1956, the frankly seductive looks and swiveling hips of Elvis Presley thrilled teenagers and horrified their parents. Although it sometimes can be difficult to discern the line between what is sexually acceptable and what is forbidden, in 1957, when Elvis Presley made his third appearance on the *Ed Sullivan Show*, there wasn't any question at all: The line ran right around Presley's waist, as Sullivan instructed his cameramen not to broadcast what he considered to be Presley's indecent gyrations.

Much of the change in sexual mores that occurred in the 1950s was driven by teens, fueled by a potent combination of hormones and disposable income. But not all of the pressure to liberalize sexual attitudes came from Elvis fans—the sexual mores for adults were also changing. By the end of the decade, *Playboy* was selling nearly 4 million copies per month and boasting to advertisers of its popularity with affluent middle-age men. With the release of *The Immoral Mr. Teas*, Russ Meyer became the King of Leer, and helped to finish off the badly waning influence of the Legion of Decency. As Rock Hudson's 1985 death of AIDS helped to underscore, the '50s were not always what they seemed when it came to sex.

Film also took ample advantage of the changes in social attitudes. Following the financial success of the various Meyer "nudie cuties" (and equally importantly, the fact that Meyer was not arrested or prosecuted), filmmakers began exploring increasingly controversial and explicit themes. During the summer of 1969, for instance, a moviegoer in most major cities could choose among *The Libertine* (a widow works her way through a sex manual), *I, a Woman, Part Two* (portraying assorted adultery, voyeurism, and fetishism), and *Therese and Isabelle* (featuring autoeroticism and lesbianism). Most significantly, moviegoers who wanted to see films like these could do so in clean, well-lighted theaters in midtown (charging a then-premium $3 and up for admission), instead of having to travel to a city's red light or tenderloin district.[41] Even Hollywood got into the act: In 1969, *Midnight Cowboy* became the first (and so far only) X-rated film to win an Oscar for Best Picture, and Marlon Brando's performance in the erotically charged 1973 film *Last Tango in Paris*[42] earned him an Oscar nomination.

The surge of explicit sexual content in mainstream entertainment was a dramatic but relatively short-lived phenomenon. The very success of hardcore movies like *Deep Throat, Behind the Green Door,* and *Misty Beethoven* led to a social and cultural backlash that forced producers and artists to tone down their productions. The changes that occurred, particularly in the five-year period from 1968 to

1973, were too sudden and too dramatic for the country to easily absorb.

In the quarter-century since the release of *Deep Throat*, the sexual content of mainstream entertainment, with the possible exception of music, has not returned to the heady days of the early 1970s. For much of that period, television networks, mainstream movie studios, and stage theaters alike saw little benefit in risking legal and social attacks to include explicit sexual conduct in their productions. Moreover, there was little impetus to do so when consumers could so easily rent videocassettes and watch essentially unlimited amounts of explicit sexual activity in their homes.

Faced with enormous competition from entertainment media in general and cable television in particular, however, the traditional broadcast networks have slowly begun incorporating more sexual content into their shows. The most widely cited example of network experimentation, of course, is the aptly named *N.Y.P.D. Blue*, which occasionally features a quick flash of one or more actor's rear ends (male and female) and side shots that show considerable portions of the breasts of female actors. *N.Y.P.D. Blue*, however, is merely the most recent example of a 20-year trend. Limited in how much skin they can show, the networks have instead chosen to use increasingly sexual themes in both drama and comedy, and have relied heavily on a combination of stronger language and tighter clothing.

Despite their efforts to evade the censors, this is not a battle that the networks are winning. Fox (which is now often listed with the so-called Big Three networks) has proved to be the most successful challenger, leading the way with *Beverly Hills 90210* (with star Shannon Doherty later making an appearance in *Playboy*), *Melrose Place*, and now the hugely popular *Ally McBeal*, all of which featured a gallery of attractive men and women dealing with a variety of sexually charged situations. Fox's use of sexual themes in its shows has been so successful in attracting viewers that Fox has been able to use its advertising revenues and syndication fees to bid heavily (and successfully) for lucrative sports broadcasting contracts that were once the exclusive province of the Big Three.

Over the last year, Fox has been challenged by two new broadcast networks, WB and UPN, both of which have tried to emulate Fox's formula. So far, at least, WB has had the most success, thanks to a combination of *Buffy the Vampire Slayer* (whose star, Sara Michelle Geller, cut her teeth as a vixen on the daytime soap opera *All My Children*), and *Dawson's Creek*, a no-holds-barred look at the sexual concerns of four attractive high school students and their equally attractive classmates. UPN, which was an early favorite of industry analysts thanks to its success in landing the latest *Star Trek* series, *Voyager*, has been slower to attract the same favorable buzz as WB. The network, however, has recently shown some ratings success (but even more controversy) with the sexually explicit *Jerry Springer Show*, and the introduction of a new and tightly body-suited character on *Voyager*, an ex-Borg named Seven of Nine (played by Jeri Ryan).

Cable movie channels like HBO, Showtime, and the Movie Channel have also proved to be potent competitors of the traditional networks, thanks to their ability to show unexpurgated versions of R-rated movies that are routinely cut by the broadcast network censors, and to produce and distribute the sort of movies that cannot be broadcast over the airwaves. For example, in 1997 HBO produced and broadcast *Breast Men,* a two-hour movie about the Texas doctors that developed the silicon breast implant. The movie featured a number of women talking about their decision to get breast implants while the camera focused on their naked torsos. In 1998, HBO began broadcasting a series titled *Sex and the City,* a bemused look at relationships and sexual activity in New York starring Sarah Jessica Parker.

Showtime, which is developing a reputation as the "Rescue Channel," has aired *More Tales from the City,* a continuation of Armistad Maupin's highly popular PBS series,[43] and agreed to show the 1995 version of *Lolita,* a film starring Jeremy Irons and Dominique Swain that for two years failed to find a U.S. distributor. The influence of cable and of competition in general is illustrated by the fact that following Showtime's decision, Samuel Goldwyn Films announced that it would distribute the controversial movie to theaters, which it did, beginning in August 1998.[44]

## THE DISCOVERY THAT PORNOGRAPHY IS SAFE SEX

The pornography industry was also indirectly boosted by the public health crises that brought a swift and sudden end to the sexual revolution. Sexually transmitted diseases, of course, have always been a concern for both public health workers and sexual revolutionaries. While serious, however, diseases like syphilis and gonorrhea were largely ignored as potential risks, in large part because both diseases are generally treatable with penicillin. Indeed, contracting "the clap" had become little more than a punch line.

The 1970s and 1980s, however, brought the specter of sexually transmitted diseases that science couldn't cure. First came the outbreak of herpes—a collection of viral infections that cause blisters on various affected regions of the body. Of particular concern for sexually active people is the fact that it is often not possible to determine if someone is infected by the herpes virus, which heightens the risk of being infected. The media devoted a lot of attention to the outbreak of herpes, and a common theme of the coverage was that the sexual revolution had run its course.

Any lingering belief that the sexual revolution was alive and well was dashed by the developments of the early to mid-1980s. Without question, herpes is a serious disease, but it is not generally life-threatening.[45] The same cannot be said for acquired immune deficiency syndrome (AIDS), a sexually transmitted disease that has become one of the leading causes of death around the world.

Although it took a disturbingly long time for the news media to recognize the import of the story, the onset of AIDS fundamentally changed public attitudes toward casual sex. A relentless drumbeat of stories have made it absolutely clear (albeit often with exaggerated statistics) that sleeping with the wrong person can be fatal.

The double-whammy of herpes and AIDS proved to be a boon for the pornography industry, as large numbers of people elected to substitute less satisfying but safer self-gratification for riskier intercourse with strangers or prostitutes.[46] The first major news story about AIDS appeared on April 11, 1983, when *Newsweek* ran a cover story with the headline: "EPIDEMIC: The Mysterious and Deadly Disease Called AIDS May Be the Public-Health Threat of the Century. How Did It Start? Can It Be Stopped?" In the three months following the *Newsweek* story, the nation's major media outlets ran 680 stories about the new disease, more than four times the total for the entire previous year.[47]

Just a short time later, on January 1, 1984, AT&T divested itself of its 22 regional operating companies ("Baby Bells"). Eager for new sources of revenue, the Baby Bells and AT&T began marketing special phone lines for the provision of audiotext services. The timing was ideal. Many Americans were looking for a sexual outlet that did not carry a risk of infection and death, and the pornography industry was in a position to offer the perfect solution. The attraction of phone sex as an alternative to physical contact is reflected in the fact that in just 12 years (1984–96), the phone sex industry went from a standing start to an estimated $1 billion per year in sales. The phenomenon of phone sex even achieved a certain cultural legitimacy with the 1992 publication of Nicholson Baker's novel *Vox*, a best-seller consisting entirely of a phone sex conversation between two people.

The adult-video industry was another sector of the pornography industry to benefit from America's newfound anxiety over sex with strangers. The onset of AIDS coincided with a significant rise in the sale of VCRs, and watching adult videos became an additional form of safe sex. Not coincidentally, the same period was marked by efforts in the adult-video industry to begin making adult videos that were aimed at couples and not just men. In 1984, for instance, former porn actor Candida Royalle began producing the Femme line of adult videos,[48] a collection of videos aimed at couples and specifically at women. Some people, including porn commentator Luke Ford, take exception to Royalle's version of pornography: "Though articulate and thoughtful, her non-exploitive non-sexist erotica is lite porn—porn for people who don't like porn. Her contributions to pornography rank with Kato Kaelin's contributions to acting."[49]

Nonetheless, Royalle's films have won a number of awards from the Critics Adult Film Association and are frequently cited as an example of a new direction in adult video. That assessment may be overblown, considering that Royalle produces only three to four videos a year compared to the 8,000 or 9,000 produced each year by the adult video industry as a whole. Nonetheless, the positive coverage that Royalle has received in the mainstream media has also contributed to a greater respectability for the pornography industry.

## SHAPING ATTITUDES: THE SEX INDUSTRY IN ENTERTAINMENT AND THE NEWS

Flip through a thesaurus under the heading for "prostitute," and a fascinating sample of epithets appear, none of them particularly complimentary. Hooker. Hustler. Harlot. Whore. Streetwalker. Strumpet. Moll. The trick, however, lies in the marketing: Cast Julia Roberts as an attractive, bubbly, drug- and disease-free prostitute, Richard Gere as a wealthy (but lonely) businessman, toss in a no-holds-barred, class-revenge-fueled shopping trip on Rodeo Drive, mix in a catchy soundtrack highlighted by Roy Orbison, and all of a sudden, a new synonym can be added to the list: *Pretty Woman* (1990), an updated Cinderella story that sold nearly half a *billion* dollars' worth of movie tickets worldwide before retiring to a lucrative existence on video store shelves ($82 million and counting).

At the time, *Pretty Woman* was simply the latest, frothiest, and most lucrative installment in Hollywood's 70-year fascination with prostitutes as film characters. In 1929, Gloria Swanson became the first actor to be nominated for an Oscar based on a role as a prostitute, the title role in the film *Sadie Thompson* (1928). Three years later, Helen Hayes won an Oscar for her portrayal of a street-walker in the title role of *The Sin of Madelon Claudet* (1931).[50] In the interven-ing years, many of Hollywood's top actresses have delivered powerful and sym-pathetic portrayals of prostitutes. Elizabeth Taylor, for instance, won an Oscar for her portrayal of a hooker in *Butterfield 8* (1960), and the following year, Audrey Hepburn was nominated for her role as escort Holly Golightly in *Breakfast at Tiffany's* (1961). Jon Voight was nominated for best actor for his role as a hustler and wannabe gigolo in *Midnight Cowboy*, and Jane Fonda won an Oscar for her role as a call girl in *Klute* (1971). The 1976 movie *Taxi Driver*, in which Jodie Foster starred as a child prostitute, led to a basketful of nominations, including best picture, best actor (Robert De Niro), and best supporting actress (Foster).

As the nation began to focus more heavily on business and personal financial success in the 1980s, Hollywood's portrayal of prostitutes began to change. Few movies more clearly make the argument that sex and business are a potentially profitable mix than the popular 1983 flick *Risky Business*. Tom Cruise, in his breakthrough movie role, starred as a high school senior and Future Entrepreneur of America. While his parents are out of town, he calls an escort service and spends an evening of delight with Rebecca DeMornay. After a vari-ety of misadventures (including rolling his father's Porsche into Lake Michigan) leave Cruise in desperate need for cash, DeMornay helps him to set up a bro-thel in his family's house to service a significant portion of Cruise's North Shore classmates. Needless to say, the movie offers a variety of happy endings: Cruise's money problems are solved, his friends all get laid (the movie conveniently ignores the minor issue of statutory rape), he goes for a late-night ride with DeMornay on the Chicago el, and a free roll in the hay for his college interviewer gets him into Princeton. In the pre-AIDS era, *Risky Business* was the perfect film to usher in a decade of unbridled capitalism and conspicuous consumption.

In the 15 years since the release of *Risky Business*, Hollywood has released a number of films featuring either sex workers or the sex business. Prostitutes have made up the bulk of the characters (*Scandal, Pretty Woman, Whore, Last Exit to Brooklyn, Milk Money, Leaving Las Vegas*), but Hollywood has also featured strippers (*Blaze, Showgirls, Striptease*), phone sex operators (*Short Cuts, Girl 6*), and the sex industry as a whole (*The People v. Larry Flynt, Boogie Nights*).

Hollywood is not alone in its depiction of the sex trade. Prostitution and sexual adventure have long been staples of soap operas, and increasingly are staples of sitcoms and evening dramas. A particularly concise laundry list of the networks' current attitudes about the sex trade were on display in the April 30, 1998, episode of NBC's hit series *Friends*. Joey (struggling actor) hires a stripper to perform at a bachelor party for Ross (divorced paleontologist friend). Joey and the stripper flirt during the evening, and she spends the night with him. When Joey wakes up in the morning, he discovers that the wedding ring he has been holding as Ross's best man is missing and the stripper is gone. Joey, his roommate Chandler (neurotic number-crunching friend), and Ross all assume that the stripper took it when she left.

After various misadventures, the three friends finally call the agency and hire the same stripper to come and perform at Chandler's office. When she gets there, they confront her and demand the ring back. She is simultaneously outraged and bemused; why, she asks the three of them, would she take a ring and jeopardize a job that pays her $1,600 a week? She then pointedly asks if any of them make that kind of money; there is dead silence, then Chandler asks her to marry him. (The three friends finally figure out that the ring was swallowed by Joey's duck.)

The nation's bookshelves have also grown more explicitly sexual. The Harlequin novel, long noted for its formulaic ripping of bodices and assorted heaving and throbbing body parts, began printing an even racier line of books in its Superromance series.[51] Writers like Judith Krantz, Danielle Steele, and Jackie Collins have sold millions of copies of their lusty romances (in 1994, 75 million copies of Krantz's novels alone were printed), and New Orleans writer Anne Rice single-handedly created the specialized but highly profitable vampire sex genre with *Interview with a Vampire* and its sequels. Other mainstream fiction explores unusual or forbidden sexual territory, including sexual torture, murder, and necrophilia (Bret Easton Ellis's *American Psycho* [1990]), phone sex (*Vox*), adultery (Robert Waller's *Bridges of Madison County* [1992]), and even incest (Kathryn Harris's *The Kiss* [1997]), to name just a few examples.

At times, of course, it has been difficult to tell the difference between make-believe and the real world. The following could easily have been a recent Harlequin book proposal:

Naive and idealistic twenty-year-old gets prestigious internship in White House. She and dashing (but aging) baby boomer president consort in the Oval Office. Suspicious White House staff arranges intern's transfer to Pentagon. Woman in whom she confides tapes conversations and turns them over to blindly ambitious special prosecutor. Havoc ensues.

President Clinton might wish that it was fiction, but the reality is that the headlines have often contributed more to the level of sexual discussion in this country than anything the pornography industry has done. In late January 1998, for instance, Ted Koppel had to warn his viewers that a particular program would involve discussions of oral sex, as did both Katie Couric on *Today* and Judy Woodruff on CNN. In an era of particular sensitivity regarding sexual harassment, the allegations about President Clinton have made water cooler discussions difficult. And all of this, of course, was before the introduction of Viagra.

## PORNOGRAPHY AND IDEOLOGY

No industry can afford to be oblivious to the social and political climate in which it operates. Even the smallest event can set off cultural earthquakes: In 1934, for instance, the American undershirt industry nearly folded after Clark Gable took off his shirt in the movie *It Happened One Night* and revealed that he wasn't wearing an undershirt.

Few industries need to be more in touch with popular culture and social attitudes than the pornography industry. The industry's primary challenge is to identify and respond to often bewildering shifts in standards of sexual attractiveness (a challenge that is complicated, of course, by the role that the industry and more mainstream media play in establishing such standards in the first place). The industry's main product is fantasy, and the object of fantasy can easily be Marilyn Monroe one year and Twiggy the next.

At the same time, the industry needs to be aware of and respond to the numerous groups and organizations that are actively seeking to restrict it or even shut it down. With the possible exception of lawyers, politicians, and tobacco company executives, few groups or industries have inspired the long-standing antipathy and scorn that have been directed toward the pornography industry. The fact that the pornography industry has not only survived but actively prospered in the face of such heartfelt opposition is a compelling commentary on the industry's ability to identify and adapt to cultural norms, to identify and serve its markets, and to take advantage of new opportunities and new technologies. In addition, the pornography industry has often been indirectly aided by the very groups opposed to it, due in no small part to public and judicial concern about the constitutional implications of the measures proposed to limit the pornography industry.

## ALTAR EGOS

It is not surprising, given the role of the church in Western civilization, that religious groups have offered some of the strongest opposition to the pornography industry (and, for that matter, to sexual content in more mainstream entertainment media as well). Religious leaders were most successful in their censorship efforts when they controlled the means of production of media; for instance, when the only printing press in the Massachusetts Bay Colony was owned by Harvard University, then a school devoted primarily to religious training.

Once religious organizations lost control over the means of production, it became far more difficult to control the sexual content of printed materials. To some degree, general religious and cultural mores helped to limit what could be read in polite society, but as the nation's population increased and the country became more diverse, commonly held values became harder and harder to identify, let alone enforce.

Despite the obvious difficulty that Comstock had with that precise problem, religious leaders did not give up in their efforts to limit the sexual content of publicly available materials. After three decades of Hollywood films that included increasingly bold use of nudity and sexual situations, it was clear that general religious disapproval and the possibility of legislative action were not sufficiently strong threats to outweigh the enormous revenues being generated. It was not until the 1930s that the anti-indecency forces realized that they could use movie revenues themselves as a lever to make the film studios listen to their concerns. When American Catholic bishops set up the Legion of Decency in 1934 to lead boycotts of films that the Catholic Church considered indecent,[52] the timing could hardly have been better: During five years of depression, film revenues had steadily declined. The boycotts were so successful that Hollywood producers agreed to create the Production Code Administration, which was designed to placate the Legion of Decency (which by now included representatives from many Protestant denominations as well)[53] by ensuring that certain sinful themes would not appear in film and that if they did, they would be offset by the depiction of a "compensating moral value."[54]

The Legion of Decency remained in operation until 1965, fighting an increasingly uphill battle against the use of sex and other mature themes in film. Toward the end of its existence, the organization's recommendations began to have a weight similar to that of the Catholic Church's *Index Librorum Scriptorum* (which, coincidentally, was also discontinued the following year).[55] By that time, objections by the league had become more badges of honor for filmmakers than marks of disgrace.[56] A popular advertising phrase, in fact, was "banned in Boston," which put potential customers on notice that a book or movie might be a little racy. With the introduction of the Motion Picture Association of America's rating system in 1968 (even though it essentially codified the status quo), the impetus for organized religious protest against the studios largely vanished.

Religious organizations did not limit their activities to film. In 1938,

American Catholic bishops founded the National Organization for Decent Literature to protest indecency in print.[57] The organization used tactics similar to the Legion's against movies to challenge publishers, booksellers, and even drugstore owners (for vending magazines and comic books) over the material being produced and sold.[58] The group's experience, however, is instructive: Although it achieved some success (by persuading, for instance, publishers Fawcett and Dell to eliminate objectionable materials), it never succeeded in establishing the type of prior review board that made the Legion of Decency so influential (at least temporarily) for films.

As studios had discovered to their dismay, movies in the 1930s were particularly vulnerable to economic boycott: They were produced in limited quantities by a limited number of studios, they were generally expensive to make, and they were shown in a finite number of locations. Books and magazines, by contrast, were largely boycott-proof: Even if a single book was targeted, there were simply too many potential retail outlets for a national boycott to be effective.

The dissolution of the Legion of Decency appeared to mark the end of organized religion's direct efforts in setting a moral tone for print, stage, or film. With declining membership, dwindling political influence, and profound cultural changes taking place, the role of religion in establishing or enforcing cultural norms diminished dramatically.

In the mid- to late 1970s, however, religion began to make a comeback in the social and political arena. A galvanizing event for religious activists was a campaign to repeal a gay rights ordinance in Dade County, Florida, in 1977. One of several ordinances passed in Florida forbidding discrimination against gays, the Dade County law sparked fervent opposition among local conservatives and religious groups around the country. The local forces were led by singer and former Miss America contestant Anita Bryant, who created the nonprofit group Save Our Children, Inc. to campaign for a referendum to repeal the ordinance. The vote on the referendum (which opponents of gay rights won by a 2-1 margin) drew national attention, and Dade County became a rallying call for conservatives and religious leaders eager to draw a line in the sand against further social liberalization.

Among the religious leaders who came to Florida to support Bryant's campaign was Jerry Falwell, a Baptist preacher from Lynchburg, Virginia. Inspired by the battle against gay rights and sensing the potential for further political action in support of conservative and religious values, Falwell returned to Lynchburg and in 1979 founded a group called the Moral Majority. The organization quickly became a potent force at all levels of American politics. Well-funded by its 4 million or so members and aided by Richard Viguerie, one of the finest mass mailing experts in the nation, the Moral Majority used a combination of high-powered lobbying and grass-roots campaigns to promote a variety of socially conservative causes, including (among others) the legislative repeal or judicial reversal of *Roe v. Wade*, increased defense spending, reduced spending on social services, tougher criminal laws and stricter enforcement, and in particular, increased restrictions on pornography.

In addition, during the first year of its existence, the Moral Majority registered millions of new and mostly conservative voters for the November 1980 election. The campaign had an almost immediate impact at both the federal and state levels, helping Ronald Reagan to defeat Jimmy Carter, and helping to elect state legislators opposed, among other things, to the ratification of the Equal Rights Amendment. The Moral Majority was also able to use the political clout it held after Reagan's election to support state and local candidates that shared its views and pushed for the appointment of state prosecutors and U.S. attorneys who would be willing to initiate obscenity prosecutions.

Despite 12 consecutive years of Republican presidents and control of the Senate for half of that period, the Moral Majority's accomplishments were modest, particularly in the realm of pornography. Instead of a national law against indecent speech or at least postal regulations with more teeth to them, religious and conservative groups had to make do with the Meese Commission, a more detailed discussion of which is set out below. With the replacement of President Reagan by President George Bush in 1988, much of the Moral Majority's enthusiasm seemed to ebb, and it was disbanded in 1989.

In its place has arisen a network of religion-based organizations that have vigorously taken up the issue of pornography in our society. Groups such as the Christian Coalition, the Family Research Council, the National Law Center for Children and Families, and Morality in Media have become deeply involved in the issue of Internet pornography and were active supporters of the 1996 Communications Decency Act. The president of Morality in Media, Bob Peters, said that his organization has been involved in the issue of computer-related pornography since the development of bulletin board systems in the mid-1980s. His own introduction to the topic came when he got a phone call in 1991:

> Somebody called from Ohio. I forget all of the details, but he was familiar with what back then was the science network. He was on it and he called to inform us that not only was adult pornography being distributed on that science network, but child pornography. And he wanted to know what legally could be done about the problem.

Peters advised his caller that it was not clear whether there was a federal law on the books at the time that prohibited the distribution of child pornography on the Internet (although he did suggest to his caller that he contact the local prosecutor about misuse of federal resources). This experience led Peters and his organization to play a role in shaping the Communications Decency Act, although he said that many of Morality in Media's suggestions ultimately were not adopted.[59] Since the rejection of that law by the U.S. Supreme Court, Morality in Media has been active in promoting the use of filtering devices and in supporting Senator Dan Coats's bill, the Child Online Protection Act, which would bar transmission of materials deemed "harmful to minors." Despite the ubiquity of the Internet, Peters remains a believer in local community standards. "With as much intelligence as computers have," Peters said, "I find it very difficult to believe that somebody couldn't program their computer to block transfer of material to certain zip codes."

The problem religious organizations face is that they are swimming against a strong consumer tide, a fact that has been implicitly recognized by the Republican Party, the religious right's most natural ally. Efforts to ban popular fiction from library shelves have also raised broad fears about the free speech implications of various legislative proposals put forward by religious groups (a point graphically illustrated in the film *Footloose*). "By my enemies, you shall know me," pornographers mutter happily, as they continue to rake in enormous revenues.

## OUR BODIES, OURSELVES: THE ROLE OF FEMINISM IN THE PORNOGRAPHY DEBATE

The same is often said about feminists and pornography, although the relationship is more complicated. A resurgence in the American feminist movement and broadly changing attitudes toward sexuality (and female sexuality in particular) were among the most important factors in the social revolution that swept across the nation in the 1960s and 1970s, particularly with respect to the issue of pornography. The strength of the resurgence stemmed from a variety of causes: Many women, including some who had important but temporary careers just 20 years earlier during World War II, were now looking to reenter the workforce after raising their children; an increasingly large number of women were attending college; the development of the birth control pill in 1960 offered women much greater control over conception and as a result, greater sexual freedom; and in 1964, Congress passed the Civil Rights Act, which although it was aimed primarily at racial discrimination also prohibited gender-based discrimination.[60]

At the same time, the popular culture was urging men and women to reexamine their attitudes toward sex and social mores. Hefner had given men a head start on the sexual revolution by introducing *Playboy* in 1953 and opening the first Playboy Club in 1960, but women began to catch up with the publication of Helen Gurley Brown's 1962 best-seller, *Sex and the Single Girl*. In her book, the 40-year-old Brown unapologetically urged women to delay marriage, have affairs with married men, and jettison the idea that "sex without marriage was dirty." For at least some women, Brown's suggestions were a welcome alternative to the discouraging life that Betty Friedan would so powerfully describe a year later in *The Feminine Mystique*.[61]

Friedan, a feminist leader and author, believed that many middle-class women, generally confined to the single career of homemaker and mother, were suffering from tremendous emotional and intellectual boredom. She argued that this boredom, which was frequently misdiagnosed as an individual problem with adjustment, was actually the result of much broader societal problems resulting from basic inequities in the treatment of women. In particular, she argued that the idealization of women as mothers and homemakers was essentially a conspiracy by men to eliminate economic competition by women.

Albeit from dramatically different points of view, both Brown and Friedan were promoting the fundamental concept of the ability of women to control their own bodies and lives. It was a concept that would play out in a variety of ways and, thanks in no small part to the issue of pornography, would lead to a profound schism in the feminist movement.

*The Feminine Mystique* led to the founding of the National Organization for Women (NOW), which Friedan headed from 1966 to 1970.[62] Her book is widely credited with galvanizing the women's movement, and NOW began actively campaigning on such issues as the passage of the Equal Rights Amendment and fuller reproductive rights for women. The spirit of the movement was captured in the title of one of the period's best-selling books, *Our Bodies, Ourselves,* a feminist health and sex manual produced by a Boston women's collective.[63] "A woman's right to choose," as NOW characterized the debate over abortion rights, was the organization's most successful campaign, culminating in the 1973 decision by the U.S. Supreme Court in *Roe v. Wade.*

At the same time that NOW was beginning its campaign to promote a woman's right to choose, Brown was advocating for the right to make very different types of choices. The success of *Sex and the Single Girl* led to her being offered the editorship of *Cosmopolitan,* which in July 1965 was a failing women's magazine based in the Midwest. In a makeover completely emblematic of the social changes taking place, Brown replaced *Cosmopolitan*'s articles on tea socials and quilting bees with uninhibited discussions of sex and relationships. The magazine's circulation rapidly grew from less than 800,000 to more than 3 million, making Brown and her concept of the "Cosmo girl" a national and international phenomenon.[64]

*Cosmopolitan* is a perfect illustration of why few industries benefited more from the change in social attitudes toward sex than the pornography industry. *Cosmopolitan* was the first magazine to target young, single women with unblushing articles about sex and relationships. Teetering itself on the edge of pornography (one can easily imagine how Comstock would have viewed articles like "Going for Multiple Orgasms" [July 1998]), the magazine helped expand the potential market for sexually explicit materials by making sex an increasingly mainstream topic of discussion. It is highly doubtful that the pornography industry's growth from 1953 to 1973 (from roughly $500 million to $2 billion) resulted in any large degree from direct purchases by women; there is, for instance, no evidence that women were purchasing significant amounts of "traditionally" pornographic materials like *Playboy* or *Penthouse.* But there is also nothing to suggest that movies such as *Midnight Cowboy* (1969), *M\*A\*S\*H* (1970), and *A Clockwork Orange* (1971), and theater productions such as *Hair* (1967) and *Oh! Calcutta!* (1969) were playing to all-male audiences.

Moreover, there is direct, albeit anecdotal evidence, that *Deep Throat*'s success resulted from the fact that it was the first hardcore pornography film to be seen by substantial numbers of women. *Time* reported that the movie's enormous revenues were due in part to the fact that "women—both alone and with men—have been lining up to see it. Many find it revolting, but some seem drawn to freckled Linda Lovelace."[65] One woman who had her doubts was Nora Ephron, who wrote in *Esquire* that "*Deep Throat* . . . is one of the most unpleasant, disturbing films I have ever seen—it is not just anti-female but antisexual as well." After seeing the film and interviewing Lovelace (who described her sudden success as "kind of a goof"), Ephron reached the conclusion that she herself was "a hung-up, uptight, middle-class, inhibited, puritanical, feminist who lost her sense of humor at a skin flick."[66]

She wasn't the only one. A large number of feminists were disturbed by the amount of mainstream attention that *Deep Throat* received (not to mention some of the themes and images in the film itself), and even more were concerned by the July 1974 launching of *Hustler*, a raw, often excruciatingly explicit magazine that abounded with misogynistic themes. Larry Flynt, who started the magazine out of his Cincinnati, Ohio, strip joint, was quoted shortly afterward as saying, "Neither Hefner nor Guccione wants to admit that people are buying skin mags for a turn-on first and for editorial quality second."[67]

The real start of the feminist antipornography movement can probably be traced to a 1976 billboard in Los Angeles promoting the Rolling Stones. The billboard depicted a woman, tied up and bruised, with the caption: "I'm Black and Blue From the Rolling Stones—and I Love It!"[68] Activists were similarly horrified two years later when *Hustler* ran a magazine cover depicting a woman being shoved into a meat grinder. The outrage these images engendered helped to fuel a variety of different feminist protests: the picketing of magazines, tours of urban sex zones, and touring slide shows to graphically demonstrate the violence inherent in much of the pornography industry's product.

The feminist antipornography movement reached its peak in 1983 and 1984, when author Andrea Dworkin and attorney Catherine A. MacKinnon combined forces to write a Model Antipornography Law.[69] The model law arose out of their testimony before the Minneapolis City Council on a proposed zoning regulation designed to limit the establishment of pornography businesses in certain neighborhoods. Both MacKinnon and Dworkin opposed the ordinance on the grounds that it implied that pornography businesses could legitimately be established in other sections of the community. They argued to the council that trying to control pornography through civil rights would be a more effective approach. The council hired them to draft an ordinance defining pornography as sex discrimination.

Under the proposal drafted by MacKinnon and Dworkin, the definition of sex discrimination would be expanded to include four activities: (1) coercion of a person into pornography; (2) trafficking in pornography; (3) forcing pornography on a person; and (4) assault or physical attack due to pornography. The purpose of the ordinance was to create both a right to recover and a remedy for someone who could prove that she had been harmed by pornography.

After an emotional public hearing, the Minneapolis City Council adopted the ordinance. Mayor Donald Fraser promptly vetoed it on the grounds that the ordinance violated the Bill of Rights in general and the First Amendment in particular. A revised version was adopted, and Fraser vetoed it again.

The MacKinnon/Dworkin model law was also adopted in Indianapolis, although the city's legislators revised the ordinance to focus solely on violent pornography (a move scoffed at by Minneapolis activists as the so-called "*Playboy* exemption"). Passage of the model law was strongly supported not only by antipornography feminists, but also by conservative and religious groups, many of which had strongly opposed women's rights. For instance, among the ordinance's ardent supporters were Greg Dixon, a Baptist minister who had been an official in the Moral Majority, and Beulah Coughenour, an ardent antiabortion activist and a member of both of Phyllis Schlafly's antifeminist groups, Stop ERA and the Eagle Forum.[70] After the city council passed the ordinance, Indianapolis Mayor William H. Hudnut III signed it into law.

Immediately after Hudnut signed the law, a lawsuit was filed by publishers, distributors, and booksellers to challenge the constitutionality of the new ordinance. Federal District Court Judge Sarah Evans Barker ruled that the ordinance was unconstitutional, and her decision was upheld by the Seventh Circuit Court of Appeals in 1985.[71] The U.S. Supreme Court declined to hear the case.

With the rejection of the model ordinance by the Seventh Circuit (which MacKinnon, with typical bombast, described as "the *Dred Scott* case of the women's movement"),[72] the efforts of antipornography feminists to create a statutory basis for attacking the economic rewards of pornography largely ceased. However, the decision did little to end the debate among women over pornography, its role in society, and their relationship to it. On one side are Dworkin and MacKinnon, arguing that pornography is inherently abusive and demeaning to women; and on the other side is a coalition of free speech feminists and sex workers who are more concerned about the constitutional threat posed by measures like the Indianapolis ordinance and who resent the assertion that no woman can voluntarily choose to participate in the pornography industry or earn a living as a sex worker.

Among the most vocal of the "my body, myself" wing of feminism is Nina Hartley, an exotic dancer and adult-video star who began stripping to earn extra money during college at San Francisco State. Hartley categorically rejects the idea that a woman cannot rationally choose to be a sex worker, and she describes the Dworkin/MacKinnon camp in no uncertain terms:

> These prudes are nothing less than the lap dogs of the right wing, which had calculatingly employed the sex-negs as willing pawns who blindly act, in a stunning example of mutual exploitation, as tools for repression in the religious fundamentalists' anti-liberation master plan. I guess a tendency for totalitarianism can overcome any other differences they may have.[73]

Hartley, who earned a nursing degree in college and is white and middle-class, acknowledges that she has options available to her that many other sex workers do not. Hartley has been aided in her argument with the so-called "sex negs," however, by the fact that the logical extension of the provisions of the Dworkin/MacKinnon ordinance is that women are fundamentally incapable of choosing to participate in the pornography industry. Regardless of their own personal feelings about pornography, many women resent the inference that they cannot decide for themselves what to do with their own bodies (which was, after all, one of the central tenets of the 1960s sexual revolution). As some antipornography feminists have begun to realize, the problem with playing ideological snugglebunnies with the religious right and social conservatives on the issue of pornography is that many of the same arguments can be used to threaten a woman's right to choose to terminate a pregnancy. In addition, a number of feminists, including most notably former ACLU president Nadine Strossen, disagree with Dworkin and MacKinnon on the grounds that their attacks on pornography are a threat to free speech in general and the rights of women in particular.

"What is wrong with this picture?" Strossen asked three years ago. "Where have they come from—these feminists who behave like religious conservatives, who censor works of art because they deal with sexual themes? Have not feminists long known that censorship is a dangerous weapon which, if permitted, would inevitably be turned against them? Certainly that was the irrefutable lesson of the early women's rights movement, when Margaret Sanger, Mary Ware Dennett, and other activists were arrested, charged with 'obscenity,' and prosecuted for distributing educational pamphlets about sex and birth control. Theirs was a struggle for freedom of sexual expression and full gender equality, which they understood to be mutually reinforcing."[74]

The irony is that while the debate over pornography rages in feminist circles, an increasingly large number of women are choosing to become both consumers and producers of pornography. By some estimates, between 40 and 50 percent of adult videos are rented by women,[75] and many of the most popular online adult Web sites are run by women. While some may continue to decry a society in which women are able to make impressive amounts of money selling images of their bodies, it is nonetheless significant that technology is making it increasingly possible for some of those women to both control the use of their images and reap the benefits.

## THE CONSERVATIVE MOVEMENT

Even before the U.S. Supreme Court handed down its decision in *Miller* in 1973, conservative activists recognized that a community of (mostly) like-minded individuals could effectively bar the sale of objectionable materials. Perhaps the best known and most effective of such groups was Citizens for Decent Literature, which was founded by Cincinnati attorney Charles Keating[76] in the early 1950s. The organization was an outgrowth of Operation Newsstand, a campaign organized by Keating to eliminate indecent materials from the city's bookstores and newsstands.[77]  By the end of the decade, Keating's group had chapters in a number of U.S. cities and towns, and Keating had earned a national reputation as a pornography fighter.

Just as groups like Keating's were building up steam to do community by community what the National Organization for Decent Literature had been unable to do at the national level, the rug was largely pulled out from underneath them by the *Roth* decision in 1957. The surge of sexually explicit materials that followed and the cultural changes that swept the nation during the 1960s made it difficult if not impossible for local or national groups to make much headway in their efforts to stamp out pornography.

Things changed dramatically in the 1970s. *Saturday Night Fever* and *Boogie Nights* notwithstanding, the 1970s were not a polyester-clad repeat of the 1960s. Sobered in part by economic difficulties (not least of which was the Middle Eastern oil embargo) and shaken by the resignation of a president, the nation was slowly becoming more conservative. Contributing to that trend, of course, was that many of the previous decade's flower children were now parents and homeowners, which tends to alter one's economic and political perspective. For other segments of society, incensed at the changes brought by the women's movement and gay pride, and horrified by the sexual content of the nation's cultural outlets, the time was ripe for both conservative and religious activism.

Conservatives found an enthusiastic ally in Edwin Meese III, President Reagan's attorney general. In 1986, Meese was instructed by the president to set up and head a commission to examine the issue of pornography in the United States, and to report back with recommendations for legislative action.

Antipornography activists remembered with particular outrage President Johnson's earlier Commission on Pornography and Obscenity, which in 1970 concluded that all laws restricting the distribution of obscene materials in the United States should be repealed.[78]  The U.S. Senate rejected the commission's report, and President Nixon declared it "morally bankrupt."[79] Commission member Charles Keating, who had been selected by Nixon to fill a vacancy in the Johnson-appointed commission, wrote an impassioned dissent, and the Senate convened hearings to determine how and why the commission had reached its startling conclusion. For Senator Strom Thurmond (R-S.C.), the reason was clear:

Some may wonder how a report that is fundamentally evil in its basic assumptions could be produced with public funds. The fact is that

President Johnson simply surrendered to the radical liberals who have taken over the Party. He chose as the chairman of this Commission a left-wing professor [William Lockhart, Dean of the University of Minnesota Law School] whose agitation for the legalization of pornography was a matter of long-established record.[80]

Determined to avoid the embarrassment to the government resulting from the 1970 commission, Attorney General Meese selected his 208 witnesses with care. Virtually all of the witnesses were antipornography, and a significant number were either law enforcement or purported victims of pornography.[81] The highlight of the parade of witnesses was an appearance by Linda Marciano (neé Lovelace), who testified that during the filming of Deep Throat, she had been physically beaten and threatened with a Walther PPK 45 automatic. Marciano's invitation to appear as a witness resulted in large part from the publication of her book Ordeal, in which she recounted the abuse and torture she allegedly suffered during the making of Deep Throat. In Ordeal, she also tried to distance herself from her contemporaneous statements about how much she had enjoyed making Deep Throat, saying essentially that she had been programmed to give such statements by her then-husband and alleged abuser Chuck Trainor.[82]

The leanings of the Meese Commission witnesses were so pronounced and the claims of injury from pornography were so outrageous that the commission's final report was generally dismissed out of hand as preordained. Moreover, since the commission did not recommend that any particular legislation be adopted to deal with problems it identified, its statutory impact was limited. The Meese Commission's report (which with its lengthy appendix of excerpts from adult literature and descriptions of porn films was itself one of the decade's most sexually explicit works) did spur Presidents Reagan and Bush to launch far-reaching prosecutorial campaigns against pornography producers, resulting in the indictment, conviction, and imprisonment of hundreds of business owners.[83] At the same time, however, the number of adult videotapes rented around the country rose from 75 million in 1985, the year before the Meese Commission, to 490 million in 1992, the last year of President Bush's administration.

The most tangible and long-lasting result of the commission's work may have been a heightened awareness on the part of the public of the dangerous potential for government censorship. The commission helped prove this point when its chief of staff, Alan E. Sears, sent out a letter on Justice Department stationery to bookstore chains, book publishers, national magazine and book distributors, cable television program distributors, and some of the country's largest convenience-variety store, drugstore, and department-store chains. The letter, which included a report from antipornography activist Reverend Donald Wildmon titled "Pornography in the Marketplace," informed the businesses that they were at risk of being identified in the commission's report as distributors of pornography, and that if they wished to avoid being so identified, they should stop selling certain materials. A number of corporations, concerned about potentially adverse publicity, complied with the Sears letter by pulling *Playboy*, *Penthouse*, *Forum*, and even *Cosmopolitan* off their shelves. Both *Playboy* and *Penthouse* sued the commission, asking that another letter be sent out retracting the allegations. The magazines prevailed, and the commission sent out a letter withdrawing the allegations of the first; however, much of the economic damage had already been done. By some estimates, sales of men's magazines dropped 20 percent following the Sears letter.[84]

The failure of the Meese Commission to provide a compelling factual basis for restricting pornography through legislation and the subsequent dissolution of the Moral Majority in 1989 did little to slow antipornography forces. In the arena of political activism, the Moral Majority was largely replaced by the Christian Coalition, a grassroots organization founded in 1988 to provide support for candidates and a conservative agenda at all levels of government. And on the cultural front, would-be censors had found an inviting new target: the National Endowment for the Arts (NEA).

Conservative attacks on federal funding of morally objectionable activities had already proved effective. In 1975, three years after the U.S. Supreme Court's decision in *Roe v. Wade*, Representative Henry Hyde (R-Ill.) introduced an amendment to an appropriations bill forbidding the use of federal funds to perform abortions. Within two years, the number of federally funded abortions dropped from nearly 300,000 to 3,000. As D'Emilio and Freedman point out, the restriction had no effect on a woman's legal right to abortion, but it substantially limited the access of poorer women.

On July 26, 1989, at a time when the Senate was not overly well attended, Senator Jesse Helms (R–N.C.) introduced an amendment forbidding the NEA from providing grants for "obscene and indecent" art. Helms's amendment was ultimately rejected by a House-Senate conference committee, but the uproar over the NEA helped the National Republican Congressional Committee in the 1990 elections and also aided Helms in his narrow victory that year over Harvey Gantt.[85] In October 1989, the Senate approved the compromise bill that required the NEA to withhold funding from any art project that it considered to be obscene within the meaning of *Miller*.[86]

One of the artists whose work helped to ignite the controversy was Robert Mapplethorpe,[87] a photographer whose frank depictions of black and white men engaged in homosexual acts of sadomasochism and autoeroticism were considered provocative by some and frankly obscene by others. In support of his amendment, for instance, Helms circulated a catalog of a Mapplethorpe show titled "The Perfect Moment," which the NEA had funded. The catalog included reproductions not only of Mapplethorpe's acclaimed portraits of celebrities and of flowers, but also of his more provocative works. Mapplethorpe's show had been scheduled to appear at the Corcoran Gallery of Art in Washington, D.C., but as the fight over the NEA gathered steam, the Corcoran's director, Christina Orr-Cahill, canceled the show just two weeks before the opening. From an economic point of view, the censorship of Mapplethorpe's allegedly pornographic images had a familiar effect: The prices for his photos went up, and the Corcoran lost nearly 10 percent of its membership. In the meantime, nearly 50,000 people paid to see "The Perfect Moment" at the Washington Project for the Arts, which agreed to exhibit the photos following the Corcoran's cancellation. On December 18, 1989, Orr-Cahill announced her resignation.

Two of Mapplethorpe's photos from "The Perfect Moment" show later became the centerpiece of a major obscenity trial that occurred, appropriately enough, in Cincinnati. The show opened on April 6, 1990, at the Contemporary Arts Center. The next morning, at the urging of various groups (including the successor to Keating's Citizens for Decent Literature and the more recently formed Citizens for Community Values), the Cincinnati police shut down the Arts Center so that they could take photographs and videotapes for use in court. Earlier in the same day, both the Center and its director, Dennis Barrie, had been indicted by a Cincinnati grand jury on the charges of "pandering obscenity" and possessing and viewing child pornography (two of Mapplethorpe's photographs depicted naked children). Legal scholars of every ideological description criticized both the closing of the gallery (which had occurred without any judicial oversight or legal process) and the indictments themselves. Artists, gallery owners, and free speech activists, meanwhile, waited nervously for the jury's verdict. To the surprise of many observers, on October 5, 1990, the jury hearing the case against Barrie and the Arts Center acquitted them of all charges.

In November 1997, a Tennessee grand jury indicted the bookstore chain for selling books featuring the works of noted photographers David Hamilton and Jock Sturges. Both books include pictures of nude children which the local state attorney considered to be obscene.[88] A state prosecutor, however, agreed in May 1998 not to prosecute Barnes & Noble for selling the photography books. A similar indictment was handed down by a grand jury in Alabama's Cobb County in February 1998. The Alabama charges were dropped in December 1998 after several state and local officials examined the books and determined that they were not obscene under Alabama law.

# THE FINANCIAL REWARDS OF PORNOGRAPHY

## THE ECONOMIC PRESSURES OF THE LAST TWO DECADES

Throughout history, there has always been a certain percentage of people who were interested in producing sexually explicit materials and a certain larger percentage who were interested in consuming them. As the history of the early Middle Ages makes clear, it has not always been possible (or legal) to satisfy those desires. That has not been a problem in the United States, however, particularly in the last 25 years. Despite the industry's fear of the effects of the U.S. Supreme Court's decision in *Miller*, pornography revenues have grown steadily, rising from an estimated $2 billion per year in 1973 to more than $10 billion (and possibly as much as $20 billion) in 1998. While much of that increase is attributable to the various technological changes that have made it easier to produce and distribute pornography, the most significant factor is the economic changes that have taken place in the United States during the same period.

In a word, the economy over the last quarter-century has been unsettling. The early 1970s featured wage and price freezes by the Nixon administration, the Arab oil embargo, and the disconcerting image of Americans standing in line on alternate days to purchase gasoline for their cars. After a brief upturn, the nation's economy headed south again in the late 1970s, just strongly enough to contribute to President Carter's loss to Ronald Reagan in 1980.

During his administration, President Reagan used a seductive combination of unsinkable optimism, tax cuts, deregulation, deficit spending and the largest military buildup in the nation's history to help jolt the U.S. economy out of its doldrums. He was aided in his efforts by the phenomenal growth of the nation's high-tech industry and by Wall Street's "merger mania," in which investment banking firms like Drexel Burnham Lambert and Kohlberg Kravis Roberts used so-called "junk bonds" to finance leveraged buyouts of struggling or cash-starved businesses.

For the architects of these deals, their lawyers, and many of their shareholders, it was an enormously lucrative period. Throughout the early and mid-1960s, the stock market did extremely well, and vast fortunes were made seemingly overnight. The mass media unabashedly ogled the nouveaux riches (*Lifestyles of the Rich and Famous*) and incorporated their lifestyles into a variety of different entertainment productions, including *Dallas, Knot's Landing,* and *L.A. Law.* The word "yuppie" made its appearance, helping to define the sensibilities of the decade.

Not surprisingly, in view of the enormous media attention given to consumption in general, the free-spending atmosphere and consumer mentality of Wall Street spilled over to Main Street. It was an ultimately destructive development, however, because real wages for the majority of Americans were not keeping up with either prices or the levels of consumption. In addition, many of the mergers were funded by junk bonds and could only be made profitable if the target companies were chopped apart and the more profitable bits sold to the highest bidder. It was not uncommon for large numbers of jobs to be lost in the process. Given these various developments, it is not surprising that during the same period of time, the nation saw a profound drop in its savings rate and an equally profound rise in its consumer debt.

In order for most families to maintain their standard of living (and to participate to some degree in the decade's consumerism), it became increasingly necessary for both parents to work. Having both parents working full-time, however, ran counter to one of the decade's most powerful social messages. Partly in response to the perceived denigration of full-time mothers by the feminist movement during the late 1960s and 1970s, and partly as a way of fueling support for tougher anticrime measures, conservative groups spent much of the decade blaming society's perceived ills on the number of women working full-time. This played directly into and amplified the guilt and unease that many parents (and particularly women) themselves felt about having leaving their children with a sitter or in day care all day. On the other hand, there were (and still are) relatively few part-time jobs that pay much above minimum wage or that offer a high enough income to pay for the benefits (such as health care) which are traditionally associated with full-time employment.

Although the economy began to revive in the early 1990s, the employment picture has not brightened significantly. Unemployment is as low as it has been in 20 years, but the mix of jobs is not as lucrative as it once was. Corporations have discovered that technology allows them to do more with fewer people, and a number of economy sectors have experienced massive layoffs in the last few years. To their surprise and delight, most corporations have also discovered that the stock market will reward them handsomely for "downsizing" or "rightsizing." Whatever the nomenclature, the net result, of course, is that fewer people are working in higher-paying jobs and fewer people have the type of financial security or benefits that they once did. Circumstances like these encourage people to take a second look at money-making opportunities that they might otherwise have once disregarded.

## NOT YOUR AVERAGE PART-TIME JOB

For sexual entrepreneurs, the primary consequence of the pornography industry's increasing prominence and economic success was to create a wider range of business opportunities. Increased demand for magazines meant more opportunities for amateur photographers to sell photos; the stunning rise in the demand for videos created increased opportunities for video producers, for actors and for makers of home movies; and Internet technology now makes it possible for men and women to create and distribute their own sexually explicit materials.

Unlike many other industries, pornography is one field in which amateurism is not merely tolerated but actually prized. Privacy has proven to be a commodity to which a price can be attached and, quite often, amateurs are perceived to have more of it to give up. That is part of the reason, for instance, for the enormous popularity of the various Web camera sites that are now available online. For a fee, an Internet user can receive periodic snapshots (usually every two to three minutes) of the interior of someone's house and see what they're doing. Activities run the gamut from housecleaning, studying, and cooking to showering, dressing and undressing, modeling lingerie, and having sex, both alone and with a partner. Although the technology is still a little rough around the edges, these are the first steps towards having not just thousands but potentially millions of online content providers.

The chief reason behind the growth in online pornography sites (both amateur and professional) is almost entirely economic: Working in the pornography industry or operating a pornography business can be lucrative. For high-tech sex workers, the pornography industry generally pays higher wages than an entry-level service job. For instance, phone sex advertisements generally offer part-time wages of between $8 and $15 per hour, while live models on adult video conferencing sites are usually paid between $25 and $50 per hour. At a time when most part-time jobs (and even a number of full-time jobs) are paying the minimum wage, the additional income is attractive. But it is not simply the income; it is also the fact that the higher wages mean that women who do this type of work can work less and spend more time on other activities, including their families and children. Although operating an adult Web site or running a phone sex business can be much more time-consuming and require a greater up-front investment than working as an operator or model, the potential return can be quite high.

Another popular reason cited for doing phone sex or being a model online is the flexibility in scheduling that such jobs offer. Much of the time, the work can be done from home and during nontraditional work hours (which is what customers are generally looking for anyway). There's no need to rush off to an office in the early morning while scrambling to get the kids to school or day care. Although some retail stores, service jobs, and offices are experimenting with flex time and job sharing, the hours of work for the vast majority of entry-level and clerical positions are usually not negotiable.

The advantages in working as a phone sex operator or as a nude model online also come at a time when technology is making such jobs safer and less inherently oppressive. For workers in many of the traditional sex occupations (particularly live strippers and prostitutes), there is a fairly high degree of risk of harassment, assault, disease, and even rape. Although there has been a wave of upscale "gentlemen's clubs" (like the nationwide line of Foxy Lady clubs), and an increase in the number of tonier "escort" services, the potentially lucrative earnings for such work come at the price of diminished personal health and safety. To a large degree, technology serves as a protective shield without diminishing the earnings potential of working in the sex industry. The telecommunications system and the Internet make it possible to become a sex worker in complete or nearly complete anonymity, and with little or no possibility of physical contact between the worker and the customer.

Admittedly, although the tech-sex biz offers some advantages over the more traditional forms of sexual commerce, many of the common complaints about sex employment still exist. Despite the relatively good wages, shifts at an adult videoconferencing company are often long with little or no opportunity for a break, the work often occurs in hastily constructed "sets" in drafty buildings, and the employees receive only a fraction of the income they generate. The hour for which a phone sex operator gets paid $15, for instance, may generate as much as $300 in revenues for the service bureau for which she works. Moreover, as the number of competitors in the high-tech pornography sector continues to grow, there is a significant likelihood that the prices companies can charge will drop, which in turn will depress wages. Over time (and the process is already beginning), a stratification similar to that in the print industry will occur. Some companies, like *Playboy*, will be able to pay top dollar for the models they hire and try to establish online brand-name recognition, while others will try to compete either on price or the outrageousness of their content.

Those drawbacks may help explain why an increasing number of women (and some men) are setting up adult Web sites of their own, in which they are the main attraction. The chief drawbacks to this approach, of course, are the loss of anonymity and privacy, as well as the cost of the necessary equipment and software. However, if those hurdles can be overcome, the advantages over working for someone else are numerous. There is greater autonomy, the same if not more flexibility in scheduling (although the total number of hours required to run one's own business are generally much greater), and the potential financial return is substantial.

Perhaps the most significant consequence of the combination between today's technological innovation and social changes is that it is giving an increasingly large number of women the opportunity to control the production and distribution of the pornography in which they appear. With extraordinarily few exceptions, the historical role of a woman in the pornography industry has been as an employee, with virtually no say over when and how images of her body would be used. Today, however, for women who can afford it (which constitutes a significant and growing percentage of the population), technology allows them to decide if and when and for what compensation they will give up some or all of their privacy.

The ability of women to participate in the pornography industry without the intervention of a (typically male) magazine editor or video producer has profound implications for the industry as a whole. Publishers like Larry Flynt have already seen the effects of the Internet, where a modem can be used to download a year's worth of *Hustler*-like photos in minutes from the Usenet or from one of the thousands of online galleries (many of which, of course, are actually from *Hustler*). The Internet has the effect of suddenly making any woman who chooses to set up her own nude Web site the head of her own *Playboy*-like channel or publisher of her own *Penthouse*-like magazine. Admittedly, the established players in the pornography industry have enormous technical, financial, and editorial resources; the saving grace of a magazine like *Playboy* may well be that people will still want to read it for the articles. But amateur Web site operators have their own enormous draw: the very realness of the images they offer and the inherent voyeurism of looking at them.

It goes without saying that setting up and appearing on a nude Web site is not an activity that everyone would feel comfortable doing. The self-published biographies of amateur site operators often reveal strong streaks of exhibition-ism. But what should also be clear is that the decision is, in today's job environ-ment, an increasingly rational economic one.

## SO JUST HOW LUCRATIVE IS THE PORNOGRAPHY BUSINESS?

The last five years are not the first time that the nation has rushed to embrace a money making opportunity, of course. On a chilly January morning in 1848, James Marshall was walking along a frozen stream bed in northern California when something caught his eye. Bending down, he picked up a small rock that glittered in the clear light. The small flecks dotting the surface of the rock sparked one of the nation's fastest population shifts, as hundreds of thousands of people rushed to California to find as many of Sutter's little gold-laden rocks as possible.

California's population explosion rivals the growth of the Internet: In 1848, when Sutter made his discovery, California's population was estimated at 14,000. Just two years later, the territory's population was more than 100,000, and by 1860, more than 380,000. Thousands of families were divided or irre-trievably broken as men and women (but mostly men) rushed off to find a for-tune in the dirt hills outside of San Francisco. It took some time for the reality to reach the public: A small number of the earliest forty-niners had gotten rich quickly, but the vast majority had made little or no profit once the easily recov-ered gold had been found. Although often significant amounts of gold remained in underground veins, the cost and difficulty of extracting it favored larger and well-established mining companies with the resources and manpower to go after it.

One hundred and fifty years later, the pornography gold rush is follow-ing a similar pattern. The lure of easy riches is drawing large numbers of people into cyberspace, and even though it doesn't involve the months or years of phys-ical separation that marked the California Gold Rush, many cyberwidows would say that the separation is no less complete. The media have played their familiar role, hyping the fortunes to be made and downplaying (or ignoring) the diffi-culties: the long hours, the start-up costs, the potential legal expenses. More important, much like the real Gold Rush, the easy moneymaking opportunities for adult Internet sites have largely disappeared, and traditional economic princi-ples have begun reasserting themselves. It is no longer sufficient, for instance, to throw a few thousand explicit pictures on a Web site, call it a "club," and start col-lecting $24.95 per month from thousands of eager customers; a great many sites today offer hundreds of thousands or even millions of images, along with a bevy of other adult resources. Although demand remains steady and may well be increasing, the supply of generic sexual images on the Internet has reached some-thing approaching the saturation point, leaving online businesses with the chal-lenge of finding ways to differentiate themselves from their competitors.

What has so caught the attention of the media is the fact that as an industry, pornography sites are among the only ones online that have consistently made money. Given the suspicious attitudes of most people toward conducting business on the Internet, the ability of one type of Web site to generate revenues (if not profits) is a cause of both wonder and envy. Less risqué sites are slowly catching up, as well-publicized businesses such as Amazon.com and Barnes & Noble increase consumer confidence in online purchases. However, there is no doubt that adult Web sites have succeeded in turning the Internet into a viable place for commerce.

It's not simply that profits are being earned by online pornography sites, it's that a *lot* of money is being earned. Forrester Research, which tracks online trends and developments, estimated that in 1996, online pornography generated revenues of about $52 million.[89] By the end of the 1996, the *Boston Globe* was estimating that online adult revenues were in excess of $100 million,[90] and calculations by Internet industry analysts in the fall of 1999 put the figure at close to $2 billion.[91] Given that only about a fifth to a quarter of the United States population even has access to the Internet today, the growth potential of the market remains very strong. Over the next five chapters, we'll look at the issues that arise in starting an adult business, review the different types of Web sites that have been set up, and evaluate the income that they are generating.

# NOTES

1. A trait that accounts in no small part for the ability of Horatio Alger, for instance, to build an entire literary career on his rags-to-riches stories in the late 19th century. American mythology, of course, can be a tricky thing, as the nation is discovering in the present wave of revisionist analysis of President John F. Kennedy. Alger, it turns out, was a minister in a small Massachusetts town who was driven from his pulpit in the wake of charges of pederasty. He moved to New York City, where the young men he met on the streets served as inspiration for his plucky heros. John D'Emilio and Estelle Freedman, *Intimate Matters: A History of Sexuality in America* (New York: Harper & Row, 1988), p. 123.
2. Frank Miller, *Censored Hollywood* (Atlanta: Turner Publishing, Inc., 1994), pp. 20–22.
3. Miller, pp. 71–82.
4. "Playgrounds," *Time*, March 24, 1961, p. 55.
5. "Think Clean," *Time*, March 3, 1967, pp. 76–82.
6. "Think Clean," *Time*, March 3, 1967, p. 80.
7. "Think Clean," *Time*, March 3, 1967, pp. 76 et seq.
8. "Hugh Hefner Faces Middle Age," *Time*, February 14, 1969, pp. 69 et seq.
9. "*Playboy* Goes Public," *Time*, September 27, 1971, p. 88. The success of the stock offering was spurred in part by the fact that the stock certificate featured a reclining nude; at the time of the offering, nearly 20,000 people bought a single share as a collector's item. New certificates (without the nude) were issued in 1990, but many shareholders refused to give up their original certificates.
10. Ebert is also remembered for his 1970 collaboration with Russ Meyer on the film *Beyond the Valley of the Dolls*, which chronicled the rise of an all-female band against a backdrop of Hollywood decadence.
11. "Family Affair," *Time*, May 10, 1982, p. 96.
12. The trial court dismissed Falwell's separate claim that Flynt and *Hustler* had libeled him, on the grounds that the advertisement clearly stated that it was a parody and thus could not

reasonably have been considered true by anyone who saw it.

13. Both Leno and Letterman have relied heavily on this principle over the last two or three years, due largely to the comedic possibilities of the O.J. Simpson trial and the Lewinsky affair.

14. *Hustler Magazine v. Falwell*, 458 U.S. 46 (1988). See *NAACP v. Claiborne Hardware Co.*, 458 U.S. 886, 910 (1982) ("Speech does not lose its protected character . . . simply because it may embarrass others or coerce them into action").

15. In a delightful irony, an important character in the film (Ruth Carter Stapleton) is played by Donna Hanover, the wife of New York City Mayor Rudolph Giuliani, a steadfast opponent of the pornography industry.

16. Dave Karger, "Porn Again Cover Up: Hollywood Is about to Unveil an Embarrassment of Movies Probing the Skin Trade," *Time*, September 20, 1996, p. 10.

17. " 'It'—Up to Date," *Time*, June 4, 1965, p. 58. Recent entrants in the "who's using whom" category include actors Erika Eleniak (*Under Siege* [1992] and others), Shannon Tweed (*Falcon Crest* and numerous straight-to-video movies), Jenny McCarthy (*The Jenny McCarthy Show* and *Jenny*, a short-lived NBC sitcom), Pamela Sue Anderson (*Home Improvement, Baywatch, Barb Wire*), and Anna Nicole Smith (*The Hudsucker Proxy, Naked Gun 33 1/3*, and a now-deceased Texas millionaire), all of whom used nude appearances in *Playboy* to boost their already established entertainment careers.

18. "Playboy FAQ–Trivia," online at http://www.playboy.com/help/trivia.html#celebrity. The Playboy FAQ is kind enough to list the month and year in which these and other celebrities appeared.

19. Michael Sauter, "Encore: There She Goes, Miss America Dethroned in 1984, Vanessa Williams Has Made a Royal Comeback," *Entertainment Weekly*, July 26, 1996, p. 68.

20. Beth Carney and Maureen Dezell, " Nancy to sue over Net image," *Boston Globe*, May 2, 1998, p. C2.

21. Katarina Witt, "Fire & Ice," *Playboy*, December 1998, pp. 174–183.

22. "Actor's Estranged Wife to Pose Nude," Associated Press, December 11, 1997. Online at http://search.newsworks.com/fquery.html?qt=pornography+industry&submit.x=7&submit.y=13. Whether Thornton's motive was really to raise male consciousness on domestic abuse or, as she also said, to show her estranged husband "what he's missing," is left for the reader to decide. Nudity has been used to help publicize issues before (for instance, the animal rights campaign "I'd rather be naked than wear fur"), but Thornton's pictorial may be a first for domestic abuse opponents.

23. "Introduction to X-Rated Videos," online at http://www.elite.net~natasha/era/movguide.htm. The most recent target of a whispering campaign was *Star Trek: The Next Generation*'s Marina Sirtis, who played Deanna Troi. The character of Deanna Troi also makes frequent appearances in the extremely X-rated amateur stories exchanged in the newsgroup alt.sex.stories.

24. See, e.g., a Web page set up by a representative of the film's owner, which has numerous photos from the film and from *Love Happy*, as well as images of various magazine covers containing articles about the film. Online at http://www.arrakis.es/~i.p.font/mm/norma.htm. A word of warning: It takes a long time for the Web pages to load.

25. For more information, visit the "Is It Marilyn?" page on the Celebrity Erotica Web site at http://celebrityerotic.miningco.com/library/weekly/aa041298.htm. The page has a number of links to other sites on the Web containing side-by-side photos from the alleged Marilyn stag film and *Love Happy*.

26. At about the time that revenues from her first film, *Behind the Green Door*, were declining, Chambers's photo appeared on Ivory Soap boxes; the film's producers, Jim and Artie Mitchell, milked the free publicity for all it was worth. An embarrassed Procter & Gamble ultimately recalled the boxes, but some still circulate as collector's items.

27. Writer and director Joe Sarno's decision to make a softcore instead of a hardcore sequel was a direct result of the confusion surrounding the U.S. Supreme Court's decision in *Miller*.

28. Luke Ford, *A History of X*, (n.d.), online at http://www.lukeford.com/indexa55.html. The rocket ride, however, was brief: Lovelace's column was dropped by Hefner, *Deep Throat II* bombed at the box office, and on January 31, 1974, Lovelace was arrested for possession of cocaine and amphetamines in Las Vegas.

29. The fake penis that Mark Wahlberg pulls out of his pants at the end of *Boogie Nights* was allegedly modeled after Holmes's 13-inch penis. Justin Plouffe, "Porn Again," *The Nassau Spigot,* 1997, online at http://spigot.princeton.edu/ns/19-7/cover-porn.html.
30. Lindsy Van Gelder, "Modems: Close Encounters of the Computer Kind," *Ms.,* September 1983, p. 61. See also Lindsy Van Gelder, "The Strange Case of the Electronic Lover," *Ms.,* October 1985, p. 94, in which Van Gelder describes her online interaction with a man who posed as Joan Sue Greene, a mute, wheelchair-bound accident victim.
31. Gerard Van der Leun, "Twilight Zone of the Id," *Time,* Spring 1995, p. 36.
32. In the spring of 1995, for instance, the volume was estimated to be the equivalent of 300 paperbacks per second.
33. John Simons, "The Web's dirty secret: Sex sites may make lots of money, but their popularity may soon taper off," *U.S. News and World Report,* August 19, 1996, p. 51.
34. Anthony Flint, "Skin Trade Spreading Across the U.S.," *Boston Globe,* December 1, 1996, p. 1.
35. Thomas E. Weber, "The X-Files," *Wall Street Journal,* May 20, 1997.
36. Matt Richtel, "Smut Purveyors Find Profits Online," *New York Times,* April 2, 1997.
37. Matt Richtel, "From Housewives to Strippers, Small Smut Sites Make Money," *New York Times,* April 2, 1997.
38. www.hotbox.com.
39. The Site, "The Virtual Hugh Hefner," Ziff-Davis TV, Inc. (n.d.), online at http://www.thesite.com/0897w5/iview/iview793jump8_082597.html.
40. Frank Rose, "Sex Sells," *Wired,* December 1997, online at http://www.wired.com/wired/5.12/sex.html.
41. See "Sex as a Spectator Sport," *Time,* July 11, 1969, p. 62.
42. *Last Tango* was originally rated "R," but the 1997 rerelease earned an NC-17 rating (the modern equivalent of "X" )
43. Maupin originally offered the sequel to PBS, which had broadcast *Tales from the City,* but the network declined. PBS is run by the Corporation for Public Broadcasting, which receives the majority of its funds from the federal government, and which has been under pressure from conservatives in Congress about the content of its shows.
44. Matthew Gilbert, "Stars defend 'Lolita' as a victim of our age," *Boston Globe,* July 14, 1998, p. C1.
45. Children born to an infected mother, however, may develop fatal infections, and it can cause potentially fatal encephalitis in people with weakened immune systems.
46. In a far more disturbing development, the British charity Save the Children reported in 1996 that in countries with high HIV incidence, men are turning to younger and younger girls in an effort to avoid the disease. Glenda Cooper, "Men turn to children for fear of AIDS," *Independent,* August 21, 1996, p. 5.
47. Randy Shilts, *And the Band Played On* (New York: St. Martin's Press, 1987), p. 267.
48. The Femme line of videos was purchased in 1995 by Adam & Eve, the largest mail order seller of adult videos. The company hired Royalle to continue shooting Femme videos for it.
49. Luke Ford, "FemPorn," (n.d.)
50. See Mike LaSalle, "Hollywood Is Hooked on Hookers," *San Francisco Chronicle,* December 3, 1995, p. 30.
51. Unlike its other series, Harlequin's Superromance series is free of restrictions on its sex scenes, and the series' books tend to be longer and more complex than the books for Harlequin's other lines.
52. Robert Sklar, *Movie-Made America* (New York: Vintage Books, 1975), p. 173.
53. Arthur Knight, *The Liveliest Art* (New York: Mentor Books), 1957, p. 240.
54. Sklar, pp. 173–74.
55. "The Index Indexed," *Time,* April 29, 1966, p. 74. As *Time* put it, "By the 18th century, it was something of a sign of excellence to be listed."
56. Frank Miller, *Censored Hollywood* (Atlanta: Turner Publishing, 1994), p. 199.
57. D'Emilio and Freedman, p. 282.
58. *Ibid.*

59. Author interview with Bob Peters, Morality in Media, June 29, 1998.

60. The language on gender-based discrimination was proposed by Representative Howard W. Smith (D–Va.), who believed that the inclusion of language on sex would help to defeat the entire bill. However, the amendment had the opposite of its intended effect; it helped attract additional support for the Civil Rights Act. Jeffrey Toobin, "The Trouble with Sex," *New Yorker,* February 9, 1998, p. 48ff. Representative Smith was no doubt dismayed that the Civil Rights Act quickly became a popular vehicle for raising suits alleging sex bias in the workplace. D'Emilio and Freedman, pp. 309–10.

61. D'Emilio and Freedman, p. 304.

62. The founding of NOW was an outgrowth of nearly a century and a half of women's activism in the United States. An organized women's rights movement slowly began growing in the early 1800s, and led to the 1848 Seneca Falls Convention, a two-day gathering organized by women's rights advocates Lucretia Coffin Mott and Elizabeth Cady Stanton. During the convention, the 100 participants (68 women, 32 men) adopted a Declaration of Sentiments, which imitated the style of the Declaration of Independence and included a list of 16 specific forms of discrimination being practiced against women. In addition, the convention also adopted 12 resolutions that demanded various rights for women, including the right to vote. In the early 1900's, the suffrage movement overlapped Margaret Sanger's campaign for reproductive rights. The two movements were natural allies: The arguments used in the two campaigns were often quite similar, and many women and men were deeply disturbed by the zeal of Comstock's attacks on Sanger and her husband. With the passage of the 19th Amendment in 1919, much of the impetus for a broader women's movement dissipated, but the efforts of Sanger and later of Planned Parenthood to make reliable information more widely available continued.

63. A new edition of this book, titled *The New Our Bodies, Ourselves: A Book by and for Women,* was published by the Boston Women's Health Book Collective in 1996.

64. *Cosmopolitan's* circulation has remained steady over the years; it still sells 2.5 million issues each month. In addition, the magazine is a market leader in each of the 27 different nations in which it is published. Brown retired after 31 years as editor of *Cosmopolitan* and was replaced by Bonnie Fuller on January 16, 1996.

65. "Wonder Woman," *Time,* January 15, 1973, p. 46.

66. Nora Ephron, "Women," *Esquire,* February 1973, p. 22.

67. "Skin Trouble," *Time,* September 22, 1975, p. 50.

68. "The War Against Pornography," *Newsweek,* March 18, 1985, p. 60; Mary Kay Blakely, "Is One Woman's Sexuality Another Woman's Pornography?" *Ms.,* April 1985, p. 38.

69. Blakely, pp. 38–44.

70. Nadine Strossen, *Defending Pornography* (New York: Scribner, 1995), pp. 77–78.

71. *American Booksellers Association v. Hudnut,* 771 F.2d 323 (7th Cir. 1985).

72. Strossen, *Defending Pornography,* p. 80.

73. Nina Hartley, "Frustrations of a Feminist Porn Star," (n.d.), online at http://www.nina.com/gauntletfin.html.

74. Nadine Strossen, "The Perils of Pornophobia," *The Humanist,* May/June 1995, p. 7.

75. Andrew Ross, *No Respect* (New York: Routledge, 1989).

76. This is the same Charles Keating who in 1991 was convicted of 17 counts of securities fraud in connection with the failure of a savings and loan. When Keating's troubles were publicized, the CDL began a series of name changes to distance itself from its founder. Today, it is known as the Children's Legal Foundation. Edward de Grazia, *Girls Lean Back Everywhere* (New York: Random House, 1992), p. 650 and asterisked note.

77. D'Emilio and Freedman, p. 283.

78. The commission was no doubt influenced by the decision of Denmark the year before to do just that.

79. de Grazia, pp. 552–55. Although it is unusual to try to prevent crime by decriminalizing the activity in question, it's something that the U.S. government has done before. When Prohibition was repealed, it wiped out the underground bootleg economy. Similarly, in states that run lotteries, the numbers racket has essentially disappeared.

80. de Grazia, p. 556 and daggered note. Senator Thurmond's characterization of Dean

Lockhart's position on pornography was clearly poetic license. The Dean's "agitation" consisted of two reasoned articles in the *Minnesota Law Review* discussing recent Supreme Court decisions on obscenity, neither of which goes so far as to advocate abolition of obscenity laws.

81. de Grazia, p. 584.

82. de Grazia, p. 588 and asterisked note. Conveniently overlooked by Marciano is her own 1974 book, *The Intimate Diary of Linda Lovelace,* which was written following her divorce from Trainor. In it, she describes the mistreatment she received from Trainor but reiterates not only her enjoyment in making *Deep Throat,* but also the fun that she is having as a star.

83. Eric Schlosser, "The Business of Pornography," *U.S. News and World Report,* February 10, 1997.

84. See de Grazia, pp. 599, 601–603. *Playboy* had a small measure of revenge when it ran a pictorial featuring women of 7-11, a chain of Southland Corporation convenience stores that pulled men's magazines from their shelves.

85. de Grazia, pp. 634–35.

86. See p. xvii of this text for the three-part test for determining whether a particular work is obscene that the U.S. Supreme Court established in *Miller v. California* (1973).

87. This account of the controversy over Mapplethorpe's works is based on de Grazia, pp. 622, 648–54.

88. Phillip Rawls, "Barnes & Noble indicted on child pornography charges," February 18, 1998, online at http://www.boston.com/globe/latest/daily/18/bn.htm.

89. Richtel, "Smut Purveyors Find Profits Online."

90. Anthony Flint, "Adults Only Spectrum," *Boston Globe,* December 1, 1996, pp. 1ff.

91. Carolyn Said, "Sex Sells on the Internet," *San Francisco Chronicle,* November 19, 1997, online at http://www.sfgate.com/cgibin/chronicle/article.cgi?file=BU3130.DTL&directory=/chronicle/archive/1997/11/19.

# 4

# THE RISKY BUSINESS OF ONLINE PORNOGRAPHY

*Whenever you wish to do anything against the law, Cicely,*
*always consult a good solicitor first.*
George Bernard Shaw, *Captain Brassbound's Conversion*

## THERE'S GOLD IN THEM THAR HILLS!

One hundred and fifty years ago, the first reports of James Marshall's discovery of gold at Sutter's Mill in California arrived in New York City via packet ships that took more than four months to round South America's Cape Horn. The reports of the discovery spread quickly by word of mouth, but the real kickoff for the California gold rush came when Eastern newspapers carried reports of President James K. Polk's 1849 State of the Union address, in which he confirmed the existence of California gold.

Despite the months-long delay in getting news stories from one coast to the other (compared to the scant seconds that Internet packets take today), the nation's nascent newspaper industry played an integral role in promoting the California gold rush, publishing a string of breathless (and often exaggerated) reports of miraculous finds and instantaneous riches. The bad news, of which there was plenty, traveled more slowly and often didn't make it into the papers at all: Of the tens of thousands of people who raced to California to search for gold, only a tiny percentage made a fortune (or even a living) from gold. Even worse, as many as 10,000 forty-niners died during the first year of the gold rush, succumbing to a combination of miserable living conditions, bad food, and poor medical care.

Over the last century and a half, neither the media nor the public has lost its appetite for gold rush stories. For instance, when the Powerball lottery exceeded $200 million in the summer of 1998, headlines from around the country  reflected the general tone of the coverage: "Lottery Ticket Buyers Go 'Crazy' over $250 Million Jackpot";[1] "Powerballers Creating Ticket Frenzy: Out-of-State Buyers Jam Lottery Outlets";[2] "Powerball Rolls on the Chaos Plateau—Chance at Quick Riches Makes Americans Light-headed."[3] Thanks in large part to the intensive coverage by the news media (most of which made only passing reference to Powerball's 80 million–to-1 odds, the regressive economic effects of lotteries, and the social costs of gambling addiction), Americans purchased more than 210 million Powerball tickets (at a cost of $1 each) in just four days. It took years to dig that much gold out of the California foothills.

The same fascination with the possibility of easy money fuels the coverage of the online pornography industry. In just the past year, for instance, articles have been published with titles like: "How to Make $$$$ with XXX" (*Wired*); "Porn Goes Mainstream" (*Time*); "Profits Push Spread of Web Porn" (MSNBC); "So, Just Who Would Run a Porn Site?" (MSNBC); "Sex Sells" (*Wired*); "Sex Sells on the Internet" (*San Francisco Chronicle*); "Sex Sites Fuel Web Payoff" (CNNfn); "Sex on the Net: Small Operators Can Make Big Killings on the Web" (*USA Today*); "Internet Indecency Thriving" (NPR); and "Smut Purveyors Find Profits Online" (*New York Times*).

While this is the first time that the economic possibilities of the pornography industry have been so favorably reported, it is not the first time that pornography has received extensive media attention. In the late 1950s and 1960s, in fact, the pornography industry even enjoyed a certain cachet. Hefner surburbanized his corner of the industry through his soft-focus pictures and businessmen-oriented clubs, and the exuberant luxuriousness of his own lifestyle obscured some of the harsher and seedier aspects of the pornography industry. At the same time, the ongoing battles to defend sexual expression in the finer arts gave the pornography industry important intellectual allies in its fight against censorship and regulation. Publishers like the Grove Press's Barney Rosset and the Olympia Press's Maurice Giradias, for instance, were praised for their courage in bringing to market such long-suppressed works as *Tropic of Cancer, Lady Chatterley's Lover, Lolita,* and *Naked Lunch.*

The media turned on the pornography industry in the early 1970s, however, as people grew increasingly concerned about the widespread availability of hardcore sexual materials. The "pubic wars" between *Playboy* and *Penthouse* and the arrival of *Hustler* stripped away much of the intellectual gloss of pornography; somehow, fighting to preserve an individual's right to look at misogynistic photos of women (let alone engage in phone sex) was less ennobling than defending their right to read *Ulysses* or *Tropic of Cancer*. Under pressure from conservative political and religious groups, the media's coverage of the industry grew steadily more critical; instead of hailing publishers of erotic literature as defenders of the First Amendment, long articles were written detailing the industry's treatment of women, the possible impact of pornography on the young, and the collateral impacts of porn shops and adult movie theaters (increased crime and urban blight).

The irony, of course, was that at the same time that the pornography industry was coming under increasing scrutiny for its alleged social consequences, its economic and entrepreneurial opportunities were exploding. Cable television, for instance, was moving away from its rural roots and attracting large numbers of subscribers in urban areas; the breakup of AT&T was making pay-per-call technology available to businesses of all descriptions; the VCR was beginning its remarkably swift infiltration into American households; and the first personal computers were marketed by IBM and Apple. There was, to be fair, some contemporary coverage of how the pornography industry was using these new technologies, but the slant of the articles was generally limited to the impact each new technology would have on the effort to control pornography. There were very few articles that highlighted the entrepreneurial potential of pornography in the late 1970s and early 1980s and even fewer profiles of successful smut peddlers.

The arrival of the World Wide Web revived the news media's fascination with the economic potential of the pornography industry. It's not simply that the media publish glowing reports about sexual entrepreneurs like Beth Mansfield, Danni Ashe, and Seth Warshavsky; such articles are a logical extension of the celebrity power that Hefner brought to pornography more than 40 years ago. It's that the media rediscovered the fact that pornography is an increasingly significant sector of the economy and that once again, pornography plays a prominent role in the adoption and development of a new technology.

The media's focus is increasingly on the remarkable growth in the number of *producers* of pornography, the number of people setting up adult Web sites, and the profits they are making. Like the reports from California a century and a half ago, there is just enough truth in the reports to swell the ranks of aspiring pornographers. For instance, while the revenues for pornography as a business sector trail such benign online stalwarts as computer software/hardware and travel, Web sex sites can in fact be lucrative: The 28,000 or so adult sites online gross at least $1 billion per year, and some observers estimate that total revenues are twice as high. It is in fact fairly easy to set up a business online, and the demand for sexually explicit materials is strong.

As with most other types of ventures, however, the reality of setting up and running a successful online pornography business is somewhat more complicated. Adult Web sites wink in and out of existence like quantum particles, and the chief reason is that many entrepreneurs mistake an exciting new medium and ridiculously low distribution costs for a new business model, one that frees them of the petty concerns that trouble entrepreneurs in the real world. As many former adult Web site operators attest, however, the real world (in the form of competitors, creditors, the Internal Revenue Service, and even law enforcement) has a nasty habit of upsetting even the most successful virtual business. As it turns out, a flourishing online pornography business is one that is not only financially successful but is also one that has met the basic commercial challenges that every new business must face—infrastructure, reliability, variety, competition, marketing, service, and value—and steers clear of the more severe consequences of peddling pornography: prosecution and conviction for copyright infringement, invasion of privacy, distribution of obscene materials, or the use of underage models.

# A RISKY BUSINESS

The pornography industry in the United States prospers on the strength of one simple economic concept: Consumers are willing to pay a premium for sexually explicit materials. Thus, for instance, *Playboy* and *Penthouse* can charge $5.95 and $6.95 per month, whereas more mainstream titles such as *Cosmopolitan* and *Vogue* (which themselves occasionally contain flashes of nudity) typically charge $3.95 and $4.95. Similarly, renting a copy of *Casablanca* might cost $2.95 at the local video store, whereas renting a grainy copy of *Debbie Does Dallas* will generally cost at least $1 more.

Various factors contribute to that premium, including the relatively large demand for sexual explicit materials, the comparatively limited number of sources,[4] and the social and political defiance implicit in the production and consumption of pornography. The most significant element in the cost of pornography, however, is the very real risk of criminal prosecution faced by each and every pornographer. Under the First Amendment to the U.S. Constitution, Americans have the right to sell or purchase pornography, but they do not have the right to sell or purchase obscenity. As hundreds of jailed pornographers have discovered, the line between what is pornographic and what is obscene shifts from county to county, and from one year to the next. It is, ultimately, a highly subjective determination. In 1954, the British philosopher Bertrand Russell told *Look* that obscenity "is whatever happens to shock some elderly and ignorant magistrate."[5] Ten years later, Justice Potter Stewart, an elderly but hardly ignorant U.S. Supreme Court justice, implicitly endorsed Russell's observation when he wrote that he could not intelligibly define obscenity, but "I knew it when I saw it."[6]

Stewart's comment underscores the problem that faces most pornographers, both online and off. In the abstract, at least, pornography is a product that is legal to produce, sell and consume. Precisely the same image, however, may be legal to sell in one area of the country and illegal in another. Even more confusingly, the legality of an image in a particular community may change if the demographics of the region change or if a new prosecutor is appointed or elected. Few other products (radar detectors are one) receive similar treatment; by and large, if a product can be sold in Georgia, it can also be sold in Oregon.

Whether there continues to be any real justification for a risk-related premium for pornography is a legitimate question. To the dismay of conservative watchdog groups, the threat of federal prosecution for obscenity has dropped sharply since President Clinton was elected.[7] Nonetheless, the cultural and polit-

ical shifts that have occurred over the last 25 years created a corps of well-organized antipornographers who are dedicated to a more aggressive policy of
enforcement at the state level and the adoption of national legislation aimed at
limiting the sale and distribution of sexually explicit materials. Antipornography
groups push for the appointment of more conservative federal prosecutors in the
hope that they will use the combination of enormous federal resources and
unsympathetic jurisdictions to rein in Internet pornography.

From the pornographer's perspective, concentrating on images of young
women makes sound economic sense. So long as accurate records are kept, the

Despite the ongoing antipornography activism, however, very few of the
numerous articles touting the economic potential of adult Web sites discuss the
very real threat of criminal prosecution or the extent to which the arrival of the
Internet complicates the issue. It is not an issue, however, that pornographers
ignore; few things are more disruptive to the operation of an adult business than
the owner's criminal trial and enforced vacation in a state or federal penitentiary.

## BUT SHE LOOKS 18!

The legal prohibition most likely to be crossed by an unwary pornographer is the
one that bars the sale or distribution of images of children under the age of 18.
Images of teens at or near their 18th birthday have proven to be a highly popular and lucrative subject for online pornography businesses. A quick search for
Web sites using the words "teen" or "schoolgirl" turns up hundreds of different
sites advertising both images and videos of teenage girls; a number of the sites,
in fact, claim that the photos they sell were taken on the model's 18th birthday.

From the pornographer's perspective, concentrating on images of young
women makes sound economic sense. So long as accurate records are kept, the
product is legal, and the closer that customers believe the models are to 18, the
heavier the demand. Although the membership cost for a teen site is generally no
higher than the cost at a nonteen site, the demand for images of young women
makes it easier for the Web site operator to attract subscribers or site traffic in the
first place, and more likely that subscribers will remain members.

Given the volume of competition even within the relatively narrow category of teen sites (in late December 1998, for instance, Yahoo! listed several
hundred adult Web sites with "teen" in the title or site description) and the
potential economic rewards, there is certainly a temptation for some Web site
operators to try to get around the age limit either by offering images of models
who look younger than 18 or by offering images of under-18 models that are
taken from a supposedly "safe" source (e.g., nudist magazines).[8] As a general rule
of thumb, however, adult Web site operators assume that *any* image of someone
under the age of 18 is ipso facto obscene and that distributing the image raises
the very real possibility of criminal prosecution and prison time.

A number of recent news reports illustrate the risks associated with the
production or distribution of nude images of children in any form. In February
1998, for instance, the national bookseller Barnes & Noble was indicted on 32

counts of child pornography in Montgomery, Alabama. The specific charges focused on two books by highly regarded photographers, *The Age of Innocence* by French photographer David Hamilton and *Radiant Identities* by San Francisco photographer Jock Sturges. Alabama State Attorney General Bill Pryor asserted that both books contain photos of nude children, and he told the Associated Press that the photographs are "designed to elicit a sexual response."[9] Barnes & Noble has been under attack in a number of areas of the country for its sale of these books, including an indictment on misdemeanor charges in November 1997 in Williamson County, Tennessee and a similar indictment in Alabama. The Tennessee charges were dropped, however, after Barnes & Noble agreed to move the books to a less child-accessible area of the store. In Alabama, state and local officials also dismissed the indictment after determining that the books were not obscene under state law.

Child pornography charges were also the basis of the 1997 ruling by Oklahoma District Judge Richard W. Freeman that the 1979 Academy Award–winning film *The Tin Drum* was obscene and could legally be seized. Following the state court's ruling, Oklahoma City police used library and video store records to track down and seize copies of the film from the public. In December 1997, U.S. District Court Judge Ralph Thompson ruled that the seizures were unlawful, and in October 1998, he declared that the film was not obscene because it did not appeal to prurient interests.

In a number of different states, including one as ostensibly liberal as Massachusetts, photography students have been interrogated or even arrested for taking nude photos of their children. While Massachusetts does not have a legal requirement that photo shops report suspected child pornography, the police will investigate if called. In November 1995, Toni Marie Angeli dropped off a set of photos of her nude four-year-old son. The owners of the shop were concerned about the photos and called the police, who met Angeli at the shop. When Angeli declined to answer questions, detectives handcuffed her and dragged her into the back room of the photo shop to arrest her. Ultimately, no charges were filed on the basis of child pornography, but Angeli served a 30-day sentence for disorderly conduct and malicious destruction of property that occurred during the arrest.

The efforts of prosecutors to stamp out child pornography are supported by a variety of federal and state laws. Under the terms of 18 U.S.C. § 2257, for instance, a pornography producer or distributor is required to check two forms of identification for each model or actor, and to maintain copies of each person's identification in the company's records. The law was passed expressly to deal with the issue of child pornography, which received considerable attention following the news that porn start Traci Lords had been arrested in May 1986 for making as many as 77 adult videos before turning 18.

In addition to the unequivocal bar against using nude models under the age of 18, federal law also prohibits the sale or distribution of images of adult women who are pretending to be under the age of 18, as well as computer-generated images of child pornography.[10] The latter ban, contained in the Child

Pornography Prevention Act of 1996, was the first time that Congress banned the sale and distribution of images that do not feature real people.

The legal risk of prosecution for child pornography is heightened by a common misunderstanding of the applicable federal law. A review of the materials available online makes clear that many adult Web site owners are under the mistaken impression that if they have not played an active role in creating an image of someone under the age of 18, they cannot be prosecuted under child pornography laws. That proves to be a dangerous misconception for pornographers. The applicable state and federal laws explicitly forbid not only the creation of child pornography, but also its distribution and even mere possession. Such provisions have repeatedly been upheld by the courts on the grounds that child pornography is not entitled to any First Amendment protection whatsoever.

## OUT OF THE BLUE: CROSS-COUNTRY OBSCENITY PROSECUTIONS

Even if an adult business scrupulously avoids displaying or distributing any images of anyone under the age of 18, there is still a risk that one or more communities around the country might decide that the business's materials are obscene. As we saw in the Introduction, the problem lies in the fact that the definition of what is obscene is generally quite subjective, and it often incorporates a moral component that varies from individual to individual and from community to community. For academics, social activists, and amateur philosophers, this makes for fascinating and long-running debates. For the operators of adult Web sites, however, the issue is one of much more immediate interest: Sell the wrong image to the wrong person in the wrong state and prison time is a distinct possibility. To make matters worse, under the terms of the U.S. Supreme Court's 1973 decision in *Miller*, each and every community in this country—every hamlet, burg, whistle stop, village, town, suburb, and city—is entitled to establish and enforce its own standards of obscenity (up to and including the limits of state law). Moreover, there is no requirement for consistency within a given state; what is considered obscene in one community may be thought merely "dirty" just a few miles away.

Pornography businesses in the real world that do not ship materials (an adult video store, for instance) have some degree of protection if they choose to traffic in sexually explicit materials, since the only obscenity standards with which they need concern themselves are those of the community in which the business is located. No prosecutor can successfully bring an obscenity case against a business in a different community if the only way to obtain the allegedly obscene materials is to travel to that adult business and bring the materials back to the other community.

The situation changes dramatically, however, if an adult business distributes sexually explicit materials by mail, telephone, or computer. In those circumstances, the business runs an increased risk that a federal prosecutor[11] from a more conservative jurisdiction will order materials from it, conclude that the materials distributed by the business to his or her community are obscene, and that the employees and operators of the business should be prosecuted accordingly. Such prosecutions can be brought, incidentally, even if the community in which the business is physically located has already concluded that the products are not obscene.

A sobering example of how such images can result in extrajurisdictional prosecution and incarceration occurred in Memphis, Tennessee. The defendants were Richard and Carleen Thomas, the owners and operators of the infamous Amateur Action, a subscription-only bulletin board system based in Milpitas,[12] California (just outside San Jose), that featured approximately 20,000 sexual images. In 1994, an undercover postal inspector in Memphis, Tennessee, joined the BBS, downloaded some sexual images, ordered an adult videotape, and sent some unsolicited child pornography to the Thomases. The postal inspector turned the materials over to the Tennessee U.S. attorney, who searched the Thomases's home and then indicted them on 11 counts of obscenity and 1 count of child pornography.[13]

The Thomases were tried before a Federal jury in Memphis, which found them guilty on all 11 obscenity counts and acquitted them of the child pornography count. In December 1994, Richard Thomas was sentenced to 37 months in prison and Carleen Thomas to 30 months. The Thomases appealed their convictions on the grounds that the court and jury should have applied the standards of the community in which their business was actually located or of cyberspace in general. In early 1996, however, the Court of Appeals for the Seventh Circuit rejected their appeal, and the U.S. Supreme Court refused to hear it. The Thomases, who have served their sentences, still face the payment of hefty fines.

There is little question that many juries would have concluded that the Thomases's products were obscene, since they specialized in images of sadomasochism and other hardcore topics, including bestiality. In 1992, however, the San Jose high-tech crime unit seized the Thomases's computers, spent several days examining the images, and concluded that none of them merited prosecution.[14]

The conviction of the Thomases in Memphis, 1800 miles from Milpitas, was of great concern to civil libertarians. They worried that the Thomases's case was a sign that the most restrictive local obscenity standard (from communities such as Memphis or Cincinnati) would end up becoming the de facto national standard, since any site on the Internet is accessible from any community in the country. In the five years since the Thomases's conviction, however, it seems increasingly likely that their case was *not* the start of a national wave of online obscenity prosecutions. Instead, the Thomases's case was a remarkable (and arguably excessive) use of new technology in the prosecution of a relatively routine obscenity case by a jurisdiction with a long history of aggressive action against pornography. Memphis, after all, was the city in which eight people were prosecuted in 1973 for their role in the creation and distribution of *Deep Throat*.

Another important factor in the Thomases's indictment and subsequent conviction is that they were among the first and certainly among the most brazen online sellers of pornography. They started their site as a bulletin board system in 1991, three years before the development of the World Wide Web. They aggressively advertised their BBS as "the nastiest place on Earth," and frequently attached extremely lewd (albeit inaccurate) descriptions to their images.[15] By 1994, they had more than 3,600 customers, each paying $99 per year for access to the Thomases's picture files.[16] While their marketing efforts were clearly a terrific success, it is not surprising that they became an attractive target for law enforcement.

Given the risk of seemingly random prosecution anywhere in the United States, it is remarkable that anyone would start a pornography business on the Internet. But there is safety to be found in two numbers: First, the more than 28,000 adult Web sites up and running make the practical likelihood of prosecution relatively small, and second, the more than $1 billion per year that online pornography sites generate helps persuade adult Web site owners that the potential economic return outweighs the relatively minor risk of prosecution. As much as they might like to do so, neither state nor federal prosecutors have the time or the resources to try to prosecute every particularly offensive adult Web site operator on the Internet.

In addition, there is a widespread awareness that the few prosecutions that take place are generally limited to the worst purveyors of pornography, primarily those that peddle child porn or bestiality. If someone starts a Web site to produce and sell photographs or videos of consenting adults in the nude or even engaged in heterosexual sex, the chances that the owner of that site will be prosecuted for obscenity anywhere in this nation are now exceedingly low. Since that describes the general nature of the product for the vast majority of the nation's adult Web sites, most online sexual entrepreneurs go about their daily affairs without looking over their shoulder to see if the sheriff is coming.

Of course, as an adult business's stock-in-trade moves further from the mainstream, the chances of being prosecuted increase. Since there are portions of this country, for instance, where it remains illegal to engage in homosexual activity even in the privacy of one's bedroom, there is some risk of prosecution by a particularly conservative community for the display and distribution of images of gay or lesbian sex. Images of sadomasochism and dominant and submissive behavior are probably in the next-highest category of risk, largely because of the combination of violence and sex (one of the legacies of the extremes to which the "roughies and kinkies" went in the 1960s). And while not automatically obscene, images of sexual behavior involving humans and animals, excrement, and incest (even implied) are by far the riskiest to peddle.

Some adult Web site operators try to reduce their risk of prosecution by refusing to accept subscribers from certain areas of the country. Many adult businesses like Adam & Eve or Xandria that ship products around the country are very careful about what products they ship to each region of the country. In some cases, in fact, an adult mail-order business will refuse to fill any order from communities or even entire states that have restrictive laws on obscenity or particularly aggressive records of prosecution. Increasingly, online businesses are following suit, particularly those that create and sell hardcore images. For instance, Zmaster, a prominent producer of legal/licensed adult images, recommends to its customers that they require each subscriber to agree to strict terms and conditions for accessing adult materials and that the Web site screen out potential customer from specific zip codes in Alabama, Arkansas, Florida, Georgia, Illinois, Indiana, Kansas, Kentucky, Louisiana, Mississippi, Missouri, Nebraska, North Carolina, Oklahoma, Pennsylvania, South Carolina, South Dakota, Tennessee, Texas, Utah, Virginia, and West Virginia.[17]

## THERE OUGHTA BE A LAW!

As most adult Web site operators are by now undoubtedly aware, there are numerous efforts to pass both state and federal legislation which would make the online distribution of sexually explicit materials much riskier. The most well-publicized effort, of course, was the passage by Congress of the Communications Decency Act (CDA) in 1996. Sponsored in part by Senator Dan Coats (R-Ind.) and former Senator Jim Exon (D-Neb.) and by Representatives Henry Hyde (R-Ill.) and Rick White (R-Wash.), the bill criminalized the knowing transmission of obscenity and/or the knowing sending or display of indecent material to children. The day the CDA was signed into law by President Clinton, the American Civil Liberties Union and a large number of co-plaintiffs filed suit to stop implementation of the legislation. After a lengthy hearing, a specially constituted U.S. District Court in Philadelphia declared that the portion of the act that barred the transmission of "indecent material" was unconstitutional. Attorney General Janet Reno appealed the court's decision to the U.S. Supreme Court, but the high court agreed in June 1997 that the efforts of the legislation to limit the dissemination of "indecent speech" were unconstitutional.[18] Writing for the majority, Justice Byron White concluded:

> We agree with the District Court's conclusion that the CDA places an unacceptably heavy burden on protected speech, and that the defenses do not constitute the sort of "narrow tailoring" that will save an otherwise patently invalid unconstitutional provision. In Sable, 492 U. S., at 127, we remarked that the speech restriction at issue there amounted to "burn[ing] the house to roast the pig." The CDA, casting a far darker shadow over free speech, threatens to torch a large segment of the Internet community.[19]

The Supreme Court's decision was a serious setback for the antipornography forces in Congress (and their supporters), but few adult Web site operators were celebrating. Immediately following the announcement of the Supreme Court's decision, Senator Coats announced his intention to introduce a revamped version of the Communications Decency Act that in his opinion would pass constitutional muster. Less than four months later, he filed S. 1482, a bill aimed at prohibiting the commercial distribution on the Internet "of material that is harmful to minors." Known colloquially as the U.S. Child Online Protection Act, the bill would require that distributors of such material block child access to it by obtaining credit card numbers or by using a system of personal identification numbers. The bill did not receive independent consideration on the floor of Congress, but instead was passed when it was attached as an amendment to a massive year-end appropriations bill in the spring of 1998.

As with its predecessor, the new act was challenged immediately by the usual suspects, led once again by the ACLU. On November 19, 1998, U.S. District Court Judge Lowell Reed issued a preliminary injunction barring enforcement of the act and scheduled a hearing for January 1999 on whether a permanent injunction should be issued. After hearing five days of testimony, Judge Reed permanently enjoined enforcement of the act, concluding in part that "the plaintiffs have established a substantial likelihood that they will be able to show that [the act] imposes a burden on speech that is protected for adults."[20] In a somewhat unusual personal statement, Judge Reed acknowledged the compelling issues raised by pornography on the Internet:

> Despite the Court's personal regret that this preliminary injunction will delay once again the careful protection of our children, I without hesitation acknowledge the duty imposed on the Court and the greater good such duty serves. Indeed, perhaps we do the minors of this country harm if First Amendment protections, which they will with age inherit fully, are chipped away in the name of their protection.[21]

Unlike the earlier bill, the Child Online Protection Act does not contain any provision for expedited review, which means that any appeal must be heard first by the United States Court of Appeals for the 3rd Circuit in Philadelphia and then (most likely) by the U.S. Supreme Court. After considerable internal debate, the Clinton Administration's Justice Department appealed Judge Reed's decision on April 1, 1999— the last day on which it could do so. A decision by the Third Circuit is not expected until the fall of 1999, and a decision by the U.S. Supreme Court (if an appeal is filed and the Supreme Court agrees to hear it) will probably not occur until the spring of 2001.

In an interview with CNN in December 1998, ACLU senior counsel Chris Hansen pointed out that enforcement of the act would mean that many nonsexual sites, including most news organizations, would be in violation of the law if they posted copies of the Starr Report on their Web sites.[22] "The Starr Report contains passages that are almost certainly in violation of this law, but you could put the report up on a government or other site if there's no advertising there," Hansen said. The ACLU attorney also pointed out the law would make it illegal for some sites to distribute "descriptive medical information about sex, genitalia, or breasts."

Peggy Peterson, spokeswoman for Representative Michael Oxley (the primary sponsor of the Child Online Protection Act in the House of Representatives), dismissed as "bogus" the concerns that the act would bar Web postings of the Starr Report. "The Starr Report," Peterson told the *New York Times*, "does not even approach the harmful-to-minors standard."[23]

If so, it is not for a lack of trying. The following, for instance, is an excerpt from Starr's description of the first sexual encounter between President Clinton and Monica Lewinsky, which occurred on November 15, 1995 (footnotes omitted):

> According to Ms. Lewinsky, she and the President kissed. She unbuttoned her jacket; either she unhooked her bra or he lifted her bra up; and he touched her breasts with his hands and mouth. Ms. Lewinsky testified: "I believe he took a phone call . . . and so we moved from the hallway into the back office. . . . [H]e put his hand down my pants and stimulated me manually in the genital area." While the President continued talking on the phone (Ms. Lewinsky understood that the caller was a Member of Congress or a Senator), she performed oral sex on him. He finished his call, and, a moment later, told Ms. Lewinsky to stop. In her recollection: "I told him that I wanted . . . to complete that. And he said . . . that he needed to wait until he trusted me more. And then I think he made a joke . . . that he hadn't had that in a long time."

It is difficult to predict right now how much, if any, of the Child Online Protection Act will survive judicial scrutiny. The "harmful to minors" standard has been upheld by federal and state courts, although not in conjunction with anything as vast and essentially private as the Internet. The only thing that can be said with reasonable certainty is that if the ruling goes against the antipornography forces, they will continue their efforts to pass federal antipornography legislation.

It is important to note that Judge Reed's injunction against the act relieves adult Web sites of the threat of federal—but not state—prosecution. Over the last few years, there has been just as much if not more antipornography legislation passed at the state level than at the federal. Most recently, legislators in Tennessee, Rhode Island, Illinois, and New Mexico have all filed legislation in this area, seeking to join a number of other states that already have or are considering laws regulating online speech.[24] It is not clear that these laws are constitutional, particularly given the U.S. Supreme Court's decision in *ACLU v. Reno*, and the ACLU's successful application of the language of the Court's opinion to help overturn state laws in Georgia, Virginia, and New York.[25]

Until a court rules that a particular state law limiting online speech is unconstitutional, however, state officials can still initiate prosecutions under it. Most state prosecutors, though, are unwilling to commit the time and resources necessary to bring a prosecution when there is a substantial risk that any conviction would be overturned. As a result, prosecutors in states that purport to regulate online speech have made little use of the laws so far. Nonetheless, the very existence of such laws adds weight to the suggestion of Web content providers such as Zmaster that online pornographers attempt to limit the areas of the country with which they do business.

# CIVIL LIABILITY

While a criminal conviction is obviously a serious penalty for peddling obscene materials, a much more concrete and immediate legal threat for most adult Web site operators is the potential for civil litigation. Inevitably, the sheer level of competition (particularly on the World Wide Web) pushes pornographers to engage in business practices that range from the irritating to the infuriating to the plainly illegal. As many legal observers have noted, the entry costs for litigation—the amount of irritation or injury that someone is willing to suffer before filing suit—have dropped at least as quickly as the cost of distributing information. In fact, litigation has become a gold rush of its own, thanks in part to multimillion-dollar verdicts for everything from spilled coffee to overturned vehicles.

In the steadily growing online pornography industry, the two most common grounds for civil litigation right now are infringements of copyright and misappropriation of trade name and trademark. The legal principles governing copyright are fairly clear-cut, even on the Internet—either a business owns or has leased the rights to the material it is distributing or it has not. The chief problem with respect to copyright online, however, is the near impossibility of tracking down every site that might have an illegal copy of a particular image. The development of electronic watermarks and software that can search the Web for images with particular watermarks will speed up the collection of information about copyright infringers, but will do little to speed up the process of sending out a cease-and-desist letter or filing suit to stop the infringement.

It is precisely this type of illegal copying that has music and video producers so concerned. The recent development of the MP3 standard for compressing music, for instance, now makes it possible to store an entire music CD in thirty to forty megabytes of storage space with no discernable loss of quality. That is still a fairly large file, but not one so huge that it can't be downloaded in a reasonable period of time, particularly by college students with access to high-speed Internet connections. The combination of improved compression techniques and faster Internet connections will continue to plague the owners of copyrighted materials.

## THE PLAYBOY DILEMMA:
## COPYRIGHT IN A DIGITAL WORLD

The very quality that makes the Internet such a dynamic medium—its ability to transport information from one corner of the globe to another in seconds—is deeply unnerving for the people who create or hold the copyright to creative works such as articles, books, photographs, songs, videotapes, films, and software. The problem lies in the fluidity of data: Once a particular creative work has been transformed into digital information, it can easily be copied and distributed hundreds or even millions of times without a single penny being paid to the copyright holder for royalties or licensing fees. Just as computers on the Internet make no judgments about the morality of the bits that they transmit, they also do not pause to evaluate whether a song (or an entire CD, for that matter) is a legal or bootleg copy.

Some of the problems with protecting copyrights online can be traced to the way in which Internet browsers work. When a computer user instructs his or her browser to visit a particular Web site (for instance, www.playboy.com), the browser looks up Playboy's address, locates the appropriate computer, and then makes a copy of the home page for Playboy, including any text, photographs, or video. The copied information is sent back to the user's computer, where the various components of Playboy's home page are arranged on the user's screen. At the same time, the copied information is stored temporarily in the user's computer (in a special subdirectory known as a *cache*) in case any of it can be used to help display other pages on the same Web site. Just in the normal course of surfing the Web, every computer user makes dozens or hundreds of copies of copyrighted material, much of which remains stored in the user's cache for days or even weeks (the precise length of time depends on how much the user surfs the Web, since older material is pushed out by newer copies). There's nothing illegal about that; an operator of a Web site effectively gives each visitor to his or her site a limited license to copy the information on the Web site so that the visitor can actually see the Web site in question. If the Web site operator refused to allow visitors to make these necessary copies, there would be no way for the visitors to actually see the Web site, which would essentially defeat the whole purpose of the Web.

There are two small problems, however. First of all, with only a little effort, someone can view the various files stored in the browser's cache (using say Adobe's Photoshop or the shareware program Paint Shop Pro), save them in another directory on his or her hard drive, and then use the images for purposes not authorized by the Web site owner: on another Web site, for instance, or in a company newsletter. Second, the Windows versions of both major browsers

(Netscape's Navigator and Microsoft's Internet Explorer) make the copying of materials online extremely easy. Text can be highlighted, copied into the Windows clipboard, and then pasted into any other Windows application. Images can be copied by the simple expedient of right-clicking on the image and selecting "Save image" from the menu options. Most other materials located on Web sites can be copied just as easily.

Illegal copying of copyrighted photos for online distribution, of course, has been a problem for *Playboy* since the first day that someone thought to hook together a personal computer and a scanner. During the heyday of the bulletin board system in the early 1990s, computer owners and BBS operators around the country wore out their scanners by converting thousands of printed photographs into electronic files that could be sent around the world in seconds. In 1992, the magazine filed suit against Event Horizons, one of the nation's largest bulletin boards, for copyright infringement and ultimately settled out of court for an estimated $500,000 payment from the BBS.

The explosive growth of the World Wide Web and the establishment of nearly 30,000 or so adult Web sites has significantly complicated the efforts of a *Playboy* or *Penthouse* to protect its intellectual property. Once, images were scattered on relatively isolated bulletin board systems (only a fraction of which amounted to any significant size); now an image that is scanned into a computer and posted on a Web page can be accessed from or sent anywhere in the world for the price of a local phone call. Thanks to the inherent capabilities of browsers and the automation capabilities of programs like PictureAgent, a single scanned image posted to an Internet newsgroup or Web site can be copied and saved by hundreds or thousands of people in a single day.

Similarly, an entrepreneur armed with a $300 optical scanner, sufficient disk space, and a couple of free days can easily copy a decade's worth of *Playboy* photos into an online image gallery. (Visits to some of the adult Web sites reveals how many individuals have done just that.) It also is increasingly easy to do the same thing with videotapes—the only thing slowing down the wholesale copying of video is the amount of disk space each video takes up and the relative slowness of Internet transmission speeds. Over the next two to three years, as new high-speed transmission methods become available, the amount of video and film available online will increase dramatically, and it is a safe bet that a significant portion of it will be illegal copies of existing commercial videotapes.

The ease with which material can be copied from Web sites or newsgroups for use in other Web sites does not make it legal, of course. Federal law prohibits the unauthorized copying of a protected work,[26] and Internet users should assume, unless explicitly told otherwise, that everything that they see online is protected.[27] Industry organizations (such as the Software Publishers Association) and individual corporations (such as Playboy Enterprises) are spending large amounts of time and money to figure out ways to police online copying, and they have shown little hesitation in pursuing both civil and criminal remedies. Although the size of the Web and the number of adult sites online may give a sense of security ("How are they going to find my little site of illegally copied *Playboy* and *Penthouse* photos?"), it is and should be illusory.

If the only means that magazines such as *Playboy* and *Penthouse* had to enforce their copyrights was to visit each adult Web site and check for infringements, the sheer number of adult Web sites would certainly offer some protection, particularly for smaller businesses. Not surprisingly, however, if software can be developed to automatically harvest images from newsgroups and the Web, then software can surely be developed to automate the search for copyright violations. A number of companies, including Playboy Enterprises, are aggressively supporting the development of software that can encode a digital watermark on images that are posted on a Web site. The leading producer of digital watermarking software is currently Digimarc Corp.,[28] which has licensed its PictureMarc software to most online stock photo agencies and a number of larger publications, including *Playboy*.[29] Using a process known as *steganography*, the software changes some of the pixels within the photo in a specific prearranged pattern unique to the owner of the copyright of the image. Many of the photo-editing programs on the market today are able to recognize digital watermarks and display ownership information when a watermarked image is loaded into the program.

As an adjunct to its PictureMarc software, Digimarc has also developed a Web spider program called MarkSpider. Web spiders are software programs that are designed to search Web sites on their own without human guidance, looking for specific information. Similar programs are used by Web search sites such as AltaVista and Lycos to compile indices of the words used in different Web sites. The MarkSpider program, however, searches Web sites for images containing specific watermarks. It visits more than 100 million separate Web pages each month, compiling a list for each registered watermark user of the sites on which their images appear.[30] Copyright holders can then examine the list to make sure that no unauthorized usage is taking place.

The owners of trademarks are also facing new challenges on the Internet. By and large, however, the structure and design of the Internet makes it somewhat easier to resolve trademark disputes. In 1983, programmers at the University of Wisconsin developed what is known as the Domain Name System, in which words can be substituted for a computer's four-part numeric address.[31] Thus, for instance, the home page of Together Networks, a Vermont Internet service provider, has an Internet Protocol address of 204.97.120.30 and a text address "www.together.net." They both will take a Web surfer to the same location, but one is much easier to remember. When a computer user types in the text version of the address into his or her browser, the software instructs the Internet service provider to contact a computer known as a root server, find the numeric address associated with "www.together.net," and connect the user to the corresponding computer.

In turn, the receiving computer looks at the address that the user is requesting, and from that address, knows what type of information to send back to the browser. For each Internet address, the first part of the address specifies the type of resource (i.e.,"www" for World Wide Web, "ftp" for File Transfer Protocol, and so forth). The second part of the address is the name of the business, individual or organization that owns the domain name (i.e., "together" for Together Networks, "microsoft" for Microsoft Corp., etc.).[32] The third part of the name indicates the type of business or organization that owns the name (i.e., "com" for commercial businesses, "org" for organizations, "gov" for government agencies, "edu" for educational institutions, and "net" for networks). Thus, if an Internet user connects to "www.together.net," the computer at the receiving end knows that the user is looking for the home or default Web page of "Together Networks," and sends the appropriate data back to the user's computer.

This universal naming system, which is one of the great strengths of the Internet, has raised some challenging trademark issues. The primary problem is that while there can be hundreds if not thousands of independent restaurants named "Main Street Grill" across the country, each happily running a business and using the same name in ads in its own community, only one of those restaurants can create a Web site with the domain name "www.mainstreetgrill.com." If more than one business has the right to use a particular name or trademark, the domain name is generally assigned to the first one to register the name.

During the first two or three years the domain naming system was in existence, Network Solutions (the company then charged with supervising domain names) did not check to see whether the person registering a trademarked name was actually entitled to it. As the World Wide Web started to grow in popularity, some savvy entrepreneurs (derisively nicknamed "cybersquatters") realized that when corporations began going online, they would want to use domain names that were similar to their real world trademarks. Cybersquatters began registering large numbers of potentially lucrative domain names (paying only $100 per name) and then held them hostage, hoping for big payoffs from companies like MTV and McDonald's.

Not surprisingly, however, many corporations with registered trademarks were unenthusiastic about paying some entrepreneur a fee for a name that they felt should be theirs in the first place. A variety of different businesses and organizations lobbied President Clinton and Congress for assistance, and in January 1996, President Clinton signed the Federal Trademark Dilution Act of 1995.[33] Under the terms of the law, an individual or business cannot use a word or phrase as a domain name if its use will dilute the distinctive quality of an existing trademark. In the four years since the law was signed, the courts have not hesitated to apply it to the activities of cybersquatters, and the speculation over trademark domain names has largely ceased. Now, in order to register a domain name, an applicant must show that he or she is entitled to use that name in commerce. Although speculation has largely died down,[34] controversy has not: it is not uncommon for two companies to each have a legal right to use a particular name or trademark, albeit in different parts of the country or different businesses. Under those circumstances, it is still generally first come, first served. For instance, Ford Motor Company would no doubt like to have the domain name "www.taurus.com," but a California software company beat them to it.

The trademark situation is complicated by the fact that Internet computers can only access those domain names that are actually registered with the Internet's central database of addresses. Unlike their human counterparts, computers are remarkably literal in their behavior: even if "www.apple.com" is registered as the domain name for Apple Computer (which it is), a computer will not know how to handle the address "www.applecomputer.com" unless it too is linked to the numeric address of Apple's Internet computer. (Compare the literal behavior of computers with the behavior of the U.S. Post Office, which over the years has grown adept at delivering letters addressed to "James Scarff, 66 Lyman Road" to *Janet* Scarff, 62 Lyman *Avenue.*) As a result, corporations such as Microsoft, Coca-Cola, Ford, or Playboy may register dozens of domain names and their variants in an effort to limit confusion and help their customers find them. In very unusual circumstances, a compromise has to be reached: so many people typed the address "www.titanic.com" into their browser, expecting to find information on the movie, that a temporary Web page was set up to offer people a choice between the real Web site for *Titanic* ("www.titanicmovie.com") and the Web site for the company that first registered the address, a California manufacturer of computer games.

The pornography industry has exacerbated trade name and trademark problems on the Internet by trying to capitalize on the literalness of computers by registering domain names that are very similar to more famous sites. For instance, a particularly popular practice of pornographers (both online and off) is to mimic or parody a nonpornographic business in an effort to trade off of that business's economic goodwill. Known as "spoofing," the process has raised a lot of concerns for both educators and librarians, who have had to deal with children accidentally (or not so accidentally) accessing inappropriate material. During the summer of 1997, for instance, the operator of a pornographic Web site registered the domain name "www.whitehouse.com" (the real address of the White House is "www.whitehouse.gov"). In part because of the similarity of names and in part because of the notoriety the site received in the press,[35] "www.whitehouse.com" generated (and continues to generate) a high level of traffic. Many people looking for the virtual tour of the White House arrive at a very different destination. A similar tactic was used to spoof NASA's Web site during the Mars Pathfinder mission; visitors who went to "nasa.com" instead of "nasa.gov" were greeted with offers to purchase access to a gallery of sexually explicit photos. Shortly after the spoof site was set up, NASA complained to the organization in charge of registering domain names, and the site was shut down.[36]

The competition among online pornography sites for customers and traffic is certainly ferocious, and the temptation to use or spoof a highly recognizable name is understandable. Although operators of adult Web sites who spoof a famous name may realize some short term benefits, they also expose themselves to possible litigation and the online pornography industry as a whole to the threat of increased governmental regulation. During the recent debates over methods for restricting online pornography, for instance, the confusion caused by sites like "www.whitehouse.com" and "www.nasa.com" was frequently cited as a justification for governmental restrictions on adult material online. Wholly apart from the legal fees incurred in defending against infringement suits, spoofing well-known commercial names simply adds fuel to the efforts to restrict the distribution of adult materials online.

The dispute over similar domain names will only intensify as browser companies and Web site operators develop new tools designed to make it easier for Internet users to locate well-known sites. For instance, in the latest versions of its browser software, Netscape has implemented a feature called "Smart Browsing." This feature allows users to type keywords (like "White House" into the address bar instead of the site's actual address ("www.whitehouse.gov"); Netscape looks up the word in database of Web sites that it created and maintains, and then connects the user to the Web site associated with the keyword(s). As the trade publication *Adult Video News* pointed out, this capability gives Netscape enormous power in determining which sites should be associated with which keywords. For instance, although both "www.whitehouse.gov" and "www.whitehouse.com" might use the same keywords (i.e., "white house"), a user who types "white house" will automatically be connected to the White House rather than "www.whitehouse.com". The owner of "www.whitehouse.com", Dan Parisi, has written to Netscape challenging its new keyword system and is currently considering a lawsuit against the browser company.

Some, of course, may not see a problem with Netscape's new feature. Smart Browsing is a relatively effective way to protect casual browsers from spoofs like "www.whitehouse.com." The system, however, is not a complete shield against pornography. For starters, entering a complete address in the browser—"www.whitehouse.com"—will take a user directly to the adult site. In addition, the Smart Browsing database will return a list of adult sites in response to certain key words that haven't been assigned to nonadult sites. Enter "xxx," for instance, and Smart Browsing returns a list of seven Web sites with "xxx" or "x-x-x" in the domain name; enter the keyword "breast," and up pops the front page for an adult Web site called "climax.com." Further experiments are left to the imagination. Clearly, however, the legal and economic implications of systems like Smart Browsing are only just beginning to be explored.

## IT MAY BE A DIRTY BUSINESS, BUT IT'S STILL A BUSINESS

Thanks in large part to the waves of downsizing that have struck the U.S. economy over the last several years, a wealth of information is available about starting home businesses in a staggering array of different fields. The shelves of the nation's bookstores groan under the weight of hundreds of different books designed to educate potential business owners about virtually every aspect of starting and running a new business. Admittedly, none of the books discusses the particular legal and social challenges faced by sexual entrepreneurs, but the basic information contained in such books as Paul Hawken's *Growing a Business* or Eric Tyson and Jim Schell's *Small Business for Dummies* is as applicable to adult businesses as it is to less salacious ventures. For example, if an online pornography business is not only going to survive but prosper, it is important that the business have a plan for operation and growth, establish good record-keeping practices, prepare a yearly budget, create and follow systems in place for handling money, and meet all state and federal tax obligations. The fact that the business's chief product is several thousand sexually explicit images or access to a live video-conference with a naked 22-year-old does not alter or eliminate the basic requirements of running the business.

## BUSINESS STRUCTURE AND CAPITALIZATION

The most profound impact of the Internet for entrepreneurs is that it makes it far easier for sole proprietors and small partners to compete on a nearly equal footing with far larger businesses than is possible on Main Street. There are two primary reasons for this trend toward parity. First, the Internet's intrinsic limitation on display space upends a fundamental retail assumption, that companies with greater economic resources are able to afford more shelf space, bigger buildings, and sports stadiums with their names on them, all of which give them a significant competitive advantage over less well-heeled competitors. On the Internet, however, every business is essentially limited to the same size storefront: the display space of each visitor's monitor. Regardless of the economic resources of a business or the amount of material it has stored on its Web site, a potential Internet customer is still only going to be able to see one screen at a time. The finite sales space available to online businesses puts an enormous premium not only on the creativity of a Web site's layout, but also on the quality of the site's products and services. As Microsoft itself discovered with its largely ignored Microsoft Network, enormous financial resources on the Internet are meaningless if consumers don't like the product.

Second, the Internet essentially wipes out the old saw "Location, location, location." The entire purpose of the Web and HTML, after all, is to relieve Internet surfers of the burden of knowing where a particular piece of information is stored. The important thing is that the information exists and is accessible across the network, not the appearance or location of the building in which the information is stored. On the World Wide Web, all Web addresses are essentially equal; from the user's perspective, there is little practical difference between the Web address for Playboy ("www.playboy.com") and the Web address for CNN ("www.cnn.com"). It takes no longer to get to one site than the other, and the pornography site is not located in a "bad" section of the Internet.

This implicit equality of Web addresses is particularly important within a particular industry. The same address parity that exists between sexual and nonsexual sites also exists between pornography businesses with enormous resources (e.g., Playboy Enterprises) and much smaller operations (as, for instance, Jen and Dave, a husband-and-wife team who operate a Web site featuring sexually explicit photos and videos of the couple). Admittedly, some Web addresses are more equal than others: A corporation the size of Playboy Enterprises can afford faster connections, bigger computers, the latest software, and a team of professionals to keep everything working, all of which help improve visitor access. Nonetheless, the basic fact remains unaltered: it is generally just as easy and quick to access the Web site at "www.jen-dave.com" as it is to visit "www.playboy.com," despite Playboy's enormous institutional advantages.[37] Moreover, as we'll see in later chapters, the constant downward spiral of technology costs makes it possible for small sites to remain competitive with much larger ones.

## MARKETING AND COMPETITION

If an entrepreneur decides to set up an adult video shop in a particular community, he or she will probably have a pretty good idea about the nature and extent of the competition. There may be one or two other independent video stores, a couple of Blockbuster franchises (which don't really compete in the category of adult films), and a half-dozen miscellaneous establishments that carry a few adult videos (e.g., convenience stores, gas stations, grocery stores). As a practical matter, however, the entrepreneur will only be competing with those stores within a few minutes drive of her own; the entrepreneur does not have to worry about what video stores on the other side of the state are doing or even (if it is big enough) the other side of the city. That makes it much easier to study the competition and figure out whether to compete on price, selection, service, or some combination of all three.

The mythical entrepreneur might also look at the economics of setting up a physical video store and decide that the advantages of running the shop on the Internet (no need for city licenses, no hassles with neighbors, no rent or mortgage, no property taxes, lower personnel and utility costs, less chance of being robbed) far outweigh those of opening a street-corner adult video store. The enormous advantages of Internet business, however, do carry one significant cost: the necessity of competing at the national and (increasingly) international level.

As we saw in the preceding section, geography has relatively little meaning online. A consumer can just as easily support a business based halfway around the world as he or she can one that is just down the street. As a result, an online business is realistically competing with every similar business in the entire world. If an adult video store in Seattle offers a popular video for the low, low cost of $19.95, the only competitors who will care are those in the immediate geographic area; the store's price cut will likely have no impact on stores in Miami or Chicago, for instance.

The situation on the Internet is precisely the reverse. Since there is no additional cost to visiting a Web site in Los Angeles or one in Boston, every online business competes with every other adult business in the same market sector. If any adult video store runs a sale on the Internet, it pressures every other adult video store to do the same thing.

The broadening of the competitive market has had a number of different consequences. One of the most obvious is to continually increase the amount of pornography online and to reduce the cost of accessing it. The myriad sites that peddle sexually explicit images compete in part by trying to offer the largest number of images (a few sites now claim to have more than a million different images available) and in part by turning their sites into minimalls of sexual activity. Standard fare for a well-equipped adult Web site these days, for instance, is a huge collection of still images, a slightly smaller collection of grainy video clips and video feeds that recall the "loops" of the early 1960s, a variety of chat rooms for sexually explicit discussion, a library of erotic stories, a sexual toy shop, and frequently, interactive video conferencing with models or couples that customers pay for separately by the minute. At one time, a monthly membership in an adult Web site with those types of resources would have cost $24.95 or $29.95; today, the cost is more typically $9.95 per month, and some sites have even dropped below that.

Despite the ferocity of the competition, however, adult Web site owners are still finding ways to distinguish their businesses. Among the most popular offerings they count on are content that is unavailable anywhere else (a typical pitch of amateur sites such as Jen and Dave); better organization of the materials on the business's Web site or on the Internet in general (i.e., comprehensive link sites); increased ease of use, so that customers can readily find what they're looking for; increased speed, so that customers wait as little time as possible for materials to download; frequent updating of material, so that customers don't see the same old stuff every time they visit the Web site; and in certain rare instances, the possibility of meeting the person or person(s) featured on the Web site. In fact, a number of individual Web site operators schedule parties where they meet and take photos with members of their online fan clubs.

Another way to effectively compete amid the throng of online pornography sites, of course, is to use an already well-established brand name. Obviously, that is not an option for most site operators, but has enabled such well-known pornographers as *Playboy, Penthouse,* and *Hustler* to quickly become three of the most heavily trafficked adult Web sites. In the summer of 1998, for instance, Playboy Enterprises CEO Christie Hefner announced that the company's main site was receiving roughly 65.5 million page views per month, or more than 2 million each day.[38] Somewhat surprisingly, despite the enormous number of visitors, the Playboy site has been unable to do what many far smaller sites have been able to do: make money. At the same time that Hefner was touting the size of the site's audience, she also announced that while Playboy Online's revenues grew to $1.6 million for the 2d quarter of 1998, the division had lost $1.5 million during the same period.

## FIGHT CENSORSHIP: HUG A LAWYER

The impressive economic resources that pornography businesses have traditionally enjoyed have given them the ability to hire top-notch legal assistance, which over the years has played a substantial role in both protecting and expanding the First Amendment freedoms that are so crucial to the pornography industry's existence. One might imagine that close association with the pornography industry would tarnish an attorney's reputation, much as often happens to lawyers who represent the mob, South American drug lords, or the tobacco companies. Traditionally, however, attorneys that represent the pornography industry have succeeded in portraying their work, both in court and out, as not so much a defense of a particular individual or business as a defense of the Constitution and the basic free speech rights of every American.

That view was strained somewhat when Alan L. Isaacman defended Larry Flynt's savage satirical attack on the Reverend Jerry Falwell in the late 1980s, and it has been further strained by Isaacman's new client, Seth Warshavsky's Internet Entertainment Group, which made headlines recently for its successful efforts to publish nude photos of the conservative talk show host Dr. Laura Schlessinger and the sexually explicit honeymoon videotape of Pamela Anderson and Tommy Lee.[39] Nonetheless, Isaacman was very sympathetically portrayed by actor Ed Norton in the 1997 movie *The People vs. Larry Flynt*.

A number of other attorneys have also gained favorable publicity for their experience and expertise in this area. One of the leading private practitioners, for instance, is Clyde DeWitt, a partner in the Los Angeles law firm of Weston, Garrou & DeWitt. A regular contributor to *Adult Video News*, DeWitt has developed a national law practice representing people in the adult entertainment industry and working on pornography-related issues. At the Electronic Frontier Foundation, staff counsel Mike Godwin has taken a leading role in opposing such legislative efforts as the Communications Decency Act, which would have restricted the distribution and dissemination of pornography on the Internet. Similarly, ACLU President Nadine Strossen, author of *Defending Pornography*, has been an aggressive opponent of laws aimed at restricting the sale and purchase of pornography. As she recently told a California conference of attorneys, academics, and sex workers, "My very strong impression is that the tide has turned." She added "Of the $10 billion sex industry, it's not ten perverts spending $1 billion a year."[40]

## THE INTERNET: A WORLD WIDE PRIMER ON STARTING AN ADULT WEB SITE

If there is one thing that will prevent the publication of an *Adult Web Site for Beginners,* it is that everything that could be put in such a book is already available to entrepreneurs online.  From the perspective of pornography opponents, it is not bad enough that the Internet has globalized the production and sale of pornography, ratcheted up its potential profits, and made sexually explicit materials readily available in every living room, library, and school in the country. What is worse is that the Internet is steadily eroding many of the traditional objections to the pornography industry, in large part because the Web has substantially reduced the social costs of learning enough about pornography and the industry to successfully run an adult Web site.

It has never been easier to research a sector of the pornography industry, learn how to compete with existing businesses, and locate product suppliers. In the so-called real world, of course, the process of learning enough about the pornography industry in order to set up and run a successful adult business was and generally still is unpleasant and often dangerous. In most urban areas, for instance, sex shops and adult movie theaters are generally segregated in seedy or rundown areas of the city, and any effort to learn about how the businesses work, how much money they make, or who supplies their products are actively and often aggressively discouraged. By contrast, a prospective pornography entrepreneur can quickly and easily access a wealth of adult Web sites from the privacy of his or her home. With a few clicks of a mouse, for instance, one can visit the Yahoo! listings under "Home > Business and Economy > Companies > Sex > Internet Services" and find companies that offer Adult Turnkey Programs (5), Age Verification Services (26), Commercial Web Site Directories, Content Providers (22), Photographs, Web Designers (4), Web Hosting (15), and Web Promotion (9). Similarly, the adult-oriented directory Naughty Linx offers an entire category devoted to adult Webmasters, including listings for Bulk Email, Billing Systems, Submissions Services, and so forth. One of the most comprehensive sites is the Webmaster section of Ynot Network (see Chapter 6), which contains links to a wide variety of Webmaster resources and even a special section devoted to new entrepreneurs called "Beginner's Luck." The scope of the material in the Beginner's Luck section is impressive, ranging from "Building an Adult Site" to "Proper Precautions," a summary of the legal risks inherent in operating an adult Web site.

In many ways, the scope of the material available on starting an adult Web site is simply an extension of the changes that have taken place offline. With the arrival of the videocassette recorder and the ubiquitous video store, it became increasingly easy to participate in the pornography industry. By the early 1990s, large numbers of so-called "mom-and-pop" video stores were adding adult titles to their stock as a way of competing against large video chains like Blockbuster, which has a corporate policy against stocking X- or NC-17-rated videos.[41] In all likelihood, none of the "mom-and-pop" video store owners, nestled in the suburbs and rural communities across the country, would have described themselves as pornographers. Nonetheless, the pornography industry quietly gained thousands of new outlets for its products, a process that helped pave the way for other types of home video fare (including cable, satellite television, and pay-per-view movies). According to *Adult Video News,* which conducted a survey of 4,000 retailers in 1997, home video generated approximately $16 billion in revenues that year. Of that total, adult home video accounted for roughly $4.2 billion, or a little more than 26 percent.

At the same time that the pornography industry was changing the suburbs, the suburbs slowly began changing the pornography industry. In 1982, adult videos got their own national trade publication, *Adult Video News,* which video store owners use to track developments in the industry. Over the years, the magazine has grown into a several-hundred-page monthly publication containing industry news, profiles of adult film stars, legal advice from First Amendment expert Clyde DeWitt, reviews, and hundreds of advertisements promoting both adult videos and their stars.[42] In 1983, the magazine created the AVN Awards, the so-called "Oscars of smut."[43]

Paradoxically, as the industry's product and production have become less and less visible to the naked eye, the industry itself is purposefully seeking a higher profile. Recognizing the social and political threats that have arisen over the last 15 to 20 years, the pornography industry is trying to do a better job of flexing its political muscle. In 1991, for instance, the Free Speech Coalition, a lobbying and trade organization for adult businesses, was founded in California.[44] The stated purpose of the coalition is as follows:

> We have a twofold mission.  First we serve to improve the quality of
> life for everyone working in or for adult entertainment businesses.
> Second, we serve to improve the external environment for the sale of
> adult entertainment products and services.

The coalition currently employs a "retired dominatrix," Kat Sunlove, as a full-time lobbyist to the California Assembly, and among its various other initiatives, helps to arrange health insurance, production insurance, and premises liability policies for members who would otherwise be unable to afford them or purchase them at all.

In addition to the Free Speech Coalition, a number of other support and lobbying groups have been formed for different segments of the adult entertainment industry. For instance, earlier this year, the San Francisco group COYOTE ("Call Off Your Old Tired Ethics") celebrated its 25th anniversary as an advocacy group for sex workers. Other active organizations are the Exotic Dancer's Alliance, PONY (Prostitutes of New York), and the Prostitutes Education Network.

No industry, however, can truly describe itself as mainstream without a collection of trade shows to hawk its wares and conferences to hold learned discussions on its past, present, and future. To the amazement of many, the pornography industry now has both. In addition to exclusively adult trade shows like AdultDex (which spun off from the better-known ComDex when the organizers decided that they did not want sexual content at their show) and IA2000, a trade show for adult Webmasters, the pornography industry now has a well-established presence at ostensibly mainstream shows for the Video Software Dealers Association, the East Coast Video Convention, and the massive Consumer Electronics Show.

Organized academic interest in the pornography industry has been somewhat slower in coming, but in August 1998, the Center for Sex Research at the California State University in Northridge hosted "The World Pornography Conference." Attorneys, academics, sex workers of various descriptions, adult video producers, and a bevy of reporters paid $175 apiece to attend seminars on the history and current status of the pornography industry. (One sample title: "A Short History of Sex Toys.") Participants also saw narrated documentaries about sex film stars and heard ACLU president Nadine Strossen deliver a keynote speech on the political challenges facing the industry. There is no word yet on whether another World Pornography Conference will be held, but somehow, it seems likely.

Over the last 40 years, the pornography industry has grown from a diffuse collection of producers and publishers to a fairly sophisticated social and political force. As the pornography industry continues to grow increasingly mainstream, the social barriers for starting an adult business will continue to drop.

# NOTES

1. *Capital Times* (Madison, Wis.), July 27, 1998.
2. *The Dallas Morning News,* July 29, 1998.
3. *Rocky Mountain News,* July 30, 1998.
4. Obviously, so many stores sell sexually explicit magazines or rent sexually explicit videos that there are (with the exception of few areas of the country) no practical impediments to obtaining pornographic materials. However, because the number of pornography outlets is smaller than the number of outlets for nonsexual materials, even the relatively minimal effort required to locate a supplier is reflected in the price.
5. Bertrand Russell, *Look,* February 23, 1954.
6. *Jacobellis v. Ohio,* 378 U.S. 184, 197 (1964) (Stewart, J., concurring).
7. One watchdog group, Morality in Media, has posted on its Web site a side-by-side comparison of obscenity prosecutions under Clinton and Reagan/Bush. Online at http://pw2.netcom.com/~mimnyc/onlysix.htm.
8. The use of photos from nudist camps and beaches is a technique first used by girlie-magazine editor George von Rosen in the 1950s. It should be noted, however, that Rosen's use was restricted to images of nude women, not children.
9. Phillip Rawls, "Barnes & Noble indicted on child pornography charges," *Boston Globe,*

February 18, 1998, online at http://www.boston.com/globe/latest/daily/18/bn.htm.

10. 18 U.S.C. § 2256. The law was cited in a number of articles as one of the primary reasons that the film *Lolita* had such a hard time finding a U.S. distributor.

11. Since federal law is applicable from one end of the country to the other, federal prosecutors have an easier time bringing prosecutions against out-of-state businesses than do state prosecutors.

12. Ironically, Milpitas is also the home of the Kansmen Corporation, maker of "LittleBrother," a software package designed to monitor employee activity on the Internet and block access to undesirable sites.

13. Edwin Diamond and Stephen Bates, "Law and order comes to cyberspace," *Technology Review*, vol. 98, no. 5 (1995).

14. Diamond and Bates.

15. If anything, they might have been indictable on consumer fraud grounds, as many of the lewdest-sounding descriptions actually led to innocuous photos.

16. Diamond and Bates.

17. See the model "terms and conditions" posted at the Zmaster Web site http://www.zmaster.com/Disclaimer.html and the "banned zip codes" at http://www.zmaster.com/bin/db/ListZipCodes.html. Zmaster also recommends that sites not permit access from a number of foreign countries, including Afghanistan, Kuwait, Iran, Iraq, Japan, Jordan, Libya, Pakistan, the Republic of China, Singapore, Saudi Arabia, Syria, and the United Arab Emirates.

18. Both the U.S. District Court and the U.S. Supreme Court noted that there was no constitutional problem with the portion of the law banning the online distribution of obscene material, since there is no First Amendment protection for obscenity.

19. Reno v. ACLU,_ U.S. _ (1997).

20. Permanent Injunction Ruling, *ACLU v. Reno,* Civil Action No. 98-5591 (E.D.Penn. February 1, 1999) (Reed, J.).

21. *Ibid.*

22. According to a recent study by the San Diego-based NetPartners Internet Solutions, Inc., an estimated 25 million people downloaded a copy of the Starr Report from the Internet. The study also found that more than half of the downloads occurred at work, costing American businesses as much as $450 million in lost productivity. The study added that the actual cost was probably higher, since the bandwidth required to download the voluminous report "undoubtedly slowed network performance and contributed to increased computer downtime." "Internet Broadcasts of Starr Reports Costs Businesses Over $450 Million in Lost Employee Productivity," *Business Wire*, October 1, 1998.

23. Joel Brinkley, "Budget Item Would Curb Internet Smut," *New York Times*, October 17, 1998, online at http://www.nytimes.com/library/tech/98/10/biztech/articles/17porn.html.

24. Jeri Clausing, "States Keep Up Efforts on Internet Restrictions," *New York Times*, Cybertimes, February 19, 1998, online at http://www.nytimes.com/library/cyber/week/021998state.html.

   As of June 1997, the following states had adopted online speech legislation of one form or another: California (obscenity and child pornography); Connecticut (harassment); Florida (child pornography); Kansas (child pornography); Maryland (child pornography); North Carolina (sexual solicitation of a minor); Oklahoma (transmission of materials "harmful to minors"); and Virginia (child pornography). Two states—Georgia and New York—have had their online speech laws overturned in court. Also, at least four states have considered such legislation but rejected it: Massachusetts, Oregon, Pennsylvania, and Washington. "State Laws That Regulate Speech on the Internet," American Civil Liberties Union, 1998, online at http://www.aclu.org/issues/cyber/censor/stbills.html.

25. "Online Censorship in the States," American Civil Liberties Union, 1998, online at http://www.aclu.org/issues/cyber/censor/stbills.html. See also Jeri Clausing, "States Keep Up Efforts on Internet Restrictions," *New York Times*, Cybertimes, February 19, 1998, online at http://www.nytimes.com/library/cyber/week/021998state.html.

26. 17 U.S.C. 101 *et seq.*

27. There are some creative works which are in the public domain, consisting chiefly of works that are more than 80 years or so old (Shakespeare's plays, for instance) and works that have been specifically created for the public domain (such as clip art). However, the mere fact that something has been posted on the Internet does not mean that it is in the public domain.

28. Digimarc's Web site is at http://www.digimarc.com.

29. Andrew Ross Sorkin, "*Playboy* Plans to Use Digital 'Watermarks'," *New York Times,* June 30, 1997.

30. Wes Thomas, "Digimarc offers the ability to find out who's using your images on their site," *Web Review,* January 9, 1998, online at http://webreview.com/98/01/09/addict/index.html.

31. "History of the Internet" (n.d.), online at http://www.ccit.arizona.edu/internet/inthist.html.

32. Each domain may also have one or more subdomains. For instance, the University of Vermont has a domain name of "uvm.edu." It also has a variety of subdomains, including "moose" and "zoo." If I want to send an e-mail to someone at UVM, the address will look like this: johndoe@moose.uvm.edu. That lets my Internet service provider know that the message is not going simply to UVM but instead to a specific computer or subnetwork at the university.

33. 15 U.S.C. § 1125(c) (Section 43(c) of the Lanham Act).

34. Speculation may have died down, but it has not disappeared entirely. Other entrepreneurs registered more generic names; legend has it that both "business.com" and "internet.com" ultimately sold for more than $100,000 each. There continues to be an active trade in generic domain names, and if you can figure out the next hot trend, you might be able to cash in. Someone's already taken "www.grunge.com" and "www.slacker.com," but tomorrow's hot domain names are still waiting to materialize.

35. Stories about www.whitehouse.com have appeared on ABC *News,* CNN, NBC's *Dateline,* and in *Newsweek.*

36. "Chrysler sues two Internet companies, alleging trademark infringement," *Boston Globe,* September 29, 1998, online at http://www.boston.com/dailynews/wirehtml/272/ Chrysler_sues_two_Internet_companie.shtm.

37. In fact, since the ease with which a site can be accessed is dependent on the ratio of traffic to the site's bandwidth, it can often be easier to visit a smaller and somewhat less well-known site than to compete with the throngs trying to get into the Playboy site.

38. Beth Lipton and Courtney Macavinta, "Playboy Deeper into the Net," July 28, 1998, online at http://www.news.com/News/Item/0,4,28598,00.html.

39. According to recent court arguments, Internet Entertainment Group has already earned approximately $8 million from the Anderson/Lee videotape through sales of videotape, CD-ROMs, and hotel movies.

40. Joel Stein, "Porn Goes Mainstream," *Time,* September 7, 1998, pp. 54ff.

41. Blockbuster, which was purchased by media giant Viacom in 1994, has been rumored to be reconsidering its stance on NC-17 movies, but no decision has been made yet. However, the company has announced that individual Blockbuster stores will begin tailoring their selections to reflect local preferences. Rob Walton, "Blockbusted," September 18, 1997, online at http://www.roughcut.com/main/godzilla_97sep3.html. Part of the reason for Blockbuster's increased flexibility may be its experience in Germany. In January 1998, the video chain announced that it was shutting down its 17 stores in Germany. A major reason for Blockbuster's failure was its refusal to stock adult movies, which account for more than a third of Germany's $400 million in annual video rentals. Nicholas Moss, "What A Flop!" *The European,* January 19, 1998, p. 31.

42. *Adult Video News* can be found on the Web at www.avn.com.

43. Jack Boulware, "The Porno Oscars," *Hotwired,* July 1996, online at http://www.hotwired.com/renevent/96/07/index5a.html.

44. The Free Speech Coalition's Web site is at: www.freespeechcoalition.org. The current president, incidentally, is Gloria Leonard, the former porn star who was one of the first to see the potential for "dial-a-porn" following the break-up of AT&T in the early 1980s.

# 5

# PHONE SEX:
# THE FIRST NATIONAL
# PORNOGRAPHY
# NETWORK

Linda Tripp: "I could never have phone sex."
Monica Lewinsky: "Oh yes you could."
The Starr Report

## HEAVY BREATHING ON WALL STREET

### THE QUIET BENEFICIARIES OF THE
### PORNOGRAPHY INDUSTRY

During the early stages of the 1996 presidential campaign, Senator Phil Gramm (R-Texas) came under attack by conservative and religious groups when the news broke that in 1974, he invested at least $7,500 in a movie directed by Mark Lester titled *White House Madness*, a scathing and generally scatological film about the last days of the Nixon administration.[1] According to George Canton, Gramm's former brother-in-law, Gramm became a fan of Lester's work when Canton showed him the rushes for *Truckstop Women*, a 1974 film featuring road-side prostitution, armed robbery and truck hijacking, numerous road violations, and significant amounts of female nudity. Canton told the *New Republic* that Gramm sent a check to invest in *Truckstop Women* and was very disappointed when he was told that the movie was already oversubscribed. Gramm made Canton promise that he would be at the top of the list of investors for Lester's next movie.

The cover story in the *New Republic* about Gramm's financial support for the arts broke on the same day in June 1995 that Gramm was scheduled to meet with the Christian Coalition to endorse the coalition's Contract with the

American Family. In a terse statement issued prior to the publication of the article, Gramm admitted investing $7,500 in a movie project, but claimed that it was for a never-completed film titled *Beauty Queens*. He said that the project had been shelved and that his investment had been used instead—without his knowledge—for a film called *White House Madness*. Canton disagreed with Gramm's version of the story, telling the *New Republic* that Gramm, when told about the plan to do a satire of the Nixon White House, was thrilled with the idea and asked to increase the amount of his investment. Canton said that Gramm was disappointed when he was told that Lester had all the funds he needed for the project.[2]

Gramm was doubtless glad that his offer was rejected; *White House Madness*, which journalist Sidney Blumenthal said "deliberately offends conservative sexual mores, shows marriage and parenthood to be hollow jokes and is filled with scenes of transvestism and bestiality,"[3] did miserably at the box office and now, 20 years later, is virtually impossible to find on videotape. Gramm's dabbling in the R-rated movie biz was not the sole reason for the failure of his campaign, but the news certainly took some of the starch out of his moral outrage and may have contributed to his fifth-place finish in the Iowa caucuses in the spring of 1996.

The irony, of course, is that many of the same people who criticized Gramm at the time for even inadvertently investing in America's sexual appetites have been doing exactly the same thing. In a reasonably diversified stock portfolio, the chances are quite good that an investor will own some shares from one or more of the nation's leading long-distance communications companies, such as AT&T (1.6 billion shares outstanding), MCI WorldCom (909 million), and Sprint (430 million). Even if an investor does not directly own long-distance telephone stocks, the chances are excellent that his or her mutual fund or pension plan does; as stalwarts of the telecommunications age, the long-distance carriers are generally considered sound investments by fund managers. What most investors may not realize is that the telecommunications industry (and particularly the long-distance sector) also has a highly profitable business relationship with the pornography industry.

When an Internet user downloads sexually explicit images from a Usenet newsgroup or visits one of the myriad Web sites that make pornography available to all comers, it looks as though he or she is getting pornography for free. But as Robert Heinlein once observed, "Tanstaafl" ("There ain't no such thing as a free lunch"). Accessing the "free" pornography online does cost; it's just that the payments are being made to companies that have not traditionally been considered as part of the pornography industry. On any given day, entire libraries of pornography are transmitted over telephone lines owned and operated by local and long-distance carriers, while hundreds of thousands of adults dial 900 or overseas phone numbers to engage in phone sex. Each transmission, whether it is in the form of text, image, voice, or video, contributes incrementally to the economic success of the telecommunications industry.

The telecommunications revolution that has occurred over the last decade has also created enormous demands for new phone lines for cellular phones, faxes, and modems. Each new line is a source of additional monthly revenues for the local phone company, ranging from the charge for the line itself to charges for excessive time spent in local calls (a common feature for heavy Internet users). Since the vast majority of residential Internet users dial local access numbers to connect to an Internet service provider (such as Vermont's Together Networks or SoverNet) or a national online service provider such as America Online, the local phone companies are the first level of the telecommunications industry that benefits from the online sector of the pornography industry.

From the local phone lines or the Internet service provider, a pornography consumer's call is then passed on to one of the long-distance phone companies in the form of either a pay-per-call or Internet traffic. The pornography-related income of long-distance carriers is far from trivial: Phone sex alone generates between $750 million and $1 billion in revenues each year, with as much as 50 percent being retained by U.S. long-distance carriers. Additional pornography-related earnings are generated by the long-distance carriers in their capacity as owners of Internet backbones (which carry virtually all Internet traffic, including pornography) or as Internet service providers (which provide users with access to the World Wide Web and newsgroups, both of which contain considerable amounts of pornography). In fact, in February 1997, *U.S. News & World Report* asserted that AT&T, thanks to its preeminence as a long-distance company and Internet service provider, is actually one of the pornography industry's highest-grossing businesses.[4] AT&T, not surprisingly, strenuously professes its disdain for both the phone sex industry and Internet pornography, but even with annual corporate revenues currently in excess of $51 billion (as of December 1998), it is doubtful that either AT&T's management or its investors would cheerfully give up the several hundred million dollars in revenue the company earns each year from a combination of phone sex and the Internet.[5]

## BREAKING UP IS HARD TO DO

The money earned by phone companies as carriers for sexual conversation is, ironically, a direct outgrowth of AT&T's battles with largely conservative administrations. Efforts to break up AT&T's perceived telephone monopoly began under Presidents Nixon and Ford, continued during the Carter administration, and culminated in 1982 when AT&T agreed with the Reagan administration to divest itself of its so-called "Baby Bells," the 22 regional operating systems that provided local telephone service, a step that took place about two years later. Overnight, AT&T went from a world-leading $150 billion in corporate assets to $34 billion. While that hardly impoverished AT&T, it left the long-distance carrier and the various Baby Bells scrambling for new sources of revenues.

A decades-old technology, audiotext, helped provide part of the answer. The practice of providing automated information by telephone began in 1928, when New York Telephone set up a system that allowed customers to call for the correct time. In 1937, New York Telephone added a weather report. Those remained the only telephone information numbers until 1974, when the company added "Dial-a-Joke," and a recorded Santa Clause message in 1975.[6]

Not surprisingly, AT&T was the first to realize that information lines could be used as a revenue producer. In 1980, it created "Dial-it" services, using a new 900 area code to help make the marketing of the services easier. Callers who dialed 900 numbers were charged a specific rate (either a flat fee or a per-minute charge) to access information. One of the first widely publicized uses of the 900 system occurred in 1980 during the Reagan-Carter debates, when the television networks set up 900 numbers to allow viewers to call in and vote for the candidate they thought won the debate. During the last of the four debates, more than 500,000 people called over a four-hour period and paid 50 cents per minute to vote, generating more than $250,000 in revenue.[7]

After the breakup of AT&T both AT&T and the Baby Bells began to aggressively explore the moneymaking potential of telephone information services.[8] In 1985, for instance, AT&T began offering information providers a "promotional compensation" of 3 to 5 cents per minute, based on the volume of calls a particular 900 line received. The following year, the Federal Communications Commission eased regulations on who could profit from 900 numbers and both AT&T and the Baby Bells increased the marketing of the information lines as entrepreneurial opportunities. To encourage entrepreneurs to lease the lines, the phone companies put the power of their billing systems behind the new services and created a pricing system that allowed entrepreneurs to bill up to $2 for the first minute and lesser amounts thereafter. The combination of high returns and well-established, reliable billing procedures proved irresistible. In 1987, AT&T alone earned $100 million on audiotext industry revenues of $225 million.[9] By 1990, industry revenues from 900 numbers as a whole crossed the $1 billion mark, a figure that rose to an estimated $7.4 billion in 1996.[10]

AT&T and local phone companies such as New York Telephone undoubtedly intended that "Dial-It" services would be used to provide such mundane information as time, weather, sports scores, movie listings, and various types of business promotions. And in fact, that is what has largely occurred: Many Fortune 500 and computer companies do use 900 numbers as highly successful extensions of their businesses, leasing lines to dispense specialized information and technical support, provide special offers, and conduct contests. In 1987, for instance, comedian Eddie Murphy asked viewers of *Saturday Night Live* to call a 900 number to vote on whether to save Larry the Lobster from the pot. 500,000 people called in (and voted to save the lobster). In 1996, MTV set up a 900 number to run a contest offering rock star Jon Bon Jovi's boyhood home as a grand prize and recorded more than 600,000 calls in a single day.

In some cases, the 900 number *is* the business. Dionne Warwick's Psychic Friends Network, for instance, had some remarkably good years: Over the course of 1995 and 1996, the Psychic Friends Network received an estimated 3 million calls, each of which cost the caller $3.99 per minute and lasted an average of ten minutes. During those two years alone, the Network grossed an estimated $120 million in revenues.[11]

For the pornography industry, the combination of a new technology and the prospect of making large amounts of easy money was like tossing a lamb into a piranha pool. Prior to the breakup of AT&T, "Dial-It" services were under the exclusive control of Ma Bell and its local phone subsidiaries. The "Dial-It" monopoly, however, was swept away with the rest of AT&T's monopoly, and the local telephone companies were forced to make the "Dial-It" numbers available to other information providers. In a lottery of 21 New York Telephone information lines in 1982, the adult magazine *High Society* was awarded one of the "Dial-It" lines. The magazine entered the lottery because its publisher, Gloria Leonard (herself a former porn star), believed that people would call to listen to suggestive dialogue read by the magazine's models. Leonard knew her audience well. By the spring of 1983, the *High Society* line was recording more than 500,000 calls per day for the sexy messages (which were changed three times daily). The lines were so successful that *High Society* negotiated to purchase two additional lines from other lottery winners.

The fact that the government was making the local phone companies give up their monopoly on "Dial-It" services did not mean that the phone companies were required to give the service away for free; the phone companies could and did profit handsomely from the content offered by other information providers, including pornographers. For instance, for each seven-cents-per-minute charge generated by the *High Society* line, New York Telephone kept five cents and paid *High Society* two cents, a profit-sharing scheme that translated into earnings by New York Telephone of roughly $25,000 per day.[12] The revenues from the phone sex lines were so impressive, in fact, that in the early 1980s, the earnings were cited by the New York Public Service Commission as a reason for denying requests for rate increases by New York Telephone.[13]

It is difficult to overestimate the enormous social and economic impact of *High Society's* successful "Dial-It" venture. When the magazine won the right to lease one of New York Telephone's audiotext lines, it effectively gained access to a new distribution network—the nation's phone system—that enabled it to provide sexually explicit dialogue and conversation not only to every community in the nation but also to virtually every home. This essentially freed the magazine from the concerns about censorship that made it impossible to sell copies in certain communities or even in entire states. For the first time, an individual interested in hearing sexually explicit material could do so without leaving the privacy of his or her home. Undoubtedly, at least some of the hundreds of thousands of calls each day to the *High Society* "Dial-It" line were from communities in which it was impossible to purchase or even find a single copy of its magazine.

The *High Society* lines were the start of an enormous and rapidly growing sector of the pornography industry. In less than 13 years, annual phone sex revenues rose from zero to between $750 million and $1 billion, an amount that constitutes an estimated ten cents on every dollar spent on audiotext.[14] In the process, numerous sex entrepreneurs got their first taste of the remarkably low distribution costs and stunning profit margins associated with electronic pornography.

## PHONE SEX AND THIRD WORLD NATIONS

U.S. phone companies such as AT&T, MCI, Sprint, New York Telephone, and Bell Atlantic are not the only companies to benefit from this country's aural fixation. The hot names in phone sex are not Kitty, Bambi, or Tiffany, but Guyana, São Tomé, and Moldova, with Gambia closing fast. They are, respectively, a small South American nation, a tiny island off the coast of the West African nation of Gabon, a former Soviet Socialist Republic in southeastern Europe, and a tiny republic on the coast of West Africa. Two things make these countries (and others like them) popular with pornographers: their relatively relaxed phone regulations and, more important, the high per-minute phone rates that U.S. customers are charged for placing calls to those countries.

In general, the system works like this: when a caller in the United States places a call to an audiotext line in a foreign country, the caller's long-distance carrier (AT&T, MCI, Sprint, etc.) calculates a billing rate for the call based on the carrier's cost of getting the call to the destination country, the amount the destination country charges for receiving the call (known as the "settlement rate"), and the carrier's profit on the transaction. The originating carrier pays the destination country its settlement rate based on the number of minutes of connection, and the destination country then pays a portion of the settlement rate to the information provider that owns or has leased the audiotext line in question.

Many smaller countries like São Tomé and Guyana have purposely established high settlement rates in an effort to boost the flow of foreign currency into their countries. The problem, of course, is that high settlement rates translate directly into high long-distance charges in the United States (and in other countries), which would normally lower the volume of calls. As previous generations have learned, however, one group of consumers unfazed by premium prices are the purchasers of pornography. Remote countries have leapt into the audiotext business because consumers (primarily from the U.S. and western Europe) have demonstrated their willingness to pay as much as $4 or $5 a minute to listen to phone sex. There are currently between 15 and 30 small countries heavily competing for a share of the audiotext market. One large service bureau, Eastern Telcom, lists the following termination points: Guyana, Canada, Moldova, Papua New Guinea, Sierra Leone, San Marino, Bolivia, Venezuela, Philippines, Hong Kong, Chile, Niue, and Saint Vincent.[15] Triton Telecom, based in Hong Kong, lists 30 termination points: Antigua, Armenia, Bulgaria, Canada, Chile, Curaçao, Diego Garcia, Dominican Republic, Georgia, Grenada, Guinea Bissau, Guyana, Haiti, Hong Kong, Israel, Jamaica, Maldives,

Moldova, Niue, Norway, Russia, San Marino, São Tomé, Sierra Leone, Solomon Islands, St. Lucia, Tuvalu, and Venezuela.[16]

The fact that such far-flung nations are used by the adult audiotext industry to make millions is a direct outgrowth of the efforts of the U.S. Congress to limit access to 900 numbers for phone sex in this country. Although the scope of Congress's legislation was ultimately limited by the U.S. Supreme Court, the confusion and concern over 900 numbers pushed the industry to find other ways to provide phone sex services. The hunt for alternatives took on a particular urgency as phone companies developed and implemented blocking technology for the 900 area code, which threatened to severely restrict the phone sex industry's revenues. In an effort to do an end run around both government regulation and blocking technology, many phone sex businesses began advertising 800 number access to their services, on the theory that while some people were willing to block access from their phones to 900 numbers, most would not be willing to block off access to 800 numbers.[17] The same theory led to the use of foreign phone numbers to provide phone sex, with the additional benefit that putting a phone sex service's content offshore lessens the chances of U.S. prosecution and gives the information provider greater freedom of content.

The challenge of policing and limiting the tremendous growth in international phone sex has been heightened by the fact that it has proved to be an important economic boon for many of the smaller nations involved. The island of São Tomé, for instance, which saw the number of calls from the United States skyrocket from 4,300 in 1991 to 360,000 in 1993, kept approximately $500,000 as its share of the $5.2 million worth of phone sex calls that Americans made in 1993. The island used the money to build a new telecommunications system.

The South American nation of Guyana has experienced even more impressive growth. In 1991, when Guyana Telephone & Telegraph (GT&T) was sold to the U.S. Virgin Islands–based Atlantic Tele-Network, Inc. for $16.5 million, it did not receive a single foreign audiotext call. The following year, Atlantic began marketing GT&T circuits to U.S. pay-per-call operations, including phone sex companies. The marketing effort was a complete success: In 1995, Guyana received 102 million minutes of foreign audiotext calls, enough to account for $91 million of GT&T's $131 million annual revenues. By June 1996, the country had already logged an additional 60 million minutes of audiotext calls.[18]

Although GT&T did see some improvements resulting from the tidal wave of foreign audiotext calls, there were some Guyanans who felt that not enough of the enormous revenues were being reinvested in the country's telecommunications system. Pamadath J. Menon, the chairman of the Guyana Public Utilities Commission, was particularly concerned about Atlantic Tele-Network's use of the money earned by GT&T. "I'm unhappy that the large cash flows are not being reinvested for the benefit of the people of Guyana," he told the *Washington Post* in 1996. Menon proposed that 15 percent of GT&T's revenues be set aside for infrastructure improvements.[19]

Like many of his countrymen, Menon was less concerned about how the money was earned: "It doesn't matter to us where the revenue comes from," he said. Most of the Guyanese population accepted their phone company's involvement in the phone sex business on the theory that the revenues from phone sex helped keep their phone rates down.[20] However, Menon's comments do highlight a common concern for countries offering termination services: the bulk of the benefits from international phone sex do not stay in the terminating countries. Due to language and cultural barriers, there are relatively few opportunities for residents to work as operators (the vast majority of calls are answered by tape machines or rerouted to operators in the originating country), and only about half of the settlement rate is paid to the host country. When the host country's phone system is run by a foreign corporation, as is the case with Guyana, the host nation's cut grows even smaller.

That state of affairs was borne out in 1997, when GT&T experienced a significant drop in its pay-per-call/phone sex revenues. Phone sex companies in the United States were experiencing increasing success through the use of credit card billing on 900 and 800 phone lines, and other small countries like São Tomé and Moldova marketed themselves as more lucrative destinations for foreign audiotext calls. At the urging of Atlantic Tele-Network, the Guyana Public Utilities Commission raised the rates (at least temporarily) for calling the U.S. from 85 cents per minute to 94. Only a few months later, however, in April 1998, the Utilities Commission announced that it was undertaking a thorough investigation of GT&T for possible malfeasance in the handling of the company. Concern over the handling of GT&T by Atlantic Tele-Network has been heightened by the fact that competition from other countries for audiotext traffic reduced GT&T's revenues by 41 percent in 1998, and by the fact that Atlantic Tele-Network is currently seeking a significant increase in the cost of basic telephone service to the island's residents.

The competition among countries for a share of the more than $2 billion spent each year on international audiotext will continue to be fierce. The willingness of consumers in the United States and western Europe to pay high per-minute charges for simple access to phone sex has had a direct impact on the ability of small nations to rebuild (or in some cases build) the telecommunications infrastructure they need to attract other types of business. Although some smaller Caribbean islands (among them Bermuda) are increasingly reluctant to be a termination point for phone sex calls, most show no signs of willingly giving up their newfound revenues.

## THE DOMESTIC PHONE SEX INDUSTRY

The U.S. phone sex industry today has a structure similar to the bookselling industry: The few large national companies have huge advertising power and technological resources, and a number of independent businesses gamely struggle to survive by finding and filling market niches and by distinguishing themselves on traditional retail criteria of price, service, and quality. The chief difference between the two industries (apart from the product, of course, although *Vox* and *The Kiss* have helped to narrow the gap somewhat) is that thanks to the impressive profit margins that exist in the phone sex industry, an independent phone sex operation can survive and prosper much more easily than an independent bookstore can.

## SERVICE BUREAUS, FRANCHISES, AND ENTREPRENEURS

Another important difference is that the book industry's largest players trumpet their names (Barnes & Noble, Borders, Waldenbooks) from one end of the country to the other. The industry leaders in audiotext, large companies known as "service bureaus," prefer to keep a far lower profile, generally hiding behind unnamed phone numbers or behind dozens of smaller businesses with essentially anonymous Web site names (e.g., www.wetgirls.com, a commercial site linked to Telecharge Audio Network, recently identified by *Forbes* as one of the nation's largest service bureaus).[21] If a major bookstore chain such as Barnes & Noble purchases a full-page ad in a national magazine, readers have no doubt about who placed the ad. By contrast, out of the dozen or more full-page ads for phone sex contained in the May 1998 *Penthouse,* not a single one carried any obvious indication as to the identity of the business(es) that purchased them. Unlike the book industry (or most other industries, for that matter), brand name identification is not necessarily an advantage for large phone sex businesses, which find it more profitable to give the impression that there are hundreds or thousands of different sources of phone sex, rather than a few dozen. In addition, as has often been the case in the pornography industry, maintaining a low profile helps reduce the risk of a possible obscenity prosecution.

Despite their anonymity, large service bureaus do play an important role in the audiotext business in general and in the phone sex business in particular. The cost of the telecommunications equipment required to handle large volumes of calls and specialized area codes like 900 and 976 pay-per-call numbers can easily run into the tens of thousands of dollars. For example, even a midsized phone sex service bureau usually requires an automated attendant system to answer the incoming calls, identify the phone number of the incoming call for billing purposes, and play a recording alerting callers to the charges for the call. In addition, the phone system must also generally have menu capability in order to enable callers to select among the different phone sex services available and to transfer the caller to that service. Lastly, phone sex operations will often implement a system capable of providing "tailored call coverage," an industry term for a phone system capable of restricting access by state or area code.

These types of resources are generally only available in what are known as private branch exchange (PBX),[22] which is a fairly costly investment; even a moderate-size one costs several thousand dollars. In turn, there is the cost of the connection to a carrier like AT&T or Sprint. For smaller businesses, the incoming call load can be handled by a number of normal phone lines connected to the PBX, but the larger service organizations typically lease a high-speed communications line (for example, a T1 line, which is capable of handling up to 1.544 megabits of information per second). The cost of a high-speed connection to a national carrier alone can cost several thousand dollars per month, which also encourages consolidation in the adult audiotext industry.

In order to recoup the cost of the equipment, most service bureaus earn additional revenues by providing access to high-speed telecommunications capabilities to other information providers. Typically, a bureau may serve as a host for a smaller phone sex business that does not have the capital to set up its own equipment or rent its own office space. In exchange for a percentage of the smaller business's revenues, the service bureau will provide office space, access to phone lines, billing, and so forth.

Another increasingly popular business model in the phone sex industry (particularly in conjunction with the Internet) is for a service bureau to recruit individuals or other businesses to serve as distributors of the service bureau's phone sex lines. Under this type of arrangement, an individual pays a fee to the service bureau and in return is given the right to market a particular phone sex number. The service bureau provides the content, handles all of the technological and administrative issues, logs the number of minutes the line is used by callers, and gives a percentage of the proceeds to the line's distributor.

How much money a distributor receives under this type of arrangement generally depends on how much advertising the distributor does. Service bureaus often provide suggestions for marketing techniques, including advertising a phone sex line on a Web site or by sending out hundreds or thousands of e-mails. In fact, the distributor model for phone sex lines is probably one of the leading sources of "spam," the much-despised unsolicited e-mail that clogs the lines and mailboxes of Internet users. A typical unsolicited phone sex e-mail:

> Tammie here, my girlfriend and I are STRIPPERS, actually we are first year college students, but we strip at night for extra money. We do good because guys really like our Tight Asses and our Big Tits. We just bought a computer and thought we would send a couple of emails out just to see if this thing really works, we are sooo bored at college—we are just sitting in our dorm room doing nothing if you want to call and talk, we love to talk about how naughty we can get at work.
> Hope you call!
> 1-800-449-7769 or 1-900-745-1107

At the other end of the 800 number is a tape recording of a breathy young woman who announces that the service is run by "Ike and Jay Inc.," is restricted to people over the age of 18, and that the cost of the call will be between $2.99

and $5.99 per minute, depending on the services selected. There is, alas, no indication if "Tammie" made the tape recording.

The cost to entrepreneurs of becoming a distributor is generally an initial onetime payment of between $500 and $2,000, depending on the service bureau in question and the number of features associated with the particular phone number. At the more expensive end, for instance, the service bureau Access Audiotext Corporation offers distributors a package deal of a five-feature 900 line and a credit-card based 800 number for $1,950. On the 900 line, callers can choose among the following services:

> *Live One on One:* Caller engages in a two-way conversation with a
> live operator/telephone actress.
> *Live Two on One:* Caller engages in a two-way conversation with
> two live operators/telephone actresses.
> *The B.J. Line:* Caller listens to provocative discussion and descriptions of certain adult fantasies.
> *DateLine/Voice Personals:* Fully automated dating system. Callers can
> place, browse or respond to recorded personal ads with intentions
> of connecting with other singles.
> *Adult Fantasy Line:* Caller listens to a fully recorded fantasy message
> narrated by a sexy female voice.[23]

In general, the entrepreneur will earn between 20 and 30 percent of each dollar generated by the phone sex lines.

Many service bureaus offer grandiose claims about both the amount of money that can be made and the ease with which it can be earned. However, it is difficult to overstate the sheer number of phone sex lines available to consumers. The print media (particularly the glossy sex magazines) are simply awash with them, and the number of phone sex lines advertised on the Internet (both through e-mail and on Web sites) is growing rapidly. Although the Internet reduces the cost of marketing a phone sex line and the size and growth of the industry makes it clear that there is a strong market for phone sex, entrepreneurs considering leasing or purchasing a phone sex line should take the time to investigate the actual payouts by the service bureau for similar lines and to plan a realistic marketing program. The competition in the phone sex business is intense.

Moreover, service bureau participation in the phone sex business is not limited to providing access to high-end telephone equipment. Most service bureaus are also content providers, hiring women and men to make tape recordings of sexual activity or to answer phones and engage in sexual conversation with callers. This is the most lucrative arrangement, of course, since the bureau does not need to share its proceeds with anyone other than the phone company providing the incoming line.

## THE INDEPENDENTS

Despite the significant market share taken up by the larger service bureaus, technology makes it possible for individuals to compete effectively in the adult audiotext business. In fact, the phone sex and adult video industries between them have offered a particularly good example of how technology is opening up multiple distribution channels for sexually explicit content. In the case of both adult pictures and adult movies, the growth of large companies made it difficult (if not impossible) for smaller companies and individuals to compete. In the so-called "Golden Age" of pornography (circa 1957–1973), starting an adult magazine or making an adult film could easily set an entrepreneur back $200,000 or $300,000. Even after the magazine or film was completed, there was still the problem of distribution, which involved competing with other well-established (and frequently well-connected) adult businesses for a small number of retail outlets or cinema screens.

Adult video, with its dramatically lower production costs, greatly expanded the number of producers of adult movies and led to the development of numerous new distribution channels, including mail order and the ubiquitous video store. Phone sex, which in theory can be produced at and distributed from any of 100 million different locations in this country, effectively shattered the model of a tightly controlled distribution system for pornography.

That is not to say that financial resources are not relevant in the phone sex industry. The greater economic resources that many service bureaus enjoy enable them to purchase more sophisticated equipment and handle a larger number of calls, which in turn generates more revenues. Having more money also translates into a greater ability to use national advertising outlets; not many independent phone sex operations are able to spend $35,000 or $40,000 per month for a four-color, full-page ad in *Penthouse.*

Nonetheless, the combination of easy access to distribution channels, the low cost of production, the relatively low cost of advertising (particularly with the advent of the Internet), the availability of reliable billing methods, and a large pool of potential employees make it possible for entrepreneurs to run a successful phone sex operation without the capital investments made by the biggest service bureaus.

One example of a successful midsize phone sex operation is "Heather's Honeys," based in San Diego.[24] "Heather," who asked to be referred to by her professional name, started her business seven and a half years ago after brief stints with a phone sex service bureau and another independent phone sex business. She began by advertising in alternative newspapers (spending between $35 and $60 per week), and then expanded onto the Internet in October 1996. At the beginning, Heather charged $25 for the first six minutes and $2 per minute thereafter.

"It worked out very well," Heather said. "I was doing a lot of the calls myself. I had a couple of girls that worked with me. I did a lot of the calls myself with different personalities." Today, Heather says that she has a number of women who work part-time for her, but only eight or so make any significant money. "I've deliberately kept my service small," Heather said. "I could have— I've certainly had the capital for years to advertise in the big glossies, and really make my business big." Heather believes, however, that keeping her business small is what has led to her 70 percent repeat call rate. Asked to compare her business to the service bureaus, Heather put it this way: "There's no kind of personal contact at all . . . and it's the man who does what he wants to do, and he hangs up on you, and that's it. There's no interaction at all. And that's what I always try to avoid with my service."

Another advantage for businesses like Heather's is that technology frees them from the geographical constraints that business owners in the real world face; at present, none of her operators lives in San Diego. "I've hired all of my girls through e-mails received on my Web site," Heather said. " I don't advertise." Many of the women looking to work for her, Heather added, have been engaging in phone sex for free with people they meet on services like America Online and decide at some point to get paid for it instead.

Heather, whose phone sex business has been her livelihood since it started, estimates that for a number of years, she was grossing between $800 and $1,000 per week, with net profits of about 80 percent. As the business has grown in the last couple of years, the expenses have risen, but so have Heather's revenues: The phone sex portion of her business alone now grosses around $4,300 per week.

The Internet has done a lot to level the playing field between the service bureaus and smaller operations like "Heather's Honeys." For relatively little money, Heather can offer not only descriptions and photos of the operators (which may or may not be how the operators actually look), but she can also offer audio samples, links to other sites (including two or three that Heather herself runs), and additional background information to help draw callers in. It is a far cry from a 1-inch-by-1-inch black-and-white text ad.

Heather agreed with the suggestion that the Internet is making it easier for people with nonmainstream sexual desires to find services that cater to their interests. "The D/S [dominant/submissive] underworld is vast on the Net," Heather said. "All your little niche sites. Your feet and your smoking and your panty fetishes and the domination/submission sites. Yessir. They're flourishing. And people are becoming much more open about it because they're realizing there are others out there like them."

One organization that has been particularly successful at helping people realize that there are others out there like them is People Exchanging Power (P.E.P.), a dominant/submissive support group founded by Nancy Ava Miller in Albuquerque, New Mexico, in 1986. Miller did not originally plan for P.E.P. to be a business, but in 1991, she found herself in need of some ready cash. Miller began meeting with submissives privately, and with the help of a friend, figured out how to use Western Union to start charging for phone sex calls. From that point on, Miller's business followed a track similar to Heather's: she handled calls herself for a couple of years and then began hiring people to handle calls for her so that she could focus more time on other aspects of P.E.P. Miller says that she generally employs between 25 and 30 women at any given time. Miller's phone sex business earns her about $70,000 per year. "It's been extremely rewarding and successful on many levels, not just financially," Miller said. "If it didn't have any other rewards, I don't know how happy I would be doing it. But it's allowed me the opportunity to do many of the things that I do best. Like I still can write. I can do public speaking."

The Internet has been particularly useful to P.E.P., which occasionally has had problems getting its advertisements for support group meetings into mainstream publications. "When I first started in Washington," Miller said, "I had trouble getting an ad in the *Washingtonian*. I have fought to get ads in various papers, and I was the first adult ad in *Washingtonian*, the *New York Review of Books*, the *Reader*. I guess [some of the publishers] thought they were outrageous. . . . They might say something like 'dominant, submissive, fetish, intelligent support group.' You know, 'May 12th at 8:00 a.m.,' or something like that. A phone number. 'Love, Nancy.'

"And so for me it didn't sound particularly wild," Miller added, "but . . . I fought for years to get into the *New York Review of Books*. I was always pestering them. And then as soon as they let me in there was a proliferation of my type of ads."

Miller succeeded in cracking the staid pages of the *Review of Books* for her support group in 1993, just as the World Wide Web was beginning to gain popular notice. The P.E.P. Web site, launched in late 1996 or early 1997, offers a dramatic example of the difference between the two venues. P.E.P.'s *Review of Books* ad was limited to black-and-white type and only advertised a nonprofit support group; P.E.P.'s Web site contains full-color photos of dominant/submissive phone consultants such as Mistress Josephine, Mistress Krystal, and Goddess Glory, who along with P.E.P.'s other counselors are available for phone conversations at the rate of $119 per hour, $99 for 45 minutes, or $89 for a half-hour. In addition, the P.E.P. Web site advertises a variety of fetish products, S&M videos, and enema paraphernalia, all items through which the *New York Review of Books* undoubtedly would have drawn a thick black line.[25]

The Internet has also helped P.E.P. become a resource for people located in more conservative communities. "There's a lot of cities that I never went to because I couldn't get the advertising in the old days prior to the Internet," Miller said. "Well, now people just get on the Internet, and they say, 'Well, there's going to be a group on the 12th of August at the Ramada, and it will be at 8 p.m., and the cost is $20, and see you there.' And a hundred people show up. Whereas before, you know, the local paper in Cincinnati may or may not take the ad."

Miller disagrees with critics who say that the Internet is making people more isolated. "There are groups all over the country now that were Internet related," Miller pointed out. "A bunch of people will get together—I guess they call it 'chatting' on the Internet. And then I guess one person after a few weeks or months or years or whatever of this says, 'Well, I'm going to be at Denny's tonight. Why don't we all get together? Or, you know, the back room of the Big Boy.' And everyone is listening, or not listening or whatever they do on a computer. Typing and interacting with one another. And so they go down to Denny's at 10 p.m. and there's 30, 80 people there. And then they just decide to meet on a regular basis every week, every month, and these so-called S&M munch groups get started. They're all over the country now."

Miller sees these informal groups as an organic outgrowth of her decade-long efforts to provide a environment in which people with dominant or submissive interests could meet. "As a matter of fact, you know, it sort of made my role as a support group leader superfluous, which is great," Miller said. "Because I always said the day that I was out of business would be the happiest day of my life because it would mean that people are getting together on their own. They're finding love. They're married. You know, they don't have to masturbate alone or be frenzied or obsessed or that sort of thing."

# PHONE SEX FOR FUN AND PROFIT

## IN THE PHONE SEX BUSINESS, A GOOD HOLD TIME IS IMPORTANT

The massive popularity of sexually oriented audiotext has resulted in a growing demand for women (and a smaller number of men) to handle the huge numbers of incoming calls, both at the larger service bureaus and the smaller independent operations. In 1997, when the phone sex industry's revenues were pegged at approximately $1 billion, an estimated 250,000 people each evening used the telephone to engage in phone sex. According to *U.S. News and World Report*, "Some calls reach a recorded message, but most are answered by 'actresses'—bank tellers, accountants, secretaries, and housewives earning a little extra money at the end of the day."[26]

In recruiting operators, phone sex business owners such as Heather and Nancy have been able to take advantage of not only American society's somewhat looser attitudes toward sex in general and pornography in particular, but also of the nation's economic uncertainty. The job pitch is certainly attractive: reasonable to good pay, flexible hours, a feeling of helping others, and the chance to act out some fantasies. Prospective employers also highlight the fact that the phone sex industry has made it possible to participate in the high earnings of the pornography industry without being exposed to some of the dangers traditionally associated with either pornography or the sex business in general: the loss of privacy and potential embarrassment of posing nude and/or appearing in an sex film; or the threat of disease from having multiple partners in a sex film.[27] The argument illustrates the further technological sanitization of pornography.

And then, of course, there is the tried-and-true advertising technique of simple exaggeration. One company ran the following ad in the November 1997 *Cosmopolitan:*

> Be an Adult Telephone Entertainer! Work from your home. Set your own hours. Make up to $7,500/month. Our book will teach you everything you need to know "plus" guaranteed employment opportunity! To order by credit card, call 1-888-845-6592, or send $19.95 + $3.00 s/h to: DITA, P.O. Box 13088, Las Vegas, NV 89112-1088.

While it is certainly possible to make that kind of money as the owner and operator of a phone sex business (particularly once the business hires additional operators), few if any operators make that much money. Far more realistic were the ads that ran in *The Village Voice* in February 1998:

> ** FANTASY TALKERS **
> Women earn $8-$12/hr doing phone sex calls. FT/PT. All hours available. (212) 741-2793.

> ** WORK AT HOME **
> Record Sex messages on the phone. $8-$10/hr. F/T - P/T, flex hrs. No experience nec. (212) 741-2793.

The hourly rates set out in the *Voice* ads are actually consistent with what most service bureaus pay phone sex operators. Shawna Gnutel, who interviewed five phone sex operators in Toronto in the winter of 1997, reported that the service bureaus there paid a base salary of $70 for an eight-hour phone sex shift. However, most service bureaus offer incentives for the amount or number of minutes logged during a shift (one bureau, for instance, would pay a $100 bonus to each operator who logged more than 200 minutes of calls over an eight-hour period) and additional incentives for keeping callers on the phone for the longest average time.[28] Gnutel reported that despite the bonuses, at least one of the women she interviewed ("Julia") rarely averaged more than $85 per shift, or a little more than $10 per hour.

In addition to the relatively low pay, the working conditions at a service bureau are usually described as unpleasant, although some operators say that they enjoy the work. Interviews are occasionally published, in fact, in which operators describe the orgasms they experienced while talking to callers. In a 1997 article for the e-zine *Fishnet,* Marlayna Dawson (an assumed name) wrote: "Although phone sex is conducted between people who never touch each other—people who, in fact, have an instrument between them at all times—that doesn't mean it isn't real sex. And it isn't only real for the guy who picks up the tab. The dirty little secret in the phone sex industry is that 'the girls' frequently get their rocks off, too."[29]  Dawson went on to say that she "had an orgasm on my very first night, while talking—or rather listening—to a particularly verbal and imaginative caller. In hindsight, I think that the very concept of what I was doing was inherently exciting to me. I was, after all, turning on men from coast to coast; it made me feel lush, sexy and powerful."[30]

In general, the working conditions in the larger service bureaus belie Dawson's report of rooms filled with happily climaxing phone sex operators. Many women report long hours, rigid time constraints, few breaks, and strict regulations, a combination that usually is not particularly conducive to male or female orgasms.[31]  In addition, the phone sex operators have to deal with crank calls, offbeat sexual requests, and occasionally misogynistic callers. Under the circumstances, it is not surprising that the average burnout rate for workers at service bureaus is about six months.

The biggest pressure for operators in the large phone sex bureaus is the fact that callers are paying by the minute. In order to maximize profits, phone sex companies stress "high average hold times," which are, simply enough, the average length of each call. The longer the callers stay on the phone, the higher the bill. The push for a high average hold time leads to a cat-and-mouse game between the operators and the callers, in which the operators try to delay climax as long as possible (often by talking about anything *but* sex) without irritating or disgusting the caller. "For the record," Dawson writes, "the national average on male ejaculation via phone sex is six minutes"[32] (whether she was joking at the time is unclear). Service bureaus use a variety of techniques, including lengthy menus, lengthy program descriptions, and financial incentives for the operators, to get more than six minutes out of each caller. Women who are particularly successful at teasing out calls earn a valuable credential. "Girls get reputations as they go from bureau to bureau," Heather said, "as being a girl who has a great average hold time."

The pressure of the work environment and the demands of the callers leave little opportunity for the operator's imagination or own fantasy. "Ninety percent of the time," Julia told Gnutel, "they just want a little bit of heavy breathing, a little bit of description. And when they come they usually hang up. So that's it. It's really straightforward. I often read while I'm doing it."[33] Heather's experience at a service bureau was similar: "[The caller's] probably not gotten the fantasy that he wanted. The girl didn't really listen to him. She was snapping gum and reading and filing her nails while she was on the phone. You know, the typical thing that they make a joke out of in the movies."

Part of the reason for operator indifference (aside from the fact, as a different "Julia" told Wendy Chapkis, that "the majority of men out there have sexual imaginations of grasshoppers")[34] is undoubtedly the realization that for the same hour of work for which they are being paid $9–10, the service bureau is grossing between $180 and $360. Even given overhead costs (telecommunication equipment, credit card processing, labor costs, office space, etc.), the service bureaus pay their employees only a small fraction of their gross revenues. In addition, the larger service bureaus replicate the same "missionary theory" of corporate management that has traditionally pervaded the pornography industry: Men at the top of the organizational chart and women on the bottom, with relatively little movement between the two.

Not all phone sex businesses are large service bureaus, of course, and the differences in working conditions between large and small shops are often significant. In general, women (and men) who work for smaller phone sex operations have the opportunity to set their own hours and to work in the comfort of their home (although some service bureaus will patch calls into an operator's home as well). More important, the smaller phone sex operations tend to offer much better pay than that offered by a service bureau. For instance, as a personal adviser for Video Alternatives, an operator is paid 50 cents per minute for each minute billed (Video Alternatives charges its callers a flat $3 per minute). An operator's pay goes up in stages depending on the number of minutes billed per month. Operators billing more than 750 minutes per month (about 3 hours per week) are paid 76 cents per minute, while operators who cross the 3,000 minute level (about 12 hours per week) are paid 95 cents per minute, which works out to an impressive $57 per hour for 50 hours work, or a gross monthly income of $2,850. Over at P.E.P., Miller pays her counselors $40 per hour (out of a $119 hourly charge), and Heather recently raised the pay of her operators to 65 cents per minute, or $39 per hour, out of an hourly charge of about $210.

The extra pay widens the pool of prospective employees. "Most of the women that work in the service bureaus," Heather said, "are undereducated. A lot of them are like single mothers desperately trying to make a living at something." As the pay scale rises, however, so do the levels of education. "A lot of [my operators]," Heather said, "are college students or housewives. And I try to pick women with good healthy attitudes who are essentially uninhibited sexually as well. They have to enjoy men. I try not to hire, you know, bitter ladies. There are a lot of them out there." The makeup of Miller's counselors is similar: "My girls are great. Most of them are college educated. They're all true dominant or submissive ladies, or switchable as they say. They're not actresses."

Perhaps due to the fairly specific interests of her service's clientele, Miller offers her counselors more guidance and training than do most other phone sex services. In addition to requiring counselors to install a second phone line, Miller also expects new employees to read both Dale Carnegie's *How to Win Friends and Influence People* and Bonnie Gabriel's *The Fine Art of Erotic Talk*. P.E.P. also provides each new counselor with a comprehensive training packet and a one-to-two–hour training session with Goddess Glory, the Executive Director of P.E.P. And each February P.E.P. brings all of its counselors to Albuquerque—all expenses paid—for seminars and workshops.[35]

## AMATEUR SEX CHAT

Not all of the phone sex occurring across the country takes place with a clock ticking in the background. As prostitutes complained at the start of World War II, it can be tough to make an honest buck when so many are willing to give it away for free. Over the past decade, a number of technological innovations have been adapted to allow nonprofessionals to talk directly to each other and engage in phone or cyber sex, obviating the need for a professional phone sex operator. Since even these services, however, carry at least a small chance of rejection or disappointment, paid phone sex operations continue to prosper and in all likelihood will continue to do so. After all, professional phone sex operators (and tape recordings, for that matter) are paid not to reject or disappoint a caller.

One of the first popular amateur pay-per-call technologies were "party lines," phone systems that allow multiple callers to join in ongoing nationwide conversations on a wide range of different topics. Party lines are a throwback to the early days of phone service, when most households were connected to a party line that let everyone on the same line listen to everyone else's conversation. But unlike the early party lines (which provided their entertainment for free), today's chat lines often cost $2 to $3 per minute, and the cost of talking coast-to-coast mounts quickly. As with other technologies, sex was an early driving force for the chat line market, accounting for as much as a third of the pay-per-call industry's $225 million in revenues in 1987.

Party lines reached their peak in the late 1980s, fueled in large part by revenues from teens who often rang up huge phone bills talking to other teens on lines such as 1-900-GO-TEENS. The chat lines, however, were a victim of their own success and of the onset of new technology. Industry excesses and overreaching were a major problem: By marketing often expensive party lines to naturally garrulous teenagers, the industry all but guaranteed outraged reactions from both parents and legislators, as media outlets gleefully ran stories of monthly phone bills in the thousands of dollars. More important, the lines helped to contribute to the introduction of 900 blocking technology, which limited the number of households from which 900 calls could be made. Use of party lines also dropped rapidly as computers and online services became more common in the late 1980s and early 1990s. The primary reason was economic: The cost of party lines compared badly to the cost of joining an online chat room on a nationwide computer service like Compuserve, Prodigy, or America Online.[36] A significant number of computer systems were undoubtedly purchased on the strength of the argument that it would reduce the family phone bill.

Another popular application of phone technology by amateurs is the use of the much-despised voice mail technology for adult personal ads. Adult voice mail systems enable callers to leave messages describing themselves and the activities in which they would like to engage, their availability to do so, their interests, and to browse through the messages that other callers have left on the system.

Such services generally charge \$1–\$3 per minute, although women are often allowed to call and place ads for free in order to ensure an adequate gender mix.

Over the past year, adult voice mail systems have been joined or augmented by so-called "virtual chat services," where amateur men and women from around the country call in and engage in phone sex with other nonprofessional phone sex callers. Among the leading companies in the field are Dick Meets Jane (New York City and others), The Buddy System (Minneapolis), and Nightline (Dallas).[37]

A virtual chat system starts out much like an adult voice mail system. For a per-minute fee, callers connect to the service, listen to voice mail messages posted by other people who are online at the same time, and post messages of their own (once a caller hangs up, his or her messages are erased). A typical message might sound like this: "Hi, I'm Rob, I'm a five-foot-ten blond surfer looking for a fun chat and a good time." If a caller hears a message that he or she finds interesting, then the caller can leave that person a message. The first person can then decide whether or not to answer. After exchanging messages, the callers can make another menu choice and begin talking directly to each other. The phone sex service blocks telephone features like *69 and Caller ID, and callers are encouraged to use first or fake names only.[38]

For "Dick Meets Jane" founders Katie Maher and Gary Baron, the fact that their service consists of two strangers having a sexy chat with each other is its chief selling point. "These days," Maher told *Cosmopolitan*, "people are a lot more comfortable being intimate with strangers. It allows you to be up front about what you want, whether it's talking, getting turned on, or even a relationship."[39]

In time, virtual chat lines will face a strong challenge from the Internet. The chief advantage for the Internet is cost: A single-20 minute phone call to even the cheapest virtual chat service costs more than an entire month's worth of unlimited Internet access. The trade-off, of course, is that virtual chat provides the excitement of actually talking to another person and leaves one's hands free for purposes other than typing. On the other hand, although the Internet is becoming an increasingly important option for telephone communications, it will still be some time before actually talking to someone on the Internet is as easy as picking up the phone.

Nonetheless, it is clear that the tremendous cost advantages of the Internet have made it an enormously popular medium for sexual conversation between consenting adults. Most of the major online services and a large number of Web sites have chat rooms where people can meet and discuss various topics. Users can remain part of the group discussion or have a private conversation with someone that they meet online.

Another hugely popular medium for sexual discussion online is Internet Relay Chat (IRC), a Unix program created in Finland in 1988 by Jarkko Oikarinen. The program is designed to allow Internet users to create online channels where people can exchange real-time messages with each other on specific topics. The program also allows individuals in a channel to talk privately with each other. The channels are located on a variety of IRC networks (EFNet, Undernet, IRCnet, etc.) that distribute the typed messages through computers known as IRC servers. Users can connect to any of the thousands of IRC channels by running software known as an IRC "client," which passes the user's messages on to an IRC server for distribution to other users on that channel. Most IRC clients are distributed as shareware; the two most popular for PCs are mIRC and PIRCH.[40]

Like many other Internet resources, IRC is not governed or administered by any central organization, although most channels have channel operators (online moderators) to make sure that basic levels of civility and good behavior are observed. The technology has proved useful for distributing information from areas of the world not easily reached by traditional media. During the Persian Gulf war in 1991, for instance, IRC was used to distribute information from the Middle East. It saw similar use in 1993 during the attempted coup against Boris Yeltsin in Moscow.[41]

If IRC users aren't reporting on war, they may well be talking about love (or at least sex). A quick search of available channels turns up dozens devoted to various sexual topics, including: #3waysex,[42] #BlackWhiteSex, #cybersex, #GaySex, #slavesex, and so forth. The conversations are generally uninhibited, all the more so because (unlike a person's voice) typed messages do not readily offer clues about the age and sex of the person actually sending the message.[43]

Despite their popularity, there is little evidence that IRC or other online chat rooms have made much of a dent in the for-profit adult audiotext market. In the ten years since IRC was created, phone sex revenues have grown from a few million dollars to $1 billion. The advantage that the audiotext industry enjoys is due in large part to the fact that there are still at least three times as many homes with telephones as homes with Internet access. It also seems fair to say that people find a live conversation (or at least listening to the sounds of sex) to be a more arousing experience than typing naughty words into a computer.

# A REMARKABLY SIMPLE PORNOGRAPHY BUSINESS

One of the reasons that the phone sex industry has experienced such explosive growth is that compared to the equipment requirements for setting up even the simplest Web site, starting a phone sex business is refreshingly simple and inexpensive: the only equipment an entrepreneur needs to establish a phone sex business is a telephone and a voice.[44] Thanks to a century of infrastructure investment and technological innovation, even the most basic telephone instantly gives a phone sex entrepreneur the ability to sell phone sex cheaply and efficiently to customers anywhere in the nation or even the world.

## TELEPHONE LINES

It is difficult to imagine any pornography business that is simpler than phone sex: If one wanted to do so, one could set up and run a phone sex business using nothing more than an existing household phone line. Doing so has the obvious advantages of simplicity and low cost: no new lines to install and no new terminology to worry about. The disadvantages of using a home phone to run a phone sex business, of course, are equally obvious: 1) If the business is at all a success, it will be difficult for noncustomers to get through; 2) Notoriety also might be a problem—marketing a phone sex line is roughly the equivalent of writing "For a Good Time, Call . . ." on every public bathroom stall in a three-state region, and using a number that could be recognized by family and friends might be embarrassing; 3) It's difficult to know how to answer the phone during "business" hours; 4) If a caller gets too persistent or is simply disturbing, it is handy to be able to change numbers without having to worry about telling family or friends; and 5) Having just one line makes it much more difficult to check credit cards while keeping the anxious caller on the line. For all of those reasons, most phone sex entrepreneurs choose to have a second line put in, and most service bureaus require operators to have a second line installed as a condition of employment.

As we've seen, there are a wide variety of different phone number and phone line systems to choose from when setting up this type of business. The most basic option, of course, is to install a second residential or business phone line. Phone sex operators who work out of their homes have a cost advantage, since the cost of installing and operating a residential line is generally cheaper than installing and operating a business line. However, the number of specialized phone numbers that are available to residential customers is generally more limited than those available to business customers, which can generally afford the cost of a PBX.

One valuable type of phone service that individual business owners consider is an 800 number, so that callers do not have to bear the cost of the call.[45] The 800 numbers generally do not have the advantage of automatic billing that 900 numbers do, but with appropriate payment options like credit cards or wire transfers, they are nearly as effective. While an 800 number can be expensive, it is virtually a necessity in a business that charges by the minute. The major drawback to using a non-800 line is that it requires callers from outside the area code to foot the bill for the call, which may discourage some potential callers and keeps the calls of others short.

For businesses, the phone companies have come up with a number of different area codes (i.e., 900, 976, 500), and most have gained widespread use in the phone sex industry. As a general rule, the cost of the equipment required to set up and operate such numbers makes them impractical for individual entrepreneurs; as we've seen, however, there are a wide variety of programs that are specifically designed to give entrepreneurs access to the benefits of the new area codes.

## TELEPHONES AND PERIPHERAL EQUIPMENT

Unlike other high-tech pornography businesses, a small or even a midsize phone sex operation places a much lower premium on the quality of the equipment used. Even the least expensive telephone is more than adequate to handle the most sexually charged conversation. If operators are spending long stretches of time on the phone (and many do), it is common to replace a handset with a headset. Not only are headsets more comfortable, they also offers the advantage of hands-free operation.

If anything, the phone sex business is more concerned about the types of telephone technology that should not be used. Despite the popularity of both cordless and cellular phones, neither is particularly well-suited for use in the phone sex business. There have been a number of high-profile interceptions of cellular phone calls recently, including incidents involving former Speaker of the House Newt Gingrich, the late Princess Diana, Prince Charles, and Tom Cruise and his wife, Nicole Kidman, as well as a report of an investigation that two Peoria firefighters—one male and one female—used their cellular phones to engage in phone sex from different rooms in the firehouse. (The results of the investigation into the alleged phone sex were inconclusive, but the two were reprimanded for playing a round of strip Ping-Pong in the station recreation room.)[46] Anecdotal reports of cordless phone conversations being picked up by other cordless phones in a neighborhood or even by nearby baby monitors are also quite common.

The fact that there have been no reports of obscenity prosecutions based on interceptions by cellular or cordless phones suggests that participants in the industry are sensitive to the risk and avoid using such devices to conduct their businesses. Most undoubtedly realize that while most prosecutors are basically willing to essentially ignore phone sex conducted on wired phones, they would be forced to take some action if X-rated conversations started pouring out of neighborhood baby monitors.

## VOICE AND TRAINING

One of the things that makes the phone sex industry so successful, despite the growth of Internet "chat" rooms, is the human element, the essential unpredictability of live conversation. While what is said and the words a sex operator uses are paramount, an operator's voice—its pitch, speed, volume, and phrasing—is also important. The ability to do different accents also helps. "Heather" said that she uses different voices to play a range of characters for her callers. "It's acting," Heather said. "It's absolutely acting. There's no choice about it."

To the extent that phone sex is acting, it is largely improvisational, with more than a pinch of on-the-fly psychotherapy thrown in. Learning occurs largely on the job, since this is not a sector of the economy that is blessed with a lot of training options (although various recent films, like Michael Lehmann's *The*

*Truth About Cats and Dogs,* Robert Altman's *Short Cuts,* and Spike Lee's *Girl 6* have offered some pointers). Operators who work in a central location for a large service bureau have a small advantage in that they can watch and hear how other operators handle calls. Heather, who started her career in phone sex at a large service bureau, agreed. "I didn't know a lot of different things—a lot of the different words, but you sort of listen to what the other girls said and kind of picked it up." Operators who work as independent contractors at home, however, often have little guidance.

Contrary to the popular perception, the content of phone sex conversations can vary widely. Some services, among them Video Alternatives's Personal Advisor program, do not even consider themselves phone sex operations. "We advertise ourselves as a CHAT LINE," the company's recruitment letter stresses, "friendly girls [and one guy] where callers can have a one-on-one conversation. How intimate you get depends on each call." In the Personal Advisor manual, operators are reminded that "there are very few callers that only want to talk about sex. Most are great friendly guys that will talk about sports, work, relationships, life and death, religion, etc. and even the weather and current events." A similar pattern is found in other smaller phone sex operations, particularly those where callers pay for a block of time instead of paying by the minute.

On the other hand, when callers are paying by the minute, as they do for most phone sex services, there is little interest in small talk and the dialogue tends to be more tightly scripted. As one phone sex operator said, "I found out that what they really want is 'huh, huh, huh, uhhh—making noises in a high-pitched voice—and saying things like 'Give me your big dick.' No, actually it wasn't 'dick,' it's always 'cock,' 'cock' and 'pussy.' The words are very specific."[47] There is a constant tension between what the caller wants to hear—the words and sounds that will help him or her reach orgasm—and the efforts of the operator to prolong the call as long as possible.

## PAYMENT

The issue of payment can be particularly challenging for independent phone sex operators. The most convenient form of payment is the credit card; in order to accept that form of payment, an operator needs to have a relationship with a credit card processing company. Many (if not most) credit card processing companies are reluctant to work with small businesses and even more reluctant to work with small, sex-related businesses (at least until the business demonstrates a consistent cash flow).[48] The chief problem lies in the so-called "chargebacks," instances in which the customer refuses to pay a particular credit charge. "Most banks," Heather said, "don't want chargebacks rates over 1 percent. Pay sites get a lot more. Way higher than that because of the monthly billing." Like many other online businesses, Heather's does not have a merchant account and instead uses a credit card processing company which will take as much as 20 percent of the amount charged as a processing fee.

There are other possibilities for operators who do not have a relationship with a credit card processor. When Nancy Ava Miller, decided to start charging for her dominant/submissive phone sex calls, a friend taught her how to get paid without having to process a credit card.

"I didn't have MasterCard or VISA capability," Nancy said. "So one day a girlfriend of mine—this was in 1990 after I officially turned P.E.P. into a business— mentioned that she was going to be visiting with a gentleman privately, and she mentioned that she was going to get a deposit from him beforehand, but he was coming right over and he was a stranger. And I said, 'Well, how? How are you going to get a deposit?' Because I knew she didn't have MasterCard or VISA capability."

Her friend said that she would have the gentleman wire the deposit using Western Union, but Nancy was skeptical about how many men would be willing to go to the trouble of wiring money. "Even the most enthusiastic person," Nancy pointed out, "if he has to drive ten miles to Western Union, by the time he gets there his little pee-pee is down. He's forgotten that he promised to send the money."

Nancy's friend explained that a guest or caller can wire money through Western Union simply by calling the company and placing a charge on his credit card. The receiving party can call a few minutes later and confirm that the money has been paid.

"So I felt my little brain start churning," Nancy said, "and the next time a gentleman called and wanted to talk, I gave him the rate, and I acted like I'd been doing it forever. And I said, 'If you want to talk, it's $50 for a half an hour. You can call Western Union' and yada, yada, yada. And the guy said okay. And I thought, 'Yeah, right.' He called me back. He said it was done. I called Western Union and the money was there." Within the week, Nancy was grossing $300–$350 per day, and after a couple of years, she was able to get credit card processing capability.[49]


## MARKETING ISSUES

As with any other business, running a successful phone sex operation depends on attracting a sufficient number of customers and keeping them satisfied. As Hamlet once observed, however, "Aye, there's the rub." Advertising is critical to operating a successful business, and the cost of marketing a phone sex business can range from a few dollars a week to many thousands per month.

Prior to the advent of the Internet, the most effective means of attracting customers was a classified or display ad, either in a newspaper or in a glossy sex magazine. While the majority of newspapers (particularly large metropolitan dailies) will not accept advertisements for certain types of businesses, including phone sex operations, many smaller newspapers see sex-related advertising as a valuable source of revenue. In fact, some members of the so-called "alternative press," like the *Boston Phoenix* or the *Village Voice,* have entire sections devoted to sex-related advertisements, including fairly explicit personal ads ("Professional gentleman into restraints, toys, creative teasing and semi-public play seeks slender woman with class, taste, exceptionally sensitive nerve endings and wicked imagination"), escort services, adult book stores, strip and massage clubs, and of course, chat lines and phone sex. Ads for phone sex are not limited to urban newspapers; in the *Valley Advocate,* for instance, a weekly alternative newspaper published in the Pioneer Valley in western Massachusetts, typical ads read:

> SARAH I'm 18, 5'1", 97 lbs, hot-redhead, big-busted, seeks horny men! Toll free! 1-800-364-6948.

> Cheating WIVES MA/CT HOME Ph. #'s. 1-900-388-5533 Ext. 152. $2.95/min. 18+.

> Intelligent B&D/S&M Fetish conversation with LOVE. Free inquiry: 617-576-9792. Also, LIVE 24 hour dispatcher. Lovely & polite lady connects you immediately with dominant or submissive lady. 818-609-9046. Love, Nancy Ava Miller. www.peoplove.com.

The cost of running a one-inch classified ad in a smaller alternative newspaper like the *Valley Advocate* is about $46 per week (less for multiple weeks), while similar classified ads in the *Boston Phoenix* or the *Village Voice* start at about $100 per week (display ads, of course, are more expensive). The difference in cost between the *Advocate* and the *Phoenix* is purely circulation: an ad in the *Valley Advocate* might be seen by as many as 28,000–30,000 people, while an ad in the *Boston Phoenix* can be seen by as many as 100,000 to 120,000 in any given week.

Ads in one of the glossy sex magazines are a whole different ballpark; getting a phone sex ad in front of *Penthouse's* several million readers takes a serious investment. Based on a recent rate card, even the cheapest black-and-white display ad (2⅛-by-1-inch) runs $2,470 per month. At the high end of the scale, *Penthouse* charges up to $40,700 per month for a four-color, full-page ad (although purchases of multiple pages can bring that down to "merely" $32,200 per page). Clearly, some companies are making enough money to justify such prices: For the May 1998 issue of *Penthouse,* for instance, the magazine sold more than a dozen full-page ads for phone sex and myriad smaller ads.

Although in its infancy, the Internet's impact on the phone sex industry will be profound, if only for the savings that it offers for advertising budgets. Most Internet service providers (ISPs), as part of their $14.95 or $19.95 monthly price, include a megabyte of storage space on the ISP's server for subscriber home pages. Depending on content, a megabyte is more than enough space to hold a number of individual Web pages, replete with photos of the phone sex operator, descriptions of special likes and dislikes, links to related sites, special offers, and so on. The cost savings can make a big difference. "I didn't put up a Web site until October of '96," Heather said. "That's when things really started taking off. It was costing me $15 a month as opposed to $300 or $400 a month to advertise."

For the $2,470 cost of a single 1-inch black-and-white classified ad in *Penthouse*, an entrepreneur can hire a Web site design firm to create an interactive Web site, completely in color and loaded with the latest Internet bells and whistles. More important, instead of having a potential audience of 4 million or so *Penthouse* readers, a phone sex company using the Internet to advertise has a potential audience of 100 million people in the United States alone and at least twice that worldwide. Heather, for instance, reports that her Web site has brought in phone sex callers from Canada, Britain, and even Australia.

In addition to expanding the potential market, the Internet also offers a Web site operator the room to advertise business sidelines. One of the limitations of using classified advertising to market a phone sex business is that the average 1-inch ad has little room for anything more than the name of the business and a phone number. On a Web page, however, there is plenty of room to offer related products for sale, including photos, videos, audio files, and even membership in an online fan club. Some operators also offer clothing (bras, panties, garters, etc.) that they have worn, allegedly, in the throes of passion.

What the Internet giveth, the Internet can taketh away. At the same time that the Internet is making it possible to market phone sex services to virtually every nation in the world, it is also making it possible for businesses in those countries to compete here in the U.S. If a caller has a yen to engage in phone sex with someone with an Irish or Australian accent, it will be increasingly easy to find the appropriate phone sex service. As competition increases online, phone sex companies are likely to try to distinguish themselves by price, convenience, and even the natural accents of their operators.[50]

# LEGAL ISSUES

## OBSCENITY

When two friends or lovers are having a phone conversation and no money is changing hands, they can say whatever they want to each other. Under most circumstances, the government has no interest in or right to monitor private conversations, regardless of how lewd or obscene the conversation gets.

The government does believe, however, that it has an interest in commercial conversations, where one person is paying for the privilege of listening to or talking to another person on the phone. This is particular true when congressmen are receiving outraged calls from constituents and businesses back home, complaining about the fact that their teenagers or employees have racked up huge phone bills without their knowledge or consent. In 1983, even before the first big surge in the phone sex industry, Congress passed an amendment to the Communications Act of 1934 which made it a crime to "to use telephone facilities to make 'obscene or indecent' interstate telephone communications 'for commercial purposes to any person under eighteen years of age or to any other person without that person's consent.' "[51] The express purpose of the legislation was to block access to sexual conversations by minors, and the legislation created a defense for phone sex providers who could demonstrate that they complied with Federal Communications Commission requirements for screening minors.

Over the next five years, the FCC promulgated a variety of regulations aimed at blocking access by minors to phone sex. After a series of court challenges,[52] the U.S. Court of Appeals in New York ruled that FCC regulations creating defenses for credit card screens, access numbers, and message scrambling "were supported by the evidence, had been properly arrived at, and were a 'feasible and effective way to serve' the 'compelling state interest' in protecting minors."[53]

In the meantime, Congress became impatient with the delay and with the fact that the Appeals Court had ruled that the FCC regulations could *not* bar nonobscene speech. In April 1988, in a move led by Senator Jesse Helms (R-N.C.), Congress amended the Communications Act again to "prohibit *indecent* as well as obscene interstate commercial telephone communications directed to any person, regardless of age."[54] Sable Communications, a Los Angeles affiliate of Carlin Communications (one of the nation's largest audiotext companies), brought suit challenging the new law, arguing that indecent phone sex is protected by the First Amendment and that Congress's bar on obscene phone sex should be overturned because it creates a "national standard of obscenity" and puts too heavy a burden on phone sex operators to tailor their speech to each community.

The Supreme Court agreed with the first argument and rejected the second. While recognizing that the U.S. government does have a compelling interest in protecting children "from the influence of literature that is not obscene by adult standards," the Court held that any regulations must be "designed to serve those interests without unnecessarily interfering with First Amendment freedoms."[55] The Court concluded that unlike radio broadcasts (which came under scrutiny in the infamous George Carlin "Seven Dirty Words" case),[56] phone sex requires a listener to take affirmative steps in order to hear the speech in question. As the Court put it:

> Placing a telephone call is not the same as turning on a radio and being taken by surprise by an indecent message. Unlike an unexpected outburst on a radio broadcast, the message received by one who places a call to a dial-a-porn service is not so invasive or surprising that it prevents an unwilling listener from avoiding exposure to it.[57]

Given that the FCC had already adopted reasonable regulations for preventing access by minors, the Court concluded that a total ban on indecent commercial phone sex was an unwarranted restriction on the First Amendment freedoms of adults.

Obscene commercial phone speech is another matter. The Court pointed out that it has repeatedly held that the protections of the First Amendment do not apply to obscene speech.[58] The Court also rejected Sable's argument that because Sable would have to tailor its message to the most restrictive community, the law in effect creates a national obscenity standard. The Court concluded that there was nothing unconstitutional about a law that prohibits the transmission of speech considered to be obscene in some communities and not in others, and said that the burden was on Sable to figure out a way to tailor its message to each community.[59]

The penalties for obscene phone sex, which can be severe, are still on the books. Fines range up to $50,000 per day for violations, and people convicted of violating the ban against obscene speech can be sentenced to federal prison for up to two years. Because of the variation in community standards, there is in fact a risk that a conversation with someone in San Francisco might be legal and the same conversation with someone in Des Moines might be highly illegal. The risk, however, is fairly small. Communities around the country that are concerned about the sexual content of phone sex simply do not have the resources to call all of the various phone sex lines to determine if the operators are engaging in obscene conversation, a fact that is partly illustrated by the phenomenal growth in the industry over the last 15 years. Even if communities did have the personnel to do so, successful prosecution would require finding the individual operator and the owners of the phone sex business employing the operator, successfully arresting them (usually out of state), prosecuting them, and then finding room in overcrowded prisons for new inmates. It is not surprising that there are neither published news reports or appellate court opinions involving obscenity prosecutions for phone sex.

Prosecutorial enthusiasm for this lengthy process is further weakened by the fact that even in the most conservative communities, there is always the possibility that the jury will not bring back a conviction of obscenity. When a Cincinnati jury, of all things, refused to find that various of Robert Mapplethorpe's photos were obscene, it undoubtedly chilled obscenity prosecutions not only in Cincinnati but in other jurisdictions as well. As a result, many jurisdictions are focusing their attention on the most serious sex-related crimes, including child pornography, and leaving the generally frustrating battle against adult pornography alone. While this may look like a victory for propornography and free speech forces, it would be a mistake to get too cocky about it. One outgrowth of the inability of communities to enforce their local decency standards is increased pressure on Congress by conservative groups to impose national limitations such as the Communications Decency Act, and it is not a battle that will subside anytime soon.

## CRAMMING AND OTHER TYPES OF FRAUD

It is not just what is being said that has created problems for the phone sex industry. A variety of high-tech scams have been associated with the industry, both by companies that provide phone sex and by people looking for ways to get it for free. Public concern over these various types of fraud have increased scrutiny on the industry and persistently raises the specter of further regulation.

In recent months, a number of reports have surfaced about a practice known as "cramming," which the *Christian Science Monitor* described as "the fastest growing scam in America." Cramming occurs when the suppliers of audiotext and phone services—not always but often sex services—charge consumers for services they did not order and bury the charges deep within the consumer's phone bill. In April 1998, for instance, the Federal Trade Commission filed suit against Interactive Audiotext Services, Inc., American Billing & Collection (doing business as ABC Services), U.S. Interstate Distributing, Inc., and four of their officers for allegedly charging customers without their consent and for failing to comply with FCC regulations that require that all service charges be disclosed at the start of a audiotext phone call.[60] In December 1997, the Public Utilities Commission of Ohio reported more than 250 complaints of unwarranted charges in a three-month period, most made by students living in group housing.[61] The National Consumers League, which began tracking cramming in 1997, reported that it was the leading complaint by consumers during the first three months of 1998.[62]

The phenomenon is already having an impact on the audiotext industry. Telephone information providers (including many phone sex services) often subcontract their billing services to companies known as "aggregators," which handle the billing for multiple smaller companies. Bell Atlantic announced a moratorium on new business from aggregators, and in July 1998, began refusing to reimburse companies that place suspect charges on consumers' bills.[63]

The phone sex industry is also often tainted by other types of criminal activity, since free access to telephone sex is often a strong motivation for theft of phone services. Some techniques, such as "phreaking" (building small electronic boxes to imitate a phone's electronic tones and thus gain free phone access) and "surfing" (cruising banks of public telephones and reading calling card numbers over people's shoulders) are well known. Less well known but equally insidious are crooks who cruise neighborhoods with cordless phones waiting to hear a dial tone. When they hear one, they park the car and use the homeowner's telephone line to dial their favorite phone sex service, leaving the unsuspecting homeowner with an often difficult-to-explain charge on their bill.[64]

Another area in which the phone sex industry has received close federal scrutiny is in the relationship between 800 numbers and foreign phone sex lines. Even given that pornography purchasers will pay a premium for their product, why, one might reasonably ask, would someone pay for a phone call to Guyana or São Tomé to get it? The simple answer is that much of the time, the caller has no idea that his phone call has been rerouted to the far corners of the earth or that the innocent-looking area code that he or she dialed is actually the area code for a small Caribbean island.

Although 800 numbers (and their newly created companion, 888) are supposed to be free to the caller, companies have figured out ways to make a caller bear the cost of using an 800 or 888 line. For instance, some 800 sex lines automatically transfer calls (without the caller's knowledge) to a number in another area code or even another country, and the caller is charged for the cost of making the second call.[65] Another common approach that fraudulent 800 numbers use is to direct callers to enter a so-called "access" code in order to gain access to the phone sex service. In reality, the access code is a second phone number also located thousands of miles away. Callers snared by these numbers cheerfully chat away on the "free" line, while the call is actually costing several dollars per minute. The first indication that the caller has that the 800 line was not in fact free is when the phone bill shows up.

Part of the regulatory measures adopted by the FCC was a provision barring phone companies from collecting for unauthorized 900 calls to other countries. The regulations do not cover 800 numbers, however, which makes it harder to persuade a phone company to strike a spurious phone sex charge to the Caribbean than to a 900 number in Los Angeles.

An increasingly popular option for phone sex businesses is to dispense with the 800 number altogether and simply advertise phone numbers located in other countries. Some of the phone numbers have the identifying code of "011," but others have innocent-looking area codes such as "809" (Dominican Republic and other parts of the Caribbean), which can easily be mistaken for domestic area codes.[66]

Some potential phone sex entrepreneurs may be tempted to dismiss these schemes as the actions of a few bad actors in the business. In general, that is probably true. The problem, however, is that schemes like these are the ones that garner the most attention and provide the greatest impetus for legislative restrictions on the industry. The phone sex business is an easy one to enter and a relatively easy one in which to make money, but it is also an industry that is scrutinized closely by Congress and the Federal Communications Commission. And unlike the Internet, telephone services have a long history of governmental oversight, which makes it far easier for the government to regulate "pay-per-call" services than the offerings on the Internet, where no such history of oversight exists.

# NOTES

1. According to the *New Republic*, Gramm's actual investment may have been as high as $15,000. John B. Judis, "The Porn Broker," *New Republic*, June 5, 1995.
2. Judis, "The Porn Broker."
3. Sidney Blumenthal, "Gramm! The Movie," *New Republic*, June 19, 1995. Blumenthal,

who somehow managed to find a copy of the movie on videotape, goes on to describe the film in some detail. The apparent glee with which Blumenthal described *White House Madness* may help explain why, three years later, Republican operatives allegedly fed false rumors to Matt Drudge that Blumenthal had a hidden history of domestic abuse

4. Eric Schlosser, "The Business of Pornography," *U.S. News and World Report*, February 10, 1997.
5. While not going so far as to actually refuse pornography-related revenues, the company has been active in efforts to control access to pornography by children. Among AT&T's recent efforts, it has reserved a special 900 exchange (555) for nonsex businesses and has been active in the development and adoption of PICS, a Web site rating system that can be used to filter out adult material.
6. Barbara Rudolph, "Who Ever Said Talk Was Cheap?" *Time*, September 19, 1988, p. 44.
7. "The Best (And Safest) Way to Profit from Pay-per-call Numbers" (n.d.), online at http://www.eastelcom.com/industry.htm.
8. A trend that has begun to affect other nominally free information such as directory services.
9. Rudolph, p. 44.
10. "The Best (And Safest) Way to Profit from Pay-per-call Numbers."
11. Recent revenues have not been so lucrative. In fact, Inphomation Communications, Inc., the company that started the Psychic Friends Network, is currently operating under a Chapter 11 bankruptcy after revenues dropped to $25 million in 1997 and $0 in 1998. "Inphomation Communications, Inc.," *Hoover's Company Capsules*, December 1, 1998.
12. "Aural sex," *Time*, May 9, 1983, p. 39.
13. Fred Bruning, "Dialling [sic] for titillation," *MacLean's*, June 27, 1983, p. 9.
14. "Adults Only Spectrum," *Boston Globe*, December 1, 1996.
15. Eastern Telcom's list of termination points is online at http://www.eastelcom.com/terms.htm.
16. Triton Telecom's list of termination points is online at http://www.tritontele.com/terminations.html.
17. The phone companies have the capability to block calls to a particular area code or overseas for any customer.
18. "Phone Sex Goes Global With Help of Technology," *Washington Post*, September 25, 1996. It should be noted, of course, that not every audiotext call to Guyana or other nations serving as termination points involves phone sex.
19. *Ibid.*
20. *Ibid.*
21. Seth Lubove, "E-sex," *Forbes*, December 16, 1996, p. 58.
22. A PBX system is essentially a miniature phone system within a business or organization. The PBX system switches calls among employees while giving everyone in the business or organization access to a common set of outside lines.
23. http://www.800900.com/adult.html.
24. The Heather's Honeys Web site is at http://www.heathershoneys.com.
25. The P.E.P. Web site is at http://www.peplove.com.
26. Schlosser, "The Business of Pornography."
27. A risk that the adult film industry asserts is actually very small, as all participants in sex films are regularly tested for a range of communicable diseases.
28. Shawna M. Gnutel, "From the Edge of the Pink Collar Ghetto: Why Women are Hanging Up On Phone Sex Work," Vol. 11, Contemporary Women's Issues Database, December 1, 1997, pp. 28–29.
29. Marlayna Dawson, "Talking Dirty: Confessions of a Phone Sex Operator," *Fishnet*, (n.d.), online at http://www.fishnetmag.com/essays/1996/11-29/conf_phone_sex.html.
30. Dawson, "Talking Dirty."
31. In fact, one of the reasons that a relatively small number of men appear in the vast majority of adult videos is that the number of men who can perform under similar circumstances is quite small.
32. Dawson, "Talking Dirty."

33. Gnutel, pp. 28–29.
34. Wendy Chapkis, *Live Sex Acts,* (New York: Routledge, 1997), p. 111.
35. Recruitment notice, P.E.P. Web site, online at http://www.peplove.com/ladies.htm.
36. Many of the computer services also charged for connection time, but the rates were usually $1 to $2.50 per hour, compared to $2 to $3 per minute. The savings offered teens a dramatic incentive to shift their allegiance from party lines to chat rooms. Using a computer for teen chat was also preferable because frequently, a computer with a modem would be installed on its own phone line, lessening conflict with parents over phone use.
37. Lori Campbell, "Phone sex and the single girl," *Cosmopolitan,* April 1, 1998, p. 130.
38. *Ibid.*
39. *Ibid.*
40. For further information on these programs and instructions on how to obtain them, see David Caraballo and Joseph Lo, *The IRC Prelude,* last updated March 20, 1998, online at http://www.irchelp.org/irchelp/new2irc.html.
41. Joseph Lo et al., "IRC FAQ," 1996–97, online at http://www.irchelp.org/irchelp/altircfaq.html.
42. Virtually all IRC channel names begin with the "#" sign.
43. While the anonymity of IRC and chat rooms makes it possible for people to explore aspects of their sexuality that they might not want to explore in the real world, it also gives sexual predators the opportunity to lure children and teens into dangerous situations. Filtering programs offer some assistance in limiting underage access to these groups, but no software is perfect.
44. Things immediately get more complicated if tape recordings are used instead of live voice, but given the enormous competition in the recorded sex business, live phone sex offers much more viable income-producing opportunities.
45. Phone companies like AT&T have been working hard to market 800 numbers to nontraditional users. Over the last couple of years, for instance, the phone companies have been pushing 800 numbers as a way for parents to help make it less expensive for their children to call home from college.
46. Brent Whiting, "Strip Game Earns Pair Reprimand," *Arizona Republic,* August 25, 1988, p. A1.
47. Julia, phone sex worker, quoted in Chapkis, *Live Sex Acts,* p. 111.
48. The success of online pornography sites has resulted in a sharp rise in the number of credit card processing companies willing to work with small adult businesses. The downside, however, is that the cost of processing can be quite steep: as much as 20 percent of the amount charged.
49. Interview with author.
50. Dialects, of course, may prove problematic. British slang words for sexual activity are only vaguely familiar to most Americans, and Australians might just as well be speaking Kurdish.
51. Sable, citing 47 U.S.C. § 223(b)(1) (A) (1982 ed., Supp. IV).
52. *Carlin Communications, Inc. v. FCC,* 749 F.2d 113 (CA2 1984) (Carlin I); *Carlin Communications, Inc. v. FCC,* 787 F.2d 846 (CA2 1986) (Carlin II); *Carlin Communications, Inc. v. FCC,* 837 F.2d 546 (Carlin III), cert. denied, 488 U.S. 924 (1988).
53. Carlin III,  837 F.2d at 555.
54. Sable, 492 U.S. at 122 (emphasis supplied).
55. Sable, 492 U.S. 115, 126, quoting *Schaumburg v. Citizens for a Better Environment,* 444 U.S. 620, 637 (1980).
56. *FCC v. Pacifica Foundation,* 438 U.S. 726 (1978).
57. Sable, 492 U.S. 115, 128.
58. Sable, 492 U.S. 115,123.
59. Sable, 492 U.S. 115, 125–126.
60. Jennifer Oldham, "L.A. Phone Sex Operation Accused of Deceptive Billing," *Los Angeles Times,* April 23, 1998, p. D1.
61. Laura Donnelly, "Phone frauds scam students," *University Wire,* January 23, 1998.
62. Jon Marshall, "Phone Fraud 'Crams' Customer Bills," *Christian Science Monitor,* May 26, 1998, p. 14.
63. Jon Marshall, "Phone Fraud," p. 14.

64. Pat Gauen, "Greedy Trick 'Slams' Phone Customers," *St. Louis Post-Dispatch,* March 2, 1998, p. 1.

65. Similar practices are being used in conjunction with the relatively new 500 area code. Sean Callebs, "FCC's hands tied when it comes to offshore phone sex," December 4, 1995, online at http://cnnfn.com/archive/news/9512/telephone.sex/index.html.

66. Over the last couple of years, some of the Caribbean islands have adopted their own area codes (for example, 441 for Bermuda, 787 for Puerto Rico, and 876 for Jamaica). The ostensible reason is to give these nations more numbers for cellular phones, modems, and fax machines, but some island phone officials admit that it is an effort to distance themselves from the stain of 809 sex calls. Shelley Emling, "Sorry, wrong number: Caribbean shies away from phone sex," *Atlanta Journal and Constitution,* August 18, 1996, p. A17. Another, more cynical possibility is that it gives the island phone systems the opportunity to participate more directly in the enormous cash stream that sex calls generate.

# 6

# THE SEARCH
# FOR
# SATISFACTION

Gratiano speaks an infinite deal of nothing, more than any man
in all Venice. His reasons are as two grains of wheat hid in two bushels
of chaff: you shall seek all day ere you find them, and, when you
have them, they are not worth the search.
William Skakespeare, *The Merchant of Venice*, I.i, 114.

We are a nation awash in information. Twenty-four hours a day, seven days a week, a vast number of media outlets produce and distribute information on every aspect of human, animal, and plant life. It wasn't that long ago that the quantity of information was somewhat more manageable; as recently as the American Revolution, for instance, it was possible for someone like Thomas Jefferson or Benjamin Franklin to have read every important book in print and to own a significant number of them (Jefferson's personal library, after all, helped found the library at the University of Virginia, and Franklin's collection formed the core of the country's first public library in Philadelphia). Over the last two centuries, however, and particularly in the last 50 years, it has become difficult to keep up with just the newspaper and magazine articles that are published on a single subject, let alone relevant books, radio reports, and television programs.

The Internet exacerbates this problem. With its low cost of entry and ease of use, the Internet allows every computer owner to become a publisher of information or a commentator on world and national affairs. In the real world, entire industries are devoted to information organization and management, so it should come as no surprise that online equivalents exist. An increasingly well-capitalized fight is taking place among a number of different online directories and search engines as they compete to become the best-known (but not necessarily the best) search engine and the most popular "portal" to the Internet.[1]

# EVERY $20 BILLION INDUSTRY CAN USE A TRAVEL GUIDE

## THE BARRIERS PUBLISHERS OF PORNOGRAPHY GUIDES FACE IN THE MARKET

Even before the Internet established itself as the worldwide storm drain of information, a market for organizers of information was already well-established. Not only are people willing to pay for assistance in organizing the vast quantities of information available, they are also willing to pay for assistance in determining what information is valuable and what is not. Members of various professional groups are constantly deluged with offers for magazines, newsletters, and seminars designed to quickly and efficiently keep them up to speed on the important developments in their fields. Consumers are urged to buy magazines and books that will tell them the best schools, kids' names, mortgages, credit cards, vacations, restaurants, and so on. Hobbyists can choose among hundreds of different checklists and price guides to help them organize their various collections. (The Beanie Baby craze alone, for instance, had already resulted in the publication of at least 14 different guides by midsummer 1998, including: *The Book of Beanie Babies, Rosie's Price Guide for Ty's Beanie Babies, The Collector's Guide for Beanie Babies,* and of course, *The Beanie Baby Phenomenon: The Retired Beanie Babies Vol. 1.* By the end of the year, the number of titles had more than doubled.) As the pool of information continues to grow, so too does the market for resources and experts to help make sense of it all.

In the pornography industry, the success of the adult videos created the market demand for guidebooks. Not only were consumers suddenly faced with hundreds and thousands of different titles to choose from, the medium was also one for which consumers expected that certain types of organizing information would be available: lists of movies by a particular director or featuring a particular star, lists of top-grossing videos, plot summaries, and even critical reviews. After all, those types of materials were routinely available for nonadult fare, so why not for sexually explicit films as well?

Initially, information about adult films or other aspects of the pornography industry was limited to articles in such magazines as *Playboy* and *Penthouse.* However, the pornography industry now uses many of the same tools and techniques that are used to organize and present information on such nonsalacious topics as finances, gardening, sports, woodworking, or personal growth. Much of this change, of course, has been driven by the phenomenal growth of the pornography industry as a whole. Increasingly, mainstream media outlets are assuming that any industry generating upwards of $20 billion in revenues also produces a volume of information and/or products that need to be sorted, organized, and indexed, and that consumers will be willing to pay for not merely for the product (which has been amply demonstrated) but also for better information *about* the product.

The pornography industry's cooption of mainstream techniques for organizing information can be seen in a number of different areas. For instance, newsletters and trade publications about various sectors of the pornography industry, once relatively rare, are now progressively more common. Not all that long ago, a newsletter like *Hot Shots,* which specializes in reviews of amateur adult video publications, would have had a difficult time identifying and reaching a potential market. Today, even the simplest pornography-related newsletter uses the same marketing tools and techniques available to mainstream publications: display advertising in relevant national publications, mailing lists of potentially interested customers, and trailers and previews on video productions. Similarly, a glossy pornography trade publication such as *Adult Video News,* although not likely to be found on most newsstands, can now find a ready market among adult video producers and the thousands of independent video stores around the country.

Another popular medium for distributing more mainstream information and expertise is the conference or seminar. Seminars on running various types of online adult businesses, once unheard of, are now routinely held at trade shows for the online pornography industry, including AdultDex, WebExpo, and Interactive 2000. At a recent Interactive 2000 conference, for instance, the list of seminars included: "Turning Audiotext Experience into Internet Dollars," "Bald Women with Long Legs: An Audiotext Marketing Scenario," "Hardware and Software: The Nuts and Bolts of the Audiotext Industry," and "Legal Issues: Offering New Internet Services and Staying out of Trouble."

One indication of the seminar potential for the pornography industry was the success of the World Pornography Conference, held at the Center for Sex Research at the University of California in Northridge in September 1998. The primarily academic conference attracted 700 people, each of whom paid $175 to listen to seminars on topics like "Feminine-Produced, Woman-Centered Pornography," "Visionary Erotica and Pornography," and "Everything You Ever Wanted to Know About the Actors and Actresses in Erotic Films and Video From the People Who Were There." Although the success of the conference can be attributed in part to home field advantage (Northridge and the communities around it are home to nearly all of the U.S. hardcore and softcore video industry), it is certainly conceivable that a similar conference would do well in other parts of the country.[2]

Books are perhaps the most common method for distributing information about most activities, and publishers leap at the opportunity to print checklists and indices of hobbies, sports, politics, and other interests. Somewhat less enthusiasm is shown for books listing sexual resources on the Internet: Between books on cyberdating and guides to online sexual resources, only about a dozen titles have been published so far, compared with the hundreds of titles listing online resources in subjects like business, finance, sports, and so on. Clearly, most publishers are reluctant to appear to be endorsing or promoting Internet pornography by publishing a book that is specifically designed to help consumers find it. In addition, the nature of the Internet itself undercuts the value of publishing a guide to Internet pornography in book form. Web sites on the Internet are inherently fluid, and adult Web sites are particularly so. Over the last five years, hundreds of guides to more mainstream sites on the Internet have been published, each of which was at least partially out of date before it even hit the bookshelves. Within six months of publication, the usefulness of a published Internet site listing (apart from helping to hold up rows of more recent Internet guides) drops precipitously. The drop in usefulness for a published Internet pornography guide would be at least as rapid.

Despite apparent publisher concerns about printing guides to pornography, however, the number of titles appears to be slowly but steadily growing: the allure of latching onto a $15 billion to $20 billion dollar market is simply too compelling, and the potential social, political, and economic risks have diminished substantially. As mainstream publishers slowly warm to the topic, it will become easier for writers to successfully propose guides to various types of pornography.

The earliest entries in this genre, not surprisingly, were guides to adult videotapes. In 1984, Robert H. Rimmer persuaded Arlington House Publishers to publish *The X-Rated Videotape Guide;* in the fall of 1998, *The X-Rated Videotape Guide VII* was published by Prometheus Books. The newest edition of the guide joined a number of other indices of the adult film world, including: *The X-Rated Videotape Star Index II : A Guide to Your Favorite Adult Film Stars* (Rimmer, Prometheus Books, 1997); *The X-Rated Gay Video Guide* (Sabin, Companion Press, 1997); and *Superstars: Gay Adult Video Guide* (Jamoo, Companion Press, 1997).

Books about sexual material on computers also got a relatively early start, at least within the context of the industry. In 1993, Phil Robinson et al. published *The Joy of Cybersex: The Underground Guide to Electronic Erotica.* One of the few pre-Internet books on the subject, the *Joy of Cybersex* focused on chat rooms (like those found on Compuserve and AOL) and on the sexual materials available from various adult bulletin board systems around the country. More recent entries include Candi Rose's *Net.Sex* (1994), Nancy Tamosaitis's *Net Sex* (1995), *Modem Love: Your Step-by-Step Guide to Sex on the Information Highway* (1995), and *Virtual Strangers: A Woman's Guide to Love and Sex on the Internet* (1996), by Elizabeth Blackstone and Denton R. Moore, and *The Woman's Guide to Sex on the Web*, by Cathy Winks (1999). Probably no surer sign can be found of online pornography's growing acceptance in mainstream circles than the fact that it is now a subject in the *Complete Idiot's Guide* series: *The Complete Idiot's Guide to Sex on the Net* was published in December, 1998.

Even strip clubs and exotic dancers are getting more attention in print. In the summer of 1998, for instance, J.P. Danko published *Live Nude Girls: The*

*Top 100 Strip Clubs in North America* (Griffin Trade Paperback), and the *Exotic Dance Guidebook* (Rivercross Publishing) was published in December 1998.

While it may be relatively difficult to find a publisher for a catalog or index of the pornography industry, that challenge pales in comparison to finding a way to distribute information about the pornography industry over the airwaves. Radio and television, with their limited number of distribution channels and close government supervision, are the least receptive media to organizers of information about pornography, something that George Carlin discovered 25 years ago when the Federal Communications Commission banned his monologue "Filthy Words" from the airwaves (a sketch in which Carlin helpfully lists the seven words that can't be said on the public airways). The radio station on which it was aired appealed the FCC's order to the Supreme Court, but the Court upheld the FCC's decision.[3]

The chief problem for chroniclers of the pornography industry is that radio and television stations depend heavily on advertising revenues, which in turn are determined by the number of listeners or viewers in any given time slot. Whether or not a particular program about pornography will be aired depends in part on the station management's own attitudes toward pornography, but more on whether management believes that the material will attract negative attention (including possible boycotts) that will damage the station's advertising revenues. Although a series devoted to the pornography industry (something along the lines of the "Great Strippers of the Southeast," for instance) would certainly attract attention and arguably a large audience, a reporter or pornography expert would probably have a difficult time persuading a radio or television network that such a series was either morally or economically justified.[4] That is precisely the type of situation that MTV reporter Tabitha Soren recently faced. In the early fall of 1998, Soren coproduced and narrated a documentary titled *I Am a Porn Star,* a behind-the-scenes look at the making of adult films. Although Soren's work was broadcast once, MTV canceled a scheduled rebroadcast, allegedly because executives felt that the documentary's material was too racy.[5]

While primly avoiding the charge of supporting or promoting pornography by broadcasting arguably positive features or documentaries about the sex industry, station executives undercut the strength of their position by running and heavily promoting popular shows that can arguably be described as actually pornographic. Among the myriad examples that leap to mind are the *Jerry Springer Show,* the *Howard Stern Show,* Fox's now-defunct *Married . . . With Children,* WB's *Unhappily Ever After,* Comedy Central's *South Park,* and (ironically enough) most of the videos that are shown on MTV. The continued existence of these shows, of course, is directly attributable to the fact that each (to a lesser or greater degree) attracts a large audience, which translates directly into higher advertising revenues for the station or network.

## THE PERFECT MEDIUM FOR DISTRIBUTING
## INFORMATION ABOUT PORNOGRAPHY

As impressive as the pornography industry's advances into the mainstream have been, it is still relatively difficult to find a major media outlet for information about the pornography industry. It should come as no surprise, then, that the Internet has become the medium of choice for organizing and distributing information about the sex industry in general and pornography in particular. A Web site with information about the pornography industry (online or otherwise) can be set up without the approval of network or publishing executives; the costs associated with distributing information via the Internet are, as we'll see, far less than those required for any other medium; and the information can be easily updated in a very short time. In addition, the information can be retrieved by individuals in the privacy of their home, which increases the likelihood that they will do so.

The pornography industry capitalizes on the Internet by publishing information that cannot easily be published elsewhere. For instance, although there are now two nationally published guides to strip clubs, the amount of material that they contain is both finite and inherently subject to staleness. Moreover, published information is both expensive and time-consuming to update. By contrast, guides that are published on the Internet can be updated in minutes and distributed instantaneously worldwide for a fraction of a cent. A quick search of the Yahoo! directory in early 1999 turned up 14 different guides to strip clubs. Titles range from "StripClubList.com" to "Nightstars" to the "Ultimate Strip Club List."

Another significant benefit of the Internet for the pornography industry is the ability to publish information that no mainstream publisher (so far) would touch. For instance, neither Amazon nor Barnes & Noble lists any book purporting to list or review escort services, brothels, massage parlors, and so on. With little effort, however, directories and guides for virtually every aspect of the worldwide sex industry can be found on the Internet. Yahoo! alone, for instance, lists 12 directories to escorts, including Callgirlz.com and Global Male Escorts. In addition, a search of AltaVista using the key words "guide," "strip," and "club" turned up more than 68,000 pages containing those three words. Although not all of the sites contain guides to strip clubs, a large number (particularly at the top of the AltaVista search results) offer detailed descriptions and reviews of strip clubs.

One indication of the power of the online pornography industry as a whole is that virtually all online directories and search engines do in fact include pornography within the scope of the materials that they organize, and many sell advertising slots to pornographers for pages that are generated by searches for sexually oriented words or phrases. (For instance, if someone searches for nude photos of a particular celebrity, a Web site that specializes in such images might pay to have its advertising banner appear when the search engine lists its results.)

The very content of online directories such as Yahoo!, Netscape, and Infoseek also helps to underscore the sociosexual changes that have occurred in this country. Is it pornography, for instance, for a general Internet directory like Yahoo! to provide extensive listings of adult sites, carefully organized by category? Probably not, or at least not any more so than a printed catalog like Henry Ashbee's *Encyclopedia Of Erotic Literature* (1877-1885),[6] the Catholic Church's *Index Librorum Scriptorum* (which admittedly was intended to warn people away from pornographic material ), or a library book catalogue that tells patrons where to find copies of *Fanny Hill, Lady Chatterly's Lover,* or *The Thorn Birds.*

What makes the distinction between a pornographic resource and a nonpornographic resource on the Internet blurrier, however, is the fact that in the real world, most printed indices or library catalogs do not accept advertisements from the adult businesses they have cataloged. By contrast, many online directories do accept adult advertising, the bulk of which is often nearly as explicit as the content of the sites they are advertising.[7] For the Internet directories and search engines, the decision to both list pornographic resources and accept adult advertisements is largely economic: Having a list of adult sites, particularly a well-organized one like Yahoo!'s, is an effective way to increase traffic, which in turn improves ad revenues. At the same time, pornographic sites are among the Web leaders in terms of actually making money, which means that adult sites are the ones most likely to be able to afford ads in the first place. In the process, however, the line between pornographer and nonpornographer gets further blurred.

There are, to be fair, a number of large Internet organizations that do not accept adult business. America Online, for instance has refused to allow adult businesses to set up shop on its service and does not accept advertising from pornographers. The same is true for Microsoft and its online service, MSN. Most recently, the Internet portal/directory Infoseek was purchased by the Walt Disney Corp. and one month later, announced that it would no longer accept adult advertising.[8] Visitors to the Infoseek directory can still locate adult materials on the service by searching with the appropriate key words, but when the list of the adult sites pops up, it is not accompanied by one or more of the garish banners that adult Web sites tend to favor. It is estimated that Infoseek's decision will cost it as much as 10 percent of its ad revenues, which in turn account for as much as 95 percent of Infoseek's overall revenues. The question that remains to be answered is whether Infoseek's action will compel other directories such as Yahoo! and Netscape to follow suit.[9] So far, there is little indication that it will.

# HOW PORNOGRAPHERS MANAGE ADULT LINKS

From the very start of the World Wide Web, people have been competing to see who can compile the most comprehensive page of links on a given topic. If someone were looking for information on science fiction books, for instance, he or she might visit "Joe's *Star Trek* Page," because she had been told that Joe's Web site has links to 300 or 400 other Web sites dealing with science fiction in general or *Star Trek* in particular. Similarly, if someone is looking for information about the Alfa Romeo "Montreal," a limited-edition sports car manufactured in the 1970s, there probably is no better place to start than the "Alfa Romeo Home Page"[10] created by Bruce Taylor, a resident of Geneva, Switzerland. A textbook example of a dedicated hobbyist's resource, Taylor's Web page does not have a drop of advertising on it. All it does have is a stunning amount of information about a single sports car model. In many ways, Taylor's Web site is the essence of what the Internet is about: the virtually free publication of quality information from one person to millions of others.

In the early days of the Web, compiling a large list of Web sites on a particular topic offered little more than bragging rights. In the spring of 1995, however, two Stanford engineering students, Jerry Yang and David Filo, decided to take time off from school and concentrate on turning their two-year-old collection of links into a business, which they called "Yahoo!" In just over three years, they succeeded in creating not just an online directory, but a publicly traded media company with a market capitalization in the neighborhood of $2.8 billion. Over the past few months, Yahoo! has established marketing deals with a variety of other online companies, including Amazon.com, E-loan, E-trade, and CDNow, and has used its brand name recognition (possibly the strongest on the Internet today) to fuel the publication of a print magazine, *Yahoo! Internet Life*. The combination of strong content and good business deals has made Yahoo! one of the leaders in online directories, averaging around 1.3 million visitors per day. In addition, Yahoo!'s brand name has helped it to persuade hundreds of thousands of people to invest in it, which has proved lucrative: Between January 2, 1998, and August 23, 1999, Yahoo!'s stock price rose from $16\frac{9}{16}$ per share to a high of 219, before dropping down to its current level of 151 or so.

## THE BIG CAT

One of the more remarkable aspects of the growth of pornography on the Internet is the fact that the leading revenue producer among link sites is a guide to online adult materials. It is not a site run by a major magazine like *Playboy* or *Penthouse*, or a major video producer like Adam & Eve or Vivid Media, nor is it published by current or former college students who developed their expertise during late-night, pizza-fueled hunts for nude pictures. Instead, the most lucrative guide to pornography on the Internet is published by Beth Mansfield, a former accountant and mother of two from Tacoma, Washington.

Mansfield began her Web site in October 1995 and decided to focus on adult links as a way of bringing as many people as possible to her Web site. The following month, she found a sponsor for her site and applied for the domain name "persiankitty.com." Within four months, Persian Kitty was receiving more than 100,000 visitors per day, and Mansfield began getting inquiries from other adult Webmasters who were interested in purchasing advertising space on her site. Mansfield initially resisted the idea, but after finding out how much advertisers were willing to pay, she agreed to accept ads. Thanks to the steady growth in the volume of visitors (within 18 months, Persian Kitty was getting more than 300,000 visitors per day, and by January 1998, the daily count exceeded 550,000),[11] the advertising revenue generated by the Web site has been impressive. The most widely circulated figures for Persian Kitty's gross revenues (almost certainly outdated) are about $80,000 per month; Mansfield estimated in April 1997 that approximately 70 percent of that figure is profit.[12]

Like more mainstream directories, Mansfield is beginning to use the brand name recognition of Persian Kitty as a basis for forming business relationships with non-Internet businesses in the pornography industry. For instance, in January 1998, Princeton Media Group (which then published such men's magazines as *Oui, Blue Boy, Leg Scene, Iron Horse, and Gent*) announced a partnership with Persian Kitty.[13] Under the terms of the deal, Mansfield agreed to develop Web sites for Princeton Media magazines and help direct traffic there, and Princeton agrees to publish a print version of the Persian Kitty Web site.[14] The magazine (which was briefly advertised on Mansfield's Persian Kitty site) combined an extensive list of adult Web site URLs from the Persian Kitty list, as well as sample photographs from featured Web sites. According to New Zealand's *OUT!* magazine, "The anticipated readership is non-webbies who want to begin exploring the Net's Great Smut Kingdom."[15] The magazine never had much opportunity to develop a readership, however, as Princeton Media ceased operations at the end of 1998.

Much of Persian Kitty's success stems from the simplicity of its design. The Web site is a straightforward and relatively unadorned listing of adult sites, with a few words of description to let visitors know what to expect. For example, on the first page that viewers see, Mansfield provides links to a number of different categories of Web sites, including: Pics of Men; Gay/Les/Bi; Erotic Stories; Sex/Relationships Advice & Info; Interesting Sites; Other Lists; CDRom/Video; Toys/Clothing; Other Products; BBS; Personals/Dating Services; Phone/Video Sex; Other Services; Age Verification Systems; Chatrooms; and Pay Sites. Without question, however, the most popular draw for Mansfield's list of links are the adult Web sites that offer access to free pornography. The popularity of Persian Kitty has given Mansfield significant power within the online adult community, since an entry in Mansfield's "Free" list can translate into 4,000 to 7,000 visitors to a Web site each day. If Mansfield puts a special tag beside the site name to indicate that it is a "new" listing, traffic can rise as high as 1,000 visitors per hour. That level of traffic can dramatically affect the success of a new Web site.

Mansfield visits each site she puts in her "Free" list to make sure that the site in fact offers free content. She also counts the number of available images (a factor that many visitors to Persian Kitty consider important) and lists other special free features, including thumbnails (stamp-size copies of online images that let site visitors see what is available without having to wait for the full-size images to load), video clips, and specific types of sexual images. "I'm probably the strangest adult cruiser there is," Mansfield told the *New York Times*. "I go and look at the structure, look at what they offer, count the images, and I'm out. It's kind of like an OB/GYN type of thing."[16] A representative sample of Persian Kitty's "Free" list reads as follows:

> NAAASTY PUSSY—12 pix, thumbnails
> [NEW] Jul 26 NAA-NAA-NAKED GIRLS—50 pix, thumbnails
> [NEW] Jul 24 NABU'S NAKED BABES—30 pix
> NADEL'S SECRET FANTASIES REVEALED—20 pix, thumbnails
> NAKED ASS CHICKS—20 pix, tour
> NAKED BLONDES—20 pix, thumbnails
> NAKED 4 U—23 pix, thumbnails, 750 pix in slideshows under video
> NAKED WEB BABE CRAWL—44 pix, some thumbnails
> NASTY SITE—25 pix, thumbnails
> NAUGHTY CO-ED CHEERLEADERS—20 pix

Although Persian Kitty does not list the most adult sites (it has entries for about 1,400 adult sites), Mansfield has succeeded in making her site one of the primary portals into the red light district of the World Wide Web. In the process, she has turned an amusing hobby into an online adult industry leader. Although Mansfield's relationship with Princeton Media Group fell apart, Persian Kitty's online accomplishments have given it the opportunity to become one of the first adult Web sites to make a foray into the more traditional pornography media.

## DIRECTORIES AND SEARCH ENGINES

Despite Persian Kitty's overwhelming name recognition in the online adult link business, the sheer volume of adult material online leaves room for hundreds of competitors. Some, for instance, purposefully style themselves along the lines of Yahoo!, with categories and cascading subcategories of headings. Others use popular search engines like AltaVista as a model.

A popular example of the directory-style adult link site is Naughty Linx,[17] a site that has received favorable attention from a variety of print publications, including *Adult Video News*, *Playboy*, *Wired*, and *Upside*. The structure of Naughty Linx is essentially identical to Yahoo!: the main page lists six main categories (Free Arts & Entertainment, Commercial Services, Regional, Information Resources, Hard Goods, and Webmasters), with various subcategories below each category that contain listings for approximately 5,000 Web sites.

When Naughty Linx lists an adult Web site in a particular category, it includes a symbol to indicate whether the link is "up" (i.e., accessible), "???"

(unreachable or too busy), or "down" (i.e., no longer in service), as well as a one-or-two sentence description of the materials available on the site. For instance, in the subcategory "Naughty Linx/Arts and Entertainment/Photography," the Naughty Linx site lists three subdirectories (Couples and Groups, Female, and Male), and descriptions of two Web sites:

> Up! Asia Carrera's Butt Kicking Homepage—[150 Free thumbnailed pictures] Asia's own site filled with hundreds of pictures of her from porn star glamour shots to her early amateur photos. Meet the nerd of porn and find out all you'd want to know about her and her movies. 15 Jul 98
> Up! Fine Art Nudes—[86 Free thumbnail pictures] This is a virtual online gallery dedicated to fine art nude photography. The site features samples from the work of several photographers, a picture gallery, and a collection of links to other art related sites. 1 Jul 98

Clicking on a link opens up a new browser window displaying the requested page. Like Persian Kitty, Naughty Linx generates revenue by putting advertising banners on its pages and by setting up reciprocal advertising arrangements with other link sites. Naughty Linx also provides Web site owners with free images linked to the adult directory, and even offers an HTML code that allows visitors to other Web sites to search the Naughty Linx listings.

On the search engine side, one recently established contender is AtillaVista,[18] a site owned by a European named Paul de K. (who requested that his last name not be used). Compared to many online pornography entrepreneurs, Paul has a fair amount of expertise in the porn business. Among his other adult ventures are a mail order business for adult video, an import/export business for adult videos and CD-ROMs, and an adult video production company.

Paul saw the potential of the Internet at an early date. "I am on the internet from 1989," he wrote in an e-mail, "and for me as I saw was it just another type of media with big possibilities." The AtillaVista Web site was launched at the end of 1997, and by March 1998, Paul and his partners were planning to quit their other jobs and focus entirely on their Internet sites (which in addition to AtillaVista include a mixture of video and free pornography sites). "We saw after the launch of AtillaVista a lot of imitators," Paul wrote. "However, we hope to raise up our traffic to 85.000/100.000 people a day within 4 months as we start our new marketing strategies."

It's unclear, however, whether the site's resources can attract that level of traffic. When AtillaVista was first set up, the site did not have the content necessary to compete with the myriad other adult search engines and directories. Sample searches on the site, for instance, turned up far fewer links than one would reasonably expect, even for a site that limits its database to adult Web sites with free content. More recent searches make clear that the same problem persists.

Despite the lack of indexed sites, however, AtillaVista does show some innovation. Paul and his crew are currently experimenting with a search engine specifically for photos; that is, users can ask the search engine to display photos matching certain key words. The idea is good but the execution needs some work: the content currently consists of sample photographs donated by various Web sites, which often results in broken links. In addition, the number of photos referenced in the database is, at least by the standards of adult image sites, on the low side (approximately 14,000 photos). Far more problematic, however, is the fact that the AttillaVista search engine relies on the descriptions created by the sites which provide the free photos. Not surprisingly, the descriptions often take poetic license with their subjects.

There are a number of other search engines that deal specifically with adult materials; Yahoo!, for instance, lists 22 different sites ranging from "Pornlist" to "Nymfoseek" to "Adultseek.com." The chief problem that AtillaVista and all of these other sites face is that not only do they have to compete with each other but also with mainstream search engines like AltaVista (the model for AtillaVista), Excite, Lycos, and Yahoo! itself. Since these much larger sites are able to compile more comprehensive indices of Web sites and have larger and faster computers on which to run the searches, they are powerful (if reluctant) competitors in the adult search engine wing of the online pornography industry.

## REVIEWING ADULT WEB SITES

### Jane's 'Net Sex Guide

Another popular approach is to eschew mass listings of adult Web sites and instead offer informative reviews of specific sites. One of the most highly regarded review sites is Jane's 'Net Sex Guide,[19] which is run by Jane Duvall and her partner, Jim. Much of the response to Duvall's site undoubtedly stems from its cheerful appearance and tone; Duvall's frank assessment of the Web sites she reviews and of the online adult industry is refreshing. In addition to receiving recognition from a number of online sources, Jane's 'Net Sex Guide was described by *Wired* in May 1998 as having "evolved into an ethics watchdog for consumers of online erotica."[20]

Prior to starting her review site, Duvall worked as a phone sex operator for Nancy Ava Miller's People Exchanging Power. "I started a self-promotion site," Duvall said, "and though I discontinued doing phone work after a very short time, the website thing snowballed. I saw areas of the adult web that needed to be addressed, and with the help of my partner, discovered our niche."[21]

On June 15, 1997, Jane and Jim officially opened their review site. At first, the site only received about 200 visitors per day, but now, Duvall's site receives over 400,000 visitors each month. Like Persian Kitty, Duvall's site generates its revenues by selling advertising space. "We have never accepted advertising on the basis of clicks," Duvall said. "[We] follow a more traditional advertising system of cost per impression, and basing it on a per thousand basis. This is what large mainstream sites like major search engines do, and it works for us."[22]

The reviews on Duvall's site are organized by category, and the list offers a good survey of the types of materials available online: Women; Amateurs; Hardcore; Lesbian; Gay Male; Models; Live Video; Fetish; BDSM; Spanking; BBW; Anime/Toons; Art/Digital Art; Asian; and Postcards. In her list of Special Sections, Duvall posts her Picks of the Week, a collection of bookmarks compiled by Duvall and her partner, and (a rarity) a list of adult Web sites specifically for women. Within each category is a chronological listing of the sites that Duvall and her partner have reviewed, with the most recent listings at the top. Unlike most other link sites, Duvall goes into extensive detail about the positives and negatives of each site. A typical review might read as follows:

> Noelle's Haven
> Mini Review—I've got a crush again. ;-) Noelle's page is very nicely d. She does the design herself (talented as well as beautiful). Every week there are a few new free pictures (thumbnails linking to larger) 8 when I was there (and an archive of the previous week) A bio, a FAQ, an erotic story of the month, and also a page where you can order photo packs, or videos of Noelle are also housed at this site. Her link list includes more than the standard commercial adult links. The members area is only $5.95/year, which is just outstanding comparatively. Members area has another 100 or so pictures (updates weekly) with descriptions for each set based on what she is wearing (or not wearing.<g>) Again, thumbnailed for ease of browsing.
> Cost: $5.00/year. Date Reviewed: 8/29/97.
> Advertising Content: Low.

Part of what makes Jane's 'Net Sex Guide so refreshing is her complete willingness to point out sites that are badly run or offer bad value for Internet users. For instance:

> Aaron's Adult Desires
> Mini Review—IF you can get past the insulting domain name (dumbwomen.com) and then manage to make it through the first 3 pages of ads without accidentally clicking one while looking for the tiny little link to go further, you'll find some pictures. 3 pages, 10 thumbnails on each, linking to larger. This site bites.
> Cost: Free. Date Reviewed: 7/22/98.
> Advertising Content: banner hell
> Categories: pics-Women

The only criticism that might be leveled at Duvall's site is the lack of a search engine for finding specific reviews on her site. The site's main strength, that it so clearly reflects Duvall's personal commitment to excellence in the adult online industry, also makes it hard for the site to keep its reviews up to date; some of the oldest reviews, for instance, are now nearly a year old, which in Internet terms is an entire generation. Duvall has re-reviewed some of the sites, but her reluctance to hire additional reviewers makes it difficult to cover both new sites and formerly reviewed sites. "While we are usually backed up in our reviews," Duvall admits, "we hesitate to bring on outside help. There are a couple of reasons for this. First, in the online world it's hard to know where someone is coming from. We don't want to "hire" someone to help that has a personal interest in any particular company. [Second,] we also plain can't afford it. . ."[23]

Like many adult sites, Jane's 'Net Sex Guide generates enough revenue to support Duvall, who says that it is her primary source of income. "Yes, it is profitable," Duvall said. "Not exceedingly profitable, but enough so that we enjoy it." Duvall frankly concedes that she could probably make more money in her former mainstream profession (she worked at a large newspaper handling national advertising accounts), but finds more enjoyment in her current work.

## Skinfinder

Among the people reading the media's breathless articles about Beth Mansfield's success was Keith McArthur, one of the three founders of Skinfinder, a combination adult search engine and rating site. McArthur, who has a background in music and the restaurant industry, stumbled across the Persian Kitty site while surfing one day with a friend. "We tripped on the site," McArthur said. "It was such a basic site. It just seemed so simple to us. And then we read an article about how much money she's making. I think it was probably one of the first major articles on her. And we thought her site was a great idea, but it was underdeveloped. It didn't save you enough time to go to other sites. And basically we just thought we would improve her idea and provide links with more information. We didn't want to get into having an adult site, per se."

After kicking the idea around, McArthur joined forces with two other people and found an investor willing to support the idea of creating a more informative guide to adult Web sites. McArthur said that the investor supplied them with an initial outlay of $15,000, which they spent over a period of two months setting up their Web site.

> We paid people to go to [adult Web sites] and rate them and kind of evaluate them on a one-to-one per-site basis. So that—paying that person, setting up the office, getting the machines and getting all the business and tax stuff taken care of, lawyers, all of that—and trying to find a merchant account that would let us process credit cards because they don't want to have anything to do with—even though

we're a text only site, they just hear 'adult-oriented material' and they freak out—all told at this point we're at about just under $15,000.

McArthur added that the investor had made a commitment to the site of up to $30,000 or $40,000, but that as the level of investment went up, so did the investor's shares in the venture. "It's incumbent upon us to keep it low so that we can maintain as much control [as possible]," McArthur acknowledged. "So those are the numbers you're dealing with when you're doing something like this. When you think about what people like Persian Kitty are making, it's easy to take the gamble."

The Skinfinder site offered a clean layout and two different ways for searching for sites: by type (free or preview), category (the various types of adult materials), and search order (rating or alphabetical); or by keyword. When the search results popped on the screen, each entry contained the name of the site, the rating given to it by Skinfinder, a range of the number of images, an assessment of the advertising density on the site, whether the images are hardcore or softcore, whether the site uses "popups" (also known as consoles), and a few brief comments by Skinfinder about the site. According to Skinfinder's own assessment, the site contained ratings for more than 1,600 adult Web sites. As of May 1999, efforts to reach the site were met with a "host not found" message, which usually indicates that the site in question is no longer operating.

As Skinfinder illustrates, setting up a successful adult business online is not solely a function of money. Despite the infusion of cash and the work invested in rating online sites, Skinfinder did not succeed in establishing a high profile on the Web for adult links. A major benefit of the site for visitors was that the advertising on the site was unobtrusive and low-key, but that was also an indication that the site was having some difficulty attracting advertisers, particularly the larger online adult sites. Skinfinder's experience underscores the extent to which the pornography industry emulates more mainstream businesses: Without an adequate marketing budget, it is difficult to attract traffic, which in turn makes it hard to attract advertisers. Since advertising revenues are all or nearly all of the income for most link sites, the level of traffic is particularly important.

## SPECIALIZED AND NICHE DIRECTORIES

### Ynot Adult Network

In addition to the general sites described above, a large number of adult link sites provide connections to specific types of sites or to sites dealing with specific topics. The relatively low start-up costs for link sites and the vast amount of material online makes specialization a potentially lucrative approach to setting up an adult business.

For 21-year-old Rick Muenyong, the founder of the Ynot Adult Network, a natural area of concentration was the community of adult Web site owners (aka "Webmasters"). The Ynot Network, which was started in September 1996, combines listings of various adult sites (with a heavy concentration on free sites) with extensive information for adult Webmasters. For instance, Muenyong runs chat rooms where Webmasters can meet and talk about various issues, offers resources for adult sites (including hosting, content, etc.), and provides a collection of online references to guide new Web site owners. According to material posted on the Web site,[24] the original purpose of the Ynot Adult Network was to provide reciprocal links among a limited number of high-quality adult sites, including a now-defunct site run by Muenyong himself. The business relationship succeeded in increasing the traffic on the various sites by a few hundred to a couple of thousand visits per day. Over the last couple of years, Muenyong has added five additional networks of adult sites; each participant can put a button on his or her Web site that links back to the home page of their network at Ynot or to other sites in the same network.

In addition to providing links among network members, Muenyong also tries to use the networks to promote better practices by adult sites. One of only a few adult Web sites to have a published mission statement, Muenyong says that his organization's goals are as follows:

> 1. To provide the most valuable service for both consumers and merchants engaged in the use or distribution of legitimate adult-related material on the web, while actively practicing and promoting all reasonable efforts to protect children from accessing potentially harmful material.
> 2. To use our power and resources, toward positive efforts which may help improve, assist, or eliminate any current or potential problems relating to the adult industry online and/or society in general.

To help promote those goals, Muenyong has created a code of ethics that each member is required to follow in the operation of their sites. Before becoming a member, an adult site must agree to comply with the code:

> 1. The YNOT Network's objective is to maintain and enforce the highest standards of ethical professional practices, making membership in the Network a recognized mark of experience, stability, reliability, integrity and competence.
> 2. We will regard as confidential all information concerning the business and affairs of the network.
> 3. We will conduct ourselves in such a professional manner as to bring credit to and enhance the reputation of our network.
> 4. We will publicize our services in a professional manner upholding the dignity of our network. We will avoid all conduct, practices and promotion likely to discredit, or to do injury to our field of endeavor.
> 5. We will strive to broaden public understanding, and enhance public regard and confidence in the Adult Internet Industry.

6. In keeping with this dedication to principle, YNOT Network members will:

    a. Follow through and complete any agreement made verbally or otherwise to any YNOT Network member, website owner or sponsor.

    b. Not disparage other members by statement or innuendo to any person outside or inside of the YNOT Network.

    c. Not display the images of any minor in a lewd or lascivious manner as defined by law.

Muenyong declined to disclose exactly how much the Ynot Web site earns from advertising, but says that it is profitable, despite the fact that he spends about $60,000 per month on advertising, staff, rent, Internet access, equipment, and so on.

## Fetishes and Other Specialized Guides

Although they do not receive the publicity or generate the revenues of a Persian Kitty or Ynot Adult Network, the bulk of online adult link sites are set up and maintained by smaller, specialized sites. For instance, Nancy Ava Miller maintains a list of "Related S&M/B&D/Fetish Web Sites!" on her P.E.P. Web site, a recent sampling of which included:

- Autumn Season
- Boston Dungeon Society BBS
- Escape—Richmond, Virginia BDSM group
- The Eulenspiegel Society—TES is a not-for-profit organization which promotes sexual liberation for all adults. Especially for people who enjoy consensual SM.
- KAP (Kink Aware Professionals)—The resource for people who are seeking psychotherapeutic, medical, dental, complementary healing, and legal professionals who are informed about the diversity of consensual, adult sexuality.

Other specialties that have their own specialized link sites include foot fetishes (FootFetishes), voyeurism (Worldwide Voyeur Top 100), homosexuality (Tor's Gay World), and lesbianism (LezLinks). In addition, both Yahoo! and Naughty Linx list a wide variety of Web sites that specialize in fetish links of all descriptions.

    There are two other enormously popular categories of adult link sites. One focuses on links to sites featuring women of particular nationalities. Among the most popular classifications are Asian (Adult Asia, Asian Girl), Oriental (NudeOrientals, Oriental Gay), African-American (Chocolate City, Ebony XXX Links), Swedish (Babes of Sweden), and Argentine (Argentina's Beautiful Women).

The other popular approach of entrepreneurs is to create a link site that concentrates on the adult resources located in a particular country, region, or even city. For instance, sites have been created for Australia (Aussie Cybersmut, Australian Hot Adult Links), Amsterdam (Erotic City of Amsterdam), New Orleans (New Bourbon), London (The Really Useful Search Page), Holland (Sex Planet), Texas (Texas Sex), United Kingdom (UK Adult Directory), Japan (Vixen), Germany (WepaPapst Erotik), to name just a few. As with other types of specialty adult Web sites, of course, there is no guarantee that the featured models are in fact from the region or even the country in question.

## RESEARCH AND REVISION:
## A SISYPHEAN TASK

The low cost of starting an online business, particularly an adult link site, is an advantage shared by every entrepreneur. As a result, there is enormous competition for traffic and the advertising revenues that the traffic generates. In addition, because of the lack of geographical constraints online, businesses are not competing with businesses in the same neighborhood or even the same county; instead, they are competing with every similar online business in the nation and around the world. This in turn gives consumers enormous leverage: A better site or a lower price is just a few clicks and a few seconds away. Customer loyalty on the Internet is an evanescent commodity.

For the operators of online businesses, the challenge is to maintain customer loyalty by developing brand name recognition for a site's unique content, quality, innovation, and/or service. In the abstract, it sounds simple enough, but in reality, running a good link site requires several hours a day for research alone. Jane Duvall, for instance, says that she spends more than 40 hours a week maintaining Jane's 'Net Sex Guide, primarily researching and reviewing Web sites. That is similar to Mansfield's report that she spends six or more hours a day visiting and appraising adult Web sites.

For operators of adult link sites, the chief challenge lies in the speed with which sites come and go on the Internet. There are tens of thousands of adult Web sites online right now and hundreds more launched each month. Keeping up with that level of information is far more than a full-time job. Even Yahoo!, which employs a large staff of surfers to identify and catalog online information, does not list every Web site or even attempt to do so. In February 1998, for instance, Yahoo's Director of Surfing Srinija Srinivasan admitted to *Wired:* "We can't possibly scale in head count to the growth of the Web.[25] I don't think users want us to be a manual attempt at what the search engines do." Mansfield, whose Persian Kitty link site is the most popular directory of adult online materials, takes a similar approach: "There's a lot more websites, adult websites out there than I will ever attempt to list," Mansfield told Ziff-Davis's *The Site.* "I try to keep at a certain level with things; I kind of term it as a jumping off point, you know, initial starting point for somebody who wants to take, you know, a surf through some of the adult sites on the Net."[26]

Some Web site operators, not surprisingly, have tried to carve out a piece of Persian Kitty's market by the time-honored technique of emulating the site's name. As a result, surfers for adult content have their choice of Persian Kitten, PornLynx, Siberian Kitty, or The Lynx.[27] Apparently feeling that all of the good cat names have been taken, some entrepreneurs have drafted other members of the animal kingdom, including Sexhound, Porndog, and The Bloated Goat.[28]

A more common approach is to set up a Web site that focuses on the same subject matter but differentiates itself from Persian Kitty in terms of either structure or content. For instance, a number of sites, like Jane's Reviewed Adult Links or Skinfinder have gone beyond simply listing sites and offer reviews or ratings of different adult sites online. Other link sites focus on niche markets, like amateurs, bondage and S&M, porn star sites, and so forth. For example, among the different directories listed by Yahoo! are: Fetish List, which specializes in "bdsm, feet, femdom, gay, latex, legs, panties, upskirts, toilet and more"; Asian Banana, which lists "categorized adult Asian sites"; and Amateur Empire, "a collection of adult amateur sites."[29]

In recent months, the suggestion has been raised that the online pornography industry has peaked. In July 1998, for instance, Jesse Berst, the editorial director at the ZDNet Anchor Desk, wrote an editorial asking "The End of Internet Sex?" Berst's article listed the various legal and legislative challenges facing the pornography industry and speculated that the days of the "Wild Wild Web" were coming to an end.

While it is unlikely that the online pornography industry can maintain its current level of growth indefinitely, the continued increase in the size of the online community should keep demand steady for a number of years to come. Moreover, as sites come and go, there will be a continued need for people who are interested and willing to catalog online adult materials.

## GENERATING REVENUE WITH LINKS

### The Ubiquitous Banner

As anyone who has spent any time on the Web realizes, display advertisements known as "banners" are virtually everywhere. Adult sites lead the way in the development and use of banners both as an advertising medium and as an income generator.

A banner is a small advertisement (either still or animated) which is displayed on a Web page. Like other advertisements, the banner ad is designed to pique the interest of viewers in a specific product or service. Unlike an ad on television or in the newspaper, however, which are essentially static, a Web banner ad is interactive. Thanks to the power of HTML, an online ad can be a hyper-text link to another Web page, which gives advertisers the ability to bring Internet users directly to their Web site. It also gives advertisers extraordinarily precise data about which advertisements attract customers and which do not.

Banners generate income for the sites that display them in one of two ways. The most common scenario is for the advertiser to pay a set amount—any-where between 2 and 25 cents—for each unique "click-through" that results from a particular site's display.[30] A click-through occurs each time an Internet user sees an ad on a particular Web site and decides to click on it. For instance, the owner of "www.rachelspix.com" might ask a Web site to display a banner ad for her site, with the agreement that she will pay 4 cents per click-through. On a given day, if the Web site has 5,000 visitors and 50 of them click on the ban-ner ad for "RachelsPix," the Web site would earn a grand total of $2 for display-ing the banner.

Banners are single-handedly responsible for a significant percentage of the pornography that is now available on the Internet. Large numbers of Web site operators have generated substantial revenues by creating Web sites that are primarily vehicles for displaying banner advertisements. The site operators then attract visitors by offering access to huge numbers of free sexual images. For the operators of such sites, the only thing that matters is generating as much traffic as possible, which increases the number of people who will click on a banner and generate income for the site. Since there are hundreds of other sites doing pre-cisely the same thing, the best and simplest way to compete is to offer increas-ingly large amounts of pornography or increasingly hardcore images.

The click-through model, however, may become a victim of its own suc-cess. The software that drives the Internet is extremely flexible, and some adult Webmasters devised creative ways to generate huge numbers of fraudulent clicks. This process, known as click-farming, has led some click-through advertisers to stop paying for raw clicks altogether and instead offer advertising sites a per-centage of the membership fees generated by the click-throughs from their site.

The entire click-through industry was rocked in late October 1998 when the largest click-through advertiser, XPics, announced that it was discon-tinuing its enormous "XCash" program.[31] The XCash program was one of the primary economic engines of the online pornography industry, offering to pay Webmasters on average 18 cents per click to advertise pornography sites. Although the precise reasons for the shutdown are unclear, it appears that XPics lost the ability to process credit card payments for membership to its various sites. Although XPics was widely criticized among Webmasters for not living up to its grandiose promises, it is undeniable that the often enormous payments offered by XPics helped persuade large numbers of people to become online pornographers.

The other common model for generating revenue on a link site is to charge advertisers a fee for space, much as newspapers or magazines do. The chief challenge has been developing the Web equivalent of television's Nielsen ratings or the circulation rates for newspapers and magazines. In the last two years, a number of different companies have been launched to accurately measure Web site traffic and to attempt to record the number of advertisement impressions delivered by a particular Web page. Given the diffuse nature of the Internet and the extensive use of cache files to speed up performance, it can be enormously difficult to accurately record the number of times a particular page is seen by Internet surfers. Nonetheless, there is tremendous interest in developing industry standards for tracking ad impressions on the Web; the more closely Web advertising emulates traditional advertising, the easier it will be to sell.

## Golden Crumbs

Sites that sell access to images or adult products online have an inherent advantage over link sites, because they can register with an adult verification service or accept credit card payments for the services and products they offer. Despite the often high processing fees charged to adult businesses,[32] the profit margin is great enough and the convenience to customers is important enough that it is still worthwhile to accept cards. A number of companies have also developed systems for processing check information online.

By contrast, the only product that link site operators have to offer is the information located on their sites and the value of the time spent organizing it, neither of which lends itself to credit card purchases. Lurking on the horizon, however, are payment systems that would allow the compilers and distributors of link sites to charge directly for the information that they compile. A number of different finance companies and Internet start-ups are working on systems for handling so-called "microtransactions," sales of goods and services that are too small to be conveniently handled by credit cards or check.

One of the most promising of the various proposals is Digital Equipment Corporation's Millicent, a system that allows Internet users to pay for transactions with electronic scrip ranging in value from 1/10th of a cent to $5. DEC tested the system in the spring of 1998, but the commercial introduction of the Millicent system has been slowed by Compaq's purchase of Digital that summer. There has also been resistance to the introduction of microcash systems because the software required to make the system work is both expensive and complicated.

If and when a viable system is finally introduced and adopted by a sufficient number of Web sites, link sites would likely be among the biggest benefactors. For instance, with an electronic microcash system (often referred to as "e-cash"), a link site operator might be able to charge as little as a single cent for each link that someone clicks on. If Mansfield were able to charge a penny for clicking on one of the links on her Persian Kitty site, for instance, and each of her 500,000 visitors clicked on a single link, she would gross about $5,000 per day, which is nearly twice her 1997 daily gross of about $2,800.

The chief benefit of an effective microcash system would be to lessen a link site's reliance on banner advertising. Banners slow down the loading of Web pages (a particular problem with adult sites), and providing another source of revenue would give Web site operators the option of getting rid of them altogether. A microcash system would also make the purchase of information more efficient. Right now, when a Web surfer visits Persian Kitty, the service appears to be free. In reality, of course, the service is subsidized by the site's advertising, and every visitor to the site "pays" for the service by waiting for the site's advertising banners to download (although, to be fair to Mansfield, the number of banners on her site is far lower than most other adult sites; she gets so many visitors per day that she is able to charge far higher rates for her ads than other sites, and therefore needs fewer banners to support her site). If a microcash system permits a site to be banner-free, then each Internet user could pay only for the information that actually interests him or her (i.e., the specific link the user is looking for).[33]

# LEGAL ISSUES FOR LINK SITES

## THE INS AND OUTS OF LINKING

The greatest legal risk for the operator of an adult link site stems is not obscenity but instead potential copyright and trademark infringement. Although the World Wide Web is predicated on a certain amount of copying (each Web page is copied to the user's computer so that it can be displayed), there are fairly clear limits to how the copied information can be used. For instance, if an Internet user visits the Playboy Web site to look at the Playmate of the Month, a copy of the image stored on the Playboy Web site is downloaded to the user's computer so that it can be displayed. Playboy gives each visitor to the Web site a limited license to display the playmate's picture on a home computer screen; that limited license, however, is not permission to use the image in another fashion (on a Web site, for instance, or in a company newsletter). As we saw in Chapter 4, the ease with which materials can be copied on the Internet often blurs the issue of ownership and is a powerful temptation for misuse. The Usenet newsgroup alt.binaries.pictures.erotica, for instance, where scanned copies of pictures from adult magazines circulate endlessly, is commonly described as "gigabytes of copyright violations."

Another tricky legal issue for link sites involves the process of linking itself. In general, a diagram of a Web site resembles a rough pyramid, consisting of a home page at the top and varying numbers of subsidiary pages below it. If a computer user types the address "www.playboy.com" into his or her Web browser, for instance, he or she will be taken to the home page of Playboy's Web site. In theory, a home page itself contains links that lead to the various other pages on the site. In order to get to photos of the Playmate of the Month, for instance, a visitor needs to go to Playboy's home page and then click on one or two intermediate pages (a process known in Web parlance as "drilling down").

The usual practice, when someone wants to create a link to a Web site like Playboy, is to use an HTML tag that lists the uniform resource locator (URL) for Playboy's home page (i.e., www.playboy.com). However, since each subsidiary page on the Playboy Web site also has a unique URL, it is possible (at least in theory) to create a link to any individual page on a Web site, thereby avoiding the necessity of going through the home page and multiple subsidiary pages to get to a particular page. It's the electronic equivalent of having a transporter beam which would allow you to drop into any store in a mall without having to walk in the front door and down the hallways.

However, just like the mall, many Web sites are set up so that visitors will see certain products or advertising on their way through the site. If a site visitor can drop directly on to a Web page that is five or six levels below the site's home page, that's five or six pages of advertising that the visitor won't see. As a result, many Web site operators strongly object to links to their sites that go anywhere but to the site's home page.

Linking to internal pages instead of the home page is particularly a problem for adult sites, since the home page usually contains the sternly worded warning that surfers under the age of 18 (or 21) should go away. The warnings typically read something like this:

> !!!WARNING!!! IF YOU ARE NOT 21, AND/OR ARE OFFENDED
> BY SEXUALLY ORIENTED MATERIAL, OR RESIDE IN AN AREA
> WHERE SEXUALLY EXPLICIT MATERIAL IS PROHIBITED,
> CLICK THE CANCEL BUTTON BELOW NOW. IF YOU ARE 21,
> AND WANT TO VIEW SEXUALLY ORIENTED MATERIAL,
> CLICK THE O.K. BUTTON BELOW.

In this particular case, if a user clicks the "Cancel" button, the user is transferred to the Webcrawler site, an Internet search engine. Most Web sites use some variant on "Enter" and "Exit," with the "Exit" button linked to some innocuous site like www.disney.com. In theory, the software that operates the Web server is set up to record the UserID of each person who clicks "OK" or "Enter," but many sites may consider it more trouble than it is worth. As a prophylactic device for blocking children, a warning page is even less effective than the rhythm method, but still, most adult Web site owners are uncomfortable with visitors simply bypassing their home page.

To force visitors to come in through the front door instead of climbing through a window, some site operators will periodically change the URLs of their internal pages (which renders links to the old addresses ineffective) or will set up their software to refuse the request of anyone who has not used the site's home page to reach a subsidiary page. Other site operators include statements on their warning page to the effect that linking to an internal Web page constitutes a de facto acceptance of the conditions contained on the warning page, although how legally binding such a statement is remains untested.

## OBSCENITY

Given the general social and political climate today regarding pornography, any adult business faces at least some risk of either state or federal prosecution. But of the various types of adult businesses operating on the Internet, a directory of adult sites and services online is by far the safest. The reason lies in the fact that most if not all of the material on an adult link site or directory consists of text, which has generally been accorded the highest level of First Amendment protection. Even if the sites listed use extremely explicit language to describe themselves (and many of them do), it is difficult to imagine any community in the United States successfully prosecuting a Web site operator for the words on an adult link site. And in fact, none of the link site operators interviewed for this book reported any problems from law enforcement or community leaders over the content of their sites.

Once the content of an adult link site strays from plain text, however, the risk of prosecution does rise slightly. Many pages of links also contain sample images from listed Web sites, and the owner or operator of the links page is potentially liable if any of the sample images are deemed to be obscene. Since the laws against obscenity do not limit themselves to the producers of obscene materials but encompass distributors as well, any site that accepts and displays an obscene image is potentially at risk.

Adult banner advertising also offers at least the slight possibility of an obscenity prosecution. Despite having a very limited amount of space with which to work, many advertising banners are extremely creative in their depiction of explicit sexual activity. There is a possibility (albeit remote) that some particularly conservative jurisdiction might try to build a case based on the visual images contained in such advertisements, or on a site's sample images.

An interesting issue arises if the link site or directory does not actually display the allegedly obscene photo, but instead simply has a hypertext link to the photo that reads something like "Sample1." The question would be whether providing a link directly to obscene material is enough to trigger criminal liability: Does the operator of the link site have an obligation to check every link on his or her site? A related question is whether liability arises if a link is provided to a site that has obscenity located on it: How much research does the operator of a link site have to do? These are precisely the type of questions that fascinate lawyers, but it is good to remember that a fascinating legal question is often an expensive legal question. While Samuel Roth and Marvin Miller may take some comfort or even pride from the fact that their names are inextricably linked to the legal history of pornography in the late 20th century, they both paid a high cost (in cash and incarceration) for the honor.

Still, of all of the *adult* online businesses than an entrepreneur could consider starting, an adult link site is the one which generally poses the least legal risk to its operator. Although the risk is low, entrepreneurs must always keep in mind that an adult link site is still "adult." In the current political climate, certainly, any adult link site will face stricter scrutiny than a link site devoted to rodeos or roses.

# NOTES

1. The concept of the portal, the current word of the day among Internet industry analysts, is to design a Web site that Internet users will rely upon as their starting place for accessing the Internet. Netscape's portal, for instance, which is the fastest growing site on the Web, currently receives more than 9 million hits per day. That level of traffic offers significant possibilities for generating advertising revenues and e-commerce revenues, and is one of the main reasons that America Online has offered to pay $4 billion to purchase the browser company. Netscape's 9 million visitors per day puts it slightly ahead of its closest competitor, Yahoo!, which has about 8.5 million visitors per day.

2. Ironically, four and a half years earlier, Northridge was the epicenter of a massive earthquake measuring 6.7 on the Richter scale. Every porn production and distribution business suffered damage from the earthquake, a circumstance that some local clergy described as divine intervention. Perucci Ferraiuolo and Mark A. Kellner, "Relief, rebuilding efforts unite churches, neighborhoods," *Christianity Today*, March 7, 1994, p. 56.

3. *Federal Communications Commission v. Pacifica Foundation*, 438 U.S. 726 (1978). For those wondering just what it was that so outraged the FCC, the Supreme Court kindly provided a transcript of Carlin's monologue as an appendix to its decision. The decision (and the monologue) can be read, among other places, on the FindLaw Web site at http://laws.findlaw.com/US/438/726.html.

4. New York's cable system does have some well-publicized adult programs on the public access channels, which might offer a potential outlet for this type of show. The chances of a review of pornography shops being shown on a mainstream channel, however, are quite remote.

5. Dave Michaels and John Douglas, "MTV Bans Porn Documentary," November 16, 1998, online at http://www.talkingblue.com/archive/mtv_bans_porn_documentary.htm.

6. Of course, Ashbee printed his three-volume set in secret (producing only 250 copies) and under the pseudonym Pisanus Fraxi, so perhaps he was worried that the *Encyclopedia* would be considered pornographic.

7. This is not an Internet innovation, of course. Urban phone books routinely carry display ads for escort services, massage parlors, and strip clubs. Even those phone books which do not allow drawings in the ads for escort services (Nashville's Yellow Pages, for instance) still carry the ads themselves.

8. The Walt Disney Corporation, not so coincidentally, has played an integral role in the efforts of New York City to clean up the image of Times Square, long a haven for a wide variety of sex shops.

9. "Infoseek Says No to Porn Ads," *Adult Video News* (n.d.; [referenced on December 17, 1998]), online at http://www.avn.com/html/avn/news/nws/ news206.html.

10. The page is located at http://www.cern.ch/TTC/montreal.html. The one drawback is that the page is quite large and can take a while to download.

11. "Internet Sex Site to Become Magazine Publisher," *OUT! Magazine*, January 30, 1998, online at http://www.nz.com/NZ/Queer/ OUT/news_ 199801/ 19980130a.html.

12. Matt Richtel, "From Housewives to Strippers, Small Smut Sites Make Money," *New York Times*, April 2, 1997.

13. Princeton Media Group, which is publicly traded (PMGIF—NASDAQ), was busy. In August 1997, it also signed a deal with Spice Entertainment for exclusive use of the "Spice"

trademark in conjunction with a print magazine, *Spice Inside,* and an online publication.

14. Justin Burrows, "Industry Snapshot: Adult Entertainment," *Hoover's Company Information* (n.d.), online at http://www.hoovers.com/features/industry/adult. html. Princeton Media's effort to latch onto the success of Persian Kitty may have come too late. The company, which published 25 adult magazines, was temporarily delisted by NASDAQ in October 1998 and subsequently announced in early November that it was unable to obtain necessary financing to continue operating. Two weeks later, Princeton Media's wholly owned subsidiaries, including Princeton Publishing and Firestone Publishing, were assigned for the benefit of creditors. The company was permanently delisted in December 1998.

15. "Internet Sex Site to Become Magazine Publisher."

16. Richtel, "From Housewives to Strippers."

17. naughty.com

18. www.atillavista.com.

19. www.janesguide.com.

20. Steve Silberman, "Porn Patrons Billed, Unfulfilled," *Wired,* May 19, 1998, online at http://www.wired.com/news/news/culture/story/12412.html.

21. E-mail with author.

22. E-mail with author.

23. Jane Duvall, "Site FAQ," Jane's 'Net Sex Guide, online at http://www.janesguide.com/tips/janefaq.html.

24. Ynot Adult Network, "Membership Information and Application", online at http://www.ynotnetwork.com/membership.html.

25. In other words: can't hire enough people to keep up with the growth of the Internet. Quote is from Chris Oakes, "Does Yahoo Still Yahoo?" *Wired,* February 11, 1998, online at http://www.wired.com/news/news/technology/story/ 10236.html.

26. "Persian Kitty," *The Site,* Ziff-Davis, August 25, 1997, online at http://www.zdnet.com/zdtv/thesite/0897w5/iview/iview793jump5_082597.html.

27. www.persiankitten.com, www.pornlynx.com, www.siberiankitty.com, www.the-lynx.com.

28. www.sexhound.com, www.porndog.com, www.bloatedgoat.com.

29. www.fetishlist.com, www.asianbanana.com.

30. The requirement that a particular "click-through" be unique is to prevent a savvy programmer from writing a program that automatically clicks on an advertisement hundreds or thousands of times to generate revenue, a process known as "harvesting."

31. Steve Silberman, "'Armageddon' for Porn Sites," *Wired,* October 29, 1998, online at http://www.wired.com/news/news/culture/story/15901.html.

32. Adult businesses are often charged processing fees as high as 20 percent of the value of a transaction, in large part due to the number of chargebacks that occur in the industry.

33. How this type of system will play out in other media is uncertain. For instance, with a viable microcash system, the *Boston Globe* might start charging its Web site visitors on a per-article basis (3 cents, perhaps, to read about last night's Red Sox game). Assuming the paper version is still being published, how many online articles will it take to equal an entire (but not completely read) newspaper? More importantly, if the paper version is not being published, the *Globe* will have cold hard numbers that make it clear which articles and which writers are the most profitable. (Something about which the *Globe* already has an idea, admittedly, through reader surveys and its existing online site.) Still, would the *Globe* reach a point at which it would discontinue less popular features or columnists? Presumably, the low cost of putting any given article online will militate against that, but the increased use of the Web will give management some interesting information for contract negotiations. ("So, Mr. Garfinkle, only 1 in 200 visitors to our Web site read your column over the last year . . .")

# 7

# HONEY, IS THAT REALLY YOU?

Blessed be the inventor of photography! I set him above even the inventor
of chloroform! It has given more positive pleasure to poor suffering
humanity than anything else that has "cast up" in my time or is like to—this
art by which even the "poor" can possess themselves of tolerable likenesses
of their absent dear ones. And mustn't it be acting favourably on the
morality of the country?
Jane Welsh Carlyle, in a letter dated October 21, 1859

In August, 1996, *U.S. News & World Report* estimated that there were as many
as 600 sites online where Internet users could purchase adult materials, and that
those 600 sites were responsible for generating an estimated $51.5 million in rev-
enues.[1] At the time, the online adult industry ranked third behind computers
and travel in volume of Internet business. The following year, Forrester Research
(analysts of online industries) estimated that sales of adult materials had risen to
between $150 million and $200 million.[2] More recent estimates have pegged
online adult revenues between $1 billion and $2 billion, or roughly 2½–5 percent of the Internet's estimated $40 billion in overall sales in 1998. The vast bulk
of the online adult industry's revenues are generated by online galleries of sexually explicit images.

## AMATEUR WEB SITES

### NAKED ON THE WEB: IS IT REAL OR MAKE-BELIEVE?

One of the most popular sexual fantasies for sale on the Internet is the idea
that average people are willing to post or set up Web sites with pictures of themselves or their spouses posing nude or engaged in sexual activity. In May 1999,
for instance, the online directory Yahoo! listed 220 entries in its subdirectory

"Home : Business and Economy : Companies : Sex : Virtual Clubs: Online Picture Galleries : Amateurs" and a search on AltaVista for "amateur nude" turns up more than 480,000 Web pages containing that particular phrase. Even given the fact that a given Web site may have multiple pages that use those terms, there are still a huge number of Web sites that purport to offer photographs of "amateur" models or describe themselves as sites that are set up and run by the women pictured on the Web site.

According to the *American Heritage Dictionary* (3rd edition), an "amateur" is defined as "A person who engages in an art, a science, a study, or an athletic activity as a pastime rather than as a profession." Determining whether a particular online model is an "amateur" or "professional" involves the same fine gradations of meaning that have plagued the International Olympic Committee for the past 40 years: Is someone a professional the moment they accept money in exchange for a nude photograph of themselves, or is there a magic threshold (30 percent, 50 percent, 80 percent of annual income) between amateurism and professionalism? Can models retain their amateur status if they charge just enough to cover expenses? To moralists, of course, there is little difference between someone who makes a living by posing nude online and someone who does it as a lark. However, the extensive use of the word "amateur" in conjunction with adult Web sites makes it clear that the distinction is a meaningful one to pornography consumers, who are clearly willing to pay for sexual images of nonprofessionals.

The obvious question, given the tremendous ease with which materials are faked online, is whether consumers are getting what they pay for. The odds are heavily against it. Any adult Web site operator can set up a page titled "Amateur High School Teachers," for instance, and there would be no way to tell whether any of the models posing had taught a day in their lives. A popular variant on this theme are the innumerable Web sites that claim to have photographs of cheerleaders, the implication being that the women pictured are high school or college cheerleaders. What these sites suggest instead is that the number of cheerleading outfits sold in this country outnumbers the actual number of cheerleaders by a factor of at least four and that cheerleading uniforms are being sold in some unusual sizes. When it comes to online photo galleries that claim to feature images of amateurs or a particular profession, a healthy skepticism is appropriate.

Another enormously popular type of adult Web site are ones purportedly set up and run by the person who appears in the photos and videos on the site. The advertisements for and descriptions of such sites should also be taken with a grain of salt.

Thanks to the easy anonymity of the Internet, there is no foolproof way to determine if the site is in fact operated by the featured model(s). Rick Muenyong, the operator of the Ynot Adult Network, estimates that the number is around 5 percent to 10 percent, with the balance run by the model's "photographer," "significant other," or by an entrepreneur who simply buys a collection of photos. Others involved in the field agree. During the research for this book, for instance, I sent an e-mail inquiry to a Susanne LaGrand, the star of a well-designed online amateur Web site.[3] In addition to offering a number of artistic nude self-portraits, LaGrand describes the history of her Web site and tells a little bit about herself:

> I am 26 years old and live in a little town in Austria/Europe. Photography is only a hobby. For my living I develop computer based training applications for various companies. I started photographing some years ago first with a little compact camera, later with a Canon EOS 500 and some others. From time to time someone is even interested in buying a poster or a puzzle of my pictures. In this case, please mail me.

A few days after the inquiry was sent, the following reply was received:

> Thanks for your mail. Basically I would be willing to answer your questions. But be aware that Susanne Lagrand—like 95% of the other amateur women online—is just a virtual person created by me, an austria [sic] internet developer and brought to life with pictures I shot of a friend of mine :) I run several small sites with similar content . . .
> If you are still interested, please send me your questions and I will answer them as good as possible.
> Thanks,
> Adi Dax

Brittany Halford, a university student in Canada who runs her own amateur Web site,[4] is even more skeptical about the number of truly amateur Web sites. "I have been involved with this for about three years now," Halford said. "That is a very long time to be doing what I am doing. I have met a lot of people on the Net through the years. And you are quite correct in the fact that most amateur/adult sites that claim to be run by women are actually not. I mean, how hard is it to find some woman to model for a few days, take 1000 pictures and pretend you are her? That could quite easily be done. And it is. You know my honest opinion on how many adult sites are actually run by women 100 percent for sure? Well, mine is one of them. And if you go to www.asiacarrera.com,[5] hers is the other one. She is legit as well."

While the number of sites actually run by women is certainly higher than two, it probably is not significantly higher. There is no denying that the traditional distribution of power in the pornography industry is present online: The images of women and the profits they generate are still largely controlled by men. There is a tremendous demand for sexually explicit images of women on the World Wide Web; to a large degree, the demand is being satisfied by the sale of large collections of photographs of women who were paid a nominal amount (if at all) to disrobe and who retain no control whatsoever over where and how their image is subsequently distributed and reap no further benefit. Still, even if only 200 or 300 women and/or couples are running their own Web sites, that represents a quantum leap in the number of women who are controlling the use of their own images and reaping the economic benefits, particularly in comparison to traditional forms of production and distribution in the pornography industry.

The fact that a few dozen or even a few hundred women own and operate adult Web sites in which they are the central attraction is obviously not a complete upending of the traditional power structure of the pornography industry. Nonetheless, the fact that so many women can and do run their own sexually explicit Web sites is testament to the impact that the Internet is having on traditional business practices. Thanks to its low entry and distribution costs, the Internet is giving some women an unprecedented opportunity to determine what images of themselves they will make available to the public, to control (at least initially) the time, place, and manner in which such distribution will take place, and to reap the bulk of the profits generated by the sale of such images.

## A FEW ONLINE BUSINESS MODELS

One result of the relatively low start-up costs for Internet businesses is that it gives entrepreneurs the ability to tailor their online venture to their interests and resources. Below are four examples of how online sexual entrepreneurs have structured their ventures. They run the gamut from a self-run image gallery to a husband-and-wife photo site that has grown into a full-service adult Web site hosting company.

### Brittany

For 21-year-old Canadian Brittany Halford, her decision to start an amateur Web site was fueled in large part by feminist disgust with the adult materials available online. "The state of the Internet adult industry drove me to do this," Halford said. "Of every 100 adult pages, 99 are crap. I wanted to make a difference, no matter how small. I just want to offer people an alternative to male run adult sites. Isn't it time a woman did this type of thing?"[6]

Halford, who began posing online about two years before starting her site, estimates that it cost her about $400 to launch her site, although that figure does not include the cost of a digital camera and 486 computer which she already owned. Since launching her site in the spring of 1998, she has purchased a better digital camera, a QuickCam, and two Pentium computers that are networked together. In addition, she uses ADSL,[7] an emerging communications technology, for her Internet access.

The site, according to Halford, is profitable, but not so much so that she can quit her job as a tech support person at a computer software company.

"The adult page is a hobby," Halford said. Like most amateur sites, the bulk of the income comes from membership fees, although Halford also has some banner advertising on her site. Unlike many amateur adult sites, however, Halford also includes picture galleries featuring photos of other models that she purchases from American and European suppliers of adult images. She also has plans to expand the site's contents: "Streaming video of me," Halford said. "That is the ticket."

As an online model, Halford had more experience with the adult online industry than many amateurs, but research was an important component of Halford's decision to start her Web site. "I used my past experience on the net modeling," Halford said, "and cruised 1000s of adult sites before I started this. I spent about a year researching, and just took the bad I saw, and made it good." Like most amateurs, Halford has taught herself the basics of HTML and does the majority of her own Web page coding, a significant factor in controlling costs.

## Oasis

If the online biographies of amateur Web site operators are any indication, a significant portion of the nude photos on the Web are there because the model in question lost a bet with her husband or boyfriend. One woman who has been able to turn a losing bet over the identity of a movie actress (she said it was Rae Dawn Chong; it wasn't) into a lucrative business is a 27-year-old Lake Havasu resident who uses the professional name Oasis.[8] After winning his bet, her boyfriend took some nude photos of her and posted them to his Web site. After seeing the positive response from visitors to his Web site, Oasis decided to set up her own site.[9]

Prior to posting nude photos of herself online, the Tulane graduate had no experience with the pornography industry. "I have worked in corporate communications for a major cable television company," she said, "as well as in book and newsletter publishing." Like most amateur Web site operators, she did not sit down with an attorney before starting her site or extensively research the adult entertainment industry. "The only research I did before deciding to delve into it myself," Oasis said, "was to check out other adult sites, see what they were doing, and to learn from what I saw there. . .what I didn't [and] exactly what I wanted to do."[10]

Oasis said that the cost of setting up her personal site was minimal. "I initially had a deal with my boyfriend and his partner to put up my site on the server they were using," Oasis said. "Other than film and developing, server space was my only overhead cost, and they took care of this for me in the beginning." The site generates virtually all of its revenues from fees that visitors pay for a members-only section of the site, and Oasis reports that it is very profitable. "We have approximately $3,000 to $3,500 in [monthly] expenses, which includes server rental and bandwidth charges, dial-up networking, paychecks, taxes, film, developing, and advertising. The site generates about $10,000 to

$12,000 a month in revenue." When Oasis started her site in March 1996, she was working full-time, but the revenues from the Web site grew to the point that she was able to quit her job in July 1997. Since then, the site has been her full-time employment.

Creating a site with that kind of monthly revenue requires a serious commitment to upgrading technology. Over the course of the last two and a half years, Oasis and her boyfriend have purchased entirely new camera equipment, including a new 35 mm camera, new lenses, two new digital cameras, and a Hi8 mm camcorder. Their computer hardware has also undergone substantial upgrades. Perhaps the biggest change (and the largest single expense) was the change in their server. Oasis and her boyfriend originally ran the site off of a personal computer running Windows NT and connecting to the Internet with a 28.8 kbps modem. As their sites became more popular, they moved the sites to a Sparc 5/85 computer in Maryland that has a T1 connection to the Internet. In the future, Oasis may add a live chat feature (where visitors to the site could engage in typed conversations with Oasis and other visitors to the site) and live streaming video, but she and her boyfriend are still evaluating the different technologies.

The success of Oasis's site sets her apart from the majority of online amateur sites, but her operation has two other unique aspects. Unlike most adult Web sites, Oasis uses a combination of online and traditional advertising to promote her site. "Generally, we market our site by placing banners and linking with Web sites of a similar nature," Oasis said. "Our best traffic[11] comes from other amateurs, as well as from various amateur link lists. We've only recently begun paying for advertising on some of the bigger Web sites, and it seems to be working out well. I've also done some more local marketing by appearing on a morning radio program and interviewing for an article in a local adult magazine."

The other unique aspect of Oasis's operation is the fact that it intentionally spills over into the real world. While most amateur Web site operators jealously guard their privacy, Oasis often organizes parties at various locations in the Lake Havasu, Arizona area, and she occasionally meets with fans. According to her online party FAQ, Oasis meets fans in a number of different settings, ranging from informal gatherings at a local bar to one-on-one dates to video shoots to large group parties.[12] Since it not uncommon for the video shoots or group parties to involve sexual activity, the FAQ makes it clear that all attending guests must supply a recent negative HIV test.

### Jen and Dave

Among the first of the amateur Web sites and one of the most widely known is Jen and Dave,[13] an adult Web site run out of Maryland by Jennifer Peterson and David Miller. In the spring of 1995, Dave purchased a computer and soon discovered that people were posting nude photographs on Internet newsgroups. "We had already taken nude photos as a couple before," the couple said in an e-mail,[14] "and decided to take new pics and post them on the amateur newsgroups. The web page got started when we got sick and tired of 'REPOST JNSHRP02, 05, 16, 22 OR I WILL KILL MYSELF' posts in the groups."[15]

The couple went "public" with their Web page around the first of October 1995, and recently celebrated their third anniversary as adult Webmasters. Much of the initial work on the site was done by Dave, but in October 1997, Jen took over management and coding of the site.[16]

Initially, Jen and Dave did not charge for their Web site, in part because they were having fun running it and in part because their start-up costs were so low. "Aside from getting pics developed and paying regular dial-up ISP fees," they said, "[our start-up costs were] zero." The site quickly became popular and before long was attracting more than 25,000 visitors per day. Citing the extra bandwidth demands, their original host shut down their site in February 1996. Jen and Dave moved their site to another host and began charging for access ($5 for six months) to help lower the volume of visitors.

Since then, Jen and Dave have expanded their Web site into a full-blown commercial venture. Their archive of softcore and hardcore photographs has grown from the initial 50 or so to more than 3,000, about 70 of which are available as a free preview of their site.[17] They have also created a CD-ROM of photos from their Web site, shot two amateur videos that they offer for sale, and have contributed images to Play with Yourself Solitaire, an adult version of the solitaire card game Klondike. Along the way, they've added a variety of equipment to assist them in the operation of the site: "two digital cameras; one video capture card; one scanner; one doomsday device; one camcorder; one new computer; one recordable CD-ROM drive; [and] one SLR camera." They have also installed a Webcam and use it for periodic broadcasts from their home.

Jen and Dave generate income from the site through the sale of memberships, videos, CD-ROMs, and limited banner advertising. The membership price has risen some since the club started: One-month subscriptions now cost $14.95, three months cost $19.95, and six months cost $24.95.[18] The couple have also produced four videos, each of which retails for $29.95; purchasers also receive a three-month online membership. The CD-ROM, which is stocked with 423 photos and 21 movie clips, costs $34.95 and comes with a six-month online membership. The combination of memberships and retail sales makes it possible for the couple to limit their on-site advertising to a small number of unobtrusive banners—a refreshing change from the majority of adult sites. Jen and Dave seemed pleased with the site's revenues: "It's profitable enough to make a living," the couple said, "but it's not like we live like kings. Expenses are reasonable, even considering that we give *far* more content (free and membership) than the average page—amateur or not."

There is no way to tell how many other amateur sites (legitimate or otherwise) have been inspired by what Jen and Dave have put online, but at least one recent Web site specifically credits the couple for their help. When a woman named Simple (one of Dave's coworkers) learned about his site, she initially gave

Dave a hard time about his "twisted porno stuff." A short time later, however, she took some nude photos with a friend and showed them to Jen and Dave. After posing in some shots with Jen, Simple asked Dave to take some of her alone and decided to set up her own Web site.[19] Over the past year, Simple's site has steadily grown: It now contains an archive of more than 400 photos and an advertisement for a nude video that Simple shot with her friend Jen. Although Simple relies more on banner advertising than do Jen and Dave, the design of her site is similar to theirs, even to the extent of using the same font. The effects of market forces can be seen in the membership fees for Simple's site: $9.95 for three months or $14.95 for six months. With a newer site and one that has fewer resources for members, Simple is not in a position to charge rates equal to those of her friends.

### Janey's Home Page

Another couple that have been instrumental in helping others develop and promote adult Web sites are Janey and Stephen Huntington, a California couple that operate Janey's Home Page. The Huntingtons started the site in February 1996 and posted sexy, albeit clothed, photographs of Janey Huntington, then a 44-year-old grandmother of two. Janey Huntington began publicizing the site on various Internet relay channels and within a couple of weeks, their site had received more than 20,000 hits. The Huntingtons decided to post more explicit photographs of Janey Huntington and began soliciting nude photographs from other models (one of whom, incidentally, was Brittany Halford). Within a year, Janey's Home Page grew to the point that it was receiving between 10,000 and 14,000 visitors per day.[20]

Today, Janey and her husband run four other adult Web sites, and Janey's Web page has become an online mall for sexual materials. In addition to photographs of herself (sold in sets of six photos for $6/set) and various models, the Huntington's site offers live strip shows, live sex shows, a catalog of adult videos, and various undergarments worn by Janey Huntington (which come packaged with photos of her wearing the enclosed item and a personal note). In addition to the charges for the various items for sale, the Huntingtons also generate revenue by selling advertising space on Janey's Home Page. The cost of putting a banner ad on the home page or main page of the photo gallery is $1,500 per month, although discounted rates are available for three- or six-month purchases. Back in 1997, the Huntingtons told the *New York Times* that the site generated between $8,000 and $10,000 per month for them. In light of the expansions that have taken place since then, it is evident that Janey and Stephen Huntington have continued to prosper with their site.

One of the most impressive additions is Janey's Web Service,[21] a Web hosting and design business that the Huntingtons run for both adult and nonadult businesses. The Huntingtons use the hosting service for their own adult Web pages and as of June 1999, for about 2000 other Web sites (the vast majority of which are sexually explicit).[22] As with other adult hosting operations, the Huntingtons offer a variety of different services, including programming assistance, graphic design, and general technical assistance. In addition, the Web hosting service offers a variety of suggestions for enhancing cash flow into an adult Web site, and it provides tutorials on some of the basics of running an adult Web site. All in all, it is a well-organized package of services that demonstrates the relatively thin line between a so-called "amateur" site (which is certainly where the Huntingtons began) and a professional operation.

# ONLINE IMAGE GALLERIES AND VIRTUAL CLUBS

## STILL GOING: THE BUNNY ONLINE

The growth of the Internet has been a challenge for the established players in the pornography industry, particularly *Playboy, Penthouse,* and *Hustler.* Each has been faced with the question of how to protect its core business—magazine subscriptions—while positioning itself to capitalize on the lucrative new technology. The somewhat erratic response of the magazines to the Internet helps to illustrate how entrepreneurs with vastly smaller resources have been able to compete on nearly equal terms with these industry titans.

Given some of the corporate problems that Playboy Enterprises, Inc. faced in the late 1970s and early 1980s, the growing importance of online bulletin boards and the Internet raised the question of whether an old bunny could be taught new tricks. In the late 1980s, the company had successfully prosecuted some high profile cases against adult bulletin board systems that were distributing copyrighted *Playboy* photographs but had not succeeded in setting up its own BBS. The company's response to the Internet, however, has been far more effective.

In August 1994, only a few months after the initial release of Mosaic, *Playboy* set up a free Web site, which allowed viewers to see a preview of each month's *Playboy,* look at a featured past issue, order *Playboy* paraphernalia, and check the listing for the Playboy Channel.[23] Two years later, PEI announced that it was adding a members-only section to its Web site. In addition to the resources available for free, members would have access to unpublished *Playboy* photos (the company has an archive of more than 9 million photographs from nearly a half-century of photo shoots), articles and interviews from *Playboy,* new content developed specifically for the Web site, special Web pages for Playmates, and a searchable database.[24]

The *Playboy* Web site has quickly become one of the most frequently visited: In October 1997 alone, the site had more than 4.3 million visitors. Although P.E.I. reported on March 31, 1999 that planned expansions in staff and investment in content had resulted in an operating loss of $2 million for the company's Online Group, the division also saw a near doubling of revenues— from $1.4 million to $2.5 million—over the same quarter in 1998. The Playboy Cyber Club now has more than 26,000 members (at a cost of $6.95/month, $18/quarter, or $60/year).[25]

Along with its Cyber Club revenues, *Playboy* also generates revenues from its site by offering advertising space on various pages and by forming electronic commerce relationships with other businesses. For instance, its Playboy Marketplace page includes pushbutton access to various publications, including *Internet Computing, PC/Computing,* and *Yahoo! Internet Life.* In addition, visitors to the Marketplace can hop over to Amazon.com, the duPont Registry (a catalog of upscale homes, automobiles and boats), or SexToys.com (an online shop for sexual aids). The Marketplace also features *Playboy* merchandise, as well as links to *Collector's Choice* and *Critic's Choice,* music and video mail-order companies that are owned and operated by Playboy Enterprises. The details of the various agreements were not made public, but reports indicate that the company expects electronic commerce to provide up to half of the Online Group's revenues by the end of 1998.[26]

Based on the contents of their Web sites, neither *Penthouse* nor *Hustler* has established the type of electronic commerce relationships on which *Playboy* is relying. What *Penthouse* has done, however, is develop business relationships with established Internet businesses to assist in the set-up and maintenance of its site. In March 1997, *Penthouse* and Bell Technology Group announced that Bell Technology would provide Web hosting services for the magazine, as well as "video streaming, firewalls and secure commerce/transaction processing."[27] The following month, Bell Technology and *Penthouse* announced that Bell Technology would assist the magazine in providing live and prerecorded adult video from its Web site. The two companies also agreed to set up Penthouse Web Hosting, a venture designed to offer design and marketing, credit card processing, shopping cart, and general consultation services to existing sites and prepackaged adult Web sites to entrepreneurs.[28]

In May 1997, *Penthouse* struck a five-year deal with Warshavsky's Internet Entertainment Group to provide live sex shows online, in which models strip and pose in response to requests typed in by viewers. Warshavsky's company produces the content and makes it accessible to *Penthouse* on special servers. The service has proved enormously popular, attracting several thousand fans daily.[29] PenthouseLive, the name of the site, is one of several so-called "private label" sites for which Warshavsky's company and IEG provides content (see Chapter 8).

On both the *Penthouse* and *Hustler* Web sites, the primary source of revenue are fees for membership in the magazine's online clubs. *Penthouse* has more extensive online offerings under a single roof, but it is also significantly more expensive. The site's fine print explains that after a one-day free trial, subscribers are charged $1 per day (billed every two months) unless subscribers e-mail

*Penthouse* and cancel their subscription. By contrast, *Penthouse* magazine currently retails on the newsstand for $5.99 per month.

The *Hustler* site takes a different approach. The main page serves as a gateway to seven different magazines produced by L.F.P., Inc., the parent corporation owned by Larry Flynt.[30] There is a brief preview offered for each magazine along with a description of the site contents, and then visitors are given the option of joining the Web site for the particular magazine. Prices range from $12.95 to $19.95 per month, with discounted rates for longer subscriptions. In general, members are given access to the current issue of the particular magazine, some material from past issues, extensive photo archives, and (depending on the magazine) video conferencing.

## THE EMPERORS HAVE NO CLOTHES

One of the things that has become evident over the last several years is that at least from the perspective of content, there is nothing that a major print publication like *Penthouse* or *Hustler* can offer to pornography consumers that they cannot find at hundreds or even thousands of locations on the Web. (*Playboy*, with its more extensive merchandise operations and deeper historical record, is a unique online destination.) In fact, from the perspective of sheer volume, Web sites have a huge advantage over print publications. Thanks to the steeply reduced entry and distribution costs, even the tiniest business can easily publish several thousand more photos than can be found in a single month's *Hustler* or *Penthouse*.

The advantages of Web publishing for pornographers are not limited to the lower costs. Entrepreneurs who use the Internet to distribute sexually explicit materials also have enormous flexibility. A Web site's contents can be completely changed in just a few short hours and once the new content is put on a Web server, it is instantly available (at least in theory) to tens of millions of people around the world. Consumers benefit as well: They don't have to visit their local newsstand or wait weeks for a new issue to arrive. When an online publisher changes its Web site, visitors immediately have access to the latest content.

Most importantly, Web publishers currently have an enormous advantage over print publishers in the type of content that they can offer. Without question, online pornography sites offer images that are far more explicit, more fetishistic, and often more illegal than are readily available to the vast majority of consumers, both within the United States and without. The most widespread example is so-called "hardcore" photographs, a term that covers a lot of ground but which is generally used to refer to photographs of actual sexual activity, i.e., genital-to-genital contact. Traditionally, well-known men's magazines such as *Playboy*, *Penthouse*, and *Hustler* have avoided publishing hardcore photos because the risk of prosecution in the nation's more conservative jurisdictions would have significantly complicated distribution efforts. However, the very prevalence of hardcore images online is slowly emboldening print publications: In December

1998, both *Penthouse* and *Hustler* eased their editorial policies and published photographs depicting sexual penetration. The change in policy resulted in the arrest of two clerks in Tulsa, Oklahoma and caused retail clerks in Utah to tape over the potentially illegal photographs, but resulted in little or no comment in the rest of the country. Jerome Mooney, a Salt Lake City attorney for Penthouse, told *Adult Video News* that the change in editorial policy was driven in part by the "new sexual standards created by the widespread availability of sexual materials on the Internet."[31]

What the Big Three do have, however, that the vast majority of other online sites do not have is tremendous brand name recognition. A strong brand name is an important business asset in general, but it is particularly important in a highly fragmented industry like the online adult trade (in December 1997, the adult site index Naughty Linx told *Wired* magazine that there were about 28,000 online sex sites, about half of which were set up for commercial purposes).[32] When *Playboy* launched its Web site, it did so on the strength of nearly 43 years as America's leading men's magazine. Both *Penthouse* and *Hustler* are similarly well-known; as a practical matter, those three sites do not have to do a minute's worth of online advertising to attract millions of visitors, many of whom find their sites simply by typing the name of one or more of the magazines into Yahoo![33] or an Internet search engine.[34]

In a legally risky business like pornography, of course, name recognition can be a double-edged sword. Magazines like *Playboy, Penthouse,* and *Hustler,* with their high degree of notoriety and large financial resources, offer a temptingly high-profile target for antipornography activists and ambitious prosecutors. The thousands of explicit Web site operators are also much more difficult to physically locate than a major organization like Playboy (680 North Shore Drive, Chicago) or Larry Flynt Publications (8484 Wilshire Blvd., Ste. 900, Beverly Hills). As a result, there is little likelihood that sites like *Playboy* or *Penthouse* will attempt to compete directly with the more explicit sites on the Web.

In order for an online adult site to effectively compete with the brand name advantage of the Big Three magazines, it needs to do some combination of the following: advertise heavily (which accounts for a significant portion of the spam that clogs the nation's e-mail boxes); establish itself as a leader in the industry in terms of innovation, content, or service; generate publicity both online and in more mainstream channels; or hope that demand for the industry's products and services is so great that consumers will not simply stick with the brands that they know but will also try less well-known content providers.

Two virtual clubs that have been particularly successful at blending these various elements are Danni Ashe's Hard Drive[35] and Ron Levy's Cybererotica.[36] The story of how 31-year-old Danni Ashe, a former stripper, turned her fan club into one of the hottest online adult sites is already becoming the stuff of Internet legend. She began dancing in Seattle nightclubs at the age of 18 and after several years of dancing, made videos of herself to sell by mail order. Ashe quickly discovered, however, that the cost of advertising was much higher than she anticipated. She worked out arrangements with a few men's magazines to exchange photo layouts for ad space; eventually the combination of the additional exposure and the advertising helped get her fan club off the ground, and she moved to Los Angeles to pursue additional modeling opportunities.

After a brief and unsatisfying stint traveling to nightclubs around the country as a "feature" dancer, Ashe returned to Los Angeles to concentrate on her fan club and modeling. In 1995, she discovered the Internet and quickly became a frequent participant in the Usenet newsgroups alt.sex.breast and alt.sex.movies. The fans and friends that Ashe made in the newsgroups encouraged her to set up a Web site to market her products, and she eventually decided to do so. She went through a series of different programmers (at a cost of about $1,400), but was unable to find one that understood the type of site she had in mind. During a vacation in the Bahamas, Ashe began reading a book on HTML that she purchased on her way out of town. During her week on the beach, Ashe taught herself the basics of HTML and created the first version of Danni's Hard Drive. Ashe's fan club revenues, the *Wall Street Journal* reported, rose almost immediately from $1,500 per month to between $10,000 and $15,000 per month.[37]

Recognizing the economic potential of her site, Ashe added a members-only section in 1995 called Danni's Hot Box that today for $14.95 per month gives subscribers access to large numbers of explicit photographs of Ashe and other models, to more than 1,400 live video feeds, and to RealAudio interviews with models and porn stars. In just over two years, Ashe's site went from grossing a little over $60,000 to more than $2.5 million in 1997. Ashe's business savvy and economic success have earned her favorable attention from a number of mainstream sources, including the *Wall Street Journal,* the *New York Times,* the *Boston Globe,* and the *L.A. Times.*

As Ashe herself points out with unconscious irony, it is no longer quite as easy to make a splash in the adult online industry as it once was. "The door isn't closing for the little guy, but it's getting more and more difficult," Ashe told Matt Richtel of the *New York Times.* "It's harder and harder to get seen unless you spend a lot on advertising." Ashe demonstrated both her business acumen and her persistence when she decided that a banner ad on Persian Kitty would be a good source of traffic and potential business. At the time, Persian Kitty was not accepting advertising, but Ashe kept writing Mansfield to ask her to sell space. Finally, Mansfield agreed to do so (and the banner for Danni's Hard Drive is often one of the first advertisements to appear when a user visits Persian Kitty).

Much of the success of Danni's Hard Drive can be attributed to the assets that Ashe brings to the business—her sense of humor, her business acumen, and her intuitive understanding of what online pornography consumers want—and to her high-profile involvement in the Web site itself. The site contains numerous photos of Ashe, for example, and she participates in many of the special features run by the site, including last January's unofficial Super Bowl half-time show ("Boob Bowl: The Superbowl of Breasts") and the May 19, 1999 release of "Bra Wars: An Intergalactic Sex Fable Starring Danni Ashe and her Jug-

I Knights." Features such as these help Ashe's site to record more than 7 million hits each day (roughly twice what *Playboy* receives on all of its sites combined), and the resulting revenues have enabled Ashe to build a million dollar Internet studio (which was first used to shoot "Bra Wars"). Like Martha Stewart, Ashe is successfully making her name synonymous with a certain level of product quality.

By contrast, the brand name recognition that Cybererotica is developing is less a function of a particular individual than a result of the business's extensive and effective online advertising. Cybererotica's owner, Ron Levy, got his start in the phone sex industry and then expanded to the Internet in the mid-1990s. By late 1997, *USA Today* reported Cybererotica had 55,000 members, each of whom was paying $24.95 per month, and Levy was grossing more than $800,000 per month.[38] Those kinds of revenues come at a cost: Levy (speaking under his user name "Fantasy Man") said in early 1997 that it took more than $1.5 million to develop the Cybererotica site and that monthly expenses ran $300,000.[39]

Danny Neufeld, a Canadian adult Web site operator, says that Levy's doing a lot better than that today. "In terms of money that changes hands you're looking at a lot more than $1.2 billion a year [total for online pornography]," Neufeld said. "[Take] Ron, for example. He runs Cybererotica. . .He runs a lot of phone sex as well. Between his sites he's got roughly 300,000 members. Okay? Now those members pay an average of $24.95 a month.[40] Okay? So by himself he moves a bit over seven and a half million [dollars] a month." Heather of Heather's Honeys pegged Levy's revenues at a much lower level—around $1.2 million per month—but agrees with Neufeld that there are at least 20 or 30 online adult Web site operators who are doing at least as well.[41]

Cybererotica's success is attributable to a combination of an aggressive banner advertising campaign, its extensive content offerings, and a commitment to make the purchase of online pornography as easy as possible. For instance, on Cybererotica's home page, Internet browsers are given the option of viewing the site in several different languages: English, Japanese, Spanish, French, German, Danish and Swedish. Visitors are given the option of paying by credit card on a secure server (i.e., one that encrypts the data it receives) or a nonsecure server (since some versions of the popular browsers do not support secure servers), by using the First Virtual electronic payment system, or by using Cybererotica's form for paying by check across the Internet (a number of different companies will process checks electronically). In May 1999, visitors who decided to sign up for a Cybererotica account (at a cost of $24.95 for one month to $59.95 for three) gained access to a wide variety of sexually explicit materials, including:

- 117,000+ video sex channels
- 160 live stripshow channels
- 375+ hidden camera feeds
- 50,000+ XXX pictures
- Five online XXX magazines

- 5,000+ erotic stories
- XXX games, chat, & more![42]

The stiff price tag associated with setting up and operating a site like Cybererotica illustrates the changing economics of online pornography. Although the cost of setting up a basic online adult site remains relatively low, the reality is that larger sites like Danni's Hard Drive, Cybererotica, and Club Love (Internet Entertainment Group's flagship) now have an enormous advantage in the resources that they can devote to marketing their sites and implementing new technology. As the online adult industry matures, it is going to be increasingly difficult for entrepreneurs to compete against the larger, more well-known sites.

## NICHE SITES

Despite the fact that at the lower end of the economic scale, pornography sites tend to wink in and out of existence like fireflies, entrepreneurs will continue to believe that they can start the next Cybererotica or Club Love. The news media help to fuel that perception: In an admittedly unscientific study conducted in early June 1998 on the MSNBC Web site, the responses indicated that approximately 15 percent of all Web users, or just under 10 million people, logged onto the Internet's ten most popular adult sites alone.[43] The MSNBC survey formed the basis of a study by the Department of Counseling and Psychological Services at Stanford University that confirmed the survey's essential finding: That on any given day, an estimated 9 million people log on to the Internet to view sexually explicit materials or engage in cybersex. The results of the Stanford study were published in the April 1999 edition of the American Psychological Association journal, *Professional Psychology: Research and Practice*.[44] Put in that context, even Cybererotica's draw of 300,000 members is only a small percentage of the interested consumers. That leaves a lot of room for other entrepreneurs, particularly in light of the fact that today, only about 35 to 40 percent of the nation's population has regular access to the Internet (and a significant percentage of that is at work, where cruising adult sites is at least in theory not permitted). The fact that there are so many people online looking for and at pornography helps to explain why the online adult industry is still so fragmented.

One effective way entrepreneurs compete against larger and better-capitalized competitors is by identifying a niche market that the larger businesses are not serving adequately. That has happened to a limited degree in the adult magazine industry—for example, there are magazines that concentrate on 18-to-21-year-olds, housewives and neighbors, large-breasted women, plus-size models, and various ethnic minorities—but the cost of starting up and distributing a national or international magazine is sufficiently great to make it uneconomical to market multiple magazine titles concentrating on a particularly narrow sexual bent or fetish. The very success of *Playboy*, after all, stems from the fact that Hefner successfully identified the sexual mainstream and marketed his magazine (and related products) accordingly.[45]

Niche markets are served to a much larger extent in the adult video industry, in large part because the cost of producing and distributing a particular video is much lower than producing a magazine (in any given year, 80 to 100 new adult magazines are started, compared to more than 8,000 new adult video titles). The lower productions costs make it much more likely that a video aimed at a small segment of the sexual marketplace will be successful.

Thanks to even smaller start-up costs, the Internet is far more like the adult video industry than print in terms of the diversity of its content. In May 1999, Yahoo! organized its listings of online picture galleries into the following categories (with the number of sites in parentheses): Amateurs (220), Anal (42), Asian (168), BDSM (469), Bestiality (19), Big Beautiful Women (BBW) (24), Black (39), Comics and Animation (39), Indian (13), Interracial (13), Latina (21), Lesbian, Gay & Bisexual (272 sites of men, 37 sites of women), Nude Celebrities (131), Older Women (30), Pregnant (19), SheMale (22), Vintage (7), Voyeurs (63), and Watersports (21).[46] Naughty Linx offers a total of 30 different categories, including Feet, Forced Infancy, Lingerie, Object Insertion, and Upskirt. Undoubtedly, a fascinating psychological and sociological study lies in the categories of photos that can be found online and the relative number of photos devoted to each sexual specialty. From the entrepreneur's perspective, however, the salient point is that there is a lot of room for competition. The following are some examples of sites that have successfully carved out niches for themselves on the sexual spectrum.

## Vintage Erotica

The Internet is breathing a second life into the erotic photographs taken by individuals over the last century. Two of the larger sites specializing in this type of sexual material are RetroRaunch and Vintage Vixens.[47] Of the two, RetroRaunch is the better known (in fact, Vintage Vixens has yet to be listed by Yahoo! in its "vintage" subcategory), but both offer fairly extensive collections of old sexually explicit photos, film clips, playing cards, postcards, and comic books. RetroRaunch's disclaimer captures the spirit of these sites: "RetroRaunch takes no responsibility for distress caused by seeing naked pictures of your grandmother."[48]

The owners of these vintage sites make clear that they are trying to find a niche for their business. The RetroRaunch mission statement, for instance, explains the site's somewhat austere appearance:

> We know you've been around the block when it comes to adult entertainment, and so have we. After seeing for ourselves the busy, messy, overdone, irritating sites out there, blighted with advertising and

tripping over themselves to give you (sell you) more, more, more!—
we elected to give you something better. We have deliberately chosen
to keep the site design simple, spare, and focused on giving you a
unique and very erotic experience.

David Ross, who runs Vintage Vixens, an adult Web site specializing in erotic
ephemera, has taken a similar approach. While the examples contained on
Vintage Vixen's home page make clear that even in the 1940s and 1950s, the
models in sexually explicit photographs were skewed toward the Barbie end of
the scale, nonetheless both RetroRaunch and Vintage Vixen offer a refreshing
glimpse into the pre-silicon era of nude photography.

When Vintage Vixens went online in the summer of 1997, it offered
access to a collection of 500 or so antique erotic photos for the fairly high price
of $24.95 per month. Today, the site contains more than 2,800 photos and costs
$19.95 per month. Ross has a working relationship with another vintage erotica
site, Eros Archives,[49] which specializes "in books focusing on erotica, fetish photography and artwork" along with "vintage men's (girlie) and fetish and bondage magazines circa 1950s–1980s."[50] Eros Archives is the primary source of Vintage Vixen's
material, although the photo gallery recently set up a section of its Web site that
is stocked with contributions from members of the site. In addition, Vintage
Vixen has a standing offer to buy or borrow examples of vintage erotica.[51]

Unlike most online picture galleries, Vintage Vixens contains virtually
no banner advertising (apart from a single banner on the home page for
Dv8nation, a separate site run by Ross).[52] The lack of advertising partially
accounts for the relatively high per-month charge (particularly in light of the fact
that the site does not offer some of the bells and whistles featured on other sites,
including live chat, streaming video, or adult video conferencing). Another significant factor is that Vintage Vixens does not have the luxury of buying hundreds or thousands of images already stored in digital form on a CD-ROM.
Every image on the Vintage Vixens site is one that Ross or a member of the site
staff has actually scanned into a computer and posted online. RetroRaunch faces
the same problem, which it explains in detail:

It isn't easy. Unlike the rest of the adult entertainment market, we
don't have the luxury of porn manufacturers churning out boatloads
of images day after day to feed the bottomless appetite of Internet.
We can't just pick up the phone and tell them to ship another gross
of cd's with a thousand pictures each. We have to research and investigate . . . telephone, e-mail, travel, and wait. When we do find
sources for our images, we often have to sort, by hand, through thousands of pictures dumped in boxes. Then scan them in, one by one.
Not to mention that the quality of the images is often so low that we
have to marshall all the image-editing skills we have just to make
them viewable (please see our announcement page for some interest-

ing information about an upcoming acquisition). Frankly, it's a pain. But we think it's worth it, and we hope you do, too.[53]

The challenges faced by RetroRaunch and Vintage Vixens in developing material for their sites illustrates one of the problems faced by online sexual entrepreneurs. While it is undeniably inexpensive (relatively speaking) to set up and operate an adult Web site, the cost and difficulty of doing so rises as a site's subject matter deviates from the mainstream. Although CD-ROM distributors do offer photographs covering a wide range of sexual practices and proclivities, the vast majority of the readily available images fall within a relatively narrow segment of the sexual spectrum. As a result, entrepreneurs who want materials for a particular niche site will either have to pay more for their raw materials, make do with less content, or develop content of their own.

## Seniors

Despite the recent appearance of various soon-to-be senior citizens in *Playboy*, the pornography industry has offered relatively few opportunities to women in their mid to late 30s, let alone women in their 40s and 50s. The industry's attitude toward older women is both a symptom of and contributing factor to society's general attitude toward aging and concepts of beauty in general. As the recent spate of May-and-December movie castings illustrate (Sean Connery and Catherine Zeta-Jones in *Entrapment,* Harrison Ford and Anne Heche in *Six Days and Seven Nights,* Warren Beatty and Halle Berry in *Bulworth*, Woody Allen and Mira Sorvino in *Mighty Aphrodite*, to name just a few), Hollywood enjoys and believes that it can market the fantasy that 20-something women are waiting eagerly to date and ideally sleep with 50-something men.[54] As numerous older actresses have pointed out, it is a fantasy that dramatically influences the scripts that are bought and the movies that are made.

Money, of course, is a significant part of the problem. With most Hollywood studios facing movie budgets anywhere between $20 million and $200 million, the pressure to take the "safe" route and cast younger female stars is enormous. Web sites, by contrast, have much more freedom to explore a broader range of female attractiveness and not surprisingly, older women are proving to be a popular category.

One of the earliest sites in this area is SeniorS EXposé, a site set up and run by Jeff Fimian, a 50-year-old semiretired salesman. Fimian got his start on the Internet by designing Web sites for auto dealers. "I was not making a living with the auto sites," Fimian said. "At the time, there were no major 'Mature Women 40+' sites and I decided to try to establish one."[55] It cost Fimian less than $1,000 to start his site, but that figure, he points out, does not reflect the hundreds of hours he put into designing and setting up his Web page, collecting material, and actually running the business.

Like most other adult sites, SeniorS EXposé features a variety of different services. Some, like the picture gallery, the personal ads, and one of the live video links, feature exclusively or primarily "mature" individuals (the minimum age for the picture gallery, for instance, is 40). The supply of mature models, however, extends only so far. The site's other live sex video feeds and phone sex links, for instance, are typical online adult offerings that feature (or at least purport to feature) the usual collection of 20-something models.

It will be interesting to see if the demand for more mature models grows over the coming years, as the Internet continues to expand and the baby boomer population ages (although recent returns out of Hollywood and Washington are not encouraging). In the meantime, Fimian has succeeded in carving out a reasonable retirement income for himself by running SeniorS EXposé. "We generate approximately $8,000 [per month] cash flow with expenses that run near $4,000," Fimian reported. "The difference is my current living."

No one is going to mistake an adult online site for Hollywood's A, B, or even C list, but the range of sexual materials online does appear to more accurately reflect the nation's sexual preferences and interests than the mainstream entertainment industry. Access to online adult materials is still affected by broader societal issues, like education, financial resources, access to computer equipment, and so forth. The dramatic drop in the cost of producing and distributing sexual materials, however, makes it possible for people whose sexual preferences are not represented by *Playboy, Penthouse,* or *Hustler* to find materials those publications ignore or to become publishers in their own right. The threat to the Big Three lies not merely in the volume of sexually explicit materials available online but also in their sheer diversity.

# LEGAL RISKS AND RESPONSIBILITIES

## "GIGABYTES AND GIGABYTES OF COPYRIGHT VIOLATIONS"

The most common risk in setting up an adult online gallery is the possibility of copyright infringement. To the dismay of such magazines as *Playboy* and *Penthouse,* a scanner and a computer make it possible to easily acquire huge numbers of sexually explicit images from printed materials. A page of a magazine, for instance, can be put on a scanner, a button or two pushed on the computer, and in seconds, a high-quality digital copy of the image is created in the computer's memory. The digital copy can be stored on a disk, displayed as "wallpaper" on the Windows operating systems, or transferred by modem in seconds to computers around the world. As thefts go, it is quick, anonymous, and virtually risk-free; there is simply no way that any magazine has the resources to track down every individual who has illegally scanned a copyrighted photo into a computer and distributed it to a bulletin board or Internet newsgroup.

Apart from the potential liability, the chief drawback to scanning in photos is that it is slow. Generally, the photos need to be scanned in one at a time, and it can take two to three minutes to scan each photo, make sure it is scanned properly, and then save it to disk. At the optimistic a rate of 20–30 scanned photos per hour, it would take a long time to build a big enough library of images to compete in today's adult Web site business. (And then, of course, there's the problem that the Web site would be a sitting duck for *Playboy's* or *Penthouse's* copyright attorneys.)

A more efficient approach (albeit one that does not solve the copyright problem) employed by entrepreneurs is to use software to harvest the scanning efforts of others. Each day, thousands of sexually explicit images are scanned and posted to Usenet newsgroups. Thanks to advances in browser technology, it is now possible to see the images that are posted as attachments to newsgroup messages, and with a simple click or two of a mouse button, save the images to a hard drive or floppy disk. Although this method is both faster and cheaper than scanning in images, it is still relatively slow and it requires wading through endless come-ons for one adult site after another.

Most sites don't specifically say that they've gotten some or all of their pictures from the Usenet. A few sites, however, take the opposite approach: Far from disguising the source of their materials, sites like X-News, Fabulous Forum, Adult Usenet Archive, Erotica-Net, Wicked News, and Mr. Skibone's Erotic Archive[56] actually advertise the fact that they have tens of thousands of images taken from newsgroup postings on their site. Some of these sites, like the Adult Usenet Archives, supplement their online earnings by selling CD-ROMs of harvested images to other entrepreneurs. For as little as $9.98, for instance, an entrepreneur can purchase a CD-ROM each month with between 5,000 and 10,000 sexually explicit images.[57] The incredibly low cost of these CD-ROMs and the ease with their contents can be posted to the World Wide Web helps explain part of the tremendous growth in online image galleries.

Most Usenet archive sites simply ignore the copyright issue, although Fabulous Forum tries to justify its site by posting the following notice on its home page:

ALL 500 IMAGES CONTAINED ON THIS SERVER ARE THOUGHT TO BE OF PUBLIC DOMAIN AND FREE OF COPYRIGHT. IF YOU OWN THE COPYRIGHTS TO ANY OF THE MATERIAL PLEASE NOTIFY MANAGEMENT IMMEDIATELY SO THAT WE CAN REMOVE THEM FROM THE SERVER.

Unlike trademarks, which can enter the public domain if used widely enough as a generic term, copyrighted works like pictures do not actually enter the public domain until their copyright expires. All creative works are copyrighted as soon as they are "fixed in tangible form,"[58] and the duration of the copyright depends on when the work in question was created. The copyright laws have changed so much that consultation with an attorney on specific images is essential, but a reasonable assumption is that any image or drawing created after 1920 is *not* in the public domain (and there may be circumstances under which pre-1920 images are also still protected).

The vast amounts of copied images online, however, are not likely to subside anytime soon. As the newsgroup archive sites recognize, the practical likelihood of being sued by any particular copyright owner for infringement is relatively small. Moreover, the cost of legal content is sufficiently large to act as an incentive for copying. On his Ynot Web site, Muenyong maintains a list of distributors who will sell images that are specifically licensed for use on the Web.[59] In addition to providing links to the various distributors, Muenyong also gives a price range for the images and notes whether there are additional fees for licenses and for exclusive use of the images. With prices for licensed images ranging from 10 cents to as much as $10 apiece, it is not surprising that many Web site operators choose to harvest images instead of purchasing or licensing them. The belief of adult Web site operators in the safety of numbers may be short-lived: the increased use of digital watermark technology will increase the likelihood that an infringing site will receive a nasty cease-and-desist letter from attorneys for *Playboy, Penthouse,* or Warshavsky's particularly proactive Internet Entertainment Group.

## INVASION OF PRIVACY

Ever since Hugh Hefner purchased a nude photograph of Marilyn Monroe and used it to launch *Playboy,* there has been an uneasy relationship between the pornography industry and celebrities. Many celebrities have found that the additional exposure of posing nude has provided a valuable boost to their careers. At the same time, many have been dismayed to discover that photographs or movie scenes that they did in the early, struggling days of their careers are pulled out of the dustbin when they become famous. After all, no one asked Monroe's permission before printing 70,000 copies of the photo of her lying naked on a red satin sheet.

It is one thing to accept payment for a nude photograph and then sign a release that permits the photographer or distributor to use the photograph as they see fit. It is, however, an entirely different thing to have clips of old nude scenes distributed online, to have paparazzi constantly shadowing one's house or marina in the hopes of capturing a topless or nude shot, to have personal photos and videos stolen from one's house and distributed, or to have one's head digitally cut from one photo and pasted onto an image of someone else's nude body.

The tabloids in England and America have made millions by publishing voyeuristic photos of celebrities. The Internet, with its fewer constraints on content, low-cost distribution and easy marketing, has created a boom market for nude and alleged nude images of celebrities. Yahoo! even has its own directory of celebrity nude sites, located under "Home : Business and Economy : Companies : Sex : Virtual Clubs : Online Picture Galleries : Nude Celebrities." Yahoo!'s listing contains dozens of different sites, ranging from Butts of the Nude and Famous to Celebrity Nudes[60] to the Ultimate Nude Celebrity Site.[61] Some of these sites are so popular that they gross between $10,000 and $80,000 per month, according to a recent report by the *Los Angeles Times*.[62]

The demand for naked celebrity skin is so great, in fact, that outright theft is a common means of obtaining material. The most common thefts, of course, occur when Web site owners scan nude celebrity photographs from various adult magazines; there certainly is no shortage of legitimate material. Another common type of theft occurs when entrepreneurs buy or simply rent videos with nude scenes in them (using convenient guides like Craig Hosoda's *The Bare Facts Video Guide* or Jami Bernard's *Total Exposure, a Movie Buff's Guide To Celebrity Nude Scenes*) and then use a video capture device like Play, Inc.'s Snappy to make a series of sexual explicit photographs out of a nude video scene. Play's own product description is a reasonably accurate description of just how easy it is:

> Just plug the stylish Snappy hardware module into your PC or lap-top parallel port. Then connect any camcorder, VCR or TV with the included cable. Watch your PC screen and when you see a picture you want, click SNAP. It's really that simple! With the press of a single button, Snappy captures breathtaking images at record-breaking resolutions up to 1500 x 1125.

The images captured by Snappy can then be handled like any other digital image. They can be stored to disk, posted to a bulletin board or newsgroup, or included in a Web site. Since Snappy retails for less than $100 and most videos can be rented for between $2 and $5, the cost of putting together an extensive and completely illegal Web site of nude celebrity shots is remarkably low.

These kinds of electronic theft are very low-risk: They usually take place in the privacy of the home, and the only risk of discovery comes if the entrepreneur then tries to make money from the copies. Remarkably, however, the demand for naked celebrity skin is so high that people will engage in much more perilous endeavors to obtain celebrity nudes. The paparazzi are the best-known examples, since they are willing to risk the wrath of surly bodyguards, the police, and the stars themselves to obtain embarrassing or revealing photos. On occasion, however, people have actually stolen the nude photographs or videos from a celebrity's home

In 1997, for instance, two thieves broke into the Los Angeles home of model and actress Elle Macpherson (known throughout the entertainment industry simply as "the Body") and stole a series of topless photographs that Macpherson had taken of herself as part of a book concept. The two men threatened to post the images on the Internet unless Macpherson paid for their return. The two men were caught and pleaded guilty to breaking and entering and extortion.[63]

Eighteen months earlier, in January 1996, Tommy Lee and Pamela Anderson discovered that a home videotape that they made during their honeymoon was missing from their home. The 40-minute video features shots from their wedding and extensive close-up footage of Lee and Anderson's private postceremony celebration, much of it shot during a wild boat ride on Lake Mead in Nevada. Still photos taken from the video made their national debut in a *Penthouse* cover story in June 1996,[64] and the couple brought suit against the magazine asking for $10 million in damages. Their suit was dismissed on the grounds that the newsworthiness of the images and the tape itself outweighed the couple's privacy. The U.S. District Court based its decision in part on the fact that other adult magazines had earlier published still photographs from the same tape.

Once the furor from the *Penthouse* story died down, so did interest in copies of the video itself. In the summer of 1997, however, an adult film producer named Milton Ingley obtained a copy of the videotape and had the bright idea to set up a Web site—www.pamlee.com[65]—to sell copies for $55 apiece. Lee and Anderson again went to court, but their efforts to stop Ingley's venture were hampered by the fact that he set up and was running his Web site from Amsterdam.[66]

In early November 1997, the videotape was obtained by Seth Warshavsky's Internet Entertainment Group, one of the largest providers of online video.[67] Lee and Anderson sought an injunction against the Internet broadcast of the sex-filled videotape, but once again, their request was turned down. As reporter Chris Stamper correctly pointed out at the time, even if Lee and Anderson had succeeded in persuading the court to order IEG to stop broadcasting their video, it would have made little practical difference to the hundreds of other companies scattered around the country that were or are selling copies of the video.

After the couple's request for an injunction was denied, IEG made the video available on two of its Web sites[68] and received more than 17 million "hits," or visits to the sites, in a single day. Visitors who agreed to become members of IEG's online clubs were given access to the entire tape through "streaming video,"[69] while those merely browsing could watch titillating tidbits. IEG temporarily pulled the video when Lee and Anderson agreed to submit the matter to arbitration, and the parties then entered into a confidential settlement agreement.[70] In a full-page advertisement in the January 1998 *Adult Video News*, IEG announced its settlement with the couple and served notice that it would take aggressive steps to police:

"ANY PIRATED DISTRIBUTION OF THE VIDEO AND WILL ALERT FEDERAL PROSECUTORS OF THIS ILLEGAL USE, CONTACT THE LEE'S ATTORNEY'S [sic] AND REVIEW ITS OWN RIGHTS TO BRING AN ACTION AGAINST THE PARTIES INVOLVED."[71]

It is completely unclear, of course, what rights IEG would have to stop anyone else from distributing the video, since IEG's rights to the stolen property are no better than anyone else's. The fact that the couple agreed to waive their claims against IEG is hardly an affirmative agreement giving IEG exclusive distribution rights. And in fact, the continuing widespread availability of the video online suggests that IEG has been no more effective in stopping the sale of the video than were Lee and Anderson.

Despite the failure of Lee and Anderson to stop distribution of the honeymoon video, other Hollywood stars are trying to stop distribution of nude photos of themselves. The most active in recent months has been Alyssa Milano, a star of Fox's *Melrose Place*. Milano and her mother Lin want to stamp out the unauthorized nude photos of Milano that circulate around the Internet. After discovering unauthorized and faked nude photos of her daughter online, Lin Milano started a company called CyberTracker (www.cybertracker.com) to assist Hollywood celebrities in tracking the use of their images online. When CyberTracker finds a site with unauthorized images, a polite but firm letter is sent asking that the images be removed.

In April 1998, Milano filed suit against a number of online firms that failed to remove the unauthorized images. Although Milano has been fairly successful (settling with two of the firms and obtaining a default judgment for $230,000 against a third), she faces the same problem that faced Lee and Anderson: The extent to which nude images of Milano (including the very images at issue in the lawsuits) have spread across the Internet may make it impossible for her to completely eliminate the use of unauthorized images.

Increasingly, it is not just the nation's celebrities that need to worry about their privacy. Thanks to scanners, every nude photograph or amateur adult video, no matter how private in concept, is now a potential addition to the vast online library of sexual images. If the subject of a photo agrees not only to have the photo taken but also to have it posted online, then there is no problem. However, if the subject does not agree or is unable to agree (e.g., she is asleep), then publicly posting such an image is a clearcut invasion of privacy. Newsgroups like alt.binaries.pictures.girlfriends are loaded with images that purport to be someone's girlfriend or spouse; although there is no way to be certain that the description of a given photograph is accurate, many of the images submitted to newsgroups or posted to voyeur Web sites appear in fact to be photos of spouses and girlfriends as opposed to professional models. Whether the image or image were posted online with the subject's permission is another matter entirely.

The Internet is even being used as an instrument of high-tech revenge. At Exwives.com,[72] for instance, disgruntled spouses can contribute nude photographs of ex-spouses, ex-girlfriends, and ex-lovers. On the main page of the site, its creators explain their motivation for setting it up:

> This site is dedicated to all the men who have been screwed over by their ex-wives. Both my friend and I have been taken for almost everything we own. So in order to get our revenge, we decided to post naked pictures of our ex-wives on the Internet for all the world to see. We also feature nasty photos of other men's ex-wives who have done the same to them. We think you'll enjoy this site, just as much as we enjoy the success of getting our revenge!

There's no way to tell, of course, whether the women pictured on the site are in fact ex-wives, ex-girlfriends, or anything else of the sort (and in the spirit of equality, the site also advertises photographs of ex-husbands and ex-boyfriends). If in fact they are photos of exes that were posted without permission, then those individuals would almost certainly be able to persuade a court to order the pictures removed from the Web site, and might well have a claim for tort damages.

## CONSUMER FRAUD

It may well be that most or even all of the images on Exwives.com are in fact legitimate; certainly, there is an ample supply of potential material and a large enough pool of disgruntled ex-spouses and ex-lovers across the nation to make the concept of the site believable. From the pornography industry's perspective, of course, it doesn't really matter. Pornography is about fantasy, and if enough people are willing to pay $34.95 per year for access to photos that they believe are of ex-wives and ex-girlfriends, then the pornography industry (and that particular Web site) has achieved its business objective.

With the vast number of adult image galleries available online, competition is fierce and many individuals will use any stratagem possible to give themselves a competitive edge, including but certainly not limited to misrepresenting the contents of their site. Does it or should it matter that a consumer (or researcher, for that matter) might be fooled into thinking a particular site is run by the woman who appears on the site? At one level, no. If a Web site succeeds in persuading its visitors that the person pictured is a Baptist minister's wife running an erotic Web site on the side, then the consumer has received precisely what he or she paid for: the fantasy that it might be true.

There is, however, an arguably legitimate consumer claim lurking in such deception. If a Web site fraudulently advertises itself as an "amateur" site, that might induce a consumer to purchase a membership in that Web site as opposed to another (which is, of course, precisely the idea). In theory, misrepresentation of goods and services is just as illegal in the pornography industry as in other consumer industries.[73]

Despite the fact that the nation's prosecutors are showing increasing interest in Internet-related crime (New York's former Attorney General Dennis

Vacco, for instance, appeared particularly intent on making himself the attorney general of the Internet), few attorneys general or state prosecutors are likely to show much sympathy for a consumer who complains that he or she was defrauded by claims made on an adult Web site. There are much more insidious and serious con games occurring online, in which consumers are completely defrauded of their money with nothing at all to show for it (whereas in the case of a fraudulent labeled adult Web site, at least the consumer got something for his or her money). Moreover, as a class of consumers, the purchasers of pornography are not seen as a particularly sympathetic group. The widely held assumption is that people who purchase pornography should realize that not everything is as it seems. There are few industries for which the phrase "caveat emptor" is more appropriate.

## CHILD PORNOGRAPHY

One of the biggest risks associated with using nonlicensed images to stock an online gallery is the possibility that some of the images might be of individuals who are under the age of 18. It is a federal crime to distribute sexually explicit images of individuals under the age of 18, and ignorance of a particular model's age is no defense.[74] The purveyors of sexually explicit images are required by federal law to maintain records establishing that each model depicted is over the age of 18.[75]

In addition to the various federal laws prohibiting child pornography, most states also have their own prohibitions. However, each state's jurisdiction is generally limited to its borders, which can sometimes be a hindrance to law enforcement. Frequently, pressure is put on Congress to pass a federal law prohibiting certain conduct specifically because states are having a difficult time responding to the conduct in question.

It is safe to say that no type of sexually explicit materials are more aggressively pursued or prosecuted than child pornography (often, in fact, to the exclusion of other materials that might arguably qualify as obscene). For the operators of online adult sites, there is enormous economic temptation to skirt the borders of legality, as consumers have demonstrated a particularly strong willingness in purchasing sexually explicit images featuring 18-to 20-year-old women. However, every reputable online resource for adult Webmasters stresses the profound legal risks of accidentally or intentionally including child pornography on a Web site.

## NOTES

1. John Simons, "The Web's dirty secret: Sex sites may make lots of money, but their popularity may soon taper off," *U.S. News & World Report,* August 19, 1996, p. 51.
2. Michelle V. Rafter, "Urls! Urls! Urls!" *Los Angeles Times,* March 17, 1997.
3. www.lagrand.com
4. www.brittspage.com.

5. Asia Carrera is a well-known porn star who recently retired and is focusing her energies on developing and promoting her Web site.

6. E-mail to author.

7. "ADSL" stands for Asymmetric Digital Subscriber Line, a technology that allows the use of copper phone lines to transmit data at speeds of up to 9 megabits per second from the Internet to a computer user (described as "downstream"), and up to 800 kilobits per second from the computer user to the Internet (described as "upstream").

8. Oasis, "Bio and FAQ," online at http://mirage.skygate.net/bio.htm.

9. mirage.skygate.net

10. E-mail to author.

11. That is, the traffic most likely to generate revenue for Oasis by signing up for her site.

12. Oasis's boyfriend, Lance, is always at such meetings, in part to prevent any unwanted behavior and in part to take photographs—a number of Oasis's fans appear in photographs with her on her Web site.

13. www.jen-dave.com

14. Jennifer Paterson and David Miller, joint e-mail to author, June 23, 1998.

15. Photographs are often posted to newsgroups in sequentially numbered series. For a variety of different reasons, it is not uncommon for a particular series of photographs to be incomplete. A significant portion of the messages in some newsgroups are requests that specific photographs be reposted so that Internet users can complete a series, much in the same way that people search for a particular baseball card.

16. The Jen and Dave Club, "Welcome," online at http://www.jen-dave.com/intro.

17. Although the photographs primarily feature Jen, Dave (or at least parts of him) also appears in a number of shots.

18. If payment is made by credit card, Jen and Dave throw in a membership to the Web site. The length of the membership depends on the amount purchased.

19. www.sexysimple.com. For the story of how Simple started her site, see "A SIMPLE FAQ," online at http://www.sexysimple.com/bio/#top.

20. Matt Richtel, "From Housewives to Strippers, Small Smut Sites Make Money," *New York Times,* April 2, 1997.

21. www.janey.net

22. www.cybererotic.com

23. "Playboy to Launch Pay Web Site," *Newsbytes News Network,* August 26, 1996, online at www.elibrary.com.

24. *Ibid.*

25. "Playboy Enterprises Reports Increased Operating and Net Income Excluding 1997 Tax Benefit," *Business Wire,* July 30, 1998, online at www.elibrary.com.

26. Bob Woods, "Playboy Inks E-Commerce Pacts," *Newsbytes News Network,* July 28, 1998, online at www.elibrary.com.

27. "BELL TECHNOLOGY GROUP: Bell Technology to provide Web hosting services for Penthouse magazine site," *M2 PressWIRE,* March 19, 1997, online at www.elibrary.com.

28. The *Penthouse* Web Hosting Services home page is http://host3.penthousemag.com/siteinfo/hosting/index.html.

29. "Internet Entertainment Group announces exclusive General Media deal for interactive peel and pose shows," *Business Wire,* May 20, 1997, online at www.elibrary.com.

30. The magazines listed include *Hustler, Barely Legal, Hometown, Dungeon & Taboo, Busty, Chic,* and *Leg World.*

31. "Penetration Pics Pose Problems," *Adult Video News* (n.d.), online at http://www.avn.com/htm/avn/news/nws/news/news208.html/.

32. Frank Rose, "Sex Sells," *Wired,* December 1997, online at http://www.wired.com/wired/5.12/sex.html.

33. As of May 1999, Yahoo! listed 90 Web sites devoted to specific playmates alone.

34. A similar dynamic exists with other types of industries online, particularly the news industry. Although there are myriad content providers online, sites run by the *Wall Street*

*Journal,* the *New York Times,* and the *Boston Globe* have a large advantage because of their brand name recognition.

35. www.danni.com

36. www.cybererotica.com. Seth Warshavsky's various clubs also fall under this general category, but will be discussed in Chapter 8 in light of the company's important role in online live video.

37. Thomas E. Weber, "The X-Files," *Wall Street Journal,* May 20, 1997.

38. Vic Sussman, "Sex on the Net," *USA Today,* August 20, 1997, p. 1A.

39. Matt Richtel, "Smut Purveyors Find Profits Online," *New York Times,* April 2, 1997, online at http://www.nytimes.com/library/cyber/week/040297porn.html.

40. Interview with author.

41. The widely disparate estimates of Levy's gross revenues illustrated the difficulty of obtaining reliable financial data about the online pornography industry (or the pornography industry in general). In December 1997, for instance, *Wired* reported that fewer than a dozen online adult business were grossing as much as $150,000 per month. Frank Rose, "Sex Sells," *Wired,* December 1997. If the online adult industry has in fact ballooned from $100 million in 1997 to more than $1 billion in 1998, then it certainly is possible that the number of multimillion-dollar adult Web sites has risen as well. For competitive and tax reasons, most adult Web site owners have little enthusiasm for discussing specific financial figures.

42. In an effort to keep its existing members and attract new ones, Cybererotica is constantly adding new materials. Just three months earlier, for instance, the site was offering less than half the number of video sex channels.

43. Andrew Quinn, "Cybersex not so hot after all, poll shows," Reuters, June 9, 1998.

44. Raymond McCaffrey, "Study: Millions Engage in Cybersex," *Colorado Springs Gazette,* March 31, 1999, online at http://www.mercurycenter.com/svtech/news/breaking/merc/docs/005081.htm#.

45. It is a sexual mainstream, of course, that *Playboy* has played a substantial role in shaping.

46. In a six month period from August 1998 to January 1999, every category increased in size, with the exception of Asian sites, which had three fewer. In addition, Yahoo! added the following categories: Big Beautiful Women, Interracial, and SheMale (sexually explicit pictures of hermaphrodites). Also interesting is that the heading "African American" was removed and the heading "Black" was added. The categories showing the fastest growth in the number of sites listed were Nude Celebrities (approximately 50 percent), Voyeurs (approximately 40 percent) and Watersports (100 percent).

47. 209.50.232.46/victoria.htm.

48. RetroRaunch home page.

49. www.erosarchives.com/

50. Eros Archives home page.

51. http://209.50.232.46/donate.htm. On the same page, Vintage Vixens also has a lengthy "Public Service Announcement" about the dangers of old nitrate film, which was used primarily before World War II and which has a disturbing tendency to self-combust and burn under unusual circumstances, including under water.

52. At present, Dv8nation contains links to Webcams featuring three different women. In an interview last spring, Ross emphasized the importance of finding a unique business angle. "I won't touch anything that even looks like a Barbie doll," Ross said. "You know, it's a waste of my time. There's so many people already doing it, so I specialize in big, heavy, fat, ugly housewives. Plain normal. You know, anything that's different from a Barbie doll."

53. RetroRaunch mission statement, online at http://www.retroraunch.com/statement.htm.

54. When Hollywood plots reverse the age casting, it is usually for providing the younger man with valuable sexual experience. The archetype, of course, is *The Graduate,* in which Anne Bancroft rounded out Dustin Hoffman's education.

55. Interview with author.

56. www.x-news.com, www.FabulousForum.com/pics.html, www.vortac.com/iah/adult.htm, www.erotica-net.com, wickednews.voyeurs.net, www.skibone.com/archive.

57. The Adult Usenet Archive, for instance, offers more than two years of monthly CD-ROMs, each containing between 5,000 and 10,000 harvested images. For less than the cost of some individual licensed CD-ROMs, an entrepreneur can purchase nearly a half-million sexual explicit images. Even putting aside the copyright problem, harvested images are notorious for their widely varying quality and rampant duplication. Still, at a millicent per image, it is a deal that is difficult for many entrepreneurs to overlook.

58. What "tangible form" means in the context of the computer revolution, where you can't actually see the bits that make up a particular image, is still being debated. Is a digital photograph, for instance, less tangibly fixed than a traditional photograph?

59. The list is at http://www.ynotnetwork.com/ho/pictures.html.

60. Surfers can choose between the "Celebrity Nudes" site at www.a1nudecelebs.com or the one at www.uap-avs.com/@celebrity.

61. www.csleuth.com

62. Greg Miller, "'Melrose Place' Star Hopes to Pull Plug on Sex Sites," *Los Angeles Times,* April 28, 1998, p. D-1.

63. "Man Admits Stealing Model's Photos," *Rocky Mountain News,* December 5, 1997, p. 85A.

64. *Penthouse* has a proclivity for honeymoon videotapes. Following the 1994 Winter Olympics, the magazine ran still photos from the wedding night video of Jeff Stone (formerly Gillooly) and Tanya Harding in a cover article for its 25th anniversary issue in September 1994.

65. Chris Stamper, "The Anderson Tapes," *The Netly News Network,* November 17, 1997, online at http://cgi.pathfinder.com/@@sDnixgYANjjgad*q/netly/opinion/0,1042, 1580,00.html.

66. The Lees were ultimately successful in getting an injunction against Ingley, and the Web site no longer offers the video for sale. Instead, it offers visitors a collection of 80 or so photographs of Pamela Lee culled from various newsgroups. In view of the fact that the site was being run outside of the court's jurisdiction, it is likely that Ingley stopped selling the video not because of the injunction but instead because competition drove the price of the video too low.

67. In interviews at the time, Warshavsky refused to say how IEG obtained the video. Lee and Anderson served a copy of their complaint for injunctive relief on Ingley, apparently believing he was responsible. Karen Thomas, "Lees fight to get sex video off Web," *USA Today,* November 11, 1997.

68. www.clublove.com and www.freesex.com.

69. "Streaming" is a technology that enables a browser or plug-in program to play sound or display video images as they are received from the source, rather than waiting for the entire file to be downloaded.

70. On March 19, 1998, IEG posted copies of the settlement agreement on its ClubLove Web site, on the grounds that Pamela Anderson had violated the agreement's confidentiality clause by telling Jay Leno on the *Tonight Show* that no settlement agreement had been reached with IEG. By its terms, the settlement agreement does not affirmatively give IEG the right to distribute the video; it simply says that Lee and Anderson waive various claims against IEG if the company chose to distribute the video (which of course it promptly proceeded to do).

71. Internet Entertainment Group, "Memo to Distributors from Internet Entertainment Group (IEG) Regarding the Pamela Anderson Lee/Tommy Lee Honeymoon Home Video," *Adult Video News,* January 1998, p. 185.

72. www.exwives.com

73. The two mottos that best summarize online activity: *caveat emptor* ("let the buyer beware") and *cum grano salis* ("with a grain of salt").

74. See 18 U.S.C. §§ 2251 et seq.

75. 18 U.S. § 2257.

# 8

# ALL THE WEB'S
# A STAGE

If I were just curious, it would be very hard to say to someone,
"I want to come to your house and have you talk to me and tell me the
story of your life." I mean people are going to say, "You're crazy." Plus
they're going to keep mighty guarded. But the camera is a kind of license.
A lot of people, they want to be paid that much attention and that's a
reasonable kind of attention to be paid.
Diane Arbus, 1971

In 1998, Jim Carrey starred as Truman Burbank in the widely acclaimed movie *The Truman Show*, a modern-day fable about a baby adopted and raised by a corporation so that his life could serve as the basis for a 24-hour television show watched by millions around the world. The movie was intended in part as an ironic commentary on our media-saturated culture and on our willingness to substitute visual stimulation for real interaction (i.e., we'll watch anything).

The true irony, however, lies in the fact that *The Truman Show* is already behind the technological curve. In the last year, numerous people have been voluntarily doing what Carrey's character was so horrified to discover had been done to him: putting some or even all of their lives on camera for people to view over the Internet. "Truth *is* stranger than fiction," Mark Twain once said, "but it is because Fiction is obliged to stick to possibilities; Truth isn't."[1]

In Washington, D.C., the fear for the last few years has been that the cable industry is on the verge of offering more than 500 channels, a development that will greatly increase the challenge of regulating content. The concern is outdated: on the Internet today, there are already thousands of different video "channels" showing a mixture of adult movies, strippers, live sex shows, and the personal lives of hundreds of people. As the cost of creating and broadcasting video content over the Internet continues to fall, the potential exists to turn every home or business in the country into its own broadcast studio.

# THE LIVE SEX BARONS

## PROFESSIONAL ADULT VIDEOCONFERENCING

### Virtual Dreams

In the fall of 1994, Tom Nyiri was having dinner with a friend and discussing the economic potential of the Internet. Nyiri, a University of Southern California dropout and computer technician, posed the question of what product or service people would be willing to have delivered electronically to their computers; the answer, Nyiri and his friend realized simultaneously, was "girls!"[2]

Less obvious was the means by which images of women from one location could be sent to subscribers or customers at another location. Nyiri's first thought was to find some way to adapt AT&T's videophone technology, but he rejected that approach on the grounds that it would limit his potential audience to people who either owned or would be willing to purchase a videophone.[3] Instead, Nyiri focused his attention on VidCall, video conferencing software produced by MRA Associates, that was designed to allow businesses to view live conferences and images of documents via modem. Nyiri's insight was that what could be done during the workday could also be done (and more profitably) after hours.

In a relatively short time, thanks to an effective marketing campaign and talk-show publicity, Nyiri's company was grossing more than $28,000 per month. Unfortunately, that was barely enough to cover expenses: The license for MRA Associate's software alone cost $10,000 per month, and he was paying models as much as $50 per hour to strip online.

The company's tremendous growth over the last two years is directly attributable to the intervention of two veterans of the phone sex industry, Edward Kinsley (the owner of Telecharge Audio Network) and Daniel Guess (the owner of a smaller Las Vegas phone sex operation). The two men purchased Virtual Dreams from Nyiri, retained him as the company's head of technology, and began the distributorship program that has proved so successful.

Despite the fact that the founding of Virtual Dreams coincided with increasingly widespread use of the Internet, Virtual Dreams's service was initially designed for direct modem dial-up: Customers used their computer modem to call an 800 number that connected the user to the Virtual Dreams computer. The Virtual Dreams software then connected the user's computer to the live video conferencing menu, which presented the caller with a list of available models. A short time ago, Virtual Dreams added an Internet-based service, "SexShow Live,"[4] which offers visitors access to eight different live sex shows. The cost ranges from $19.99 for 30 minutes to $39.99 for unlimited access during a single 24-hour period. The Internet-based show is considerably less expensive than the dial-up service, which costs $5.99 per minute plus a nonrefundable $9.95 setup charge. In addition, there is a five-minute minimum on all calls ($29.94 regardless of how quickly a caller is satisfied). The cost differential is explained by the fact that the dial-up service is one-on-one, while the Internet-based sex shows are broadcasts that do offer interactivity—the strippers and performers exchange typed messages with viewers—but no exclusivity. Thus, Virtual Dreams can have dozens or hundreds of people watching a single show at a time, which allows the company to bring the cost down to as low as 2.7 cents per minute and still make a profit. The combination of dial-up and Internet video conferencing, with some phone sex numbers thrown in for good measure, is in fact quite profitable: In December 1996, *Forbes* estimated that Virtual Dreams was grossing in excess of $1 million per month. The magazine also estimated that operating expenses consumed only half of that amount.[5]

## Internet Entertainment Group

About the same time that Nyiri started Virtual Dreams, a 22-year-old named Seth Warshavsky first saw interactive video on a site operated by a Canadian company, Sizzle. Warshavsky also thought that live video sex could be a lucrative endeavor. "Initially," Warshavsky told Ziff-Davis's *The Site*, "we thought they had an incredible site, except they weren't really aggressively doing anything with it—it wasn't aggressively marketed or anything. And initially we wanted to form an alliance with them or a partnership with them where we'd market their product for them."[6] When the negotiations between the two companies failed to produce an agreement, Warshavsky and his business associates began developing their own video conferencing software called InWeb, a process that turned out to be much more expensive than they expected. When they began, Warshavsky expected the development of the software and Internet site to cost a couple of hundred thousand dollars. By the time the site was launched in January 1996— originally under the name "Candyland.com"[7]—Warshavsky and his associates had invested more than $2 million in the development of InWeb and marketing costs for their site.

Much of the money required to develop InWeb and an interactive video Web site came from Warshavsky's early but successful foray into the pornography business. In 1990, at the age of 17, Warshavsky dropped out of high school in Bellevue, Washington, and moved to Seattle. While watching late-night television with a friend named Josh, Warshavsky saw an ad for a phone sex business. Convinced that they must be making a large amount of money, he and Josh borrowed $7,000 using credit cards and founded J&S Communications in less than a month.[8]

Using the phone number 1-800-GET-SOME (a number Warshavsky boasts he still has), J&S Communications began marketing phone sex services.

When people called, Warshavsky had an answering service take down the caller's credit card information and then page Warshavsky with the caller's phone number. Warshavsky would then give the number to a woman so that she could call the client back and have phone sex with him. It was a cumbersome system, but a lucrative one. In a relatively short time, J&S Communications was logging between 50 and 60 customers a day at $39.95 per call. Warshavsky bought out his friend at the end of their first year, and went on to become one of the major players in the phone sex business. By 1995, in fact, revenues for his phone sex business were estimated to be at the $60 million mark.[9]

The phone sex business, already under attack by Senator Jesse Helms for its use of 800 numbers, received a further blow in September 1995, when the FCC issued an advisory against the use of 10-XXX numbers, a billing system used extensively by the phone sex industry to route phone sex calls overseas and away from the disapproving gaze of federal regulators and legislators. Although the FCC's efforts to restrict the spread of phone sex by banning 10-XXX numbers was ultimately unsuccessful (thanks to the industry's discovery of foreign exchanges), the short-term impact of the government restriction was severe, and it left Warshavsky hunting for a less scrutinized industry.

The Internet in 1995 was precisely the type of economic playground for which Warshavsky was looking. With the World Wide Web little more than a year old, the actual number of potential competitors online was relatively low, an ideal situation for a well-capitalized entrepreneur. Moreover, much of the Internet community was still clinging tenaciously to the Internet ideals of free and open exchange of information. This utopian mind-set offered little impediment to an entrepreneur unconcerned about the idealistic visions of the online community. When Warshavsky's Candyland site went online in January 1996, he was already well-positioned to be one of the leaders in the online pornography industry.

In the past four years, Warshavsky has demonstrated a keen business sense when it comes to online sexual materials. Using an aggressive marketing campaign (including extensive use of banner ads and click-through payments), Warshavsky has managed to make his company's 30-plus Web sites, including the flagship Club Love, into some of the most popular stops on the Internet. As early as August 1997, for instance, Warshavsky claimed that Internet Entertainment Group was recording more than 6 million visitors a day and that 50,000 people had signed up to become members of the Club Love site. By May 1999, Warshavsky was reporting that Club Love's membership exceeded 115,000, each paying $24.95 per month for access to the site's photos, videos, adult videoconferencing, and other sexually oriented resources.[10] Thanks to a number of high-profile stunts by Warshavsky and IEG, the number of daily visitors has often spiked well above 6 million. When "Club Love" first posted nude photos of radio moralist Dr. Laura Schlesinger (which IEG purchased from an old boyfriend), for instance, Warshavsky said that the site's traffic shot up to 14 million visitors per day. [11]

## THE ECONOMICS OF ADULT VIDEOCONFERENCING

Adult video conferencing has been a lucrative endeavor since its introduction in late 1994. The rates charged by Web sites for interactive videoconferencing typically range from $2.99 to $5.99 per minute, and sites report that some customers spending as much as $6,000 in a single month to exchange typed electronic messages with a particular model. For Barbara Bailey, the owner of PleasureGirls and 11 other adult videoconferencing sites, the reason for the large expenditures is simple: "They fall in love," she told the *L.A. Times.*[12]

Adult videoconferencing sites charge as much as they do for their services in large part because they can—both the novelty and the privacy are compelling attractions—but also because the significant start-up and operational costs associated with offering such services limit the number of potential competitors. For instance, when Tom Nyiri founded Virtual Dreams, one of the Internet's largest suppliers of adult videoconferencing, it took loans totaling $25,000 to get his business off the ground, and even then, the company barely survived its first year.[13]

Virtual Dreams has survived and prospered by striking deals with other adult Web sites to distribute the shows produced by Virtual Dreams. In a typical arrangement, an entrepreneur pays Virtual Dreams a franchise fee (approximately $3,000 in 1996). In return, Virtual Dreams helps the entrepreneur set up a Web site featuring interactive modeling and sex, which the entrepreneur then markets on the Internet and in his or her local area. Visitors to the Web site pay as much as $5.99 per minute to participate in the adult videoconferencing, which appears to be produced by that particular Web site. In reality, the Web site visitors are watching content produced at the Virtual Dreams studio in its San Diego or Las Vegas studios (the latter is a 30,000-square-foot complex that Virtual Dreams built in late 1996 and early 1997, after revenues for its product crossed the $1 million-per-month mark). The entrepreneurs are paid up to 30 percent of the fees generated by their Web site, and Virtual Dreams keeps the rest. In June 1997, Virtual Dreams had a list of more than 200 different distributors of its adult videoconferencing, and CEO Daniel Guess (not only a phone sex industry veteran but also a Republican) is intent on adding more.[14] In addition, the company is making arrangements with studios around the world (so far chiefly in Europe) to help provide 24-hour access to interactive strip shows.[15]

The distribution model employed by Virtual Dreams offers a number of advantages, not only for pornography businesses, but for more mainstream businesses as well. The first and most important, of course, is that it helps to increase Virtual Dreams's cash flow. In return for a relatively low investment in Web page design and some additional models in San Diego or Las Vegas, Virtual Dreams has greatly increased the number of people marketing its product. Second, the distributor model has the effect of coopting potential competitors by offering a low-cost alternative to setting up a full-blown interactive videoconferencing operation. It is a lot easier for an entrepreneur, for instance, to come up with a few thousand dollars to purchase a Virtual Dreams package than it is the $25,000, $50,000, or even $100,000 required to set up an adult videoconferencing studio. Third, it reduces the pressure on companies like Internet Entertainment Group and Video Dreams to develop and establish brand identity with consumers amid an apparent sea of adult videoconferencing sites. In late August 1998, for instance, Yahoo! listed 222 different videoconferencing Web sites under the heading "Home : Business and Economy : Companies : Sex : Adult Services : Videoconferencing." On Yahoo!, Virtual Dreams is just one listing among many, but if it in actuality provides content to and profits from a majority of the adult videoconferencing sites on the Yahoo! list, then it need not spend large sums of money promoting its own site. The distributer program set up by Virtual Dreams has been emulated by a number of other adult videoconferencing companies, including Bailey's Cyber Sex World (which claims on its Web site that more than 500 different sites on the Internet use one or more of the company's video services),[16] and Warshavsky's IEG-run sites.

Club Love, the IEG flagship, was an early leader in the concept of "upselling," a technique that involves charging visitors a relatively minor amount to access a site and then persuading them to spend money on additional goods and services once they've signed up. On the Club Love site, subscribers were initially charged $9.95 per month for access to a library of photographic images and for the right to purchase a wide variety of other goods and services. For instance, a visitor might pay $4.95 for a movie, $4.95 for a day's access to personal ads, or $7.95 for a day's worth of access to sexually oriented games such as Strip Blackjack.[17] But the Whopper of his Club Love site, Warshavsky told *ABC News*, was the $29.95 IEG charges customers to watch 15 minutes of a live sex show; the Whopper with Cheese, a half-hour's access for $49.95.[18]

Another significant source of income for IEG is a distributorship program similar to the one run by Virtual Dreams. IEG has relationships with more than 1,400 Web sites to promote or distribute the live video content that the company produces in Seattle, including exclusive arrangements with large pornography companies like *Penthouse* and Vivid Video, one of the top producers of adult videotapes.[19]

The combination of an extensive distribution network for its original content and aggressive upselling on its own Web sites has proved particularly lucrative for IEG. According to published interviews with Warshavsky, the annual revenues of his company have risen steadily, from $7 million in 1996 to $20 million in 1997 to $50 million in 1998. The site charges $35 per month for access to the site and has approximately 5,000 subscribers, which adds more than $1.5 million each month to IEG's gross revenues. Amazingly, the company's revenues are expected to double again in 1999 to $100 million, with profits of roughly $35 million.[20] Since IEG is a privately held corporation, however, there is no way to verify those figures.[21]

Even industry giants, however, are not immune to price wars, and the trend in the online pornography industry is definitely away from separate charges for different services. Online customers would apparently prefer to pay a higher but comprehensive charge rather than a low admission charge and additional fees for individual services. As a result, Club Love now offers memberships at $24.95 per month (although the optimistic can sign up for a year's access for about $175). The membership fee includes access to all of the services and attractions for which Club Love used to charge separately, including the once-pricey live sex shows.

How well IEG has made the shift to a flat-fee arrangement and how accurate Warshavsky's revenue claims are may become apparent in the relatively near future. The company is presently engaged in negotiations with investment bankers and undergoing an audit in preparation for making an initial public stock offering. Warshavsky's hope is to raise sufficient capital (in the $300 million to $1 billion range) to enable him to purchase other online adult sites and to expand into developing mainstream communication technologies, including high-speed Internet connections and interactive television.

There is some skepticism about whether IEG in general and Warshavsky in particular can attract enough support on Wall Street to go public. Few doubt, given the popularity of online pornography, that IEG's revenues are at least close to what Warshavsky is describing, which makes IEG one of the most profitable Internet sites in operation. Given that other Internet-related businesses have successfully gone public despite a conspicuous lack of profits (Infoseek, for instance, which lost $25 million in 1997 and $5.7 million in 1998, traded at about $36-½ per share in June 1999, giving it a market capitalization of more than $2.25 billion), IEG would appear to have the numbers to support an initial public offering.

More problematic is the taint associated with Internet pornography, a cause not helped by IEG's broadcast of the Pamela Anderson/Tommy Lee video and the Dr. Laura Schlesinger photos, or Warshavsky's well-publicized offer (along with Bob Guccione) of $3 million to Monica Lewinsky for a nude or seminude photo appearance on Club Love and in *Penthouse*.[22] Warshavsky also brings to the table a difficult reputation in both the online sex industry and the phone sex industry, where the collapse of his phone sex business in 1995 left hard feelings and claims of unpaid creditors. Similar charges of slow or nonexistent payments have also dogged IEG, problems which Warshavsky dismisses as a one-time issue stemming from a surge of "bogus credit card charges" in 1997.[23]

What may help IEG's prospects for staging an initial public offering is Warshavsky's growing role as a spokesman for online adult entertainment. In February 1998, for instance, he testified before the Senate Commerce, Science, and Transportation Committee at a hearing on Internet indecency, where he was described by Senator John McCain (R-Ariz.) as "the Bob Guccione of the 1990s."[24] Warshavsky, who appeared at the request of the committee, offered a proposal called the Dot Adult Act, which would have created a new extension for domain names called ".adult."[25] Warshavsky also called for the mandatory inclusion of so-called "v-chips" in computers and passage of legislation requiring access barriers to screen out children.

Warshavsky's legislative proposal received little attention from the senators, who instead grilled Warshavsky on the ease with which children can access material on the Internet in general and on Club Love in particular. While it is not clear that Warshavsky is the ideal poster child for the online adult industry's efforts to police itself—despite his testimony to the contrary, his Club Love site has offered full frontal nudity and images of sexual activity on its preview pages, which can be accessed by anyone who stops by the site—IEG's economic resources will continue to thrust that role on the 25-year-old entrepreneur. The stakes, of course, are huge, because if IEG can follow Playboy Enterprises, Inc. (trading at $21-$^{9}/_{16}$ on August 23, 1999), Metro Global Media ($1-$^{15}/_{16}$), or New Frontier Media ($6-$^{9}/_{16}$) onto Wall Street, it will have enormous resources available to shape itself into a leading multimedia content provider in an increasingly digital world.

The consolidation that has taken place in terms of content provision and the sheer cost of setting up adult videoconferencing sites will continue to prop up the per-minute price for the time being, but the enormous competition within the industry makes it difficult for companies to continue charging upwards of $360 per hour for an online videoconferencing service. Already, it is possible to find adult videoconferencing services for as little as 50 cents per minute, and a few of the larger online sex providers (like Cybererotica, for instance) are offering interactive video services as part of a flat $24.99 monthly membership fee.

Narrowing profit margins in the adult videoconferencing business will make it even harder for entrepreneurs to compete directly against well-established operations like Virtual Dreams and IEG. A smaller profit stream will extend the period for return on investment, which will make it harder for entrepreneurs to raise the capital needed to set up and run competing operations. Even if entrepreneurs are able to raise the money, the advantage that companies like Virtual Dreams or Cyber Sex World have in the number and scope of their online business relationships makes adult videoconferencing a very crowded field. While demand for adult videoconferencing remains high, the large number of existing businesses makes it more expensive for a start-up business to establish a market presence.

In the short term, at least, these various factors help make the distributor model an attractive option. The risk associated with paying a few thousand dollars to Virtual Dreams or Cyber Sex World for a "promotional partnership" is much lower than the risk associated with starting a competing business, and at the rate of $1.80 per minute (a site operator's typical cut), an entrepreneur requires a little more than a day's worth of business in order to recoup his or her initial investment. Even with a distributorship, of course, making any serious money requires a lot of work in terms of Web site maintenance and marketing. Nonetheless, compared to the challenges of setting up a studio, hiring models, and so on, a distributorship is a far simpler proposition.

## STRIPPING IN CYBERSPACE

One group of people who are undoubtedly feeling the pinch of narrower profit margins in the live sex and adult videoconferencing sectors are the women and men who work as strippers on adult videoconferencing sites. When Nyiri founded Virtual Dreams in 1994, his two models cost him $400 per day each, or around $50 per hour, which works out to an annual full-time salary of $100,000.[26] By the middle of 1997, *Time* magazine was reporting that Virtual Dreams's dancers were paid about $40,000 per year with benefits (approximately $20 per hour, or 1/18th of the money earned by Virtual Dreams).[27] One of Virtual Dreams's competitors, Warshavsky's IEG, was reported to pay a similar amount to its online strippers.[28] Twenty dollars per hour, however, may now represent the high end of the online stripping trade; it is not uncommon, for instance, to see ads offering as little as $10 or $15 per hour for online strippers.

Even though the distribution of both power and money in online conferencing companies tends to emulate real-world establishments (i.e., most of the businesses are run by men, and the employees are women), online conferencing companies are stressing aspects of the work environment that are unusual in an industry not generally hailed for its sensitivity to women's issues. For instance, two fairly typical advertisements in New York's *Village Voice* (February 3, 1998) illustrate the efforts of some videoconferencing businesses to appeal to a wide range of potential employees:

Make Big Money Now
Here's Your Chance to Be a Star. The nation's hottest Internet Service, CUN-TV[29] is looking for sexy, adventurous females to perform live. No Experience Necessary. Flex hours. Safe, Clean, Midtown Location. No Customer Contact. Immediate Hire. Call Asia: 212-696-2502.

World's Largest Internet Site
Is seeking attractive girls, lesbian couples, tv/ts and hot guys. You must be upbeat, enjoy chatting & be reliable. AM/PM shifts available. Perfect for young moms & students. We are open 24 hrs. Safe midtown location. No computer exp. nec. No customer contact, no dancing. No standing on your feet all day. $15/hr. plus tips. Limited openings call Maureen: 212-688-3555 x 1040. Our company does business with Playboy, Spice and Falcon video. Check out our hot

sites at www.peepshow. com, www.4gay.com, www.shemale.com

Thanks to the nature of the technology, at least some of the advertised claims are true. Adult videoconferencing and live shows do remove the possibility of physical contact with the customers, and site technicians can act as electronic bouncers, disconnecting and refusing access to customers who make threatening or illegal suggestions (e.g., asking models to simulate sexual activity by a child). In addition, because adult videoconferencing studios are not open to walk-in traffic, they do not raise the zoning concerns that live strip joints do, and thus can be located in less seedy, less threatening urban areas. Perhaps most importantly, the anonymity of the Internet means that online stripping virtually eliminates the possibility of stalking by infatuated customers.

The extent to which other types of claims are true will depend on the business in question. Because of technological demands, it is generally not possible for models to work out of their homes the way phone sex operators can, so models must travel to the studio and work there. In addition, some online strippers have reportedly been required to work lengthy shifts in tiny cubicles with few if any breaks. In a typical day, online models may answer as many as 200 calls from men around the world.[30]

The same technology that makes online stripping safer can also make it both awkward and uncomfortable. Since online video transmissions do not take place at the same rate as video or television, sudden movements on the part of the models can make the transmission appear jumpy. With real-time audio conversations in their infancy, some online strippers have to interrupt their routines to type messages back and forth with customers. The computers themselves help to make the work environment uncomfortable: Since each cubicle is loaded with a computer and cameras, adult videoconferencing businesses generate a lot of heat, not all of which is good for the operation of computers. In order to prevent system failures, businesses use powerful fans or air conditioners to lower the temperature, which is fine for clothed techies but less fine for naked models writhing on a couch or gym mat.

Perhaps most disturbing is the power shift that often accompanies adult online videoconferencing. In live strip joints, generally speaking, customers come to watch the show that the dancers choose to put on; various beefy bouncers are usually on hand to enforce a basic civility between patrons and dancers. By contrast, online videoconferencing is often marketed as an opportunity for customers to "direct" the performance of the models, a slightly more polite way of saying that customers are given the opportunity to order models around. A model can refuse a specific request, of course, without fear of direct physical reprisal from the customer (who may be thousands of miles away), but more problematic are the economic consequences of being labeled uncooperative, ranging from a loss of tips to unemployment. Services that charge $180 and up per hour can ill afford to employ uncooperative performers, and at $15 to $20 per hour, there is no shortage of women willing to work as an online models. The steady demand for these relatively safe and modestly lucrative jobs gives adult videoconferencing businesses powerful leverage in dictating the conduct of their employees.

# THE WEB CAM PHENOMENON

The world's most famous coffeepot resides in a hallway outside the so-called "Trojan Room" of the University of Cambridge Computer Laboratory in Cambridge, England. In 1991, graduate students and members of the Computer Lab's "coffee club" grew tired of traipsing up and downstairs only to discover that the hackers on the second floor of the lab had drained the pot. Two students, Paul Jardetzky and Quentin Stafford-Fraser, pointed a video camera at the coffeepot, ran wires from the camera to a computer with a frame-grabber[31] attached, and wrote the software necessary to distribute and receive images of the coffeepot.[32] (A student's interest in the project, needless to say, was directly proportional to his or her distance from the coffeemaker.) In early 1994, images of the Trojan Room coffeepot, as it is known, were made available on the World Wide Web and by the end of the year, more than 150,000 people from around the world had stopped by the Web site to see if the pot was half-empty or half-full.[33] The pot still percolates for a worldwide audience today (provided, of course, that the light in the room is on).[34]

Four years later, there are thousands of Web cams in operation, showing everything from the Boston skyline to daycare facilities to the most explicit sexual activity. It is a rapidly growing phenomenon, one that offers everyone with a computer and an Internet connection the opportunity to turn their home into a worldwide broadcasting studio. Not surprisingly, there are a lot of people who are using the technology to satisfy their own exhibitionist tendencies and/or the voyeuristic tendencies of others (particularly those who are willing to pay to do so).

## CU-SEEME

One of the least publicized uses of Web cams is to provide images for use with CU-SeeMe, a program first developed by Cornell University in 1992 for use on Macintosh computers. A Windows version of the software with audio was released in August 1995. The CU-SeeMe software is designed to send video and audio signals from one computer to another using the same software. Users have the option of connecting directly to each other (by typing each computer's unique Internet Protocol address into the software) or to special computers known as reflectors, which take the video and audio signals from a single computer and make them available to multiple viewers. Once connected to a reflector, the CU-SeeMe software can open up a separate video window to show the transmissions of each person broadcasting to that reflector.

The visual equivalent of Internet Relay Chat, CU-SeeMe was originally developed to provide low-cost business videoconferencing and long-distance education, and most of the existing 200 or so reflectors are used for those types of activities. Like so many other technologies, however, CU-SeeMe has also been put to more erotic purposes. On any given evening, people around the country use this technology to pose nude in front of each other, engage in mutual masturbation sessions, or even watch each other having sex. It is a high-tech version of "I'll show you mine if you show me yours." To speed up transmissions and to minimize the impact on business use of CU-SeeMe, a number of the reflectors are exclusively used for adult transmissions: Adult XXX Amateur Club, Backdoor, Bev's Café, Biker Bar, Club Flash, to name just a few.[35] Not surprisingly, directories for adult CU-SeeMe reflectors and extensive instructions on using CU-SeeMe are available on the World Wide Web.

The transmission of sexually explicit images using CU-SeeMe is a little different from most online pornography. Typically, the display of nudity and sexual activity on the Internet flows in only one direction, from the producer to the consumer. Even when a model is in the midst of a hot-and-heavy typed conversation with a videoconferencing customer, he or she cannot see the customer or what the customer is doing. For CU-SeeMe users, however, the expectation is exactly the opposite: Not only do users expect to be able to see each other, but the custom is that if someone is participating in an adult conference that features nudity, he or she will also be broadcasting nude images of himself or herself (which probably accounts for the smaller number of people using CU-SeeMe for erotic purposes). While it is in fact possible to use the CU-SeeMe to look at others without broadcasting nude or even clothed pictures of oneself (a practice known as "lurking"), most adult reflectors discourage the practice by refusing to allow a CU-SeeMe user to receive images unless he or she also is transmitting video images (the software is specifically designed to detect if a computer user is broadcasting or merely lurking).

Unlike many other types of sexual material online, adult CU-SeeMe has remained relatively free of commercial activity. Although there have been some efforts to set up and run commercial adult CU-SeeMe reflectors, they have not been particularly successful. The relatively small number of users, the technical challenges of dealing with occasionally balky CU-SeeMe reflectors, and the somewhat erratic video quality have proved to be powerful disincentives for consumers. Nonetheless, businesses keep trying. One of the few current contenders right now is a business called CU-Central,[36] which is attempting, in their words, to bring "organization, security, and availability to the adult CU-SeeMe community." The company's scheme for doing so is to set up six adults-only reflectors—"The Doorway," "The Lounge," "The Game Room," "The Stairway," "The Hallway," and "The Upstairs"—and charge admission depending on the level of access that a particular user wants. Still, the challenge of providing an organized and consistent online experience is highlighted by the fact that CU-Central offers free admission to its reflectors for single women and for couples. CU-Central said in August 1998 that it had 950 members, but there is no information available on the breakdown of the site's memberships by gender, age, or for that matter, any other criteria.

Although commercial adult CU-SeeMe activity has experienced only sporadic success, the steady growth of the technology overall illustrates the Internet's impact on the distribution of information. Prior to the invention of the World Wide Web (and more specifically, the invention of such software as CU-SeeMe), an individual's ability to distribute live video was severely limited. Videoconferencing has been around for some time, of course, but studio access can run several hundred dollars per hour and the potential audience is quite small. Cable channels and broadcast networks offer access to potentially enormous audiences, but a combination of regulatory and fiscal barriers limit the broadcast of sexual materials to just a few channels. Local cable access channels offer an inexpensive outlet for some sexually explicit live video (New York's *Midnight Blue* and the *Ugly George Hour of Truth, Sex, and Violence* are two particularly well-known examples), but the number of public access channels is limited, and cable operators retain the ability to reject patently obscene broadcasts.

By contrast, the chief factor affecting an individual's ability to distribute live video over the Internet is his or her budget. The cost of most of the equipment, at least by the standards of the broadcast industry, is relatively minimal: a computer powerful enough to run the hardware and software needed to broadcast images over the Internet can be purchased for less than $1,000; new digital Web cameras retail for about $100, and an Internet connection can be had for as little as $9.95 per month (although $19.95 is more typical). The cost of the software is even less expensive. In the interests of promoting better use of desktop videoconferencing, Cornell University made the decision to provide its CU-SeeMe software free to the public.[37] An enhanced version of the software (which includes technical support not easily obtained from Cornell) is available from White Pine for about $70.[38] Even with the commercial version of CU-SeeMe, the total cost of setting up a computer system to distribute live video on the Internet is less than $1,500.

Obviously, that is not an insignificant amount of money; part of the reason that only about 50 percent of U.S. households have computers at all is that a $1,000 to $1,500 purchase is not in the budget of many families. Nonetheless, when one considers that in 1995, Westinghouse paid $5.4 *billion* to purchase CBS (which has a potential audience of roughly 235 million Americans but which in the last sweeps period of 1998 averaged 13.7 million viewers per evening), paying $1,500 for access to a worldwide broadcasting network and a potential audience of more than 100 million people is an amazing bargain.

## GLASS HOUSES: THE GROWING POPULARITY OF HOME WEB CAMS

A far more successful business model for online sexual entrepreneurs has been to use Web cams to upload periodic images of their homes and activities to a Web site. Since visitors to the Web site can view the images without special software (both major browsers are designed to automatically display images contained on a Web site) and without having to necessarily broadcast naked images of themselves, these one-way broadcasts are far more popular with the majority of Internet users than CU-SeeMe.

Although the cost and complexity of setting up a home-based Web cam is greater than most other home-based adult Web sites, it remains a comparatively open market. The relative lack of competition represents a real opportunity to individuals who are willing to put time, effort, and money into maintaining the site and who are willing to give up their privacy, which is of course what makes these sites so compelling to so many. While bandwidth remains a hurdle (it is not unusual, for instance, for a moderately popular home cam to distribute up to a gigabyte of information or more per day), technological changes will eventually make the distribution process both easier and less expensive.

Online exhibitionism received its first major boost in 1996, when a Dickinson College student named Jennifer Ringley became one of the first to set up a Web cam to show people how she was living her life. Ringley had been chatting with a friend about the "Fishbowl Cam," a famous Web cam site featuring periodically updated images of someone's office fish tank, and became fascinated with the idea of setting up a human fish bowl. She initially limited access to her Web cam images to a half dozen friends or so, but after getting a positive response, she made it generally available to the Internet community. In a fairly short time, Ringley began receiving a half million hits a day on her Web site, which she dubbed "JenniCAM."

Following graduation from Dickinson, Ringley moved to Washington, D.C., to work as a freelance Web page designer. She has continued and expanded JenniCAM, adding a second camera to cover a different portion of her apartment ("JenniCAM II"), and adding streaming video technology ("JenniSHOW"). The technological improvements are funded by the $15 annual subscription fee that Ringley charges for access to faster Web cam upgrades (the free Web cam updates every 20 minutes, the subscription Web cam every 2 minutes).[39] Although Ringley's decision to charge the relatively nominal amount for access to her Web cam was primarily motivated by the cost of the bandwidth required to handle the traffic generated by her site, the volume of subscription fees is great enough to provide her with a comfortable living.

Although Ringley's intent in setting up and running JenniCAM was not particularly mercenary (the $15/year charge is roughly 1/12th of what most other Web cam sites charge, and Ringley briefly stopped accepting new members), it did not take long for other people to realize that what Ringley had really accomplished was to figure out a way to get people to pay to watch her sleep. The notoriety that her site gained led to numerous imitators and even earned Ringley a guest spot on the CBS show *Diagnosis Murder*. In an episode titled "Rear Window '98," which aired on November 12, 1998, Ringley played the operator of a Web cam site who is murdered online.

One of the more amusing offspring of the JenniCAM is a parody created by Web site designer Wes Denaro. In designing his site (called WesCAM, of course),[40] Denaro closely emulated the layout and font that Ringley used in setting up her site. Unlike JenniCAM, which brings visitors into Ringley's home, WesCAM is limited to shots of Denaro sitting at his cubicle at work. Nonetheless, his site still attracts more than 5,000 visitors per day.[41]

In an interview with the *Boston Globe,* Denaro said that the idea to create WesCAM grew out of his office's fascination with JenniCAM. "We all started watching JenniCAM, and a couple of my co-workers were completely obsessed with her," Denaro said. "It was the first online cam we found. All day I'd hear someone yell out 'Jenni's home' or 'Jenni's changing.' All day they'd watch and watch." Rumor has it that Denaro's co-workers were not the only ones fixated on JenniCAM: *Entertainment Weekly* published a report that director Peter Weir was so fascinated by JenniCAM that he sent Ringley anonymous e-mails during the shooting of *The Truman Show.*[42]

What makes JenniCAM so compelling, apparently, is the sheer normalcy of the images. As Mark Glaser wrote in a column for the *Los Angeles Times,* "So what's the big deal? I suspect many voyeuristic men are lurking, waiting for Ringley to undress for bed. There is occasional nudity, but mainly it's real life, which means endless phone calls, sessions at the computer and plodding hours when Jenni is asleep."[43] In her online Frequently Asked Questions page, Ringley specifically rejects the idea that her JenniCAM is pornography:

> Pornography is in the eye of the beholder. Myself, I do not think this constitutes pornography. Most often, pornography is defined as something explicit which is made with the clear intention of arousing the viewer. Yes, my site contains nudity from time to time. Real life contains nudity. Yes, it contains sexual material from time to time. Real life contains sexual material. However, this is not a site about nudity and sexual material. It is a site about real life.[44]

Needless to say, not everyone agrees with Ringley that the worldwide broadcast of one's private activities is appropriate or morally acceptable. In a speech to Catholic bishops for a March 1998 conference titled "The New Technologies and the Human Person," Leo Hindrey, the president of Telecommunications, Inc.,[45] told the assembled prelates that the Internet had the potential to function as an "electronic pew," but that it could also be "stunningly immoral." As an example of the Internet's immorality, the TCI executive specifically cited Jennifer Ringley and her JenniCAM, despite the fact that he had never visited Ringley's site.[46]

## Marketing Voyeurism

Despite the concerns of Hindrey (who may also be worried about the threat that the Internet poses to cable viewership), Ringley is probably correct that her site is not pornographic, let alone legally obscene. Hindrey's ignorance about the content of JenniCAM is evident in the fact that even in March 1998, it was possible to find far more sexually explicit Web cams then the JenniCAM; more

explicit material, in fact, can regularly be found on a number of the cable channels carried by TCI, including HBO, Cinemax, Showcase, and MTV. Hindrey
also apparently neglected to mention to the U.S. bishops that in 1995, Playboy
Enterprises launched the first international Playboy TV channel in a joint venture with Flextech plc, a U.K. entertainment company that is majority-owned by
a subsidiary of TCI and British Sky Broadcasting Ltd.[47] Just on skin content
alone (let alone sexual activity), there is no comparison between the mildest
evening of programming on Playboy TV and JenniCAM.

Admittedly, the fact that TCI itself profits from the distribution of sexually explicit materials does not undercut Hindrey's essential point, that there are
images and content on the Internet that far surpass Playboy TV in their explicitness. As with other technologies, the freedom of access to the Internet and the
relatively low cost of producing and distributing Web cam images is evident not
only in the number of sexually explicit Web cam sites on the Internet but also in
the diversity and explicitness of the sexual content.[48]

The evolution of Web cam sites has followed the growth of online
pornography in general. As JenniCAM grew in popularity, not surprisingly,
numerous imitators sprang up. Most emulated Ringley's approach, in which
nudity is an infrequent but natural part of her daily activity. It took no time at
all, of course, for some Web cam operators to realize that they could boost the
amount of traffic to their site (and thus increase the advertising rates for banners
on their sites and/or the number of potential members) by increasing the amount
of nudity and sex that visitors could see. In the two and a half years since Ringley
started JenniCAM, literally hundreds of different Web cam sites have been set
up, the majority of which contain either nudity or sexual content. In the process,
Web cam sites have settled on a fairly typical structure: an introductory page, a
guest cam that updates every 10–30 minutes, a members-only cam that updates
every 20–60 seconds, a gallery of archived images taken by the Web cam, a page
of frequently asked questions, and usually a page of links to other adult sites or
sexually explicit Web cams. In some cases, like Ringley's JenniCAM, the Web
cam is the primary focus of the Web site; in other cases, like Jen and Dave, a Web
cam is a later addition to an existing image gallery site.

Sexually explicit Web cam sites generally fall into one of three general
categories: "amateur" sites, featuring women, men, and couples for whom the
Web site is their first experience as nude models; "professional" sites, which feature models with previous experience in the adult entertainment industry and/or
models working full- or part-time for an online pornography business; and
"voyeur" sites, which feature video images of men and women who do not know
that they are being recorded,[49] let alone that the images are being distributed
around the world over the Internet.

The largest number of sexually explicit Web cams are those that advertise themselves as "amateur." The phrase "amateur," needless to say, is far more
hype than guarantee: There is no way to tell if a particular Web cam model derives
all of her income from her site, or if the site is merely a part-time hobby. Again,

it may not really matter. Web cams are the quintessential medium for persuading consumers that they are paying for the privilege of viewing someone's private activities, regardless of the fact that the model in question is generally giving up her privacy quite willingly. The number and apparent popularity of Web cam sites is clear testament to the power of voyeurism as a source of sexual fantasy.

The designation "amateur" also has little if anything to do with the explicitness of the sexual content of a particular Web cam site. While some "amateur" Web cam sites contain little or no nudity, it is equally true that many "amateur" Web sites contain sexual activity that is as extensive and as explicit as adult videoconferencing sites with "professional" models. Typically, most "amateur" Web cam sites feature individual women posing nude or masturbating, although a growing number also feature men, couples, and even groups.

As the popularity of individual Web cam sites has grown, it did not take long for online pornography businesses to see the economic potential of the new technology. "Amateur" sites were quickly joined by sites operated by individuals and businesses that make no pretense of amateur status. Adult-film stars like Lori Michaels (also a *Penthouse* pet) and Shanna McCullough, for instance, use live appearances on Web cams they have set up to help promote their videos. Similarly, large online pornography businesses such as IEG and Cybererotica have created Web cam sites based on specific themes, among the most popular of which is the college coed dormitory cam. So popular are dormitory cams, in fact, that IEG runs a banner advertisement offering payments toward room and board and even tuition for female college students willing to live in a dormitory outfitted with 31 cameras that constantly transmit images to the Internet. One such site, Voyeur Dorm,[50] already exists and is populated by five female college students. The site charges $35 per month for access to the site and has approximately 5,000 subscribers, which adds more than $1.5 million each month to IEG's gross revenues.

Appearing on ABC's *Good Morning America* on May 20, 1999, the women in the dorm appeared pleased with the arrangement and defended the site. As one put it, "This is our life. You pay to watch it, and, you know, if you don't want to see it, don't watch."[51] Warshavsky's innovative approach to campus housing, however, has attracted unfavorable attention from local authorities. *Good Morning America* reported that city officials in Tampa, Florida, where the five students live, consider Voyeur Dorm to be an adult entertainment business. A hearing has been scheduled on whether the dorm has to move outside Tampa city limits.

## WEB CAM DIRECTORIES, NETWORKS, AND REVIEWS

A sure sign of the growing popularity and sheer volume of these types of sites is the growing number of Web sites specifically designed to catalog, organize, and even review Web cam sites. (One can imagine a somewhat surreal dialogue between critics Gene Siskel and Roger Ebert: "Gene, I thought the life we saw today was well-intentioned but dull." "You're right, Roger. The dialogue is awful, and the plot is worse. I'm giving this life a big thumb's down.") Even *Playboy* has caught wind of the new trend in online exhibitionism: In its September 1998 issue, it published a brief article about Web cam sites and included a nice mention of The Nose's HomeCams Page, a listing of nearly 1,200 Web cams.[52]

Most sites listed on the Nose's HomeCams site are set up along the same lines as Ringley's, with a GuestCam that refreshes every 10–20 minutes and a Member's Cam that refreshes every 1–2 minutes. In addition, the sites usually offer members a variety of additional services, including access to extensive galleries of images saved from the Web cam, live chat sessions, and even private CU-SeeMe sessions.

Another site that specializes in sexually explicit Web cams is Top Cams,[53] a site that not only lists adult Web cams but also attempts to rank them by the amount of interest that they generate. In a typical setup, Top Cams will list a Web cam on its site and ask the Web cam operator to put a link to Top Cams on his or her site. Top Cams then uses software to measure the number of visitors in (i.e., that click on the Top Cams link on the Web cam operator's site) and the number of visitors out (i.e., that click on the link to a particular Web cam in Top Cams's list). In January 1999, the most frequently visited sites in the Top Cams list received between 4,000 and 6,000 visitors per day.

Since Top Cams focuses on sexually explicit Web cams, its list of 163 Web cam sites is smaller than other more general Web cam lists. Nonetheless, the list offers well-organized and thorough information about each Web cam site, including a sample picture (which may or may not be sexually explicit), a link to the site, the information on the number of visitors in and out, and a brief description of what is on the site. Top Cams does not purport to review the sites—the descriptions are actually written by the Web cam operators themselves—but each paragraph generally contains enough information to make it clear what each site offers. In addition, each listing contains a content category ("girl," "guy," "couple," etc.), the Web cam's refresh rate (i.e., the frequency with which the image is updated), and the operator's description of the amount of nudity (ranging from "almost" to "whenever horny" to "HELL YES").

One relatively new site that purports to offer objective reviews of Web cam sites is Webcam Magazine,[54] which was established on the Web in late December 1998. Webcam Magazine reviews sites based on a variety of criteria, including: the quality of the Webcam, member site, guest site, originality, speed, content, overall. In addition, the site offers interviews with Web cam site operators, answers to frequently asked questions about Web cams, and an article titled "Spice Up Your Sex with a Webcam," a *Cosmo*-esque piece that suggests that peering into the sexual habits of others may provide couples with some ideas for their own sex lives.

The real challenge for most Web cam site operators is not setting up the site but successfully marketing it. Even in the relatively small universe of sexually explicit Web cam sites, the competition is stiff, and it can be difficult to attract both attention and traffic. To overcome this problem, some Web cam site operators affiliate themselves with networks of adult Web cam sites. In exchange for a percentage of the revenues generated by the Web cam site, the network handles the promotion of its members' sites, handles the creation and maintenance of photographic archives, and processes payments.

A typical example is the AmateurCam Network,[55] a site that features 17 individual Web cams. The site operators (all of whom happen to be women) run the Web cams from their homes, typically appear online in lingerie or in the nude, and generally promise to appear online at specific times during the day (or night). Visitors to the AmateurCam Network pay either $9.95 or $12.95 per month to subscribe to a particular model's site. In return, members get access to a Web cam that refreshes every 60 seconds, access to an archive of images from the Web cam, the ability to send the model e-mail, and the ability to participate in live chat sessions with the model and other members. The network has recently added streaming video on some of its sites at a cost of about six cents per minute. Some of the time, the models act as if the Web cam doesn't even exist. Most of the time, however, the models specifically put on shows for their Web cam audiences, ranging from nude chat sessions to showers/baths to explicit sexual activity. The AmateurCam Network has captured the voyeuristic nature of Web cams in its motto: "Get to know them. Watch them. It really is fascinating."

One of the largest distributors of Web cam images is Ifriends,[56] a site that collects and organizes material from a wide variety of different Web cams. A significant portion of the available material is adult, ranging from "Girls Home Alone" to "Guys Home Alone" to "Threesomes/ Groups," but Ifriends also offers live Web cam feeds on relatively benign subjects like "Psychics/Advice," "International Conversation," and even "Cooking." Although the adult Web cam feeds are clearly the primary focus of Ifriends, its inclusion of nonsexual topics may be a harbinger of the future. As bandwidth costs continue to fall, it will become increasingly easy for people to create and distribute online videos on an essentially infinite number of topics. For instance, someone who thinks that he or she makes a particularly good Thanksgiving turkey might broadcast their holiday preparations. Similarly, others might broadcast online shows dealing with everything from gardening to automobile repair to personal investment. That process is already occurring with text—hundreds of thousands of people have written up their expertise and put it on a Web page—and the same thing will happen with more visually oriented skills.

In the short term, the most profitable Web cams remain those that offer nudity and/or sexual activity. Web cam operators that sign up with Ifriends charge varying amounts (generally between 99 cents and $1.99) per minute for access to their Web cam feeds; the money earned by a particular Web cam feed is split 50/50 between Ifriends and the Web cam operator(s). In addition, Ifriends encourages Web cam operators to sign up friends to distribute Web cam feeds through Ifriends, and offers to pay a commission of 1 percent of the sales of each site that is signed up. Ifriends claims that some Web cam sites earn as much as $2,000 per week for part-time work, a claim that is not easily verified.

# THE LEGAL RISKS AND RESPONSIBILITIES OF ONLINE ADULT VIDEO

## OBSCENITY

Obviously, anyone who distributes sexually explicit images is at some risk for a possible obscenity prosecution. The use of the World Wide Web to distribute such images simultaneously increases and decreases the risk of prosecution. Since the Web is accessible in any jurisdiction in the country, a federal prosecutor could attempt to prosecute a Web cam site operator for violating federal laws against the transmission of obscenity over telephone lines (using the obscenity standards of the state in which the federal prosecutor is based). That is precisely what happened, of course, to Richard and Carleen Thomas in 1994, when they were prosecuted in Memphis, Tennessee, for violating Memphis obscenity standards, despite the fact that their Amateur Action Bulletin Board System was physically based in northern California.

At the same time, adult Web site operators have a number of institutional advantages over bulletin board operators. First, there are simply so many adult web sites. While companies that make filter programs put the number of sexually explicit Web sites at more than 100,000, most objective estimates put the total at between 30,000 and 40,000. With that many adult Web sites in existence, an offended jurisdiction would have the resources to pursue the distributors of only the most egregious and offensive material, which typically means child pornography.

Another advantage generally enjoyed by adult Web site operators is that it can be relatively difficult to determine the physical location of the site or its operator(s). Unlike a bulletin board system, the general location of which is readily determinable from the board's area code and exchange, the physical location of a Web site is not readily determinable from its IP address. There are certainly tools that can be used to track down the physical location of Web sites, but the process is somewhat more complicated than calling the phone company to find out the location of a particular phone number. Moreover, Web site operators who are concerned about potential illegality have available to them a variety of software tools that can make it extremely difficult to locate either a Web site or its operator.

Prosecution of most Web cam sites is also unlikely because the majority do not offer images that could be considered obscene in even the most restrictive jurisdictions. While there are a large number of Web cam sites with sexual material, most limit themselves to nudity, which puts them on a par with magazines like *Playboy* or *Penthouse*. A general rule of thumb is that penetration is required before images of heterosexual activity will be considered "obscene," and even then, the majority of jurisdictions in the country would decline to prosecute (in general, less latitude is shown for images of homosexual activity, or images of bestiality). By that standard, the operators of most Web cam sites live R-rated lives (occasional nudity and sexual situations), with occasional NC-17-rated interludes that may or may not appear on camera. An interesting question can be raised about whether it is somehow more "obscene" for a "real" person to appear nude or sexually active online, as opposed to someone who is a pornography professional. In all likelihood, however, it would be difficult to make that type of distinction stand up.

It does not take much effort, of course, to find Web cam sites that specialize in broadcasts of sexual intercourse. Most such sites are certainly flirting with the boundary between pornographic and obscene, and a number clearly cross it. Nonetheless, even the most graphic Web cam site is unlikely to be prosecuted for obscenity absent some active suspicion that the people portrayed on the site are under the age of 18.

Obscenity may not be the only potential liability for Web cam site operators. A remote but intriguing possibility is that a Web cam site operator could be prosecuted for appearing nude in public. Most jurisdictions have laws that prohibit public nudity, and an argument could be made that appearing nude on a Web cam that can be accessed from a particular jurisdiction is the virtual equivalent of appearing nude in that jurisdiction. Since most such laws are merely misdemeanors, the cost and effort of actually prosecuting a Web cam operator for public nudity would almost certainly outweigh the deterrent effect. Nonetheless, the question throws into graphic relief the unresolved issue of where activity in cyberspace actually takes place.

## COPYRIGHT

The risk of copyright violation for the producers and distributors of a Web cam site is generally much lower than for the operators of a virtual club or online image gallery. The copyright in the live images created and distributed by a Web cam site is owned by the people producing and distributing the images. Regardless of whether a site is distributing intermittent images or streaming video, a live Web cam broadcast largely eliminates copyright concerns.

If anything, the more challenging copyright issue for Web cam site operators is protecting their own copyright in the images that are distributed. The majority of Web cams in use today are used to distribute a photographic image every 30 seconds or so. It is a relatively simple matter for a Web site visitor to save and then redistribute the images just like any other photograph. Capturing and redistributing streaming video is moderately more complicated but certainly not impossible. While virtually every Web cam site contains explicit warnings about copyright, cam operators face the same challenges that every other producer of Web content faces: preventing the unauthorized use of protected materials.

As bandwidth capacity increases and processors grow more powerful, it will be easier for individual entrepreneurs to become distributors of streaming video. As long as the images being broadcast are produced by the site owners, the copyright analysis remains the same: The site operators are the owners of the copyright to the live broadcast. For some entrepreneurs, however, the temptation will be to increase the materials on their site by broadcasting adult videos without permission.

The chief protection that adult videotape companies have today against the unauthorized distribution of their product is the fact that setting up video feeds is both challenging and expensive. In order to distribute just one adult videotape via streaming video, an entrepreneur has to successfully link together a playback device, a video capture card, a fairly powerful computer, and software to store and compress the video to a manageable size and length.[57] In addition, an entrepreneur must be able to either set up and operate a streaming video server (which also requires a fairly powerful computer and full-time, high-bandwidth Internet connection) or rent space on someone else's streaming video server.

Online pornography sites with the economic resources to do so, of course, already have extensive offerings of adult videos (Cybererotica alone, for instance, today offers more than 18,000 channels of streaming adult video). In general, though, larger sites have an economic incentive (i.e., their prominence increases the threat of large legal fees and penalties for copyright violations) to work out licensing arrangements with adult video producers and distributors that give them permission to broadcast the videos. Smaller adult Web sites, which have already shown a propensity for scanning and distributing large numbers of copyrighted photos, may not feel that the risk of copyright litigation is great enough to justify the cost of actually licensing an adult movie before broadcasting it on a Web site.

## MINOR MODELS

For most Web site operators, setting up and operating a Web cam reduces one of the more serious risks of involvement in the pornography industry: the possibility that the site will unwittingly distribute the image of someone who is under the age of 18. As long as the people operating the Web site and appearing on camera are themselves adults, there is little or no risk that the site will accidentally distribute an illegal image. Public Web site operators with minor children, of course, have to be careful that their children never appear on camera unclothed, and may want to establish a policy that they never appear at all. It is one thing to use a Web cam to show Grandma and Grampa images of an 18-month-old having a bath in the kitchen sink, but another thing altogether to put that type of image on the Internet for public consumption.

If a Web site operation grows and models are hired to offer either live sex video or adult videoconferencing, then the issues of age are the same as with still photographs. Federal law requires that proof of the age of all models appearing nude or participating in a sexual explicit production be maintained and stored in a central location where they can easily be produced. As most adult Web site operators are aware, this is certainly one area in which state and federal law enforcement agencies are devoting enormous resources.

One copyright issue that is often overlooked in the production of amateur videos in the real world is the use of music. As the amateur video handbook from Video Alternatives stresses, the use of music in the background of a video is a violation of copyright unless the producers of the video have specific permission to use it. It is one thing, for instance, for a Web site operator to ask a friend to play or record some original music to use in the background; it is another thing altogether to have a CD or cassette tape playing while the video is being recorded. Video Alternatives warns potential contributors that it will mute out the sound of music from any videos it receives unless there is clear proof of permission. Since it is often difficult to edit out only music, much of the other sound on the tape is lost as well. The same rules apply to online video distribution.

## INVASIONS OF PRIVACY

One of the reasons that sites such as Voyeur Dorm are popular is that they offer visitors the titillation of peeking in on private activity, like a woman's dormitory. Selling the fantasy of voyeurism, of course, is not illegal (as long as the models are over 18, of course). It is a consistent practice of sexual entrepreneurs, however, to challenge the boundaries of what is legal and/or in good taste. Novelty, after all, is an important element of a pornography purchase: the novelty of seeing a new person unclothed, for instance, or the novelty of a new sexual situation or fantasy. Entrepreneurs quickly came to the conclusion that if consumers are interested in and willing to pay for staged voyeurism, then they would be even more likely to pay for access to real electronic voyeurism.

It should go without saying that before someone's image appears in a photo or video used on a Web site, a Web site operator should have that individual's permission to do so. In reality, however, illicit images and videotapes of people are becoming an enormously popular Internet attraction. Thanks in no small part to the end of the Cold War and the success of filmmaker and conspiracy maven Oliver Stone, manufacturers of so-called "spy" cameras (tiny devices with fish-eye lenses) have been aggressively marketing their products to amateur conspiracists for the past decade. With the advent of the Internet and its apparently insatiable demand for new sexual material, the radical fringe has been joined by both professional and amateur pornographers, who are discovering an impressive (albeit illegal) array of places in which to conceal the tiny cameras. A quick search of either Yahoo! or AltaVista illustrates the imagination and creativity of pornographers. The leading locations are women's locker rooms and changing rooms, but also popular are cameras concealed in the ceilings of women's bathrooms or in the toilets themselves ("toilet cams"), under a desk in an office ("secretary cams"), or in a book bag or other sack for use on busy city streets, malls, or amusement parks ("upskirt cams"). Another recent "innovation" are cameras that are allegedly concealed in the offices of doctors conducting ob/gyn exams. Cybererotica alone advertises that its members can see images from more than 180 hidden cameras. While some so-called "voyeur" cams are undoubtedly staged by a photographer or Web site, there can also be little doubt that many women (and some men) have unwittingly had nude photos of themselves distributed to a worldwide audience.

The most common types of unauthorized private images are illicit videotapes or photographs of an individual's sexual partner or family members, which are then contributed or sold to a Web site specializing in voyeuristic images. The most common tactic, according to the online reports, is to conceal a digital camera or video recorder under an artfully thrown pile of clothes in the bedroom; a close second is to wait until a spouse or partner has fallen asleep. Others claim that they left their camera in plain view and told their partner that the camera's blinking red light meant that the camera was simply recharging. At a site like Voyeur Web,[58] for instance, visitors can look at a variety of still images that have been contributed to the site and read a brief description of how the photos were taken.[59] A typical entry (from a January 12, 1999 posting) reads as follows:

> Hi Igor—love the site and finally have a contribution for you. My wife's best friend is gorgeous with a great body. Our bathroom has an old vent (piece of board with 10mm holes drilled in it) leading to the attic. She came to stay over once, so when she was headed to the bathroom, I got (quietly) into the attic, turned the light off and set the video camera going. By zooming in a bit, I managed to get the camera to focus on her rather than the holes in the vent—but you can still see the vague shape of the vent in the pictures—sorry about that! It was incredibly exciting finally capturing her on video (I've had first hand views of up skirts and down blouses in the past) and I recently got a Miro PC/TV card which allowed me to create an avi file of the footage, from which these stills are taken. At the time these pictures were taken, my wife and kids were only just downstairs finishing off breakfast—I was 'sorting out the loft' allegedly. Just as I'd finished taping—my 4 year old daughter came up the stairs shouting to me and I only just managed to move away from the vent area in time to avoid discovery!

Attached to this recitation were three photos of the naked torso of a woman, shot from above; the images are blurred in a manner consistent with the contributor's statement that they were shot through a grate.

The scope of the problem was driven home in April 1998 when ABC's *Primetime Live* did an exposé on landlords who spy on and even videotape their tenants,[60] using equipment similar to that offered for sale in the Voyeur Shop.

During the course of the show, *Primetime Live* reporter Sylvia Chase interviewed a number of tenants who had discovered that they had been videotaped by their landlords. For most, a major concern was whether copies of the videotapes were being sold around the country. "There could be thousands of copies of the video-tape," said Dennis Neuser, a tenant in Alaska who discovered that he and his wife had been videotaped while in the bathroom of their apartment. "He could have put it on the Internet. No one knows."[61] Neuser's instincts were accurate. Chase reported that copies of similar illicit videotapes were readily available in sex shops from New York to Anchorage, and that voyeuristic videotapes can also be purchased on a number of sites on the World Wide Web.

Homes are not the only source of voyeuristic images. Unbeknownst to most people, there are an enormous number of security cameras in use around the world, and an increasing number of communities are adding security cameras in public areas as means of augmenting more expensive and overworked police forces. Where there are video cameras, there are generally videotapes, and where there are videotapes, there is the possibility of reproduction and distribution. In England, for instance, where video surveillance is already a $250 million-a-year business, there is a booming market for videos of surveillance film outtakes, including shots of people committing crimes, acting crudely, or even having sex in places where they thought they would not be observed. Industry experts say that current surveillance technology is capable of taking much sharper pictures than most people realize, giving camera operators the ability to identify specific faces, license plate numbers, and even printed text in someone's hand.[62] In the fall of 1998, the Security Industry Association held a conference to discuss the privacy concerns raised by security cameras. The industry, however, has rejected suggestions that the sale of security cameras and "spy cams" be halted until protective legislation can be adopted.[63]

As both camera and Internet technology continue to grow in sophistication and speed, the number and intrusiveness of illicit or surreptitious photographs will grow. In August 1998, for instance, Lucent Technologies announced that it had successfully integrated all of the technologies required for a video camera onto a single quarter-inch chip, which analysts expected would lead to the development of high-quality video camera with lenses no larger than a marble. Despite the innovation, the new chip is expected to sell for less than $50, leading to the production and sale of a wide range of tiny but affordable devices capable of capturing video images.

The Internet's greatest strength—the fact that it has become a vast repository of readily accessible information—only exacerbates the problem of electronic voyeurism. In the days before the Internet, a budding voyeur would have had to find a bulletin board that specialized in voyeurism or perhaps purchased a book on surveillance photography from a fringe press like Loompanics. Today, however, a vast amount of information about voyeurism is only a local phone call away. The scope of the information on voyeurism alone is staggering: Not only do Web sites provide access to images and videotapes from concealed cameras, but they also give instructions on where to purchase the best cameras and where to hide them, as well as detailed instructions on building specific types of spy sites. (One extreme example is a set of instructions on how to conceal a spy camera on the inside of a toilet, which can then be used to snap pictures while the toilet is in use.)

Economic forces help to drive the accumulation and distribution of information online. Sites such as Voyeur Web try to boost their usefulness to their consumers (and thus the amount of traffic they receive) by artfully blending a large archive of images with extensive technical information (suggestions on cameras, strategies for obtaining voyeur shots, and video capture software). In addition, Voyeur Web has tried to solidify its market position by setting up an online store for surveillance equipment. Billed as a source of "technology for amateur photographers and surveillance," the Voyeur Shop[64] offers visitors their choice of digital cameras, Web cams, video capture devices, surveillance equipment, minirecorders, covert cams, and video transmitters.

In addition, the Voyeur Shop offers extensive information on how to take voyeur-style photos using different types of equipment. One topic that the Voyeur Shop covers in particularly thorough detail is the infamous "X-ray" capability of the various Sony video cameras equipped with a NightShot feature. When used with a specialized filter in low-light conditions, Sony NightShot cams appear to make some clothing layers translucent. (Samples of the resulting photographs are periodically posted to Voyeur Web and other voyeur sites.) Shortly after the discovery was made of the Sony cam's enhanced (and avowedly unintended) capabilities, the manufacturer announced that it was altering the Nightshot technology to make it more difficult to take "X-ray" photos.[65] In the interim, however, camera shops were deluged with calls of consumers interested in purchasing the camera.[66]

Law enforcement is largely incapable of investigating and prosecuting high-tech Peeping Toms. Most of the dressing rooms in the country, after all, generally resemble each other and lack any identifying information. Moreover, the chances that a surreptitiously photographed person will discover his or her photo online is extremely small. Law enforcement has an easier time making a case when the photographs or videotapes are taken from a specific and recognizable location, like an apartment house. But even then, ABC's Chase reported, prosecution of the Peeping Tom landlords is hampered by outdated or nonexistent laws. Most of the nation's legislatures have not yet squarely addressed this issue. While individuals can seek civil penalties for violations of privacy or for the intentional infliction of emotional distress, the lack of specific statutory prohibitions make it difficult for law enforcement to deal with the problem. The Alaskan landlord who videotaped his tenants, for instance, was charged with misdemeanors in conjunction with the taping (his thefts of tenants' bra and panty sets, however, were considered felonies).[67]

The challenge facing lawmakers, of course, is that technology moves so much faster than the wheels of legislation can easily turn. When a legislative body like Congress does try to act swiftly, it runs a serious risk of overreaching, of adopting a solution that is so broad and overly inclusive that it causes more problems than it solves. Widespread invasions of privacy are unquestionably a serious problem, but it will be incumbent on legislatures to craft statutes that do not unnecessarily stifle permissible speech at the same time.

# NOTES

1. Mark Twain, "Pudd'nhead Wilson's New Calendar," *Following the Equator* (Hartford, Conn.: American Publishing Co., 1897).
2. Seth Lubove, "E-sex," *Forbes,* December 16, 1996, p. 58.
3. Lubove, "E-sex," p. 58. Given the efforts of Panasonic and Pioneer to boost sales of DVD players by encouraging the production of adult DVDs, and given AT&T's tacit (and profitable) participation in the phone sex industry, it is mildly surprising that AT&T did not think of this approach itself.
4. www.virtualdreams.com.
5. Lubove, p. 58.
6. "The Virtual Hugh Hefner," *The Site*, Ziff-Davis TV, August 25, 1997, online at http://www.thesite.com/0897w5/iview/iview793jump8_082597.html.
7. Warshavsky lost a well-publicized trademark fight with Hasbro over the domain name "Candyland.com," which Hasbro successfully claimed was an infringement on its trademark of the same name. See *Hasbro Inc. v. Internet Entertainment Group, Ltd.,* 40 U.S.P.Q. 1479 (1996).
8. Frank Rose, "Sex Sells," *Wired,* December 1997, online at http://www.wired.com/wired/5.12/sex.html.
9. Rose, "Sex Sells." The partnership did not end amicably; a court battle ensued over rights to a call-routing system. Barton Crockett, "Inside an 'XXX-files' kingdom," MSNBC, July 23, 1998.
10. Karl Taro Greenfeld, "Taking Stock in Smut," *Time,* April 19, 1999, p. 43.
11. Al Martinez, "The Naked Truth," *Los Angeles Times,* November 6, 1998, p. B1.
12. Michelle V. Rafter, "Urls! Urls! Urls!" *L.A. Times,* March 17, 1997.
13. Lubove, p. 58.
14. Daniel Eisenberg, "Sex, Bytes and Video Dates," *Time,* June 1, 1997, p. 32.
15. Lubove, p. 58.
16. See http://www.cybersexworld.com/opportunity.html.
17. Thomas E. Weber, "The X-Files," *Wall Street Journal,* May 20, 1997. Numerous articles since have made mention of the fact that Warshavsky has hung a framed copy of Weber's article on the wall behind his desk.
18. Peter Coogan, "The Web's Porn King," *ABCNews.com,* August 22, 1998.
19. Barton Crockett, "Inside an 'XXX-files' Kingdom," MSNBC, July 23, 1998.
20. Greenfield, p. 43.
21. Barton Crockett, "Profits Push Spread of Web Porn," MSNBC, July 23, 1998.
22. "Internet porn site chips in another $1m for Lewinsky photos," *Nando.net,* February 6, 1998, online at http://www.techserver.com/newsroom/ntn/info/020698/info12_28875_ noframes.html.
23. Barton Crockett, "Inside an 'XXX-files' Kingdom."
24. Senator McCain in turn was quoting from Frank Rose's article in *Wired.* The comparison was apt, given that Warshavsky's offer to Monica Lewinsky had been made only four days earlier.
25. The suggestion has also been made to create a ".xxx" domain name, but the proposal is opposed by some companies (most notably, *Playboy*) who are leery of being associated with anything labeled "xxx."
26. Lubove, p. 58.
27. Eisenberg, p. 32.

28. Matt Richtel, "Smut Purveyors Find Profits Online," *New York Times*, April 2, 1997.

29. www.cun-tv.com.

30. Daniel Eisenberg, p. 32.

31. A "frame-grabber" is a device that electronically clips snapshots from a video source like a video camera or VCR and stores it in a computer's memory. The popular Snappy device, which is so popular for transferring the nude scenes of celebrities from videotape to the Internet, is a frame-grabber.

32. Simson Garfinkel, "Credit the Coffee Pot," *Boston Globe*, June 25, 1998, p. D1.

33. *Ibid.*

34. The Web site for the Trojan Room coffeepot is located at http://www.cl.cam.ac. uk/coffee/coffee.html.

35. A list of the available reflectors, along with a brief description, is online at http://ccwf.cc.utexas.edu/cgi-bin/cgiwrap/streak/scan.

36. www.cu-central.com.

37. The download site for the Cornell software is online at http://cu-seeme.cornell.edu. The trade-off for free software is often (as is the case here) a lack of technical support.

38. The White Pine Web site is http://www.wpine.com/Products/CU-SeeMe.

39. Mark Glaser, "Cybertainment: For Those Who Like to Watch, Home Webcam Provides Picture of Private Lives," *L.A. Times*, January 8, 1998, p. F 41.

40. wescam.inline-design.com/live.html.

41. Christopher Muther, "All the World's a Stage," *Boston Globe*, July 21, 1998., online at http://www.boston.com/dailyglobe/globehtml/202/All_the_Web_s_a_stage.htm.

42. Dave Karger, "Tru Lives: Who needs Jim Carrey? Real-life versions of The Truman Show indulge the exhibitionist and the voyeur in us all," *Entertainment Weekly*, June 12, 1998, p. 87.

43. Glaser, "Cybertainment."

44. Jennifer Ringley, "General FAQ," online at http://www.jennicam.org/faq/generalhtml. Ringley's choice of words is particularly apropos, given the popularity of MTV's *Real World* series, a show about an artificially constructed life (six to seven preternaturally attractive house-mates selected from a cattle call of thousands of potential participants) that due to broadcast constraints (even by the relaxed standards of cable) is unable to show as much of the "real world" as the simplest Web cam.

45. Tele-Communications, Inc. (TCI) is the nation's second-largest cable company, with more than 10 million subscribers (it trails only Time-Warner). In the summer of 1998, TCI agreed to a buyout by AT&T for $48 billion. Final approval of the deal is still pending.

46. Jonathan Dyson, "Ready for your close-up?" *Independent*, October 31, 1998, p. 42.

47. Playboy Enterprises, Inc., SEC 10-K filing, June 30, 1997.

48. The diversity in the number and content of the Web cams online is not matched (at least so far) by a similar diversity in the featured models. At the beginning of 1999, for instance, there were very few African-American, Latino, or Asian Web cam models. Given the slow but steady growth of online sexual materials featuring minorities, however, it is likely that minority presence in Web cams will also grow.

49. "Recorded" seems like an inapt word, until one realizes that a Web cam is neither used to "film" someone (no film) nor to "videotape" them (no videotape).

50. www.voyeurdorm.com

51. Gina Smith and Diane Sawyer, "Voyeur Dorm," *Good Morning America*, May 20, 1999.

52. Mark Glaser, "Just Say Cheesecake," *Playboy*, September 1998, p. 30, online at http://www.playboy.com/magazine/current/english/wired.html. The Nose's site is located at server 06.option.net/homecams/index.html.

53. www.topcams.com.

54. webcammagazine.com/home.htm.

55. www.nakedmodels.com.

56. www.ifriends.net.

57. There are an increasing number of online firms (for example, Encoding.com) that for a fee will take videotape and convert it to a digital format suitable for transmission over the Internet. The cost of hiring a firm to do the conversion, a process known as encoding, ranges anywhere

from $2 to $10 per minute of videotape.

58. voy.voyeurweb.com.

59. The usual caveat about everything on Internet, of course, applies to so-called voyeur photos and videos. There is no way to know whether any of the materials were in fact illicitly taken; they might just as easily have been taken with the full knowledge and consent of all involved. One of the things that makes online pornography so successful, however, is the willingness of consumers to believe the fantasies that are offered.

60. Sylvia Chase, Diane Sawyer, Sam Donaldson, "Rooms with a View," *Primetime Live*, April 1, 1998.

61. Chase, et al., "Rooms with a View."

62. Chris Oakes, "Electronic Eyes Get Smaller," *Wired*, August 14, 1998, online at http://www.wired.com/news/news/technology/story/13740.html.

63. *Ibid.*

64. www.voyshop.com.

65. The company announced that it would alter the cameras to prevent the NightShot technology from being used during the day. However, as the Voyeur Web site points out (as did many news articles), the company's alteration can be overcome by the simple expedient of putting black tape over the camera's light-sensing device, thereby fooling it into thinking that it is nighttime.

66. Chris Reidy and Hiawatha Bray, "Camera can bare too much; Sony calls halt to shipments," *Boston Globe*, August 13, 1998, p. 1.

67. Sylvia Chase, et al., "Rooms with a View."

# 9

# THE FUTURE
# OF ONLINE SEXUAL
# ENTREPRENEURSHIP

It is change, continuing change, inevitable change, that is the dominant
factor in society today. No sensible decision can be made any longer
without taking into account not only the world as it is, but the world as
it will be. . . . This, in turn, means that our statesmen, our businessmen,
our everyman must take on a science fictional way of thinking.
Isaac Asimov, *My Own View*

As this is written in 1998 and 1999, it is sobering to realize that just five years
ago, only a small number of scientists around the world had any idea that a new
means of connecting computer users was about to make its debut. It is entirely
safe to wager, however, that none of them had any idea that the World Wide
Web, as the new software tool was christened, would so rapidly become such a
powerful economic and social force. Considering the essentially unpredictable
effects that other technologies have had (the role of printing in the Protestant
Revolution, for instance, or the influence of television on the 1960 U.S. presidential race), it is probably impossible at this early stage in the technology's history to fully anticipate the impact that it will have. It seems likely, for instance,
that although today only about 50 percent of the nation's households are
equipped with computers,[1] it will not be long before both the computer and
Internet access are nearly as ubiquitous as the television and the telephone (both
of which can be found in more than 95 percent of U.S. households).[2] In fact,
there is quite a strong probability that future households will use devices that are
a combination of some or all of our present communication tools, putting the
functional equivalent of a printing press and film studio in each household. The
question, of course, is that if everyone has a voice, will anyone be heard?

In the online pornography industry, the chief question is the extent to
which consolidation will occur. For most online businesses, the entry costs will
remain low and in fact may drop even further. As the number of online busi-

nesses of all descriptions continues to grow, however, it will be increasingly difficult for new businesses to successfully market their goods and services. Online directories, search engines, and link sites (all of which have their own economic agendas) will defray the cost of marketing to some extent, but as the volume of material online continues to grow, the ability to conduct Webwide marketing campaigns will grow steadily less affordable. The Internet corollary of a tony address, vast distribution networks, and economy of scale will be the ability to engage in ubiquitous advertising and to develop and implement the latest technological improvements.

# LOOMING IMPROVEMENTS IN TECHNOLOGY

### FADING PHOTOGRAPHS

For the last century and a half, the photograph has been an integral part of our cultural landscape, an important part of our personal, political, and societal history. Since France released the details of Daguerre's invention, literally billions of photographs have been taken, recording everything from prom night jitters to crime scenes to the birth of new galaxies.

Throughout that period of time, the experience of viewing photographs has largely been one of delayed gratification. A photographer takes a photo and then must wait while the photograph is developed, a process that could be as long as a few weeks (back when photographers sent off both their film and cameras to Mr. Eastman for developing) or as short as two minutes (using Mr. Land's Polaroid system). As many people have discovered, the combination of film and developing can make photography an expensive hobby or business.

Thanks in large part to the growth of the Internet, the use of film and photographic paper as the mechanisms for recording images is being challenged by devices that largely dispense with both. As we saw in earlier chapters, online entrepreneurs are making increasing use of both digital cameras and digital video recorders, which can be used to take photographs or make videos and transfer them directly to a computer. Once stored in a computer, the images can then be made available to a worldwide audience for little or no cost. Already, a large number of adult Web sites, including online video companies like IEG, are using high-end digital video equipment[3] which dramatically reduces the time and cost of putting both images and video online.

Consumers and entrepreneurs will benefit from the increased competition in the digital imaging market. In an effort to maintain their market share, traditional camera companies such as Canon and Olympus are using their optical experience to develop digital cameras. At the same time, companies with experience in other types of computer technology, such as Epson and now Logitech (which recently purchased the QuickCam from Connectix) are making forays into the digital imaging business. As is typically the case, the producers of digital imaging technology are competing on both features and price: As cameras with higher and higher resolutions are introduced, the cost of lower resolution cameras steadily falls. In the summer of 1998, for instance, cameras with resolutions equal to or in excess of Super VGA[4] quality were available on the market for as little as $700.

Photographic film and prints are not going to disappear in the immediate future, any more so than the paperback book. It is still far more expensive and awkward to display a collection of digital family photos than it is a series of snapshots (compare the cost and convenience of an inexpensive photo album and a set of snapshots—$20–$30, tops—to the cost of taking and displaying a comparable number of digital photos—$1,500 or so for a digital camera and computer). In the not-so-long run, however, the low cost of electronic bits versus film will favor digital technology. Once a digital camera is purchased, the cost of each additional photo approaches zero, which means that the savings in both film and development costs can fairly quickly repay the cost of the initial hardware investment. Moreover, the ease and convenience of displaying digital photographs will only grow. Digital cameras themselves can be used to display the photographs they take, and given the shrinking size of both laptop computers and personal digital assistants, it is only a matter of time before a pocketbook or suit coat pocket-size device is marketed that can serve in part as an electronic photo album.[5] A similar product development track can be seen in publishing, where there are a number of different so-called "electronic" books now in production. These devices are about the size and weight of a thick paperback and can download a number of books through a computer attached to the Internet. More advanced versions allow readers to mark their place, search for specific words, and annotate their texts. Economics and durability, however, still favor actual paperbacks. The new devices cost $200–$300 each and readers still have to pay for the texts. Moreover, a paperback that has been dropped into the pool can still be read (once it dries); dunking is not recommended for most electronic devices.

The most immediate benefits of the changes in digital technology will be experienced by those interested in using such technology to produce their own Web site content. However, even those sites that rely on content produced by third parties will see the benefits of decreased cost of both taking pictures and filming videos. Right now, the price for many of the photo collections on CD-ROM includes the cost of shooting and developing film and scanning the finished slides or photographs. With more widespread use of digital imaging technology, those intermediate steps will be largely eliminated.

## THE BANDWIDTH SWEEPSTAKES

The ability of Web site operators (adult or otherwise) to inexpensively produce images and video is meaningless without the ability to efficiently distribute them. At present, the vast majority of Internet users are limited to connection speeds between 28.8 kbps and 56 kbps (although the practical ceiling is generally around 50 kbps). As the internet continues to grow in popularity and demand for bandwidth increases, a number of different industries are, however, investing enormous sums of money to develop and implement faster connection technologies.

The so-called Baby Bells have been among the primary beneficiaries of the rapid growth of the Internet. Much of the benefit has been indirect—the installation of additional phone lines, the increase in charges for local calls—but the Baby Bells have also used their considerable resources to compete in the Internet service provider market. The phone companies have enjoyed an inherent advantage, since the technology for transmitting information from one computer to another of necessity has relied on the phone system.

Until the introduction of the World Wide Web, there was relatively little demand for significantly faster transmission speeds. The availability of large numbers of sexually explicit images did help fuel a market for faster modems, since the time spent downloading images during a long-distance call to a BBS was an important issue. However, given the relatively low numbers of BBS users and the virtually complete disinterest of the corporate world, there was little or no impetus for the development of other types of transmission technology.

The Internet, however, has changed all of that. In a little more than five years, the number of World Wide Web users in the U.S. alone has risen from zero to more than 100 million. Although growth will slow some over the next few years (depending to a large extent on computer prices), there is very little likelihood that it will stop altogether. More importantly, the technological structure of the Internet is such that when an access provider connects to the Internet, it gives its customers access to everyone else connected to the Internet. In a remarkably short time, Internet connectivity has become a multibillion-dollar business, one that few communications companies can afford to ignore. As the Web has grown more complex and consumers have indicated a willingness to pay for faster transmission speeds, the users and developers of faster communication technology—cable, satellite, and even electrical lines—have seen an opportunity to claim some of the business for themselves.

## Ask Not for Whom the Baby Bells Toll

When it comes to Internet connectivity, the bulk of the profits earned by Baby Bells are indirect, in the form of local usage charges collected when Internet users call their local ISPs and spend an average of 20–30 minutes online. All or nearly all of the Baby Bells also offer their own ISP services, but unlike their monopoly on local phone service, there are several thousand ISPs competing with the Baby Bells for business.

What initially appeared to be an enormous institutional advantage for the Baby Bells in the Internet sweepstakes—a world-leading network of millions of miles of copper cable—has instead proved to be the phone industry's biggest challenge. As engineers and technicians have worked to make modems faster, they have discovered that copper phone wire has some intrinsic speed limits that are difficult to overcome. The advances that have been made have been impressive nonetheless: When the World Wide Web was first introduced, the average modem speed was 9,600 bps and a large percentage of computer users were still using either 4,800 bps or 2,400 bps modems. Four years later, the minimum modem speed generally available is 28 kbps, and 56 kbps modems are available for less than $50.

The phone companies, aware of the practical limitations of copper wire, have been working on a variety of technologies to transmit data at faster speeds. Even before the growth of the Internet, phone companies had developed Integrated Services Digital Network (ISDN), a technology that uses a pair of linked data channels to provide transmission speeds of up to 128 kbps. However, the phone companies have done a miserable job of making the installation of ISDN lines both easy and relatively inexpensive. As a result, computer manufacturers have been slow to manufacture the devices necessary to connect personal computers to ISDN lines. The lack of sales volume at both ends of the business has helped to keep the cost of ISDN high, which in turn has further delayed the technology's slow adoption. Things have improved slightly for ISDN in the last year: It is available in 100 percent of the nation's urban areas and 70–80 percent of more rural areas, prices for both installation and equipment have fallen, and the speed with which ISDN lines can be installed by the phone company has risen dramatically. Nonetheless, the phone companies appear to have missed a decade-long opportunity to further solidify consumer reliance on telephone technology.

One technology currently preventing faster adoption of ISDN is the slow spread of another telephone company technology, digital subscriber lines (DSL). DSL offers a number of important advantages over ISDN, including a far faster potential speed (up to 8 mbps compared to 128 kbps) and the fact that the technology can be used over existing phone lines. However, it is unclear how quickly DSL will be available to significant portions of the country, and as with most new technologies, the initial cost is likely to be high. More important, phone companies have been reluctant to implement DSL technology because the technology will compete directly with the phone companies' extremely profitable business in high-speed T-1 and T-3 access lines. (By way of example, T-1 lines transmit data at approximately 1.54 million bits per second, while DSL tops out at between 7 million and 8 million bits per second.) The Baby Bells are feeling the heat from cable and satellite access providers, however, and have been urging the Federal Communications Commission to allow them to offer DSL services through unregulated affiliates or subsidiaries. The proposal faces considerable opposition from long-distance carriers and from the nation's cable companies, which fear that if the FCC proposal is implemented, it will give the Baby Bells a monopoly in high-speed access to the Internet.

## Internet on Cable

Why are the Baby Bells so concerned about the competition from cable? The chief reasons are speed and infrastructure. With a theoretical[6] maximum transmission speed of up to 10 mbps, cable offers the tantalizing prospect of nearly instantaneous Web surfing. In addition, cable is aided in its efforts to compete for Internet connection business by the fact that it has a vast network already installed: Roughly 67 percent of American households are wired for cable.

The drawbacks to cable, however, are nearly as profound as the speed it offers. In addition to the technological and security concerns raised by the shared nature of cable traffic, using cable for Internet access is an expensive proposition. While most ISPs today charge between $9.95 and $19.95 per month for Internet access (a figure that some believe must rise), cable access right now is generally priced between $29 and $49, a figure which usually includes the cost of leasing a cable modem from the cable company. In addition, cable companies often charge a $50 to $100 installation fee. Moreover, the majority of cable systems are designed for one-way traffic, from the cable company to users. In the absence of a fairly expensive equipment upgrade by the provider, cable modem users must still use a phone line to send data from their computer to the Internet. And finally, using a cable modem means that the cable company becomes the ISP. Users can generally access their e-mail from their old ISP, but the trade-off for the faster speed of cable lines is fewer potential ISPs. Aware of the threat from cable, non-cable ISPs are petitioning the Federal Communications Commission to bar cable companies from requiring customers to use the cable company as their ISP. Not surprisingly, the cable companies reject the need for any further regulation.

## Satellites

In the summer of 1998, a *Washington Post* reporter traveled to Toksook Bay, a Yup'ik Eskimo village in western Alaska, to see a demonstration of a satellite Internet feed set up by Alaska Wireless, a start-up company providing access to the village's 700 residents.[7] The two-way satellite dishes offer access at speeds up to ten times the average telephone modem and can be left on all day for nearly instantaneous Internet access.

Other satellite systems offer even faster Internet transmissions, although most (like DirectPC) suffer from the same unidirectional limitation faced by the majority of cable systems. More advanced systems will offer bidirectional transmissions, although it is likely that there will always be a disparity in the speeds with which information is received and the speed with which it is sent. As with cable, the use of a satellite system for accessing the Internet will limit the choice of ISP to one: the company actually providing the access. In addition, some users may be reluctant to put a satellite dish (even one of the new 8-inch so-called "pizza dishes") on the side or roof of their house.

The efforts by Alaska Wireless to provide Internet connections without resorting to highly expensive land-based transmission systems like phone wire has raised concern in the offices of United Utilities, an Eskimo-owned phone company that holds a monopoly on local phone service in the sparsely populated area. In exchange for the monopoly, United Utilities has an obligation to provide local phone service to all residents, an infrastructure challenge that United Utilities allegedly borrowed more than $22 million to meet. The company is concerned that the technology being installed by Alaska Wireless will cost United Utilities both customers and revenues that it needs to repay the infrastructure loans.[8]

The Alaskan utility has good reason to be concerned. As it grows increasingly easy to use the Internet not only to access voluminous amounts of information but also to conduct telephone conversations, it will be possible for Internet service providers of all descriptions to become de facto phone companies. Undoubtedly, companies like United Utilities will be working strenuously to prevent that from happening. Whether Congress or the courts can act quickly enough to respond to market forces, however, is still an open question.

## Electric Utilities

One of the more creative possibilities for Internet access is to use the nation's extensive electric wires to provide Internet access. This idea is still in the formative stages, but is generating a lot of buzz in utility circles. Electrical power is transmitted at 60 Hz over copper wires, the same medium used to transmit phone conversations. In theory, data can be transmitted along the same lines at different frequencies, up to a maximum speed of about 1 mbps.

Not surprisingly, a number of technical issues need to be resolved. The use of electrical wires for the transmission of data has seen its most complete testing in Britain, which has an electrical grid that is constructed differently than the one used in the U.S. In particular, the U.S. makes far greater use of transformers to transfer electricity from high-power lines to local distribution lines, and it turns out that transformers wreak havoc with data signals.[9] Nonetheless, the use of electrical lines for Internet connectivity is getting a very serious look, particularly by municipalities that speculate that Internet profits could be use to check or even reduce electricity rates.

## BIOFEEDBACK, TELEDILDONICS, AND VIRTUAL REALITY

A few years ago, the hot trend in motion picture theaters was "SenSurround," a combination system of speakers and bounceable seats that together were supposed to give moviegoers the illusion of being *in* the movie. More recently, IMAX movie theaters have attempted to create a sense of virtual reality by wrapping moviegoers in an eight-story screen.

Until recently, the only senses engaged by computers were sight and hearing (and even hearing was relatively underutilized, given the tinny nature of most early PC speakers). Over the last couple of years, however, significant amounts of time and money have been spent in an effort to develop computer peripherals that utilize other human senses, or provide a more complete sensory experience for the senses we can use (i.e., more finely detailed photos, moving video, stereophonic sound, etc.).

## Biofeedback

The pornography industry has been relatively slow to adopt biofeedback technology, but as we'll see, that is changing. Much of the pioneering work in biofeedback has instead been done on behalf of the gaming industry, particularly for those who use a joystick to fly a fighter plane or control an action figure. Among the current leading competitors in the so-called "force feedback" industry are Microsoft's Sidewinder Force Feedback Pro Joystick (which retails for about $150) and the Force FX by CH Products (approximately $189). The general theory behind both devices is the same: Motors in the base of the joystick respond to software commands from the game, translating action on the screen into varying levels of resistance and movement in the joystick.

What may be of much greater interest to the pornography industry is the fact that biofeedback systems are being designed for increasingly larger portions of the body. In the August 1998 issue of Computer Gaming, for instance, BSG Labs, Inc. ran an advertisement for Intensor, its new combination chair and sound system. BSG built the speakers for the high-powered sound system directly into the chair, so that the vibrations from the sound of the game travel up and down the user's spine. Although BSG's intended market is clearly the numerous PC game players, it is likely only a matter of time before an enterprising online adult site makes use of Intensor's capabilities. BSG's own ad copy offers a hint of what might lie ahead:

> Be advised. With Intensor, you'll not only hear your games like never before, you'll also feel them. In your back, in your legs. You'll feel sensations in places you never even knew you had. Which means every engine rev, every explosion, every kick will seem more real than you may want it to. So it's important to note that under this type of extreme duress, screaming in high-pitched tones for one's mommy is quite common.[10]

A quieter biofeedback peripheral that may have broader and more immediate appeal is the FEELit mouse. Introduced at the 1997 Fall Comdex show in Las Vegas by Immersion Corp., the FEELit mouse uses proprietary "I-Force"[11] technology to give users tactile feedback while using the mouse. For instance, when users click on and drag an icon on the desktop, the icon gives the illusion of weight. When users click on the side of a window to expand it or shrink it, the software creates the impression of pulling on a rubber band. In addition, Web pages can be designed to give the FEELit mouse the sensation of sliding over different textures and surfaces, or over hills and down valleys. Logitech, one of the largest manufacturers of computer mice, announced in August 1999 that it was planning the release of Wingman Force Feedback Mouse. The $99 Wingman Mouse will be one of the first widely available peripherals to use the FEELit technology.

The fact that these devices are not widely supported (if at all) by adult Web sites is purely a function of economics. Putting photos or video on a Web site makes economic sense for adult entrepreneurs because every Web browser is designed to display those types of data. As a result, every Web surfer owns the software necessary to become a customer. By contrast, before a Web surfer can use a biofeedback device online, a site's software must be written (or rewritten) to include the specific codes used by each device. Software companies or Web sites will only go to the trouble of doing so if there is a sufficient customer base for a particular biofeedback device to justify the time and expense of doing so. While there is certainly a large enough pool of PC game players to justify the expense of incorporating biofeedback commands into games, that same pool of consumers is not large enough to justify the same expense for adult Web sites (particularly since the majority of joystick users are under the age of 18).

A more comprehensive and more exciting type of tactile research is taking place at universities around the world. Known as haptics, it is the study of how people use the sense of touch to experience the world. In 1993, for instance, a team led by an MIT undergraduate named Thomas Massie invented a device called "PHANToM" ("Personal Haptic Interface Mechanism"). The PHANToM is a small device shaped like a thimble. On the inside of the device are three small motors that can be programmed to cause sensations of texture and movement on a user's finger.

A short time after he invented the PHANToM, Massie and his wife, Rhonda, set up SensAble Technologies to manufacture and market the device. By December 1997, the company had sold more than 200 of the $20,000 devices, chiefly to other researchers;[12] the company sold its 400th less than a year later.[13] According to Dr. A.M. Srinivasan, the director of MIT's Touchlab and a leading touch researcher, using the PHANToM for cybersex "is not the focus of anyone's research," although he conceded that "[i]f we get very good at designing haptic interfaces, it probably will happen."[14]

Researchers are also working on a subtler and more precise technology to induce tactile sensations on the skin. Known as micro-electro-mechanical arrays (MEMS), the technology consists of a grid of thousands of tiny actuators or rods, all individually controllable. Programmers can write software to control the movement of the actuators to simulate surface textures, motion, etc. To date, only small grids of actuators have been constructed; the goal is to use MEMS to construct gloves or even entire bodysuits, a target that researchers assign to the"long-term future."[15] It is safe to assume, however, that as that future draws closer, one of the industries that will be standing on the doorstep waiting for the announcement will be the pornography industry.

## Teledildonics

That is not to say, of course, that the pornography industry is not making its own contributions to tactile research. At the Erotic USA conference in New York City in April 1999, SafeSexPlus.com made a splash when it demonstrated its new technology for controlling sex toys across the Internet. In order to experience "teledildonics" (or "cyberdildonics," as SafeSexPlus.com describes the process), a computer user attaches a sex toy to an SSP Converter Box manufactured by SafeSexPlus.com. The company markets a number of devices, including vibrators and a male-oriented toy called "Robo-Suck," that are specifically designed to connect to the SSP Converter; for those computer users who don't want to replace their favorite sex toys, SafeSexPlus.com offers instructions for wiring the devices to the SSP Converter.

Once the appropriate sex toy is hooked up, the SSP Converter is attached to the user's computer screen with suction cups. The box is positioned over a specific area of the screen, the brightness of which can be controlled by a remote partner. Using a small window on his or her computer, the remote part-ner can increase or decrease the brightness of the screen underneath the SSP Converter, which in turn makes the sex toy go faster or slower. SafeSexPlus.com proudly proclaims the social benefits of its invention: "SafeSexPlus.com is healthy. You'll never catch a sexually transmitted disease at SafeSexPlus.com. Nobody will die of AIDs [sic] through SafeSexPlus.com. Could divorce rates even improve, as traveling husbands or wives use SafeSexPlus.com with their spouses to satisfy their mutual libidos?"

The company sells its SSP Converters for $25 and has an online store stocked with a variety of controllable sex toys for both men and women. The software to control the devices is provided free by SafeSexPlus.com, and will allow a couple to engage in one-on-one, private sex play across the Internet. The technology has been adopted by the Ifriends Network, which has reconfigured its software to accommodate the new technology. Now, Ifriends subscribers can receive remote stimulation from online exhibitors or return the favor. According to SafeSexPlus.com, a cyberdildonics chat room has been established on Ifriends and a lively debate is ongoing about which Ifriends exhibitor "gives the best Internet."

## Virtual Reality and Cybersex

The idea of blending virtual reality and sex has been an enormously popular one in the science fiction community for years, as the use of the Holodeck in *Star Trek: The Next Generation* demonstrated. As conceived by the show's creative team, the Holodeck is a computer-controlled environment on the U.S.S. Enterprise that users can program to simulate any environment or activity they choose. The ship's computer then uses incredibly sophisticated material-generation technology to create tangible objects and individuals with whom the ship's personnel can interact. The Holodeck was a frequent plot device for the show, which used it to explore questions of what is real and what is not (with occasional hints at the possibilities of cybersex).

In 1995, the Fox network took the concept of virtual reality and built an entire show around it. The short-lived *VR5* featured Lori Singer as a young woman who was able to call people on the telephone and interact with them in a virtual reality created by her imagination.[16] Virtual reality has also played an important role in a number of recent Hollywood film productions, including *Lawnmower Man, Total Recall, Virtuosity, The Matrix,* and *eXistenZ.*

*Star Trek, VR5,* and the aforementioned movies contemplate a type of three-dimensional virtual reality in which users are able to physically move around and interact with the artificial world. That type of full-immersion virtual reality is enormously complicated and in all likelihood will not be available for decades, if ever. Some progress, however, has been made in developing systems and devices that allow the mind to fool itself into thinking that the rest of the body is participating in an artificial world.

The simplest of these systems are text-based worlds, often referred to as multiuser dungeons (MUDs) or multiuser simulated environments (MUSEs), in which computer users adopt characters, play roles, interact with other users in real-time in a virtual world. The author of a particular MUD or MUSE sets the basic parameters for the game (i.e., jungle, dungeon, unexplored planet, etc.), but the course of the game and the specific interaction among the players is completely unscripted.

Not surprisingly, a significant portion of the imaginary activity that takes place online is imaginary sex. Some MUDs, in fact, are specifically designed by their authors to promote cybersex among the players; one popular MUD consists of nothing more than a hotel and a lobby.[17] Like the real world, unfortunately, not all cybersex is necessarily gentle. In one well-publicized incident on a MUD called LamdaMOO, a New York University student figured out how to control the online characters of two women. He then described his character and the two female characters as participating in various sexual acts, and made it appear that the two female characters were enjoying themselves. The originators of the female characters acknowledged that the "cyberrape" posed no actual physical threat but said that it was "extremely annoying and disconcerting."[18]

As systems grow more visual, both the illusion and potential impact of such behavior is heightened. A number of companies (including a number of arcade game manufacturers) have created helmet-based systems that can be used to project and view images of an artificial world.[19] When combined with position-sensing gloves, the users of such systems can pretend to "pick up" objects in the artificial world and move them around. This type of system was the focal point last season of an episode of NBC's popular comedy *Mad About You.* The episode raised the question of whether actor Paul Reiser's electronic hanky-panky with a programmed version of supermodel Christy Brinkley constituted infidelity.

Led once again by gamers, headset systems for virtual reality will continue to drop in price and grow in popularity. Undoubtedly, some Web sites will use the technology for displaying adult movies and games, on the theory that they can create the illusion that viewers are not simply watching a movie, but are actually on the set. Headset systems and big screens, however, are simply different ways of experiencing a medium that already exists. The online pornography industry's big plunge into virtual reality will not occur until other senses (in particular, touch and smell) can be added to the experience.

## CHANGING FINANCIAL CONSIDERATIONS FOR SEXUAL ENTREPRENEURS

One of the things that must make the publishers of sexually explicit magazines such as *Playboy* and *Penthouse* nervous is that the skin magazine trade is one of the few distribution channels for pornography that has failed to drop in cost. Forty-five years ago, the cost of a single issue of *Playboy* was 50 cents at the newsstand; today, the same publication costs $5.95. Not only has the rise in price run counter to the downward trend experienced by most other forms of pornography distribution (another exception being adult movie ticket prices), but print publications have also committed the cardinal sin of outstripping inflation (all other things being equal, *Playboy* should cost about $3.05 per copy in 1998).[20] The rise in the price of a copy of *Playboy* is not entirely the magazine's fault; the rise in the cost of paper alone accounts for a significant portion of *Playboy*'s current price. Nonetheless, the increased cost leaves *Playboy* and other adult magazines vulnerable to industries that have not and are unlikely to experience similar price increases.

Adult videos are a good example of the typical trend in the cost of distributing pornography. In the mid-1970s, in the earliest days of the video revolution, the producers of adult films and loops were able to repackage their old materials and retail the sexually explicit videotapes for prices as high as $300. Even as late as 1982, *Penthouse* carried ads for sexually explicit videos that ranged in price from $70 to $100 per video. And then came the VCR boom: Within five years, the prices for sexually explicit videos in *Penthouse* ads dropped to as little as $2, with most ranging in price between $9.95 and $29.95. By 1989, ads for videos had largely disappeared from *Penthouse*, in part because it was no longer cost-effective for the producers and distributers of adult videos to purchase *Penthouse* ads, and in part because more cost-effective channels for distributing adult videos were available (including both direct mail and video rentals). Similar price reductions have occurred with daguerreotypes and photographs, phone sex, computer bulletin boards, and sexually explicit CD-ROMs.

Precisely the same dynamic is occurring online. Like the camera and the telephone, the computer and the Internet are relatively accessible technologies. Although even the cheapest computer system is certainly more expensive than either a phone or a camera, the costs continue to fall, and even the most basic computer systems today are capable of handling much of the work required to set up an adult Web site. For the majority of Americans, the cost of equipment does not pose a significant barrier to joining the online pornography industry, and numerous media reports about the potential earnings have encouraged entrepreneurs to do so.

As a result, there is tremendous competition for the $2 billion or so spent annually for pornography on the World Wide Web (a figure that will continue to grow as more people go online; the most recent studies estimate that more than 100 million Americans now have access to the Internet). When there is extensive competition in an industry, one of three things tends to happen: Businesses specialize in order to carve out niches for themselves, businesses cut prices (sometimes devolving into an often ruinous price war), and some businesses (particularly in the pornography industry) push the limits of what is legally and socially acceptable.

In just over four years, competition among the thousands of online image galleries alone has driven prices steadily down from a high of $29.95 to $39.95 to an average of $4.95 to $9.95 per month, and some sites, relying entirely on advertising revenues, offer free access to their adult content. Multimedia sites, which generate revenues through both ads and memberships, have settled into the $4.95 to $19.95 range per month, and prices for adult videoconferencing are holding steady (at least temporarily) at between $2.99 and $5.99 per minute. (The first cracks in the pricing structure for adult videoconferencing, however, are starting to appear. Some of the larger online adult sites [Cybererotica, for instance] are beginning to bundle adult videoconferencing with the other services offered to members. As more and more sites follow suit, it will be difficult for companies such as Virtual Dreams to justify the high per-minute costs.)

As with other mediums, the drop in prices for online adult materials is largely a function of competition, both among the Web sites themselves and among the various businesses that provide necessary products and services. For instance, a review of hosting services for adult Web sites shows a wide range of prices for setup costs, storage, and data transfer fees. The same is true for companies that provide Web content, including photo collections, video feeds, and even adult video conferencing.

One consequence of decreased entry costs for setting up and running an adult Web site, of course, is that it makes it easier for prospective entrepreneurs to do so. Unfortunately, the prices that entrepreneurs can reasonably charge for online adult materials have fallen faster than the cost of the materials themselves. Just two or three years ago, when online adult entrepreneurs could easily charge $29.95 per month for a few thousand photos, the profit margins were significant. Today, even a popular site such as Cybererotica can charge only $19.95, and in order to charge even that much, must offer thousands of video feeds, tens of thousands of still images, live videoconferencing, adult chat, games, and so forth.

While it is certainly still possible to make money producing and distributing pornography on the Internet, it now takes more time and more money to start and run such sites than it did just a few years ago. For the vast bulk of online adult entrepreneurs, the gold rush is effectively over.

# LEGAL CHALLENGES TO ONLINE PORNOGRAPHY

Despite the fact that the United States is an avowedly multicultural nation of more than 260 million people, the ambivalence of Christianity as a whole and Puritanism in particular toward sexual activity is woven deeply into the nation's social and legal fabric. For those who might be tempted to gloat that the Internet represents a final victory over sexually repressive elements of America's cultural past (or at least its white, Anglo-Saxon Protestant cultural past), it is instructive to recall the mid to late 1970s, when a widespread easing of sexual mores played a substantial role in the rise of the Moral Majority and the subsequent election of President Reagan. For an industry that can attribute a significant portion of its profits to challenging or flouting social mores, the potential for political and legal backlash is a real threat.

The online adult industry, unlike pornographers of 25 years ago, is aided by two important factors: First, the social and cultural climate has changed significantly since the Moral Majority was founded, and second, the industry is blessed by its enemies. In the glee following their electoral triumphs in 1980 and 1982, religious and social conservatives developed overly inflated opinions not only of their political power but of the extent to which they had the support of the American people. The combination of political overreaching and some impressive sex scandals involving religious leaders Jim Bakker and Jimmy Swaggart helped to undercut much of what those groups were trying to do. Despite these setbacks, however, the religious right and social conservatives remain powerful voices in American politics, and have retained much of their influence in both the House and the Senate. As the legislative success of the Communications Decency Act of 1996 illustrated, their efforts to restrict the pornography industry have not ceased.

## THE SON OF CDA AND OTHER FEDERAL INITIATIVES

The June 1997 decision of the U.S. Supreme Court rejecting the indecency provisions of the Communications Decency Act came as a blow to antipornography forces, but it did not take them long to regroup. When Congress returned after its summer recess that year, Senator Dan Coats (R-Ind.) introduced legislation that would prohibit commercial Web sites from distributing to people under the age of 17 any material that is "harmful to minors."[21] Known as the Child Online

Protection Act or CDA II, the bill would apply to any "communication, article, recording, or writing" that depicts "in a patently offensive way with respect to what is suitable for minors, an actual or simulated sexual act or sexual contact, actual or simulated normal or perverted sexual acts, or a lewd exhibition of the genitals." In an effort to get around the Supreme Court's objection that the Communications Decency Act was fatally vague, the bill also requires that any allegedly criminal material must "lack serious literary, artistic, political, or scientific value," which is one of the requirements of the Court's 1973 *Miller* decision.[22] In order to avoid prosecution, Web site operators displaying potentially offensive materials would be required to obtain age verification, most typically through the use of credit card numbers. Anyone convicted of violating the law would be subject to fines of up to $50,000 and imprisonment for up to six months.[23]

Following the adoption of the new bill by the Senate in July 1998, Harvard Law professor Lawrence Lessig (who briefly served as an adviser to the U.S. District Court in the Microsoft antitrust case) told the *New York Times* that he thought the revised bill could pass constitutional muster. "It is a much closer question," Professor Lessig said, "and quite possibly the Supreme Court will uphold it."[24] Professor Lessig based his opinion on a number of factors: the bill addresses only Web sites, instead of trying to establish a single rule for every type of Internet resource; the standard set forth in the bill—"harmful to minors"—is one that the U.S. Supreme Court has endorsed in other circumstances; the bill was passed at a time when the use of adult verification services and credit cards is generally less burdensome for adult sites, most of which already use one or both; and the bill redefines "minor" to mean anyone under the age of 17, which essentially eliminates the perceived flaw in the CDA that it was too restrictive for most college freshmen.

A similar bill was eventually passed by the House of Representatives in the fall of 1998 and a compromise version of the Child Online Protection Act was included in an Omnibus Appropriations Act that was sent to the White House and signed by President Clinton on October 21, 1998. The following day, an ACLU-led coalition of rights groups, booksellers, medical professionals, and the media filed suit against the implementation of the bill in U.S. District Court in Philadelphia. On November 19, 1998, U.S. District Judge Lowell Reed issued a temporary restraining order against COPA, finding that the plaintiffs had demonstrated a likelihood of success on the merits of at least some of their claims.

Judge Reed permanently enjoined enforcement of the act in February 1999. The Justice Department has appealed that decision to the Third Circuit Court of Appeals. A decision is not expected until sometime in early 2000.

In addition to COPA, members of both houses have introduced legislation, the Childrens' Internet Protection Act, which would require schools and libraries that receive federal funding to install software on "computers with Internet access to filter or block material deemed to be harmful to minors." The legislation was defeated in 1998, but was reintroduced in 1999 by Senator John

McCain (R-Ariz.) and Representative Bob Franks (R-N.J.). Under the terms of the legislation, schools that fail to install filtering software lose their eligibility for federal funds. The law also provides that "the determination of what material is to be deemed harmful to minors shall be made by the school, school board, library or other authority responsible for making the required certification."

Requiring filtering programs on school and library computers will have little immediate effect on online sexual entrepreneurs, but to the extent that such legislation encourages the development and implementation of Web site rating programs, sexual entrepreneurs may slowly find it more difficult to distribute their materials, since it will be easier for ISPs, search engines, and online directories to weed out adult sites.

## STATE EFFORTS TO RESTRICT PORNOGRAPHY

At the same time that Congress was considering and passing the Communications Decency Act, a number of states were adopting similar laws. According to the ACLU, at least 12 states—California, Connecticut, Florida, Georgia, Kansas, Minnesota, Montana, Nevada, New Mexico, New York, Oklahoma, and Virginia—have all adopted legislation that to one degree or another limits free speech on the Internet.

When the U.S. Supreme Court ruled in 1997 that the Communications Decency Act was unconstitutional, the Court's ruling did not directly affect the status of state laws limiting Internet speech. However, under the terms of the Fourteenth Amendment, states may not adopt and enforce any law which would abridge a person's First Amendment rights:

> No State shall make or enforce any law which shall abridge the privileges or immunities of citizens of the United States; nor shall any State deprive any person of life, liberty, or property, without due process of law; nor deny to any person within its jurisdiction the equal protection of the laws.[25]

Since the state laws aimed at limiting the spread of pornography online also implicate the First Amendment right to free speech, *ACLU v. Reno* sets the standards by which similar state laws are judged.

So far, at least, federal courts have been persuaded that the various state statutes challenged by the ACLU have impermissibly infringed on the right to free speech set out in the U.S. Constitution. In three states—Georgia, New York, and Virginia—the statutes limiting Internet speech have been overturned by the courts, and the ACLU is currently involved in litigation in New Mexico, where it recently received an injunction preventing the implementation of the state's Internet censorship law. The New Mexico bill, Senate Bill 127, is particularly sweeping: It creates criminal penalties for the "transmission of communications that depict 'nudity, sexual intercourse or any other sexual conduct.'" In ruling on the ACLU's request for a preliminary injunction, U.S. District Court Judge C. Elroy Hansen concluded, *inter alia,* that the ACLU would be able to prove the following:

> a. The New Provision, on its face and as applied to Plaintiffs, violates the First, Fifth, and Fourteenth Amendments, and the Commerce Clause of the United States Constitution. See generally *Reno v. American Civil Liberties Union,* 117 S.Ct. 2329 (1997); *American Libraries Ass'n v. Pataki,* 969 F.Supp. 160 (1997).
> b. The New Provision violates the First and Fourteenth Amendments of the United States Constitution because it effectively bans speech that is constitutionally protected for adults. See *Reno,* 117 S.Ct. at 2346 (holding that the federal Communications Decency Act "effectively suppresses a large amount of speech that adults have a constitutional right to receive" in order to deny minors access to potentially harmful speech).
> c. Defendants have failed to satisfy their burden to demonstrate that the New Provision will directly and materially advance a compelling governmental interest. See, e.g., *Sable Communications of Cal., Inc. v. FCC,* 492 U.S. 115, 129-31 (1989).
> d. Defendants have failed to demonstrate that the New Provision constitutes the least restrictive means of serving its stated interest. Id.; *Reno,* 117 S.Ct. at 2346-47.

Notwithstanding the success of the ACLU in challenging restrictions of free speech online, state legislators have persisted in their efforts to do at the state level what the Congress was unable to do at the federal. The position of the ACLU on such legislation is summed up on the organization's Web site:

> Laws that try to keep adult materials away from minors end up reducing all online content to that which is suitable for children—the Supreme Court declared this outcome unconstitutional in *Reno v. ACLU.* Similarly, the use of blocking software at libraries prevents both adults and teenagers from getting access to valuable speech like sex education materials, abuse recovery discussions, and speech about lesbian and gay issues.[26]

When the ACLU persuades a court to overturn a particular statute on free speech grounds, that has its own chilling effect: It helps to slow down the passage of similar legislation in other jurisdictions, and in some cases, stops it altogether. Online entrepreneurs can rest assured, however, that many of the state legislatures will attempt to find constitutionally acceptable limitations that can be placed on adult Web sites.

## TOWARD THE MOST LOCAL OF
## COMMUNITY STANDARDS

The shivers that ran through the online community in July 1994 when Richard and Carleen Thomas were convicted of obscenity by a federal jury in Memphis, Tennessee, have largely subsided. The predicted wave of online obscenity prosecutions arising out of the nation's more conservative jurisdictions never materialized. Instead, in the intervening years, law enforcement's attention has been directed almost exclusively at child pornography. Like Mount Etna, the prosecutorial threat raised by the Thomas conviction has never really vanished; occasional rumbles are heard, but the population on the slopes of the mountain has grown so fast that it is essentially impossible for law enforcement to keep pace. Unlike real-world volcanoes, however, a number of organizations are actively engaged in trying to get the volcano to erupt by urging a more aggressive attitude by federal and state prosecutors toward alleged obscene materials on the Internet.

On its Web site, for instance, the watchdog group Morality in Media summarizes a variety of articles discussing the state of the pornography industry. The statistics and views expressed in the articles show that during the Reagan and Bush administrations:

1. Sales were curtailed;
2. Reagan and Bush were viewed as being tough on porn;
3. The industry was "on a downward trend."

But, during the Clinton/Reno administration:

1. Sales have skyrocketed;
2. Clinton and Reno are viewed as soft on porn;
3. The sky is the limit.[27]

From October 25 to November 1, 1998, Morality in Media coordinated its annual campaign called "White Ribbon Against Pornography," an effort to pressure the U.S. attorneys general in each of the 93 federal districts to aggressively pursue obscenity cases. Although aimed at obscenity generally, the campaign also targets alleged obscenity on the Internet.

Even before Morality in Media's annual letter-writing efforts, the Justice Department was reexamining its efforts on Internet obscenity. On June 10, 1998, Deputy Attorney General Eric Holder sent a memo to all U.S. attorneys advising them that the "[i]nvestigation and prosecution of Internet obscenity is particularly suitable for federal resources."[28] Holder reminded the Attorneys General that when the Supreme Court overturned the Communications Decency Act of 1996, it left in place the provisions that bar the use of the Internet for the sale and distribution of obscene materials. "Prosecution of cases involving relatively small distributors," Holder said in his memo, "can have a deterrent effect and would dispel any notion that obscenity distributors are insulated from prosecution if their operations fail to exceed a predetermined size."[29]

A few months earlier, on February 10, 1998, Senator Dan Coats (R-Ind.) had testified before the Senate Commerce Committee in support of S. 1482, the Child Online Protection Act. During his remarks, he pointed out that not all of the Communications Decency Act had been overturned:

> Key portions of the CDA, in particular those outlawing on-line obscenity, or hard-core pornography, were left unchallenged, thus providing the opportunity to prosecute the worst offenders. Unfortunately, the Clinton Administration Justice Department has not prosecuted a single case under the obscenity ban. Not one. This is a sorry track record.

Despite the urging of Senator Coats and Morality in Media, however, there appears to be little enthusiasm in the Clinton Justice Department for pursuing prosecutions for Internet obscenity, other than those involving child pornography. That might change if Vice President Al Gore succeeds President Clinton; his wife, Tipper, was one of the founders of the Parents Music Resource Center, an organization aimed at persuading record companies to label albums and CDs that contain sexually explicit or violent lyrics.

Much of Clinton administration's disinterest in obscenity prosecutions may lie in the risk that a successful online obscenity prosecution could result in a single jurisdiction setting the legal obscenity standard for the entire Internet. The 1973 *Miller* decision was predicated in large part on the idea that individual communities were in the best position to determine whether, in the words of the Court, a "work, taken as a whole, appeals to the prurient interest" and whether a "work depicts or describes, in a patently offensive way, sexual conduct specifically defined by the applicable state law." The emphasis on local standards gave each community the opportunity to determine what type of sexually explicit materials, if any, would be available within its borders. Thus, for instance, a jurisdiction like Memphis, Tennessee, could make the determination that the movie *Deep Throat* was obscene, while the issue never came up in places like New York and San Francisco. Much of the justification for relying on the local community standard was that communities had both a right and a duty to protect their citizens from unwanted exposure to obscene materials, and to protect the community from the collateral effects of having adult businesses in town, including the attraction of undesirable elements, increased crime, and decreased property values.

The Court's deference to "local community standards" did require national distributors to either avoid certain jurisdictions or engage in self-censorship to limit the risk of prosecution. In the case of movies, it was a relatively simple matter for distributors to avoid certain theaters; the limited number of theaters involved made that type of distribution decision practical. In the case of national publications like *Penthouse* and *Penthouse,* however, it was easier, safer, and ultimately more lucrative to change cover art, for instance, than to stop selling magazines in entire cities or states. In either case, the threat of prosecution by more conservative jurisdictions helped to limit the range of sexual materials available, not only in more conservative jurisdictions, but to a lesser degree, in more liberal jurisdictions as well.

A much-debated question is whether the *Miller* standard is still relevant following the development of the Internet. Unlike with other types of media materials, the publisher of an adult Web site does not make a conscious decision to ship his or her content to different parts of the country; instead, the Web site owner makes the material available on the Internet, where it can be accessed by Internet browsers from anywhere in the world. Even assuming that a Web site operator has an obligation to prevent certain people from visiting an adult site,[30] it can be extremely difficult to determine the geographic origin of a visitor; even if the Web site's software successfully identifies a visitor's user name or e-mail address, "johnadams@aol.com" could just as easily live in Pensacola or Juneau. Requiring a credit card can be useful (Web sites can refuse purchases by cardholders from specific areas), and some adult Web sites attempt to reduce their risk by asking visitors for their geographic address, or by posting stern warnings that residents of certain states should stay away. However, it is questionable whether those types of measures would survive an obscenity prosecution.

The Internet also poses in fairly stark terms the extent of a local government's obligation or duty to protect its citizens from themselves. While it can be argued that a local government can and even should protect its citizens from the unwanted risk of seeing explicit sexual materials in a storefront or bookstore window along Main Street, it is less clear that the same obligation exists to protect citizens from what they might see on their personal computer screens in the privacy of their homes. In addition, the purchase and consumption of pornography from the Internet dramatically reduces the visible effects of pornography on a community. When someone uses a computer to access pornography on the Internet, it does not increase the risk that a criminal element will be attracted to the community nor does it decrease the property values of surrounding homes. Both antipornography and religious groups argue that pornography causes other types of damage that communities do have an interest in stopping: domestic abuse, child abuse, sexual assault, the general decline of morals, and so on. However, the connection between the consumption of pornography and those types of social problems is much more difficult to demonstrate than the drop in property values caused by the opening of an adult video store.

The case before the U.S. Supreme Court in the summer of 1999 involving the Communications Decency Act did not address the *Miller* standard directly, and the Court declined to hear the appeal of the Thomas's conviction, in which the issue was raised. It will not be until a jurisdiction attempts to prosecute a World Wide Web site for obscenity that the conflict between a virtually instantaneous and essentially private distribution system and local community standards can be squarely presented to the Court. The question can then be asked whether the appropriate "local community standard" for sexual materials is one that governs conduct only in public or extends as well into each person's home.

# SEXUAL MORES IN THE NEW MILLENNIUM

## AN INCREASINGLY SEXUAL SOCIETY?

Predicting the pace of technological change can be challenging (there is always the possibility of an unforeseeable breakthrough), but predicting the general trend is not particularly taxing, particularly when it comes to computers. The constants of the last half-century have been faster speeds, greater capacity, and generally lower cost. There are occasionally anomalies, of course, such as the sudden surge in memory prices in 1996, but upward price movements in computers or computer components can generally be traced to a specific event, like the burning of a large East Asian chip manufacturing plant.

Far trickier to predict are the ebbs and flows of social attitudes toward sex in general and pornography in particular, especially in a large and multicultural nation such as the United States. Although the general trend over the last two centuries has been toward a more liberal attitude on sex and sexual materials (one shudders to think what Cotton Mather or Jonathan Edwards would have thought about MTV's *Loveline*, for instance, or Fox's *Married with Children*), the transition has not been the steady progression that has marked technological change, but more of a drunkard's walk, lurching from one extreme to another with an occasional step backward.

The chief concern for sexual entrepreneurs, of course, is that some of the social shifts can be potentially damaging to their business interests. Running a pornography business when Ed Meese was the U.S. attorney general, for instance, was a risky proposition, and the campaign by New York's Republican Mayor Rudy Giuliani to drive sex shops not only out of Times Square but off the island of Manhattan altogether has cost adult businesses hundreds of thousands in legal fees in what now appears to be a losing cause.

The concern of religious and social conservatives over the nation's increasingly liberal attitudes toward sexual materials is fueled by changes in virtually all segments of the entertainment industry. Even prime-time television, the most strictly regulated medium, features language, sexual situations, double entendres, provocative clothing, and even flashes of nudity that would have been virtually unthinkable 15 or 20 years ago.

In particular, the volume of sexual materials on the Internet and the ease with which those materials can be accessed by children threaten to spark the kind of backlash that led to the growth of the Moral Majority in the late 1970s. Public concern and media attention to the issue has been so great that Congress went so far as to adopt a statute (the Communications Decency Act of 1996) that most commentators and not a few legislators agreed at the time was flatly unconstitutional. In one of its relatively rare unanimous decisions these days, the largely conservative Supreme Court agreed.

While online sexual entrepreneurs can obviously take some comfort from the Court's decision in *ACLU v. Reno (I)*, the risk of adverse political developments will remain high in the coming years. The invention of the World Wide Web and its phenomenal growth has coincided (fortunately for the industry) with a Democratic administration, including a Justice Department less likely (as Senator Coats complained) to initiate obscenity prosecutions for online materials other than child pornography. But the industry certainly has no guarantees that future administrations will be either as accommodating or distracted. In the normal course of events, one might reasonably expect that the raging sexual scandal and impeachment of President Clinton and fund-raising questions involving Vice President Gore would create a serious risk that the White House will wind up in Republican hands in the year 2000. However, the 1998 midterm elections were widely viewed as a rebuke of Republican efforts to unseat President Clinton; even more startling, his approval ratings reached all-time highs on the weekend following his impeachment by the House of Representatives (a development which adds additional fuel to conservative and religious arguments about the decline of American values). Even if the Republicans continue in 2000 the self-immolation that they began in 1997 and 1998, online sexual entrepreneurs should avoid getting too cocky. After all, the Communications Decency Act was based on an amendment first introduced by Jim Exon, a conservative Democratic senator from Oklahoma.

The public's reaction to the details of Clinton's trysts (so luridly laid out in Ken Starr's report to Congress) may be the most optimistic sign for electronic pornographers. Clearly, the expectation of conservative legislators and syndicated columnists such as Mona Charen and Cal Thomas has been that the revelations about the president's conduct would so outrage the American public that support would grow not only for impeachment but also for his removal from office. But the country has shown a surprising willingness to distinguish between the president's public performance (of which they strongly approve) and his private life (of which they strongly disapprove but don't want to hear anything further about). Increasingly, the idea that even the president is entitled to a personal life that is free from the intrusions of either the media or a special prosecutor lends implicit support to the idea that what people do with their computers in the privacy of their home, regardless of where that home is physically located, is their own business. That attitude can only benefit the online pornography industry.

## SEXUAL CAPITALISM IN THE MEDIA

The attitudes of the public and Congress toward online pornography are complicated by the reactions of other types of media to the growth of the Internet. As ABC, CBS, and NBC have discovered to their dismay, entertainment consumers have finite amounts of time and money. As the public's media options have expanded, older media such as the television networks and theaters have lost revenues and market share to newer competitors.

As we saw in earlier chapters, a significant reason for the loss of market share by older media is the fact that new entertainment technologies are generally not subject to the same degree of government or even industry regulation. While less regulation has a number of different implications, the highest-profile consequence is often increased sexual content. Cable television generally has a higher level of sexual content than broadcast television, sexually explicit videotapes are more readily available than sexually explicit adult films, and the Internet trumps them all.

This would be largely an interesting academic discussion were it not for the fact that the purpose of each medium is to sell its products to consumers. Although the conscious decision of consumers to spend their time and money on one medium rather than another is the result of numerous factors (cost, convenience, privacy, etc.), there is little doubt that when presented with a choice, consumers have as a general rule chosen to spend time and financial resources on the medium offering the highest levels of sexual content and convenience of access. Hence the success of cable television at the expense of the traditional networks; hence the virtually complete triumph of videocassettes over adult movie theaters; and hence the stunning growth of the Internet.

The broadcast networks in particular have responded to this economic reality by straining at the leash of government regulation, trying to squeeze as much sexual content as possible into a medium in which none is supposed to appear. With market share and ad revenues plummeting, there can be little doubt that *N.Y.P.D. Blue's* derriere of the week is merely the first crack in the facade of the government's regulation of sexual content on broadcast television.

The implications for the online pornography industry are twofold. First, more explicit television broadcasts or even Hollywood theater releases would represent, at least in theory, increased competition for the pornography industry. In reality, it is highly unlikely that broadcast television can or will change fast enough or far enough to even begin to approach the content available on cable, let alone what is available on videocassette or on the Internet.[31] To a lesser degree, the same is true of the movie industry; although the limitations on sexual content are largely self-imposed, the industry has shown little enthusiasm for significantly loosening restrictions on sexual content, and most theater owners offer little support for films with an NC-17 rating.

The more significant risk for the online pornography industry arising out of efforts by broadcast television to compete on sexual content is that it will help to further spur the legislative and electoral efforts of political conservatives. Regardless of their precise market share, the shows that are broadcast by television networks have a high cultural profile. When a show like *N.Y.P.D. Blue* is launched, it can have a political and social impact that is disproportionate to the number of people actually watching. In 1997, in fact, the television industry was compelled by social activists and the threat of Congressional legislation to adopt a rating system to alert parents to the content of its shows. By some accounts, however, all that the implementation of a television rating system has accomplished is to provide political cover for the networks as they increase the explicitness of their programs and to provide children with an easy-to-use guide for finding materials that their parents didn't want them to see in the first place.

The irony, of course, is that in the networks' stampede to compete the explicitness of cable, video, and the Internet, they are ignoring their enormous creative and financial advantages. The networks have the resources available to them to produce superb works of comedy and drama, but even in this, they are ceding their advantage to cable (as the often terrific original movies on Lifetime, Showtime, and HBO amply demonstrate). There is little doubt, however, that the continued commercial viability of ABC, CBS, and NBC will depend on finding ways to develop and broadcast content that is competitive with the offerings of cable networks and premium movie channels, because that is clearly the direction in which the viewers are moving. What impact the efforts of the broadcast networks will have on the nation's social and political landscape remains to be seen.

## DE FACTO DANES?

Thirty years ago, a Presidential Commission recommended that state and federal laws against pornography and obscenity be scrapped, as they had seen in Denmark a few years earlier. An angry President Nixon rejected the commission's recommendation and chastised the commission, saying, "American morality is not to be trifled with."[32]

Today, technology is on the verge of accomplishing at least part of what the commission recommended.[33] Individuals with access to a personal computer can see materials in the privacy of their home that in many cases are impossible to obtain in the communities in which they live. If capitalism is an ongoing financial plebiscite, then the online pornography industry's growth from little more than a dirty picture trading society in 1994 to a $1 billion–$2 billion industry in 1998 is a telling commentary on American attitudes toward legal restrictions on adult materials.

The challenge for traditional media outlets lies in the numbers. At the end of May 1999, the number of Americans online crossed the 100 million mark, or just over 40 percent of the total population. Although the rate of growth, which has already fallen precipitously from the stunning levels of

1994–95, will continue to slow, there is no reason to think that people or businesses will suddenly stop using the Internet. Early predictions that the Internet would choke on its own growth have proved to be exaggerated, computer prices continue to fall, transmission speeds continue to rise, and the current generation of schoolchildren are being taught to think of the Internet as a natural source of information and entertainment. A growing synergy of communications devices and transmission methods may well make the Internet an integral part of virtually every household.

As the number of Internet users continues to grow, so too will the revenues of the online pornography industry. In the last quarter-century, the revenues of the pornography industry overall, by conservative estimates, have quintupled, rising from roughly $2 billion to more than $10 billion (and less conservative analysts put the estimate closer to $20 billion). Since the Internet makes the distribution of pornography cheaper and faster and its consumption more private, there is absolutely no reason to think (absent unusually restrictive legislation) that the online pornography industry will not continue to garner a reasonable percentage of the money spent on the Internet. Clearly, the industry's success to date demonstrates the willingness of pornography consumers to use the Internet for commercial transactions.

It is important to remember that 45 years ago, it was a single entrepreneur that laid the foundation of the pornography industry as we know it today. Hugh Hefner could not have thrived in our capitalist society if the public was unwilling to purchase the product he was offering. Over the last several decades, the continued growth and survival of his business has depended on his ability and that of his management to respond to the desires of the public. Precisely the same dynamic is occurring with online pornography. The newly born industry (which includes some old offline stalwarts) is succeeding because hundreds and thousands of entrepreneurs are offering to the public a product that the public is willing to purchase, and moreover, is willing to purchase it through a technology about which most people are highly suspicious. It is difficult to imagine that the efforts of these entrepreneurs will not have at least as profound an effect on the nation's sexual mores as did Hefner a half-century ago.

## NOTES

1. James Coates, "Computer industry anticipates heavy demand this holiday," *Washington Times*, November 30, 1998, p. D24.
2. Michael Fitzgerald, "Case: We've only just begun," ZDNN, December 10, 1997. Online at http://www5.zdnet.com/zdnn/content/zdnn/1210/262053.html.
3. Peter Coogan, "High Tech Wizards Find a Home: Porn Paves Web Progress," *ABCNews.com*, August 25, 1997, online at http://www.ientertain.com/porntech0825.index.html.
4. Super Video Graphics Array ("SVGA"), also known as "extended VGA," is a video standard that is capable of displaying an image ranging from 800 x 600 pixels to 1600 x 1200 pixels, with a palette of up to 16.7 million colors. (By contrast, the human eye is generally capable of distinguishing approximately 19 million colors.)

5. That may not entirely be good news; it's one thing to sit through a forced showing of 15 or 20 snapshots during an airplane flight or cab ride. It's another thing altogether to sit through an electronic slide show of 200–300 digital images.

6. Cable is a shared resource. As the number of users of a particular cable line increases, the transmission rate does fall.

7. Doug Fine, "Eskimos Warm to Digital Age," *Washington Post*, August 9, 1998, p. C1.

8. *Ibid.*

9. Ashley Dunn, "Electrical Lines Could Zap Data to (and Through) Homes," *New York Times*, February 4, 1998.

10. "The Intensor Survival Guide," BSG Labs, Inc., *Computer Gaming*, August 1998, pp. 63–65.

11. More information on I-Force is available at www.forcefeedback.com.

12. David Kohn, "Device Brings New Sense of Purpose to Tactile Research," *New York Times*, December 27, 1997.

13. Sensable Technologies, "Company History," online at http://www.sensable.com/history.htm.

14. Kohn, "Device Brings New Sense of Purpose To Tactile Research," *New York Times*, December 27, 1997.

15. Tom Standage, "Connected: In touch with your feelings," *Daily Telegraph*, December 2, 1997, p. 7.

16. Television shows, particularly those dealing with science fiction, live long and prosper on the Internet, where fans can compile frighteningly detailed guides to individual episodes, debate the relative merits of characters, draft alternative plots, and collect photos of the show's stars.

17. Joshua Quittner, "'Virtual Sex—A Byte of the Forbidden Fruit," *Newsday*, November 7, 1993, p. 7.

18. *Ibid.*

19. Another popular application of this technology is for use in flight simulators, a much less expensive and safer alternative to (although not a complete replacement for) training flights.

20. woodrow.mpls.frb.fed.us/economy/calc/cpihome.html.

21. Courtney Macavinta, "Life after the CDA: Censorship," December 23, 1997, online at http://www.news.com/News/ Item/0,4,17596,00.html.

22. *Ibid.*

23. Maria Seminerio, "Congress Ready for Cyberspace Fight," December 8, 1997, online at http://www.zdnet.com/zdnn/content/zdnn/1208/261308.html.

24. Carl Kaplan, "New Anti-Pornography Measure Could Pass Constitutional Test," *New York Times*, July 31, 1998.

25. U.S. Constitution, Fourteenth Amendment, § 1.

26. American Civil Liberties Union, "Online Censorship in the States," 1998, online at http://www.aclu.org/issues/cyber/censor/stbills.html.

27. "Chronology of the Growth of the Hardcore Video Porn Racket," Morality in Media Web site, online at http://pw2.netcom.com/~mimnyc/porngrow.htm.

28. Declan McCullagh, "Justice Plans Net Obscenity Crackdown," *Netly News*, June 29, 1998, online at http://cgi.pathfinder.com/time/daily/article/0,1344,13855,00.html.

29. *Ibid.*

30. By analogy, could a video store in New York City be prosecuted for obscenity for selling a copy of *Deep Throat* to a Memphis tourist?

31. This is particularly true if the Republicans win the next presidential election; there is little likelihood that the Federal Communications Commission would countenance network broadcasts of explicit sexual content under a Republican president.

32. Edward de Grazia, *Girls Lean Backward Everywhere* (New York: Random House, 1992), p. 560.

33. The Commission's head, Dean William B. Lockhart said that the Commission's "most important recommendation was that [the U.S.] should plan and develop and finance a massive program of sex education for young and old, to cover everyone's needs, designed to insure a healthy attitude towards sex and a sound understanding of our sexual nature." de Grazia, p. 560.

# INDEX

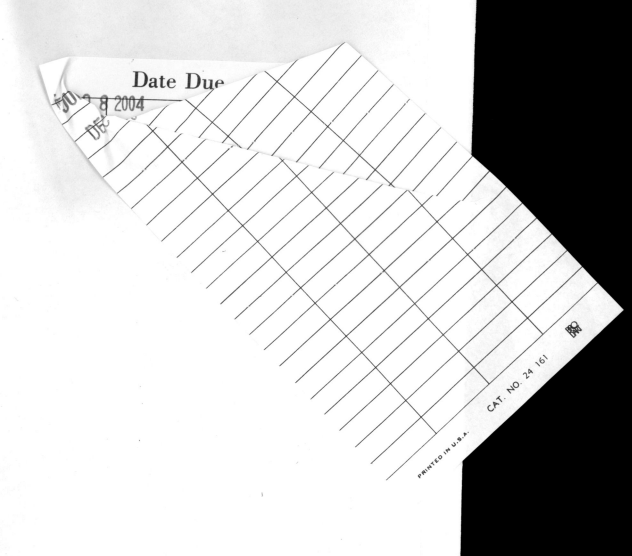